SPANISH

SECOND LANGUAGE ACQUISITION

State of the Science

SPANISH
SECOND LANGUAGE
ACQUISITION
State of the Science

BARBARA A. LAFFORD
AND
RAFAEL SALABERRY

EDITORS

GEORGETOWN UNIVERSITY PRESS
WASHINGTON, D.C.

Georgetown University Press, Washington, DC 20007
©2003 by Georgetown University Press
All rights reserved.
Printed in the United States of America

10 9 8 7 6 5 4 3 2 1   2003

This book is printed on acid-free recycled paper meeting the requirements
of the American National Standard for Permanence in Paper for Printed
Library Materials.

Library of Congress Cataloging-in-Publication Data

Spanish second language acquisition : state of the science /
Barbara A. Lafford and Rafael Salaberry, editors
      p. cm.
Includes bibliographical references and index.
    ISBN 0-87840-907-6 (pbk. : alk. paper)
1. Spanish language—Study and teaching—Foreign speakers.   2. Second
language acquisition.   3. Spanish language—Grammar.   I. Lafford,
Barbara Armstrong.   II. Salaberry, M. Rafael.
PC4127.8.S63 2003
468′.0071—dc21   2002013809

dedication

To my mother, Kathleen, with eternal gratitude
for her faith, courage, and love,
which have always sustained me,
 and
To my husband, Peter,
my aunt and uncle, Sarah and Horace Worman,
my grandmother, Ardis Lee Armstrong,
my great-aunt, Genevieve Wilkins,
and my mentor, Linda R. Waugh
for their faith, love, and constant support.
—Barbara A. Lafford

To María José
 and
Julian Sebastian
—Rafael Salaberry

Contents

Part I: Linguistic Topics: Products

Part III: Methodological Perspectives

List of Tables and Figures

Tables

Figures

Preface

The increasing popularity of Spanish in colleges in North America has generated a demand for courses at both the undergraduate and the graduate level on Spanish SLA (second language acquisition) and its application in the classroom. The present volume is primarily intended as a reference tool for second language acquisition researchers; graduate students in SLA, second/foreign language pedagogy, or linguistics programs; and practitioners and pedagogues who teach diverse second and foreign languages and want to keep up with research trends in the field of SLA (with particular attention given to Spanish). The book can also be used as a basic text in a graduate course on Spanish SLA for students who have some background knowledge of linguistics.

The division of the study of second language acquisition into an investigation of products (i.e., specific elements of language, such as phonemes, morphemes, syntactic and discourse patterns, and their appropriate pragmatic use) and processes (i.e., how second language systems are gradually formed through language processing and production mechanisms) is applied here to categorize studies involving Spanish L2 data. The first six chapters of the book deal with products of Spanish SLA (i.e., phonology, tense/aspect, subjunctive, clitics, lexicon, pragmatics/discourse), and the next three chapters focus on the processes involved in SLA (from generative, cognitive and sociocultural theoretical perspectives). The last chapter investigates the effect of different instructional approaches on the second language acquisition process. Because the studies analyzed in the products chapters are empirical ones grounded in SLA theory, some of the material covered there also appears in the process (theoretical) chapters and is cross-referenced.

The overview of research on the Spanish linguistic topics (products) covered in the proposed volume could be easily incorporated into a variety of undergraduate teaching methods and applied linguistics courses as well as graduate courses on SLA. The chapters on theoretical perspectives (processes) would be of great interest to scholars and graduate students working on theses or dissertations who seek an understanding of broad theoretical issues in SLA. Finally, the effect of different instructional approaches on learners' abilities in the target language (Spanish) is a topic of interest to all present and future teachers of the language.

We owe a debt of gratitude to family, friends, and colleagues for their personal support and encouragement during this project. We wish to thank Peter Lafford for his technical assistance and tireless efforts in putting together the final manuscript for submission to

Georgetown University Press. In addition, we want to acknowledge the editorial and research assistance we received from Diana Chin, Sarah Neal, and Julie Sykes (Arizona State University graduate students in Spanish SLA/Applied Linguistics) in the preparation of the original manuscript.

Of invaluable assistance as well were the reviewers (established, publishing SLA scholars who must remain anonymous) of each of the chapters. Their insightful comments were extremely valuable in the creation of the book's quality of analysis and its depth and breadth of coverage of Spanish SLA studies. We also acknowledge the assistance of Gail Grella of Georgetown University Press and thank her for her patience and wisdom.

Finally, we express our gratitude to Arizona State University for granting Barbara A. Lafford a sabbatical leave to work on this book project, and to David W. Foster and Deborah Losse, chairs of the Department of Languages and Literatures, for their support. Recognition also goes to the Department of Hispanic Studies at Rice University for their continued encouragement of Rafael Salaberry to commit the time to carrying out this project and to the School of Humanities for the Presidential Research Grant offered to tenure-track professors.

Introduction

BARBARA A. LAFFORD   Arizona State University

RAFAEL SALABERRY   Rice University

1.0   Purpose of the Volume

In recent years, the number of studies of the acquisition of Spanish as a second language has increased substantially. However, most of this research in the United States has been disseminated in professional journals such as the *Modern Language Journal* and *Studies in Second Language Acquisition* or in edited volumes (e.g., Andersen 1984b; Meisel 1986; Van-Patten, Dvorak, and Lee 1987; Freed 1995) in which the focus also encompasses languages other than Spanish. Although some applied linguistics journals in Spain and Latin America do publish articles almost exclusively based on Spanish issues (for example, Mexico's *Estudios de Lingüística Aplicada,* Spain's *Revista Española de la Lingüística Aplicada,* and Chile's *Lenguas Modernas*), *Hispania* and *Spanish Applied Linguistics*[1] have been the only major journals in the United States to accept second language acquisition[2] (SLA) or applied linguistics articles dealing exclusively with Spanish (or Portuguese) data.

Edited volumes on various aspects of Spanish linguistics that contain papers on Spanish SLA (e.g., Morgan, Lee, and VanPatten 1987; Hashemipour, Maldonado, and Van Naerssen 1995; Salaberri Ramiro 1999) or that contain selected conference papers from meetings held on the acquisition of Spanish as a first and second language (e.g., Glass and Pérez-Leroux 1997; Pérez-Leroux and Glass 1997; Leow and Sanz 2000; Montrul, in press) sometimes appear. However, no other single published volume brings together the different lines of research on Spanish second language acquisition (SLA) proposed in this text.

The purpose of this volume is to provide a "state-of-the-science"[3] overview of Spanish SLA studies carried out in the last quarter of the twentieth century and the beginning of the twenty-first. Each chapter reviews general SLA trends on the topic in question (studies carried out using second-language [L2] data from many languages in different language learning contexts) and then discusses in detail empirical investigations carried out on the acquisition of that aspect of the target language by L2 learners of Spanish. Each chapter will answer the following questions using research investigating the acquisition of Spanish as a second language:

- Where have we been?
- Where are we now?
- Where should we go with our research agenda for the twenty-first century?

This volume will also be the first book to give a broad, panoramic view of current research trends in SLA before presenting a critical overview of major works on Spanish SLA that reflect those trends. Such a review is needed to synthesize and distill the vast amount of information that abounds in the field of SLA and to place the studies done on Spanish SLA in a broader context. In addition, this volume is organized to make this research very accessible for scholars looking for research on certain aspects of Spanish SLA[4] (e.g., phonology, tense/aspect, subjunctive, clitics, lexicon, pragmatics/discourse), specific approaches to the L2 data (e.g., generative, cognitive, and sociocultural), and the role of instruction in the development of Spanish L2 systems.

The coverage of Spanish SLA research in this volume does not presume to be exhaustive. However, the authors have done their best to include touchstone articles in each subfield that discuss the most pressing and interesting issues in that area. The contributors were given the liberty to select the articles they felt were appropriate representations of work done in their subfield; thus, it is inevitable that some readers will take issue with the choices made by authors for inclusion or the exclusion of certain works in this volume. However, we felt that it was important to allow the individual authors to craft the scope of their chapters and develop their arguments accordingly. Sometimes research on languages other than Spanish are included in the volume because of their importance in treating key issues for the establishment of the research base of a given subfield. Notably absent in this state-of-the-science volume are contributions by Roger Andersen and Bill VanPatten, pioneers in Spanish SLA research, whose commitments prevented them from participating.

2.0 The Development of Spanish SLA Research

According to the framework established by Lafford (2000) for categorizing major paradigm shifts in the study of Spanish applied linguistics in the twentieth century, empirically based SLA research did not begin until after the mid-1960s, when scholars began to inform their understanding of the second language acquisition process with studies in cognitive psychology (Ausubel 1968) and formal linguistics with a nativist base (Chomsky 1965).[5] Second language studies in this period (1965–79) also involved the collection and analysis of data gathered from L2 learners themselves.

This practice differed from that of the prior era (1945–65), in which scholars and applied linguists used (mostly written) first-language (L1) data taken from authentic materials from the target culture (e.g., contemporary books and periodicals) and some data gathered from native speakers of the L2 via oral interviews and written questionnaires to inform pedagogues of the workings of the target language. Scholars of the period, influenced by behaviorist psychology (Watson 1925; Skinner 1957) and structural linguistics (Bloomfield 1929; Bloch and Trager 1942), assumed that L2 errors were the result of a transfer of L1 habits.[6] As a result, linguistic creativity in the L2 classroom was limited in hopes of training the second language learner to mimic and memorize (mim-mem) native speaker patterns of linguistic behavior through the use of mechanical drills and dialogues (Audiolingual Method).

However, Chomsky's (1959) review of Skinner's (1957) *Verbal Behavior* pointed out that the process of language learning could not be entirely accounted for in a Behaviorist stimulus-response model. Chomsky's "poverty of the stimulus" argument stated that children learning their native language create sentences they never encountered per se in the input to which they were exposed, and could not possibly be simply imitating what they heard. (Carroll 2001 discusses the limited relevance of this argument for adult L2 acquisition in particular.) This ability to create (sometimes imperfectly) with the language began to be recognized as an important part of the language learning process, inasmuch as it was with this type of output creation that children created and tested hypotheses about the language they were learning (Creative Constructionism; cf. Dulay and Burt 1974).

With the publication of Corder's (1967) treatise on the significance of learners' errors, scholars began to recognize that L2 errors were produced from many sources (e.g., transfer, overgeneralization, analogy). Corder pointed out that errors inform teachers about learners' progress, provide evidence to researchers on how languages are learned, and allow learners to test their hypotheses about how the target language is structured. Selinker (1969, 1972) brought the notion of a learner's cogent rule-governed transitional L2 system *(interlanguage)* into the discussion of SLA.[7]

In the 1970s, SLA research was dominated by researchers using interlanguage (patterns of total usage, not just errors) data to study the order of acquisition of English morphemes in second language contexts by children of various ages (Dulay and Burt 1974; Fathman 1975) and adults (Bailey, Madden, and Krashen 1974). These studies provided evidence against Behaviorism in favor of a theory of creative constructionism, in which learners (regardless of age) followed certain universal patterns of development in the construction of their interlanguage. Spanish first language acquisition morpheme order studies (see Van Naerssen 1980) also appeared in the 1970s. However, the Spanish second language studies during this period were based on an error analysis (e.g., Lindstrom 1976; Gunterman 1978) rather than an interlanguage approach.

Lafford's (2000) framework points out that the last paradigm shift in L2 research in the twentieth century began in the early 1980s, when scholars began to look more closely at the use of learners' second languages in their social contexts. In this last era of the twentieth century (1980–99), scholars were heavily influenced by sociolinguistics (interlanguage variationist models based on the work of Labov 1972 [Tarone 1983; Major 1987]), discourse and pragmatic analyses (interactionist paradigms proposed by Hatch 1978a and 1978b and Long 1981) and sociocultural learning theory (Vygotsky 1962). During this era, scholars continued the earlier interest in investigating the inner workings of the learner's mind within Universal Grammar (Chomsky 1965) and Minimalist frameworks (Chomsky 1981, 1995). In addition, they gave attention to underlying cognitive processes at work during the acquisition process (e.g., L2 operating principles [Andersen 1984a, 1990]; processing principles [MacWhinney 2001; Pienemann 1998; Skehan 1998; VanPatten 1996]; noticing items in the input [Carroll 2001; Schmidt 1990]; and the need for the learner to focus on form [DeKeyser 2001; Doughty 2001; Long 1991).

The *product-process* dichotomy (explained in the preface), which has been applied to Spanish SLA studies during this last era, will be used to categorize the Spanish L2 studies presented in this volume. This opposition is reflected in the organization of the book and is explained in the next section.

2.1   Products of Spanish SLA

The first six chapters of the book provide overviews of current research on the acquisition of certain products of Spanish SLA by adult learners. The following section summarizes the contributions of each of these chapters to understanding the field of Spanish second language acquisition.[8]

2.1.1   Chapter 1 (Phonology): "Staking Out the Territory at the Turn of the Century: Integrating Phonological Theory, Research, and the Effect of Formal Instruction on Pronunciation in the Acquisition of Spanish as a Second Language"

A. Raymond Elliott begins this chapter on the acquisition of Spanish phonology by adult learners of Spanish by reviewing intrinsic, biological, or learner variables apparently involved in L2 phonological acquisition: the effect of age on child and adult acquisition of L2 phonological systems (the Critical Period Hypothesis, involving notions of brain plasticity and cognitive reorganization), gender, affect and attitude, and field independence/dependence in relation to L2 pronunciation. Subsequently, he explores several hypotheses, theories, and models that attempt to account for L2 phonological acquisition: the Contrastive Analysis Hypothesis; the Similarity Differential Rate Hypothesis; interlanguage phonological theory (including the Markedness Differential Hypothesis); and phonological variation as explained by social context (Tarone's Interlanguage Continuum and Major's Ontogeny Model).

A unique feature of this study is the synopsis of selected L2 phonological studies carried out in the last four decades, with special attention given to the ones using Spanish L2 data. Table 2.1 systematically provides the following information on each L2 phonological study listed: name of researcher and purpose of the study; the type of subjects used and the specific L2 being acquired, the training received, and whether or not the study's results were significant at the $p < .05$ level or not (S = significant, NS = not significant). The role of formal instruction in pronunciation rounds out this chapter. According to Elliott, a more integrated and practical theory of second language phonological acquisition must be developed that eventually will serve to modify classroom methodologies in order to enhance the acquisition of Spanish pronunciation. Elliott concludes the chapter by offering several suggestions for possible avenues of future research on L2 phonological acquisition.

2.1.2 Chapter 2 (Tense/Aspect): "The Development of Tense/Aspect Morphology in Spanish as a Second Language"

Silvina Montrul and Rafael Salaberry provide the reader with an introduction to the intricacies of tense-aspect marking in verbal morphology and a general overview of the studies that have attempted to account, in theoretical terms, for the potential stages of development that seem to accompany the acquisition of past-tense verbal morphology. The topic is especially appropriate for inclusion in a volume that deals with the state-of-the-science knowledge about the field for two main reasons. First, the notions of tense and aspect appear to be the type of overarching phenomena that can span several components of a grammatical system (i.e., morphology, syntax, semantics, discourse, pragmatics). Therefore, a thorough understanding of the developmental processes that explain the acquisition of tense and aspect will be crucial to test any overall theory or model of second language acquisition—and the development of Spanish in particular. Second, and no less relevant, is the resurgence of research dedicated to this topic in the last decade.

The authors highlight the complexity of the Spanish tense/aspect system from the point of view of English native speakers. Their analysis focuses on the evidence submitted to account for some of the prevalent theoretical models about the development of verbal morphology. Among such models, Montrul and Salaberry discuss substantively the Primacy of Aspect Hypothesis, as well as recent proposals stemming from the minimalist program. The authors conclude the chapter with suggestions for future lines of research on the questions raised in this chapter.

2.1.3 Chapter 3 (Subjunctive): "The Development of Subjunctive and Complex-Syntactic Abilities among Foreign Language Learners of Spanish"

Joseph G. Collentine critically reviews the research conducted to date on the acquisition of the Spanish subjunctive. Although studies examining subjunctive development by native speakers of Spanish and Spanish-English bilinguals in the United States receive some attention here, this chapter focuses its efforts on investigations involving foreign language (FL) learners of Spanish. Additionally, because one of the key predictors of subjunctive development may be the learner's abilities to generate complex utterances, this chapter also probes works on the acquisition of complex syntax (from a structural and a formalist perspective) and the effects of short-term memory limitations on the processing of such utterances. In this review of Spanish L2 subjunctive studies, Collentine refers to his syntactic foundation hypothesis, which states that the acquisition of the ability to process complex syntax establishes certain prerequisite developmental conditions for the acquisition of the subjunctive. Thus, if students need to control some aspects of Spanish syntactic structure before being able to process the subjunctive for intake, it is not surprising that this grammatical category (mood) is acquired quite late vis-à-vis other morphological phenomena (i.e., tense/aspect). Collentine suggests that research on the subjunctive may be the strongest *cohesive* body of empirical evidence to support the notion that relatively complete acquisition of any grammatical phenomenon may require both input- and output-oriented teaching strategies to language processing. The author concludes by delineating some of the strengths and shortcomings of the studies reviewed, proposing suggestions for future research.

2.1.4 Chapter 4 (Clitics): "Cognitive and Linguistic Perspectives on the Acquisition of Object Pronouns in Spanish as a Second Language"

James F. Lee provides an overview of empirical research on the acquisition of object pronouns (clitics) by classroom learners of Spanish as a second language. Like the subjunctive research Collentine reviews in the preceding chapter, the study of the acquisition of clitic pronouns brings together issues of morphological acquisition and the ability to process and produce complex syntax. Lee categorizes the work in this area as falling under two rubrics: processing incoming information (decoding meaning) and producing language samples (encoding meaning). Under processing, Lee reviews studies that illustrate the effect of the first noun strategy, that is, the tendency of learners to assign subject role to the first noun they encounter in a string even if that noun is a grammatical object. Lee points out that VanPatten developed the widely known processing-instruction approach to classroom instruction (altering the way learners perceive and process linguistic data in the input; cf. Lee and VanPatten 1995) as an attempt to counteract this particular L2 learner strategy. Under the production rubric Lee discusses case study comparisons of naturalistic and classroom learners that investigate learners' use of clitics when expressing ideas. The next section of the chapter examines the research on clitic acquisition carried out within generative syntactic frameworks. Lee points out that the empirically based L2 studies that examine Spanish object pronouns from a linguistic perspective demonstrate that learner data are an important source of information for supporting and refining generative theories of syntax. The chapter concludes with a section on possible directions for future research in the acquisition of Spanish clitic pronouns.

2.1.5 Chapter 5 (Lexicon): "The Acquisition of Lexical Meaning by Second Language Learners: An Analysis of General Research Trends with Evidence from Spanish"

Relative to the amount of L2 research produced to date on grammatical issues, Barbara Lafford, Joseph G. Collentine, and Adam S. Karp point out that the acquisition of the lexicon has received less attention by SLA scholars. Nevertheless, they note that the study of L2 vocabulary acquisition has gained momentum in the last fifteen years, albeit mostly with databases gathered from learners of languages other than Spanish (e.g., English, German, and French as a second/foreign language). They first provide a general overview of the acquisition of lexical phenomena across second languages before detailing the studies on L2 lexical acquisition that have been carried out using Spanish data. Using Henriksen's (1999) microconnectionist view of the L2 lexicon that expands N. Ellis's (1994) macro model, the authors distinguish between three types of knowledge of a word: partial/precise knowledge; depth of knowledge about the word; and receptive/productive dimension. In their review of Spanish L2 studies within this framework, the authors note that most L2 lexical studies based on Spanish may be classified under the partial/precise knowledge category (e.g., studies of the acquisition of *ser/estar* and *por/para*). The last section of the chapter reviews the research on ways in which L2 vocabulary acquisition can be facilitated (e.g., vocabulary learning strategies, such as word frequency lists, guessing from context, inferring meaning from glosses and the use of dictionaries, multimedia cues, and semantic mapping). The chapter concludes with a critical look at the limitations of the works reviewed and suggestions for future research in the area of Spanish L2 vocabulary acquisition.

2.1.6 Chapter 6 (Pragmatics/Discourse): "Pragmatics and Discourse Analysis in Spanish Second Language Acquisition Research and Pedagogy"

Dale A. Koike, Lynn Pearson, and Caryn Witten provide an overview of research in the acquisition of L2 pragmatic and discourse competence using data collected from learners of Spanish. Like the lexical acquisition literature discussed in chapter 5, research in the acquisition of pragmatic and discourse features has not been as copious as that devoted to morphological and grammatical phenomena. However, considering the importance currently being afforded research that investigates a learner's use of language in various social contexts (cf. Lafford 2000), it is not surprising that the number of second-language pragmatic (i.e., the interpretation and use of situationally appropriate linguistic forms) and discourse (i.e., the ability to construct coherent and cohesive oral and written discourse structures) studies rose sharply in the 1990s. The authors begin with an overview of the theories that have had great impact on pragmatic and discursive studies. Owing to their belief that advances toward the acquisition of target language discourse and pragmatics by L2 learners and analyses of cross-cultural and linguistic behavior by SLA researchers must be based on knowledge of native speaker norms, the authors first provide a brief overview of relevant studies of Spanish L1 pragmatics and discourse. They then examine several recent Spanish SLA studies focusing on these issues. These works are critically reviewed in terms of their theoretical bases and frameworks, their research designs and methodologies of data collection, their discussions of the data, their conclusions, and their contributions to the field of Spanish SLA. Finally, the authors propose directions of future research in Spanish SLA pragmatics and discourse analysis.

2.2 Processes Involved in Spanish SLA

Although a study of the products of SLA provides many valuable insights into the acquisition process, it is only through the analysis of the processes involved in SLA from a more global, interdisciplinary perspective that scholars can make stronger predictions about the types of processing involved in the acquisition of a second language. Gass and Selinker (2001) note the advantages and disadvantages of such an interdisciplinary approach. Multiple perspectives on the same data provide a richer understanding of the phenomena at work; however, Gass and Selinker propose that "multiple perspectives on what purports to be a single discipline bring confusion, because it is frequently the case that scholars approaching second language acquisition from different (often opposing and seemingly incompatible) frameworks are not able to talk to one another" (xiv).

To stem this confusion, the processes section of the book analyzes the contributions and insights of three different theoretical perspectives that have dominated the research of

Spanish as a second language during the last two decades of the twentieth century: linguistic (generative), cognitive, and sociocultural. The order of presentation of these chapters follows a trajectory from a nativist perspective in which Universal Grammar plays an important role in establishing constraints on the creation of possible L2 grammars (chapter 7) to a look at how the learner's cognitive processes interact with the input received by the learner (e.g., hypotheses about the second language that affect the way second language *input* is apperceived, comprehended, converted to *intake* and becomes a part of the developing Interlanguage system) (chapter 8), and it ends with a discussion of the importance of sociocultural interaction between the learner and other speakers of the target language in the development of second language competence (chapter 9).

2.2.1 Chapter 7 (Generative Perspectives): "Current Issues in the Generative Study of Spanish Second Language Syntax"

Liliana Sánchez and Almeida Jacqueline Toribio review recent developments in the area of Spanish second language acquisition from the perspective of generative grammars (Government and Binding Theory and the Minimalist Program). The authors open with a succinct overview of the conceptual and analytical tools of the framework and identify some of the prevailing themes in generative second language research. As a point of departure, they highlight what is labeled "the poverty of the stimulus argument": the linguistic data available to children underdetermine what they learn, and therefore children must be innately endowed with cognitive structures specific to language. When transferred to the environment of second language acquisition, many interesting questions arise that lead to a lively debate on the relevance of innately determined knowledge instantiated in Universal Grammars: no access to Universal Grammar (UG), partial access to UG, and full access to UG.

In order to address this debate, the authors provide a very coherent review of the literature with a primary focus on studies carried out to analyze the development of four prominent properties of Spanish grammar: null categories, clitics, word order, and predicate argument structure. Sánchez and Toribio expand their analysis with a review of three topics that they consider hold great promise for future study in generative syntax: language attrition, language variation, and child and adult bilingualism. Their analysis of these topics is enticing and provides readers with a substantial number of research ideas that hold promise to revolutionize a number of areas of our field that go beyond the generative analysis of syntax.

2.2.2 Chapter 8 (Cognitive Perspectives): "Cognitive Perspectives on the Acquisition of Spanish as a Second Language"

Paola E. Dussias presents a well-articulated overview of the current research on the effect of various general cognitive processes that are relevant for the analysis of second language learning in Spanish (e.g., perception, memorization, and information processing). She also provides a more in-depth analysis of one particular area of research that is informative of the state-of-the-science knowledge of cognitive approaches with regard to L2 Spanish acquisition in particular: sentence processing among Spanish-English bilinguals. Dussias provides an analysis of various theoretical models that have been central to the advancement of our knowledge in this particular area of inquiry of L2 acquisition. In doing so, she analyzes the relevance of various dichotomies for the development of prevalent hypotheses of the field: form versus meaning, conscious versus unconscious, explicit versus implicit teaching, natural versus academic environments, and the like. Dussias's in-depth analysis of sentence parsing and sentence processing among Spanish-English bilinguals represents a useful case study that shows how several cognitive processes come together in the process of second language acquisition as a whole.

Dussias's investigation of the question of the learnability of Spanish as a second language from a cognitive perspective highlights the importance of a very broad area of research that spans several fields (some of them, such as artificial intelligence, fairly recent). Dussias is careful, however, to point out that general cognitive processes interact with other components of the learning process in general: linguistic and sociocultural components. (These are discussed in detail in the other two theoretical chapters of this volume, 7 and 9.)

2.2.3 Chapter 9 (Sociocultural Perspectives): "Sociocultural Theory and the Acquisition of Spanish as a Second Language"

Marta Antón, Frederick J. DiCamilla, and James P. Lantolf examine the role of sociocultural theory within an overall research agenda that attempts to investigate and understand the acquisition of Spanish as a second language as a cognitive phenomenon. As Vygotksy (1962) originally proposed, sociocultural theory accounts for the relationship between language and mind. One of the principal claims of the theory states that language functions as the central mediating device for human cognitive activity. This function is assumed to originate externally in social interaction and to become gradually internalized in early childhood. The theory recognizes a Zone of Proximal Development, a metaphor to describe the opportunities to learn that novices can access through collaborative interaction with experts. With regard to adult classroom SLA, the concept of scaffolding (the expert takes control over portions of the process that are beyond the learner's level of expertise) is particularly important and is discussed in detail in this chapter.

The authors divide their review of sociocultural studies into different sections: private speech, lexical organization, reading comprehension, language play, and collaborative interaction. Finally, they argue that the L2 that is used by learners in a collaborative setting—as opposed to noncollaborative settings—is used as the principal mediating device to negotiate meaning, form, procedures, and goals. That is, language is used as a cognitive tool, and not simply as a communication medium.

2.3 Theoretical Issues

2.3.1 Chapter 10 (The Role of Instruction): "The Role of Instruction in Spanish Second Language Acquisition"

Second language acquisition research over the last thirty years has attempted to examine and quantify the relationship between an array of classroom procedures and numerous instructional outcomes. To bring together the theoretical issues discussed in this volume,

Charles Grove analyzes the most prevalent approaches to instruction that aim to facilitate Spanish SLA. Given that the scope of the topic is so broad, Grove focuses on some hypotheses that seem to have captured the attention of practitioners. In more specific terms, Grove selectively describes the role of grammar instruction of years past and its new embodiment in the notion of a *focus on form* (as opposed to *focus on forms*), the relative importance ascribed by different scholars and practitioners to pedagogical activities that focus on different stages of the acquisition process (i.e., input, intake, the integration of new knowledge and output), and the role of various types of social interaction in instructed SLA (e.g., modified input through feedback, tenets of sociocultural theory). Outside of the scope of Grove's treatment are several aspects of teaching methodologies (e.g., the role of testing, the teaching of cultural and discourse competencies—as opposed to the prevalent centrality of morphology and syntax) that were not included owing to space limitations. It is important to point out, however, that Grove's chapter touches on the potential new paths that future studies may choose to pursue in order to bring about sound pedagogical approaches toward Spanish second language acquisition. Grove's chapter will be of use to both classroom researchers and teaching practitioners, especially in teacher training programs where aspects of second language acquisition theory, research, and instructional practice are integrated with the goal of mentoring teaching professionals who wish to make informed pedagogical choices to meet better the needs of their students.

3.0 Application of Spanish Second Language Research

It is hoped that the appearance of this state-of-the-science volume on the research that has been carried out on Spanish second language acquisition will facilitate the work of applied linguists and pedagogues in their interpretation and application of the results of these studies to the teaching of Spanish as a second language. As pointed out in the methodological chapter in this volume, there is a great need for more constructive dialogue among second language researchers, applied linguists and practitioners. For instance, more SLA scholars could work with (or become) applied linguists in order to be actively engaged in the application of their research (including, but not limited to, research on various instructional design features) to the creation of pedagogical materials and to the testing of these materials in classroom learning contexts. On the other hand, more pedagogues could be trained to evaluate SLA research and conduct their own "action research" in order to inform their choice of materials and activities in the classroom, i.e., more teacher-training programs need to include required courses in second language acquisition and in Spanish applied linguistics.

In closing, we would like to point out that constructive dialogue between scholars and practitioners is but the first step towards a more comprehensive understanding of how second language acquisition occurs and what instructional design features and practices will facilitate this process. Indeed, the realities of classroom instruction cannot easily be compressed into the type of research design that most studies reviewed in the following chapters describe. Therefore, it is not easy to reach overarching conclusions that practitioners could follow in the form of a recipe of "best activities" or a brochure of "best teaching practices." In fact, more recent theoretical approaches to the study of Spanish second language acquisition (e.g., sociocultural) have pointed out the need to recognize and address the needs of individual language learners who possess a unique set of goals, abilities, and motivational levels.

Indeed, the dialogue among scholars, applied linguists and practitioners needs to lead to *action*— a true collaboration between these groups in which they work together on specific projects that have definable outcomes (e.g., materials development, curriculum design), keeping in mind the various "stakeholders" in this process: researchers, program administrators, teachers, and learners. Only through this kind of collaboration can true advances in the fields of Spanish second language acquisition, applied linguistics, and pedagogy be accomplished.

NOTES

1. *Spanish Applied Linguistics* ceased publication in December 2001.

2. The phrase *second language acquisition* has been defined in different ways by scholars in the field. Ellis (1994:11) notes that often the term refers to a case in which "the language plays an institutional and social role in the community (i.e., it functions as a recognized means of communication among members who speak some other language as their mother tongue)"— for example, English taught to international students in the United States. However, Ellis (1994:2) also defines the learning of a foreign language as learning that "takes place in settings where the language plays no major role in the community and is primarily learnt only in the classroom," for example, English learned in Japan. For the purposes of this volume, we will follow Ellis's lead in following common usage by employing the phrase *second language acquisition* as a neutral, superordinate term to refer to both types of learning (1994:12).

3. We believe that the systematic study of the products and processes involved in the acquisition of a second language may take many forms, and that the studies reviewed in this volume adhere to the principal characteristics of the "scientific method"—that is, hypothesis formation, observation, and experimentation and theoretical elaborations. Other major criteria used to determine the relevance of the material to be included in the chapters of this volume were the high quality of the research and the work's focus on issues central to the understanding of second language acquisition, with particular attention to those studies carried out using Spanish L2 data.

4. Because of space limitations, this volume does not include some important topics in Spanish SLA that have not been researched extensively—for example, Andersen's (1984c) study of the acquisition of Spanish gender in a second language context.

5. "Paradigm shifts" are defined by Lafford (2000) as "rules and assumptions that underline foreign language teaching that occurred as the twentieth century progressed." See Kuhn (1970) for a discussion of paradigm shifts in scientific theories.

6. The linguistic sources used in what Lafford (2000) calls Era I (1900–44) to inform applied linguists came from traditional grammars and traditional Spanish literary texts. Faculty psychology, which believed that the mind was a muscle that needed to be exercised, informed

the grammar-translation method of foreign language teaching, prevalent during Era I. Stern (1983) notes that the nineteenth century was characterized by two currents that continued into Era I of the twentieth: inductism and grammar translation on one hand and deductism and the direct method on the other.

7. Many scholars have proposed terms similar to Selinker's interlanguage—for example, Nemser's approximative systems (1971), Corder's idiosyncratic dialects/transitional competence (1971), and Tarone's capability continuum (1979).

8. Even though there is no separate chapter devoted only to syntactic issues, this area of Spanish L2 research is covered extensively in chapters 3 (subjunctive), 4 (clitics), and 7 (generative approaches).

WORKS CITED

Andersen, R. W. 1984a. One-to-one principle of interlanguage construction. *Language Learning* 34.4:77–95.

———. 1984b. *Second languages: A cross-linguistic perspective.* Rowley, MA: Newbury House.

———. 1984c. What's gender good for anyway? In *Second languages: A cross-linguistic perspective,* ed. R. Andersen, 77–99. Rowley, MA: Newbury House.

———. 1990. Models, processes, principles and strategies: Second language acquisition inside and outside of the classroom. In *Second language acquisition—Foreign language learning,* eds. B. VanPatten and J. F. Lee, 45–68. Clevedon: Multilingual Matters.

Ausubel, D. 1968. *Educational psychology: A cognitive view.* New York: Holt, Rinehart and Winston.

Bachman, L. 1997. *Fundamental considerations in language testing.* Oxford: Oxford University Press.

Bailey, N., C. Madden, and S. D. Krashen. 1974. Is there a "natural sequence" in adult second language learning? *Language Learning* 24.2:235–43.

Bloch, B., and G. L. Trager. 1942. *Outline of linguistic analysis.* Baltimore: Waverly Press.

Bloomfield, L. 1929. *Language.* New York: Holt, Rinehart and Winston.

Carroll, S. 2001. *Input and evidence: The raw material of second language acquisition.* Amsterdam: John Benjamins.

Chomsky, N. 1959. Review of *Verbal behavior* by B. F. Skinner. *Language* 35:26–58.

———. 1965. *Aspects of a theory of syntax.* Cambridge, MA: MIT Press.

———. 1981. *Lectures on government and binding.* Dordrecht: Foris.

———. 1995. *The minimalist program.* Cambridge, MA: MIT Press.

Corder, S. P. 1967. The significance of learners' errors. *International Review of Applied Linguistics* 5:160–70.

———. 1971. Idiosyncratic dialects and error analysis. *International Review of Applied Linguistics* 9:149–59.

DeKeyser, R. 2001. Automaticity and automatization. In *Cognition and second language instruction,* ed. P. Robinson, 125–51. Cambridge: Cambridge University Press.

Doughty, C. 2001. Cognitive underpinnings of focus on form. In *Cognition and second language instruction,* ed. P. Robinson, 206–57. Cambridge: Cambridge University Press.

Dulay, H., and M. Burt. 1974. Natural sequences in child second language acquisition. *Language Learning* 24.1:37–53.

Ellis, N. 1994. Vocabulary acquisition: The implicit ins and outs of explicit cognitive mediation. In *Implicit and explicit learning of languages,* ed. N. Ellis, 211–82. New York: Academic Press.

Fathman, A. 1975. Language background, age, and the order of acquisition of English structures. In *New directions in second language learning, teaching and bilingual education,* ed. M. K. Burt and H. Dulay, 33–43. Washington, DC: TESOL.

Freed, B. F., ed. 1995. *Second language acquisition in a study abroad context.* Amsterdam: John Benjamins.

Gass, S., and L. Selinker. 2001. *Second language acquisition.* Mahwah, NJ: Lawrence Erlbaum.

Glass, W. R., and A. T. Pérez-Leroux, eds. 1997. *Contemporary perspectives on the acquisition of Spanish: Production, processing and comprehension,* vol. 2. Somerville, MA: Cascadilla.

Gunterman, G. 1978. A Study of the frequency and communicative effects of errors in Spanish. *Modern Language Journal* 52.5:249–53.

Hashemipour, P., R. Maldonado, and M. Van Naerssen, eds. 1995. *Studies in language learning and Spanish linguistics in honor of Tracy D. Terrell.* San Francisco: McGraw-Hill.

Hatch, E. 1978a. Acquisition of syntax in a second language. In *Understanding second and foreign language learning: Issues and approaches,* ed. J. C. Richards, 34–69. Rowley, MA: Newbury House.

———. 1978b. Discourse analysis and second language acquisition. In *Second language acquisition: A book of readings,* ed. E. Hatch, 401–35. Rowley, MA: Newbury House.

Henriksen, B. 1999. Three dimensions of vocabulary development. *Studies in Second Language Acquisition* 21:303–18.

Johnson, M. 2001. *The art of non-conversation: A reexamination of the validity of the oral proficiency interview.* New Haven: Yale University Press.

Kuhn, T. 1970. *The structure of scientific revolutions.* Chicago: University of Chicago Press.

Labov, W. 1972. *Sociolinguistic patterns.* Philadelphia: University of Pennsylvania Press.

Lafford, B. 2000. Spanish applied linguistics in the twentieth century: A retrospective and bibliography (1900–99). *Hispania* 83.4:711–32.

Lee, J. F., and B. VanPatten. 1995. *Making communicative language teaching happen.* New York: McGraw-Hill.

Leow, R., and C. Sanz. 2000. *Spanish applied linguistics at the turn of the millennium: Papers from the 1999 conference on the L1 & L2 acquisition of Spanish and Portuguese.* Somerville, MA: Cascadilla Press.

Lindstrom, N. 1976. Good errors and bad errors: An insight into growing semantic astuteness. *Hispania* 59.3:469–73.

Long, M. 1981. Input, interaction and second language acquisition. In *Annals of the New York Academy of Sciences,* vol. 379, *Native language and foreign language acquisition,* ed. H. Winitz, 259–78. New York: New York Academy of Sciences.

———. 1991. Focus on form: A design feature in language teaching methodology. In *Foreign language research in cross-cultural perspective,* eds. K. de Bot, R. Ginsberg, and C. Kramsch, 39–52. Amsterdam: John Benjamins.

MacWhinney, B. 2001. The competition model: The input, the context, and the brain. In *Cognition and second language instruction,* ed. P. Robinson, 69–90. Cambridge: Cambridge University Press.

Major, R. 1987. A model for interlanguage phonology. In *Interlanguage phonology: The acquisition of a second language sound system,* eds. G. Ioup and S. H. Weinberger, 101–24. New York: Newbury House/Harper and Row.

Meisel, J. M. 1986. *Adquisición de lenguaje/Aquisição da linguagem.* Frankfurt: Vervuert.

Montrul, S. In press. *Fourth Conference on the acquisition of Spanish and Portuguese* and *Fifth Hispanic Linguistics Symposium.* Somerville, MA: Cascadilla Press.

Morgan, T. A., J. F. Lee, and B. VanPatten, eds. 1987. *Language and language use: Studies in Spanish.* New York: University Press of America.

Nemser, W. 1971. Approximative systems of foreign language learners. *International Review of Applied Linguistics* IX.2:115–23.

Pérez-Laroux, A. T., and W. Glass, eds. 1997. *Contemporary perspectives on the acquisition of Spanish: Developing grammars,* vol. 1. Somerville, MA: Cascadilla Press.

Pienemann, M. 1998. *Language processing and second language development-processability theory.* Amsterdam: John Benjamins.

Salaberri Ramiro, M. S. 1999. *Lingüística aplicada a la enseñanza de lenguas extranjeras.* Almería: Universidad de Almería.

Schmidt, R. W. 1990. The role of consciousness in second language learning. *Applied Linguistics* 11.2:129–58.

Selinker, L. 1969. Language transfer. *General Linguistics* 9:67–92.

———. 1972. Interlanguage. *International Review of Applied Linguistics* 10:209–30.

Skehan, P. 1998. *A cognitive approach to language learning.* Oxford: Oxford University Press.

Skinner, B. F. 1957. *Verbal behavior.* New York: Appleton-Century-Crofts.

Stern, H. H. 1983. *Fundamental concepts of language teaching.* London: Oxford University Press.

Tarone, E. 1979. Interlanguage as chameleon. *Language Learning* 9.1:181–91.

———. 1983. On the variability of interlanguage systems. *Applied Linguistics* 4:142–63.

Van Naerssen, M. 1980. How similar are Spanish as a first language and Spanish as a foreign language? In *Research in second language acquisition,* eds. R. C. Scarcella and S. D. Krashen, 146–54. Rowley, MA: Newbury House.

VanPatten, B. 1996. *Input processing and grammar instruction in second language acquisition.* Norwood, NJ: Ablex.

VanPatten, B., T. R. Dvorak, and J. F. Lee. 1987. *Foreign language learning: A research perspective.* Rowley, MA: Newbury House.

Vygotsky, L. S. 1962. *Thought and language.* Trans. E. Haufmann and G. Vakar. Cambridge, MA: MIT Press.

Watson, J. B. 1925. *Behaviorism.* New York: W. W. Norton.

Part I

Linguistic Topics: Products

1

Phonology

Staking Out the Territory at the Turn of the Century: Integrating Phonological Theory, Research, and the Effect of Formal Instruction on Pronunciation in the Acquisition of Spanish as a Second Language

A. RAYMOND ELLIOTT   University of Texas at Arlington

1.0   Introduction

Research on the acquisition of second language phonological skills suggests that several factors influence one's ability to acquire native or near-native pronunciation. The purpose of this chapter is to provide a panoramic and historical overview of phonological acquisition theory, empirical research, and the role of formal instruction in pronunciation during the second half of the twentieth century, with particular attention to studies using Spanish L2 data. Synthesizing phonological theory in relation to past and current research will prove to be particularly fruitful for understanding underlying factors involved in the acquisition of second language phonological systems.

This chapter will first review intrinsic, biological, or learner variables that appear to relate to L2 phonological acquisition: the Critical Period Hypothesis (child and adult acquisition of L2 phonological systems and the effect of age); brain plasticity and cognitive reorganization; gender; affect and attitude; and field independence/dependence in relation to L2 pronunciation. The chapter will then explore a number of theories that have accounted for Spanish L2 phonological acquisition: the Contrastive Analysis Hypothesis; the Similarity Differential Rate Hypothesis; the Markedness Differential Hypothesis; and phonological variation as explained by social context, Tarone's Interlanguage Continuum, and Major's Ontogeny Model, subsequently revised as the Ontogeny-Phylogeny Model. Finally, this chapter will discuss several studies examining the role of formal instruction in pronunciation. It is my hope to develop a more integrated and practical theory of second language phonological acquisition that will eventually serve to modify classroom methodologies in order to enhance the acquisition of Spanish pronunciation.

2.0 Learner Variables

2.1 The Effect of Age: Child versus Adult Acquisition of Pronunciation

Studies in both first and second language acquisition support the notion of a *critical* or *sensitive period* for acquiring linguistic skills, after which complete native or nativelike mastery of the language becomes quite difficult. Penfield and Roberts (1959) proposed that "for the purposes of learning languages the human brain becomes progressively stiff and rigid after the age of nine" (236). Later, Lenneberg (1967) claimed that the critical period of L1 acquisition correlated with the process of hemispheric lateralization, which, according to his research, is complete by the onset of puberty. Although empirical evidence seems to support the effect of brain lateralization on L2 acquisition and phonological development, there is apparent disagreement in terms of when cognitive reorganization or cerebral lateralization begins and what the direct consequences are.

Krashen (1972) and Krashen and Harshman's (1972) reevaluation of Lenneberg's data modifies his claims for the critical period and L2 acquisition. Krashen and Harshman claim that lateralization or hemispheric specialization is complete much earlier than puberty and should not be a barrier to native or near-native acquisition of a second language phonological system for adult learners. In fact, they conclude that Lenneberg's data support the hypothesis that lateralization occurs before the age of five, as opposed to puberty, and that children older than five can achieve nativelike pronunciation of a second language. Krashen (1982) notes, however, that neurophysiological or maturational changes, coupled with affective factors and cognitive operations, may account for the apparent differences between child and adult L2 acquisition. Schulz and Elliott (2000:118) add that individual learner factors such as motivation, attitudes toward the target language, intelligence, cognitive style, introversion, extroversion, ego permeability, and background knowledge, among other factors, may also affect language learning (Skehan 1989) and play a role for both younger and older learners.

Few areas in second language acquisition have drawn as much attention as the apparent differences between child and adult learners. Researchers have examined the critical period in relation to adult acquisition of L2 morphology (Johnson and Newport 1989; Patkowski 1980), morphosyntax (White and Genesee 1996; DeKeyser 2000), syntax (Johnson and Newport 1989; Patkowski 1980); lexical acquisition (Strozer 1994; Schulz and Elliott 2000) and pronunciation (Oyama 1976, 1982; Seliger 1978; Krashen, Long, and Scarcella 1979; Scovel 1981, 1988; Patkowski 1990; Tahta, Wood, and Loewenthal 1981; Flege, Munro, and MacKay 1999; Loewenthal and Bull 1983; Snow and Hoefnagle-Höhle 1977; Olson and Samuels 1973; Tun and Wingfield 1997; Elliott 1995a, 1995b, 1997). Others have examined the critical or sensitive period and ultimate attainment in relation to an adult's age of arrival and length of residence in the target language country (Oyama 1982; Schulz and Elliott 2000; Moyer 1999), mastery of grammatical structures in terms of production and recognition (Coppieters 1987; Harley 1986; Johnson and Newport 1989; Patkowski 1980), amount and quality of native-speaker input (Flege and Liu 2001), and the effect of formal instruction.

With regard to child-adult differences and the acquisition of L2 phonology, Scovel (1969:245) observed that adults, when learning a second language, "never seem capable of ridding themselves entirely of foreign accent." According to the Critical Period Hypothesis, with the onset of puberty, the second language learner experiences a cognitive reorganization associated with cerebral lateralization that consequently results in permanent neurophysiological changes and loss of brain plasticity. Scovel (1969) maintains that loss of brain plasticity explains the fundamental difference between children and adults when acquiring a second language phonological system. He states that the "same plasticity that accounts for the ability of the child to relocate speech to the nondominant hemisphere accounts for the plasticity that must be evident in the neurophysiological mechanisms underlying the productions of the sound patterns of a second language" (252). He argues that the "simultaneous occurrence of brain lateralization and the advent of foreign accents is too great a coincidence to be left neglected" (252).

Almost without exception, researchers, second language teachers, and learners believe that children are better language learners than adults in the long run. Many L2 studies (Oyama 1976, 1982; Seliger 1978; Krashen, Long, and Scarcella 1979; Scovel 1981, 1988; Patkowski 1990; Tahta, Wood, and Loewenthal 1981; Flege, Munro, and MacKay 1995) have shown that childhood and early adolescence is the best age range for successful language acquisition in terms of rate of learning and ultimate attainment (McLaughlin 1987:29). Research studies by Kenyeres (1938), Oyama (1982) and Tahta, Wood, and Loewenthal (1981) all found that younger learners were more successful at L2 phonological acquisition. Counterevidence to this claim was found by Loewenthal and Bull (1983) and Pennington and Richards (1986), who attributed these findings to the effects of the social situation on phonological performance. Other studies examining child-adult differences in L2 acquisition have favored the adult language learner, indicating that "older is indeed better" (Genesee 1976, 1988; Neufeld 1978; Snow 1983, 1987; Ellis 1985; Flege 1987; Loewenthal and Bull 1983; Snow and Hoefnagel-Höhle 1977; Olson and Samuels 1973; Tun and Wingfield 1997).

Long and Scarcella (1979) note that on careful comparison of the child-adult studies a definite pattern emerges: older is apparently faster initially, but younger is better in terms of ultimate attainment. Subsequent research by Genesee (1988), Snow (1983, 1987), Ellis (1985), and Flege (1987) supports this claim. In addition, Long (1990) notes that although the ability to acquire a second language diminishes with age, there may be several different critical periods for different components of L2 acquisition. Long (1990:280) adds, for example, that "native-like morphology and syntax only seem to be possible for those beginning before age 15" but that the critical period for phonological acquisition may be earlier.

Scovel (1969, 1988), Walsh and Diller (1981), and Seliger (1978) concur with Long, noting the existence of several critical periods that govern various aspects of L2 acquisition, each closing at different times. The ability to acquire native pronunciation of the L2, for example, appears to be the first to diminish at or around the onset of puberty. Scovel (1988:108) argues that L2 pronunciation appears to be the only skill that is truly constrained by the critical period. Unlike other L2 skills, such as morphology, syntax, or lexical acquisition, L2 pronunciation has a neuromuscular basis, requiring neuromotor involvement and a physical reality, thus making it more vulnerable to maturational constraints.

Strozer (1994) proposes that the acquisition of L2 vocabulary may be the only area of L2 acquisition that does not appear to be affected by maturational constraints and that adults, like their child counterparts, have equal chances for acquiring the L2 lexicon. Schulz and Elliott's (2000) study of a fifty-seven-year-old woman's acquisition of Spanish over a five-month period seems to support such a claim. This study found statistically significant decreases in the number of lexical problems for the adult learner during a five-month stay in Colombia. They note that measurements of the adult's lexical acquisition in pre- and post-tests showed that she suffered from "less interference from French, used fewer English words, engaged in less nonsensical word formations, mispronounced or misspelled fewer words, and used fewer words inappropriately" (114). Schulz and Elliott's findings should be interpreted with caution since Schulz is an expert in applied linguistics. The authors maintain, however, that her experiences learning Spanish were "not unlike any other mature adults who are motivated to learn a second language" (116). Although personal accounts can provide valuable insights into language learning and acquisition processes, Schulz's diary entries are nevertheless subjective (117) and reflect the experiences of an adult who has considerable experience in learning and teaching languages. The findings of this research cannot, therefore, be viewed as generalizable to other mature adults who are learning an L2 who are lacking said experience.

Although scientific empirical studies coupled with considerable anecdotal evidence have led to recurrent claims regarding a sensitive period for L2 phonological acquisition and child-adult differences, researchers (e.g., Flege, Munro, and MacKay 1995) note that there are some children who, in spite of having acquired the L2 prior to the critical period, may never achieve native or nativelike pronunciation. Aside from the few anomalous cases, it appears, however, that ultimate L2 phonological acquisition is constrained for most by biological differences related to age. Although adults may have an advantage initially, it appears that children eventually surpass their adult counterparts and are more successful in acquiring native or nativelike pronunciation.

2.2 Gender

L1 studies focusing on gender differences in relation to pronunciation ability have shown that women in Western societies tend to use more formal and prestigious phonological patterns when speaking their native language (e.g., Wolfram 1969, Trudgill 1974, López Morales 1983, Silva Corvalán 2001). Major (2001) notes that similar findings have been reported in SLA research on pronunciation and gender. Weiss (1970), Gussenhoven (1979), Broeders (1982), and Hiang and Gupta (1992) found that females had better pronunciation than did males and that females were more likely to use prestige forms in comparison to their male counterparts.

Some studies in L2 acquisition have focused on gender as an explanation for individual differences when learning/acquiring a second or foreign language. Researchers have speculated that females, in comparison to males, tend to be superior language acquirers. With regard to L2 pronunciation, Asher and García (1969) note that females have an initial advantage over males when acquiring target language pronunciation. On the other hand, Suter (1976) found a nonsignificant correlation between gender and subject accuracy of English pronunciation indicating that females were not better than males. Likewise, Elliott (1995a) reported a nonsignificant relationship between gender and subjects' scores for pronunciation accuracy by native English-speaking college students learning Spanish on four different L2 pronunciation tasks: word repetition exercises, word reading exercises, sentence repetition exercises, and a free elicitation exercise.

Although anecdotal evidence seems to suggest that females have better L2 pronunciation than do males, empirical research provides preliminary evidence that this relationship is indeed negligible and does not support such a claim.

2.3   Affect and Attitude

Teachers and researchers have long recognized the importance of attitude in language acquisition. Mantle-Bromley (1995:373) views *attitude* as consisting of three main components: *affect*, for example, the degree to which a student likes or dislikes the target language and/or the target language culture; *cognition*, what a particular person knows or believes about the attitudinal object, regardless of the veracity of such beliefs; and *behavior*, defined as the L2 learner's intentions or actions relating to the attitudinal object. Mantle-Bromley maintains that a combination of affective reactions, cognition, and behavior constitutes one's "overall attitude toward the language and culture" (373).

Previous studies examining target language pronunciation have provided preliminary evidence suggesting a linear relationship between learner attitude and the acquisition of native or near-native pronunciation. Harlow and Muyskens (1994:146) note that students "worry about pronunciation a great deal because they feel insecure about how they sound to other people." Consequently, students might be reluctant to imitate the target language sound system. Aronson (1973) maintains that "attitudinal, cultural and socio-psychological factors" play an important role in the acquisition of an L2 phonological system. Furthermore, Aronson (1973:324) notes that student motivation for acquiring native or near-native pronunciation is diminished when certain L2 intonation patterns carry tacit connotations with which the student does not want to mark himself. He concludes that some native American English speakers' resistance to acquire the Castilian /θ/ can be explained by examining the phonetic environment in which this sound occurs. Because the environment of the Castilian /θ/ coincides with that of the undesirable English lisp, American English speakers are reluctant to produce this sound in Spanish. He states that "[it] is the cultural, social connotation of lisping that causes the American student to resist to a greater or lesser degree acquiring the proper pronunciation [of the Castilian /θ/]" (325).

In his study focusing on pronunciation accuracy of university students studying intermediate Spanish as a foreign language, Elliott (1995a, 1995b) found that subject attitude toward developing native or near-native pronunciation, as measured by the Pronunciation Attitude Inventory, was the most significant variable in relation to target language pronunciation. The study revealed that subjects who were more concerned about their pronunciation of Spanish as a foreign language tended to have better mastery of the target language allophones. This finding lends credence to an earlier claim by Suter (1976), who found that subject concern for acquiring proper pronunciation in English correlated significantly with ESL subjects' scores in English pronunciation.

It would appear then, as suggested by empirical research to date, that attitude or subject concern for successful mastery of the L2 phonological system plays a pivotal role in phonological acquisition. As such, Elliott (1997) argues that teaching Spanish pronunciation during the initial stages of language acquisition may conversely increase student concern for developing native/nativelike pronunciation. This, in turn, will help to lower students' affective filters by making them feel less anxious about speaking. With renewed confidence in the way they sound, students might be more likely to seek out native speakers with whom to converse. More contact with native speakers translates to greater amounts of target language input, which will serve to enhance our students' mastery of the second language phonological system.

2.4   Field Independence/Field Dependence

Field independence/dependence (FI/D) is defined as a cognitive style that represents the "extent to which the person perceives part of a field as discrete from the surrounding field as a whole, rather than embedded in the field; or the extent to which the organization of the prevailing field determines the perception of its components; or, to put it in everyday terminology, the extent to which a person perceives analytically" (Witkin et al. 1977:6–7). A *field independent* individual "may be described as relying on an internal orientation, whereas a *field dependent* person relies on external orientation" (Jamieson 1992:492).

Although it is difficult to determine to what extent cognitive style influences L2 acquisition, researchers examining the FI/FD as a predictor have reported the following findings: (1) field independence correlates significantly to traditional classroom activities such as those found in grammar-based methodologies; (2) FI relates to student scores on linguistic, integrative (e.g., cloze passages), and communicative measures (Hansen and Stansfield 1981); and (3) FI has a minor relationship to tests that measure reading comprehension. Hansen and Stansfield (1981) note that biases result from individual cognitive styles insofar as field independent students are favored over their field dependent counterparts in cloze passage performance.

With regard to Spanish L2 phonological acquisition, Elliott (1995a) found that field independence related significantly to pronunciation accuracy on different types of L2 pronunciation tasks. He reported that FI individuals tended to have better target language pronunciation of Spanish allophones on more controlled discrete word and sentence pronunciation repetition exercises. FI was also significantly related to pronunciation accuracy with free speech data when the subjects' attention was focused on communicating meaning over pronunciation. Furthermore, he maintains that subjects who had more formal instruction in Spanish had more accurate pronunciation of the target language; however, the relationship between pronunciation accuracy and total number of years of formal study of Spanish was lost in a multiple regression analysis when factors such as attitude and FI were taken into consideration.

In a follow-up study, Elliott (1995b) proposed that the overall effect of cognitive style and FI in relation to Spanish pronunciation accuracy could be eliminated, or at least diminished, when students are taught in a way that appeals to all learning styles and preferences. By employing a multimodal methodology, differences in pronunciation ability of the target language as they related to FI were neutralized due to the type of formal instruction provided. In other words, by employing a variety of instructional techniques designed specifically to account for learning-style variation, teachers and curriculum designers recognize the importance of learning styles from the outset and lessen the role that cognitive style plays in L2 acquisition.

3.0 Theories of Phonological Acquisition

3.1 The Contrastive Analysis Hypothesis

One of the best-known hypotheses of language acquisition in the 1960s and early 1970s was the Contrastive Analysis Hypothesis (CAH). Highly influenced by Behaviorism, a major underlying tenet of CAH was that language acquisition consisted of habit formation and that errors in the L2 could be easily traced to the learner's first language. Under the precepts of contrastive analysis, researchers systematically compared two or more languages in order to determine both similarities and differences. Consequently, it was believed that similarities would present L2 learners with little difficulty insofar as these features could be easily transferred from the L1 to the L2. Conversely, it would be possible to account for L2 errors by examining areas in which the L2 structure differed significantly from the L1. By identifying dissimilar structures between the native and second language, it would be possible to pinpoint critical areas where errors would likely occur in morphology, phonology, syntax, and semantics. Furthermore, by knowing problematic areas it would be possible for teachers and curriculum designers to tailor language curricula in order to meet the anticipated needs of specific L1 populations.

Extensive research on CAH led to two separate schools of thought or positions regarding this hypothesis: the strong and weak versions. Under the strong version, or the *a priori* approach, researchers and teachers believed that systematic comparisons of L1 to the L2 would enable one to predict all errors that L2 learners would produce. Two major problems surfaced from the strong version: CA predicted errors that never occurred, and errors that did occur in L2 production could not be traced back to the learner's L1 nor remotely explained by CA. In fact, it was noted that learners sometimes produced sounds that were not found in either the L1 or L2 (Flege 1980; Berger 1951; Nemser 1971a, 1971b; Dickerson 1974; Elliott 1997). The weak, or *a posteriori* approach, started with an analysis of learners' L2 errors and subsequently attempted to identify the source of the errors through a systematic comparison of the native language to the target language.

With regard to phonological acquisition, Weinreich (1953) claimed that interference on a phonological level can occur in the following ways:

1. Sound substitution: An L2 learner tries to use the closest sound equivalent from the L1. For example, a native English-speaker may substitute the English alveolar /t/ for the Spanish postdental variant. Likewise, a Spanish speaker typically substitutes the Spanish trilled r for the English retroflex.

2. Phonological processes: Research has shown that allophonic differences are more difficult to acquire in comparison to phonemic ones. For example, Elliott (1995b) has shown that it is much easier for subjects to acquire the Spanish voiced alveolar trill than it is to learn when or when not to use the voiced nonfricative continuants [b d g] or learning when to voice the phoneme /s/ when it comes before a voiced consonant.

Hardy (1993) made a similar claim when she studied a native Spanish speaker when acquiring pronunciation of English. She found that it was easier for her subject to master sounds that were not already present in his language than it was to learn the allophonic differences in relation to phonetic environments in which the sound occurred. Flege (1991, 1992, and references therein) has addressed this issue at length and has proposed that "equivalence classification" may account for this difficulty. That is, when the learner is confronted with L2 sounds that are similar to L1, the learner may equate the two and substitute the L1 sound during L2 speech.

3. Underdifferentiation: The L2 has sound distinctions that are not present in the L1—for example, a native speaker of English using [d] for [d] and [đ]; [b] for [b] and [b̞] or [R] for [r] and [rr] in Spanish.

4. Overdifferentiation: The L1 has distinctions that the L2 does not have. Major (2001) notes that although this alone may not contribute to a foreign accent or to nonnative pronunciation of the second language, it results in a different mental representation that differs from that of a native speaker. For example, in Spanish the phoneme /d/ has two basic allophones, [d] and [đ], whereas in English these sounds represent two different phonemes. Therefore, English learners of Spanish may have trouble acquiring these two Spanish sounds as allophones of one phoneme. Major notes that the "reasons for these psycholinguistic differences are that allophones are usually not at the level of consciousness of a native speaker, while phonemes are" (2001:32).

5. Reinterpretation of distinctions: According to distinctive feature theory, languages consist of features that are either primary or secondary. For example, in English, vowel quality is primary while length is secondary. Therefore, American English speakers do not hear vowel length differences in word pairs such as *sheep* versus *ship* and *beet* versus *bit* and will frequently experience difficulty in learning languages in which vowel length is primary and vowel quality is secondary. Such cross-linguistic differences between primary and secondary features can lead to misinterpretation and consequently result in mispronunciations of the target language.[1]

6. Phonotactic interference: Phonotactic interference occurs when sound patterns differ from the L1 to the L2. Such differences can result in the modification of syllable and word patterns to match those of the L1. Major (2001:32) notes that a Spanish speaker may add an initial 'e' sound to English words that begin with an "S+cons" cluster, resulting in mispronunciations such as: "estudent" for "student," "estop" for "stop," and "eslave" for "slave."

7. Prosodic interference: Prosodic interference occurs when L1 and L2 prosodic features (e.g., tone, rhythm, and stress) differ. This typically results in modifying L2 prosodic features to match the L1. Prosodic interference is especially noticeable between syllable-timed versus stress-timed languages, for example, English and Spanish respectively.

Drawing upon the tenets of the CAH, Stockwell and Bowen (1965) proposed a hierarchy of phonological difficulty in their contrastive study of the sounds of English and Spanish. Table 1.1 provides an example of the hierarchy they proposed ordered from the most to the least difficult. According to their hypothesis, one should be able to predict difficult Spanish L2 sounds based on whether the allophones are present or absent in the L1 and if present, whether the sound is obligatory or optional.

Table 1.1

Stockwell and Bowen's (1965) Hierarchy of Phonological Difficulty

Native Language	Target Language	Degree of Difficulty
Ø	Obligatory	Difficult
Ø	Optional	
Optional	Obligatory	
Obligatory	Optional	
Obligatory	Ø	
Optional	Ø	
Optional	Optional	
Obligatory	Obligatory	Easy

Stockwell and Bowen (1965) maintain that sounds not present in the native language (English) but present and obligatory in the target language (Spanish) will pose the most difficulty to L2 learners. For example, the hierarchy predicts that a native speaker of English would have considerable difficulty learning to pronounce the Spanish trilled r in words like *ropa* and *carretera*. On the other hand, sounds that exist in both languages and are obligatory will be the easiest to learn. For example, a nonnative speaker of either language should acquire the 'n' sound with relative ease because both Spanish and English have the voiced alveolar nasal [n]. Considering the two polar extremes, the model predicts that new and unfamiliar sounds will be the most difficult to learn and sounds that exist in both languages will be easy to master.

Subsequent research in L2 phonological acquisition, however, has provided preliminary evidence that is contrary to this claim. Hardy (1993) found that it was easier for her subject to learn new sounds not present in Spanish, his native language. For example, learning to use the English v was easier than it was to correct faulty pronunciation due to positional constraints (e.g., learning to pronounce z in word initial position) or to differences in allophonic rules between the two languages (e.g., learning when/when not to use fricative d). Furthermore, Elliott (1997) found that native English-speaking students acquiring Spanish at a large midwestern university evidenced statistically significant improvement in their pronunciation of the voiced alveolar trill following fifteen weeks of instruction in pronunciation in comparison to the subjects' acquisition of the voiced stop and nonfricative continuant allophones. Elliott (1995b, 1997) found a pattern that was strikingly similar in all analyses—phonemic differences were much easier to acquire than were allophonic differences. In other words, sounds that differ in comparison to English due to positional constraints, such as the n assimilating to a bilabial or the voicing of the s to a voiced consonant, evidenced little to no improvement as a result of instruction, even though pronouncing these sounds should be easy for native English speakers. In this case, CAH would have failed to have predicted both Elliott's and Hardy's findings.

Both Hardy and Elliott's findings lend credence to Major and Kim (1999), who proposed the Similarity Differential Rate Hypothesis (SDRH). According to the precepts of the SDRH, "dissimilar phenomena are acquired at a faster rate than similar phenomena and that markedness [to be discussed at a later point] is a mediating factor that slows rate" (Major and Kim 1999:152). That is to say, sounds that are not present in the learner's L1 phonological system appear to be early-acquired features, whereas similar sounds, those that exist in both L1 and L2, tend to be late-acquired. What Major and Kim propose is quite contrary to the predictions made by Stockwell and Bowen (1965) in their application of CAH to Spanish phonological acquisition.

3.2 Markedness Differential Hypothesis

Several researchers (Eckman 1977, 1987; Eckman and Iverson 1993; Carlisle 1988, 1994; Castino 1992; Cebrian 1997) have examined markedness as a means of explaining the acquisition of second language phonological systems. In his study of markedness and phonological acquisition, Eckman incorporates the concept of typological markedness or the notion of "relative degree of difficulty" (Eckman 1977:320) into contrastive analysis theory. Eckman (1977:320) defines markedness thus: "A phenomenon A in some language is more marked than B if the presence of A in a language implies the presence of B but the presence of B does not imply the presence of A." For example, the voiced nonfricative continuants in Spanish [b d g] imply the presence of their voiced stop counterparts [b d g] but not the reverse; therefore [b d g] are the marked forms and will consequently be more difficult to acquire.

Three major predictions regarding L2 acquisition are made by the Markedness Differential Hypothesis (Eckman 1977:321):

1. Areas of the target language that differ from the native language and are more marked than the native language will be difficult.

2. The relative degree of difficulty of the areas of the target language that are more marked than the native language will correspond to the relative degree of markedness.

3. Those areas of the target language that are different from the native language but are not more marked than the native language will not be difficult.

Larsen-Freeman and Long (1991) note that Eckman's MDH has not received the attention that the theory warrants. Future research might benefit from reexamining this theory in relation to phonological acquisition in order to refine it and generate more precise, albeit more complex, hierarchies of phonological acquisition. This in turn would enable teachers and researchers to identify more easily those sounds that are more difficult to acquire and perhaps tailor instruction accordingly.

Furthermore, recent empirical research (Elliott 1997) has provided preliminary evidence that hierarchies of sound acquisition as predicted by the MDH appear to reflect natural orders of sound acquisition and universal phonological principles as posited by Jakobson (1968). For example, Elliott (1997) examined the effect of formal phonological instruction in Spanish and subject Spanish pronunciation, improvement or otherwise, from the beginning to the end of the semester. Elliott (1995b, 1997) found that with regard to the acquisition of the nonfricative continuants [b d g], the intervocalic 'b' was the only continuant to improve. On a universal scale, Jakobson (1968) notes that fricatives are more marked than their stop counterparts and consequently are more difficult to acquire.

What Elliott (1995b, 1997) did not expect, however, was that some subjects in the experimental group evidenced idiosyncratic behavior by replacing the stop 'b' with the fricative variant, thus resulting in overgeneralization of [b]. Furthermore, other subjects sporadically used the stop and fricative 'b' ([b b]) in free variation without any noticeable consistency. Although both the MDH and Jakobson's theories of universal phonological principles would have predicted the late acquisition of the nonfricative continuants, the theories would not have predicted subject overgeneralization of [b] nor usage of the stop and fricative 'b' in free variation. In fact, no other theory to date has been offered that could explain or predict overgeneralization of target language sounds. Perhaps future research in the area of perception, production, and systematic reorganization of the learner's L2 phonological system might explain overgeneralization as well as other phonological idiosyncrasies.

3.3 Major's Ontogeny Model, The Ontogeny Phylogeny Model, and Tarone's Continuum: Social Context and Phonological Variation

Pennington and Richards (1986) note that disparate results obtained in L2 pronunciation research are due in part to variation in experimental design, and particularly to varying models of phonological instruction provided. Furthermore, they maintain that "phonological performance in the target language is affected by communicative demands of the situation or task in which the learner is engaged" (217). Drawing on theoretical research by McLaughlin, Rossman, and McLeod (1983), Pennington and Richards view L2 phonological learning from an information-processing perspective in which subject pronunciation varies on a continuum ranging from conscious attention to automatic processing. They state that when L2 learners feel stressed, for example, during a public presentation, "performance conditions may inhibit access to automatic processing" (217). The consequence of such stressful social situations is a diminished ability to perform and a decrease in accurate L2 pronunciation.

Similarly, Tarone (1983) argues that a learner's interlanguage will evidence systematic variability on a continuum ranging from careful to vernacular speech styles. Vernacular styles produce "the most regular and systematic phonological and grammatical patterns" (Tarone 1979:181), whereas careful styles are susceptible to target and native language interference. Tarone (1979:186) argues that whenever "a speaker is systematically observed," careful speech will result. If experimental subjects are aware they are being tape-recorded, their speech will not be "monitor-free" and will constitute a more careful style that, according to Tarone, will evidence more target and native language interference.

Considering the effect social context may have on L2 production and pronunciation, Tarone notes that researchers are faced with an experimental paradox: How to get good recorded data without bringing about a style shift from the vernacular to careful speech styles? She states that "if we get good recorded data, we get bad data in the sense that the speaker has focused attention on speech and style-shifted away from the vernacular, which is the most systematic interlanguage style and therefore what we may want to study" (1979:188). Drawing on Labov's (1969) "Observer's Paradox" and his five methodological axioms, Tarone maintains that research into the systematic nature of interlanguage is possible only if researchers are constantly aware of its extreme sensitivity to context and attempt to control for its "chameleon-like nature" (188).

Major's (1987) Ontogeny Model, on the other hand, predicts that transfer errors are more frequent in casual speech but decrease as speech becomes more formal. Major (1987:107) states that "speakers are able to correctly produce sounds and words in isolation, but in running speech they slip back into L1 patterns." The Ontogeny Model claims that over time, transfer processes decrease, while developmental processes are at first infrequent, later increase, and still later decrease. Although researchers knew that transfer and developmental factors played an important role in L2 acquisition and had been aware of them for nearly twenty years, Major (2001) notes that before the Ontogeny Model, no theory existed that could explain their interaction.

Recent research supports Major's claims. Elliott (1997) found that students learning Spanish evidenced more transfer errors during a free elicitation exercise in which subjects described one of two familiar pictures. According to Major, free elicitation exercises are less formal than word/sentence repetition or word reading exercises and would therefore evidence more transfer/interlingual errors. Elliott (1997) reported that as students focused their attention on communicating meaning as opposed to their pronunciation, more transfer errors emerged, such as the retroflexion of [r] and [rr], diphthongization, vowel lengthening, and the use of stops in fricative environments. Similar findings were reported by Volker (1996) and Derwing, Munro, and Wiebe (1998).

Major (2001) has revised the ontogeny model to include the concept of "the life cycle of whole languages" or language groups, which takes into account issues such as historical development, dialectal variation, language shift and maintenance, language loss, and language contact, to name a few.

4.0 The Acquisition of Spanish L2 Pronunciation

Major (2001) notes that four levels of investigation are possible in the study of phonological acquisition: (1) individual segments (e.g., being able to pronounce the [r] in *pero* and the [rr] in *perro*); (2) combinations of segments, (e.g., the ability to pronounce a triphthong in a word such as *apreciáis*); (3) prosodic or paralinguistic features consisting of stress, rhythm, tone, and intonation; and (4) global accent: the overall accent of the nonnative speaker. The majority of empirical studies thus far in Spanish appear to have examined pronunciation ability as it relates to transfer (Zampini 1994), the grapheme-phoneme effect (Zampini 1994; Elliott 1995a, 1995b, 1997), perception and production (Rosenmann 1987; Zampini 1998a), subject mimetic or mimephonic ability (Reeder 1997), and subject ability to pronounce individual sounds such as the pronunciation of stops (Nathan 1987; Zampini 1994; González-Bueno 1997) and voiceless stops and trills (Reeder 1997).

Few of these studies have used subject mimetic ability as a measure of Spanish L2 pronunciation. For example, Rosenmann (1987) compared fifty English-speaking children and fifty young adults' ability in auditory discrimination and oral production of Spanish sounds. While she hypothesized that children would perform better than adults, statistical analyses of the data indicated that adults were superior in both auditory discrimination and sound production. For the pronunciation portion of her study, subjects were instructed to repeat Spanish words after a native speaker model. None of her subjects had ever been exposed to Spanish nor had used it as a natural means of communication. For them, the words they repeated were nonsensical and meaningless. The apparent superiority of adults' pronunciation or repetition of "nonsensical" words led Rosenmann to claim that adults are more efficient and successful at learning a second language owing to their cognitive advantage and level of maturity—a finding that does not support the critical age hypothesis. In addition, judges were instructed to rate subject pronunciation of particular allophones as either good or bad. Such a rating scale does not enable researchers to examine intermediate stages of phonological development as do other studies by Suter (1976) and Elliott (1995a, 1995b, 1997). Research examining L2 phonological acquisition and development should employ subjects who have had at least minimal exposure to the target language as a natural means of communication. Mimetic ability, in my opinion, is not the equivalent of natural phonological development and should not be regarded as such.

With regard to the effect of transfer, most recently referred to as cross-linguistic influence, Zampini (1994) found that native language transfer hampers English speakers' acquisition of the Spanish voiced spirants [β ð ɣ]. She notes that this is especially true for the Spanish allophone [ð] given its phonemic status in English. In addition, Zampini found that the grapheme v interferes with the acquisition of the Spanish [b] and [β] allophones, leading to less accurate pronunciation in formal reading tasks. In order to combat the adverse effects of transfer and spelling, Zampini recommends oral exercises that focus on allophonic and phonemic differences between Spanish and English and on differences relating to orthography as well. Elliott (1995b) made a similar proposal to Zampini's with respect to teaching pronunciation in a communicatively oriented classroom. He shows that improvement in Spanish pronunciation for adult learners is possible by employing a multimodal methodology that accounts for individual learning style variation. The methodology aims to promote a metalinguistic awareness based on interlingual allophonic and phonemic similarities and differences as well as an awareness of the grapheme-phoneme relationship.

Zampini (1998a), in addition, examined the relationship between perception and production in the acquisition of Spanish /b/ and /p/. In her study, she examined voice onset timing of /b/ and /p/ in Spanish and English. She found that students in an advanced undergraduate course in Spanish phonetics showed significant gains toward nativelike ability in both production and perception; however, she did not find a statistically significant relationship between production and perception.

In a follow-up study, Zampini (1998b) found that thirty-two second- and fourth-semester English-speaking students of Spanish acquire the nonfricative continuants [β ð ɣ] in predictable stages that correspond to a prosodic hierarchy (for a detailed account of the theory of prosodic phonology, see Selkirk 1980 and Nespor and Vogel 1986). She found that subjects tend to spirantize these sounds much more frequently when they occur within words (e.g., *estudio*) than they do across word boundaries (e.g., *bastante dificil*). When addressing the limitations of her study, Zampini notes that students may be aware of environments in which spirantization occurs, but may be hampered by their inability to speak the language fast enough. Consequently, she recommends developing pedagogical materials that move beyond simple contrastive analysis of Spanish and English phones and control the phonetic environment in which these sounds appear in order to facilitate learning.

5.0 The Effect of Formal Instruction on L2 Phonological Acquisition

Emphasis on the acquisition of second language phonological skills in the classroom has varied over the last century depending on the preferred method of instruction. Under the precepts of the Grammar Translation Approach (1930s through the 1950s), which focused heavily on the development of metalinguistic knowledge (i.e., the ability to describe the L2 linguistic system), reading, and writing, pronunciation received only peripheral attention.

With the onset of the Audiolingual Approach in the 1950s, pronunciation was no longer relegated to the back burner and was given great importance by both researchers and teachers. Based on the behaviorist premise of habit formation and mimicry/memorization, audiolingualists believed that all errors evidenced in the L2 could be traced back to the first language (this belief was especially true with regard to L2 phonological systems). The prevailing belief that orthographic conventions impeded correct target language pronunciation resulted in an effort to diminish the grapheme-phoneme effect. The first chapter of the Modern Language Association Spanish textbook *Modern Spanish* (1973) focused entirely on the second language phonological system. In this chapter, students learned detailed rules regarding the articulation of target language sounds. Concepts such as allophone/phoneme and point, place, and manner of articulation as well as rhythm, stress, and intonation were presented to the students. Students received additional pronunciation practice outside the classroom by completing listening and repetition exercises in the language laboratories.

With the advent of more communicative approaches to language learning and instruction in the 1980s, explicit instruction in target language pronunciation became a thing of the past and was generally limited to the preliminary chapters of language textbooks or found in the back pages of the textbook appendixes. While it may appear that researchers had examined almost every facet of language acquisition in relation to the Communicative Approach, the acquisition of pronunciation fell to the wayside and consequently suffered from serious neglect in the communicative classroom. Terrell (1989) notes that proponents of the Communicative Approach simply "have not known what to do with pronunciation" (197). He suggests that this is because "neither the Europeans nor the North Americans have devoted much time to the study of acquisition of sound systems" (197). On a more practical note, he argues that students' "pronunciation habits will ultimately depend on the ability to attend to and process input" (208) and can be enhanced through the use of advanced organizers and meaningful monitor activities for both beginning and advanced students.

Celce-Murcia (1987:6) believes that pronunciation can be taught by using tasks that "focus on meaning, using activities such as role playing, problem solving and games." Drawing on Celce-Murcia's (1987) concept of meaningful pronunciation activities, Terrell states that students should be presented with communicative activities that present phonemic contrasts, such as Spanish /p, t, k/. While completing such activities, students are instructed to carefully monitor their production of these sounds without aspiration (Terrell 1989:212). However, the question of the potential benefits of teaching pronunciation in the classroom remains.

Research studies examining the effect of formal instruction in pronunciation have yielded seemingly contradictory results. Formal instruction in pronunciation of a second or foreign language for the adult learner can: (1) have *no* relationship to pronunciation ability (Suter 1976); (2) have *beneficial* effects on pronunciation accuracy (Murakawa 1981; Neufeld and Schneiderman 1980; Elliott 1995a, 1995b); (3) have possible *negative* effects on pronunciation ability leading to the overgeneralization of sounds (Elliott 1995b). In addition, Elliott (1995b) found that when pronunciation is not taught in lower division Spanish courses, there is a slight decrease in subjects' pronunciation ability. McCandless and Winitz (1986:361) found that "extensive auditory input in the beginning stages of second language learning results in improved pronunciation relative to traditional procedures of language instruction." They add that given sufficient auditory exposure before attempting to communicate will increase the likelihood of an adult achieving nativelike pronunciation. Neufeld (1977) reported similar findings showing a positive effect of extensive listening on target language pronunciation before making attempts to communicate in the foreign language.

A synopsis of several empirical studies examining the effect of formal phonological instruction and/or pedagogical intervention is presented in table 1.2. It is important to note that although several of the studies report statistically significant improvement in pronunciation, none of the studies, except for Neufeld's (1977), claim that subjects had acquired pronunciation indistinguishable from that of a native speaker. Furthermore, only two of the studies surveyed (MacDonald, Yule, and Powers 1994; Suter 1976) reported a negligible relationship between phonological instruction and/or pedagogical intervention and the acquisition of an L2 phonological system. Suter's (1976) findings must be interpreted with caution because the variable he used for "formal instruction" solely indicated whether the subjects had ever received formal instruction in pronunciation. Suter did not, however, assess the quality or type of instruction that was provided.

Several conclusions can be garnered from the research examining the effect of formal instruction in L2 pronunciation and phonological development. First, formal instruction in L2 pronunciation appears to relate significantly to improvement in pronunciation, or at least with regard to the production of individual sounds. In general, subjects benefited from formal instruction in pronunciation; however, their improvement appears to fall short of native or nativelike L2 pronunciation. The issue of long-term effects of pronunciation instruction remains unanswered and appears to warrant further investigation. Most studies, be they ESL or modern languages, focus on incremental changes in L2 pronunciation shortly after formal phonological instruction or training has taken place. However, whether learners retain the effects of instruction over the long term (six months or more after training concludes) is not known.

Second, it is quite possible that the studies surveyed merely corroborate previous research on formal instruction which report a beneficial effect in terms of rate of L2 acquisition. It would be premature to address the beneficial effects of pronunciation instruction in terms of ultimate level of attainment. Future research might benefit from determining

Table 1.2
Studies in L2 Phonological Acquisition

Researcher	Purpose of study	Language	Subjects and Language	Type of Training	Results	S/NS*
Pimsleur (1963)	To evaluate student pronunciation of the French uvular /R/ after 50 minutes of auditory discrimination training	French as a second language	High school students learning French in Los Angeles	Experimental group subjects were asked to differentiate between American and French pronunciation of problematic sounds. Duration of training: 50 minutes.	Training was effective for French words ending in nasal vowel phonemes /ã õ ẽ/ but not effective for /o/ and /oᵘ/. Inherent differences in these sounds resulted in effective treatment for some and not for others.	S/NS
Suter (1976)	To identify variables that relate to pronunciation ability	English as a second language	61 nonnative speakers of English	Incidental classroom training as indicated on self-report.	Formal classroom training in pronunciation did not relate to pronunciation accuracy.	NS
Neufeld (1978)	To determine the effect of extensive auditory exposure on subsequent ability to pronounce Japanese and Chinese	Japanese and Chinese as a foreign language	20 adult learners of Japanese and Chinese	Students were provided with ample auditory exposure before production practice of Japanese and Chinese.	Many were classified as possessing native or near native pronunciation.	S
Murakawa (1981)	To determine the effect of phonetic instruction on the articulation of individual phonemes	English as a second language	Native Japanese speakers learning English in the US	Intensive phonetic training. Duration of training: 12 weeks.	Significant improvement in articulation of individual phonemes.	S
De Bot and Mailfert (1982)	To evaluate the effect of visual feedback denoting pitch changes in relation to English intonation	English as a foreign language	10 native French speakers learning English	Pretest/posttest design. Duration of training: 13 minutes.	Training in perception of intonation resulted in improved production of English intonation.	S

Table 1.2

Studies in L2 Phonological Acquisition (continued)

Study	Purpose	Language	Subjects	Description	Findings	
McCandless and Winitz (1986)	To examine the relationship between auditory practice and pronunciation performance in second language acquisition	German as a foreign language	40 American-English speaking university students learning German	End of year comparison of pronunciation accuracy among students studying under four different methodologies: (1) native speakers; (2) students of a comprehension class; (3) traditional approach; and (4) a control group. Duration of training: 240 hours.	Subjects in the comprehension group are rated higher in quality of speech production than were those of the traditional or control group; auditory exposure is an important consideration in the learning of native-like pronunciation patterns.	S
Mastreit (1987)	To evaluate the effectiveness of pronunciation instruction for L2 learners of French	French as a second language	8 native Catalan-speaking students: 6 females and 2 males studying at L'école de Traducteurs et d'Interprètes	Instruction provided was based on the verbo-tonal method, which depends on body movements to promote L2 acquisition and diminish nonnative accent. Duration of training: 3.5 months.	Statistically significant improvement was found in both sound discrimination and oral production of the L2.	S
Rosenman (1987)	To investigate the question of age in relation to second language learning	Spanish as a foreign language	50 first graders and 50 twelfth graders randomly chosen from Muncie, Indiana	Subjects were provided with auditory discrimination tests using minimal pairs in Spanish and an oral production test using words that differed in only one sound. No specific training in pronunciation was provided.	A multivariate analysis of variance indicated that adults were superior in both auditory discrimination and oral production in comparison to children.	S
Castino (1992)	To evaluate the effectiveness of formal knowledge of phonetics in relation to L2 learners' pronunciation of Spanish as a foreign language	Spanish as a foreign language	40 third- or fourth-year university students enrolled in a Spanish phonetics course	Pre- and posttest pronunciation scores were compared for students when (1) reading a dialogue and (2) engaged in spontaneous communication. Subjects received instruction regarding point, place and manner of articulation of Spanish phonemes.	L2 learners evidenced improved pronunciation of Spanish phonemes following extensive instruction in and increased comprehension of Spanish phonetic theory.	S

Table 1.2

Studies in L2 Phonological Acquisition *(continued)*

Researcher	Purpose of study	Language	Subjects and Language	Type of Training	Results	S/NS*
Hardy (1993)	To evaluate predictions regarding ease of phonological learning by employing controlled single-subject experimental methodologies common to speech-language pathology while focusing on the acquisition process by a second language learner	English as a second language	25-year-old male native Spanish speaker from Madrid, Spain, enrolled in intensive English language classes for six months while in the U.S.	Contrast training with minimal pairs. Duration of training: 6 months.	Minimal pair training resulted in immediate phonological improvement, however, when training was removed improvement was no longer apparent.	S
MacDonald, Yule, and Powers (1994)	To compare pronunciation, improved or otherwise, in relation to four different pedagogical practices	English as a second language	123 native English-speakers judged pronunciation of 23 adult Chinese ESL learners before and at two times subsequent to each of the four conditions	(1) traditional drills; (2) self-study with tapes; (3) interactive activities; and (4) no intervention.	No one intervention related to improvement in pronunciation of English by the Chinese learners.	NS
Ganschow and Sparks (1995)	To examine the effect of an academic year of direct instruction in the phonology/orthography of Spanish on the native-language skills and foreign language aptitude of high school women identified as at risk and not at risk for learning a foreign language	Spanish as a foreign language	14 at-risk women and 19 not-at-risk women	At-risk students were taught using a multisensory structured language approach with direct and explicit teaching of phonology/orthography in a highly structured, step-by-step fashion (Williams 1987). Not-at-risk subjects did not receive special instruction in pronunciation. Duration of training: 1 academic year.	Pre- and posttest comparisons between groups showed that the at-risk students made significantly greater gains than students in the not-at-risk group who did not receive such instruction. At-risk learners continued to lag behind not-at-risk learners in FL aptitude.	S
Volker (1996)	To examine the effect of formal instruction in German pronunciation for college students after 15 weeks of instruction	German as a foreign language	2 German classes at Southwestern university	The teaching of phonetic principles to help subjects predict sound occurrence; listening comprehension and articulation exercises. Duration of training: a 3-hour class per week for 15 weeks.	Pronunciation instruction resulted in improved pronunciation and spelling.	S

Table 1.2

Studies in L2 Phonological Acquisition (continued)

Study	Language	Subjects	Treatment	Results	S/NS
Elliott (1995a, 1995b, 1997)	To examine the effect of formal instruction in Spanish pronunciation	Spanish as a foreign language	66 Native-American English-speaking university students learning Spanish	Multimodal: formal instruction in pronunciation over a sixteen week period. Duration of training: 15 weeks.	Subjects in the experimental section experience statistically significant improvement.	S
González-Bueno (1997)	To test the hypothesis that formal instruction in the pronunciation of Spanish stops to native English speakers will result in improved pronunciation in comparison to control group subjects who did not have such instruction	Spanish as a foreign language	60 Native-American English-speaking students at Pennsylvania State University	5–10 minutes of formal instruction in the pronunciation of stops over a 15-week period.	Subjects in the experimental section experience statistically significant improvement as measured by a significant decrease in voice onset timing (VOT) in their pronunciation of /p/ and /g/ but not with /b, t, d, k/.	S with mixed results
Derwing, Munro, and Wiebe (1998)	To evaluate the effect of formal instruction in ESL pronunciation following 11 weeks of pronunciation instruction	English as a second language	48 ESL students	3 groups receiving different type of treatment: (1) segmental accuracy [teaching of individual sounds and syllables]; (2) Global focus [prosodic features including stress, intonation and rhythm]; (3) no pronunciation instruction. Duration of training: 11 weeks.	All groups improved their pronunciation of English as a Second Language, however, the segmental group's improvement was statistically significant.	S
Elliott (1999)	The effect of formal instruction in Spanish pronunciation on the order and accuracy of phonemic acquisition	Spanish as a foreign language	66 Native-American English-speaking university students learning Spanish	Multimodal instruction of particular sounds listed by teachers as contributing most to a foreign accent. Duration of training: 15 weeks.	Spearman rank order correlations comparing ranking of allophones for subjects in experimental and control sections did not change.	S

*S = significant, NS = not significant

whether students with formal instruction in L2 pronunciation have a greater chance of acquiring native or near-native pronunciation in comparison to those students who have not had such instruction. Research findings to date appear to support such a claim. In addition, we might also find that formal instruction in pronunciation is instrumental in enhancing student progress in other areas of L2 acquisition such as listening comprehension and even speaking. Consequently, further research in this area might reveal that formal instruction in pronunciation may ultimately enhance nonnative speaker communication with linguistically naive native speakers.

Third, although recent research (Murakawa 1981; Volker 1996; Castino 1992; Elliott 1995b, 1997) reports that adults benefit from formal phonological instruction, preliminary evidence suggests that there exists a natural order of sound acquisition and that this natural order remains unaltered due to instruction (Elliott 1999). Researchers should turn their attention to formal instruction in pronunciation in relation to universal phonological principles, Eckman's Markedness Differential Hypothesis, Major's Ontogeny-Phylogeny Model, and the more recent Optimality Theory.[2] Research of this nature might provide clues as to the existence of an interlanguage phonological system similar to those found in the acquisition of morphemes and other grammatical structures. In turn, we might be able to classify the interlanguage phonological system in terms of sounds that are early- or late-acquired and tailor classroom instruction accordingly.

Fourth, as researchers, we must not lose sight of the underlying fundamental, albeit practical, reason for carrying out empirical studies of this nature—the classroom. One of the most important findings of the current literature review is that pronunciation instruction, traditionally underemphasized in lower-division language courses, appears to be especially beneficial for adult foreign language learners who, according to students and teachers alike, rarely benefit from such instruction.

Several helpful and empirically tested techniques that can be easily incorporated into language curricula have come to light in the present review. These techniques include but are not limited to: (1) providing phonetic instruction of concrete rules about point, place, and manner of articulation as tested by Murakawa (1981), Ganschow and Sparks (1995), Volker (1996), Castino (1992), and Elliott (1995b, 1997); (2) providing extensive auditory exposure, (e.g., listening passages with student attention focused on sound over meaning), as per Neufeld (1978), McCandless and Winitz (1986), and Terrell (1989); (3) presenting sound distinctions through the use of articulatory facial diagrams as demonstrated by González-Bueno (1997) and Elliott (1995b, 1997); (4) tailoring instruction to focus on not only those sounds that are different or nonexistent in the students' target language but also those sounds that are similar in both the L1 and L2 as demonstrated by Murakawa (1981), Volker (1996), Hardy (1993), Castino (1992), and Elliott (1995b, 1997) and elaborated upon by Major and Kim (1999) in their discussion of the Similarity Differential Rate Hypothesis; and (5) providing students with immediate feedback in order to prevent phonological fossilization.

Fifth, I believe that both teachers and researchers need to recognize the effect that task has on L2 pronunciation. Research on pronunciation has shown that pronunciation ability varies on a continuum ranging from careful to vernacular speech styles. Vernacular styles tend to be more regular and systematic (Tarone 1979:181), whereas careful styles are more susceptible to both target and native language interference. As such, we should have more realistic expectations with regard to an adult's pronunciation of the L2 and expect varying degrees of accuracy when students are reading and/or speaking the second language.

Sixth, and finally, missing from the current body of research are studies examining differences between naturalistic and classroom phonological acquisition. Future research might reveal underlying universals that govern sound acquisition, whether in the classroom or in the target-language country. Several interesting proposals have been made on this topic, however, more empirical research is needed in order to substantiate such a claim.

6.0   Conclusion

The purpose of this chapter is to provide an overview of L2 phonological theory, research, and the effect of formal instruction in L2 pronunciation during the second half of the twentieth century, with particular attention paid to studies using Spanish L2 data. In this chapter we have examined what I view as several important theories that attempt to explain L2 phonological acquisition: biological and/or learner variables (e.g., the Critical Period Hypothesis; brain plasticity; cognitive reorganization; gender; affect and attitude; field independence/dependence); the Contrastive Analysis Hypothesis; the Similarity Differential Rate Hypothesis; the Markedness Differential Hypothesis; phonological variation as explained by social context, Tarone's Interlanguage Continuum, and Major's Ontogeny-Phylogeny Model. This chapter did not, however, cover other theories that, in addition to those discussed here, may provide further insight to L2 phonological acquisition (e.g., Phonological Translation Hypothesis [Flege 1981]; Motor Theory; Speech Perception Theory; Connectionism; Universal Grammar; Speech Learning Model; and Optimality Theory). As researchers carry out more investigations on L2 pronunciation and phonological acquisition, it is possible that the research generalizations offered in this chapter will be viewed differently and eventually modified. Clearly, further research into the nature of phonological acquisition and the teaching of pronunciation is needed.

As we move into the new century, prospects for future research appear bright. Questions addressing the existence of a natural order of phonological acquisition, natural versus classroom acquisition of L2 pronunciation, hierarchies of sound difficulty as well as the relationship between perception, production, and systematic reorganization of the learner's L2 phonological system remain unanswered. In order to progress in the pedagogical arena, and specifically in the teaching of pronunciation, we must first investigate those areas of phonological acquisition that remain unanswered. Findings from future research will prove to be particularly fruitful in helping us design both foreign and second language curricula as well as in making decisions regarding the sequencing of instruction and in the selection of classroom materials. As teachers, our ultimate goal should be to provide quality instruction that is effective in improving L2 phonological acquisition, especially for the adult learner—a goal that would be impossible to achieve if we were artificially to divorce theory and empirical research from practical classroom application.

NOTES

1. For a more in-depth discussion of reinterpretation of distinctions, see Major 2001.

2. Prince and Smolensky (1993) were the first to propose Optimality Theory (OT), which proposes that phonological systems consist of rankings and universal constraints and determine the phonetic shape of a word with an underlying representation known as input. OT claims that there is a set of constraints shared by all speakers and listeners. These constraints are general or natural tendencies of language that in some cases can be violated. Not only does OT allow researchers to make more specific hypotheses in relation to the effects of transfer, but it also enables us to determine the interaction between transfer and developmental processes in addition to how these processes change over time (Hancin-Bhatt and Bhatt 1997). To my knowledge, no research to date has focused on OT as an explanation for L2 acquisition of Spanish phonology.

WORKS CITED

Aronson, H. I. 1973. The role of attitudes in the learning of foreign languages. *Modern Language Journal* 57:323–27.

Asher J., and R. Garcia. 1969. The optimal age to learn a foreign language. *Modern Language Journal* 53:334–41.

Berger, M. D. 1951. The American English pronunciation of Russian immigrants. Ph.D. diss., Columbia University.

Broeders, A. 1982. Engels in Nederlandse oren: Uitspraakvoorkeur bij Nederlandse studenten Engels [English in Dutch Ears: Pronunciation preference in Dutch students of English]. *Toegepaste Taalkunde in Artikelen* 9:127–28.

Carlisle, R. S. 1988. The effect of markedness on epenthesis in Spanish/English interlanguage phonology. *Issues and Developments in English and Applied Linguistics* 3:15–23.

———. 1994. Markedness and environment as internal constraints on the variability of interlanguage phonology. In *First and second language phonology,* ed. M. Yavas, 223–49. San Diego, CA: Singular.

Castino, J. M. 1992. Markedness as a predictor of difficulty in the second language acquisition of Spanish phonology. Ph.D. diss., University of Pittsburgh.

Cebrian, J. 1997. Markedness and phrasal domain in the transferability of voicing rules in Catalan-English interlanguage. In *New sounds 97: Proceedings of the Third International Symposium on the Acquisition of Second Language Speech,* eds. J. Leather and A. James, 47–54. Klagenfurt: University of Klagenfurt.

Celce-Murcia, M. 1987. Teaching pronunciation as communication. In *Current perspectives on pronunciation: Practices anchored in theory,* ed. J. Morley, 1–12. Washington, DC: TESOL.

Coppieters, R. 1987. Competence differences between native and near-native speakers *Language* 63.3:544–73.

De Bot, K., and K. Mailfert. 1982. The teaching of intonation: Fundamental research and classroom applications. *TESOL Quarterly* 16:71–77.

DeKeyser, R. M. 2000. The robustness of critical period effects in second language acquisition. *Studies in Second Language Acquisition* 22:499–533.

Derwing, T., M. J. Munro, and G. Wiebe. 1998. Evidence in favor of a broad framework for pronunciation instruction. *Language Learning* 48:393–410.

Dickerson, L. J. 1974. Internal and external patterning of phonological variability in the speech of Japanese learners of English: Toward a theory of second language acquisition. Ph.D. diss., University of Illinois.

Eckman, F. R. 1977. Markedness and the contrastive analysis hypothesis. *Language Learning* 27:315–30.

———. 1987. Markedness and the contrastive analysis hypothesis. In *Interlanguage phonology: The acquisition of a second language sound system,* eds. G. Ioup and S. H. Weinberger, 55–69. Cambridge, MA: Newbury House.

Eckman, F. R., and G. K. Iverson. 1993. Sonority and markedness among onset clusters in the interlanguage of ESL learners. *Second Language Research* 9:234–52.

Elliott, A. R. 1995a. Field independence/dependence, hemispheric specialization, and attitude in relation to pronunciation accuracy in Spanish as a foreign language. *Modern Language Journal* 79:356–71.

———. 1995b. Foreign language phonology: Field independence, attitude, and success of formal instruction in Spanish pronunciation. *Modern Language Journal* 79:530–42.

———. 1997. On the teaching and acquisition of pronunciation within a communicative approach. *Hispania* 80.1:96–108.

———. 1999. The effect of formal instruction in Spanish pronunciation on the order and accuracy of phonemic acquisition. Paper presented at the American Association of Teachers of Spanish and Portuguese Annual Conference, Denver.

Ellis, R. 1985. *Undertaking second language acquisition.* Oxford: Oxford University Press.

Flege, J. E. 1980. Phonetic approximations in second language acquisition. *Language Learning* 30.1:117–34.

———. 1981. The phonological basis of foreign accent: A hypothesis. *TESOL Quarterly* 15:443–53.

———. 1987. A critical period for learning to pronounce foreign languages? *Applied Linguistics* 8.2:162–77.

———. 1991. Perception and production: The relevance of phonetic input to L2 phonological learning. In *Crosscurrents in second language acquisition and linguistic theories,* eds. T. Huebner and C. A. Ferguson, 249–89. Amsterdam: John Benjamins.

———. 1992. Speech learning in a second language. In *Phonological development: Models, research, implications,* eds. C. A. Ferguson, L. Menn, and C. Stoel-Gammon, 565–604. Timonium, MD: York Press.

Flege, J. E., and S. Liu. 2001. The effect of experience on adult's acquisition of a second language. *Studies in Second Language Acquisition* 23:527–52.

Flege, J. E., M. J. Munro, and I. R. A. MacKay. 1995. Factors affecting strength of perceived foreign accent in a second language. *Journal of the Acoustical Society of America* 97:3125–34.

Flege, J. E., G. H. Yeni-Komshian, and S. Liu. 1999. Age constraints on second-language acquisition. *Journal of Memory and Language* 41:78–104.

Ganschow, L., and R. Sparks. 1995. Effects of direct instruction in Spanish phonology on the native-language skills and foreign language aptitude of at-risk foreign language learners. *Journal of Learning Disabilities* 28.2:107–20.

Genesee, F. 1976. The role of intelligence in second language learning. *Language Learning* 23:267–80.

————. 1988. Neuropsychology and second language acquisition. In *Issues in second language acquisition: Multiple perspectives,* ed. L. Beebe, 81–112. Cambridge, MA: Newbury House.

González-Bueno, M. 1997. The effect of formal instruction on the acquisition of Spanish stop consonants. In *Contemporary perspectives on the acquisition of Spanish,* vol. 2, *Production, processing, and comprehension,* eds. W. R. Glass and A. T. Pérez-Leroux, 57–76. Somerville, MA: Cascadilla Press.

Gussenhoven, C. 1979. Pronunciation preference among Dutch students. Paper presented at the Second International Conference on the Teaching of Spoken English, University of Leeds.

Hancin-Bhatt, B., and R. M. Bhatt. 1997. Optimal L2 syllables: Interactions of transfer and developmental effects. *Studies in Second Language Acquisition* 19:331–78.

Hansen, J., and C. Stansfield. 1981. The relationship of field-dependent-independent cognitive styles to foreign language achievement. *Language Learning* 31:349–67.

Hardy, J. E. 1993. Phonological learning and retention in second language acquisition. In *Confluence: Linguistics, L2 acquisition and speech pathology,* ed. F. R. Eckman, 235–48. Amsterdam: John Benjamins.

Harley, B. 1986. *Age in second language acquisition.* Clevedon: Multilingual Matters Ltd.

Harlow, L. L., and J. A. Muyskens. 1994. Priorities for intermediate-level language instruction. *Modern Language Journal* 78:141–54.

Hiang, T. C., and A. F. Gupta. 1992. Postvocalic /r/ in Singapore English. *York Papers in Linguistics* 16:139–52.

Jakobson, R. 1968. *Child language, aphasia and phonological universals.* Netherlands: Mouton.

Jamieson, J. 1992. The cognitive styles of reflection/impulsivity and field independence/ dependence and ESL success. *Modern Language Journal* 76:491–501.

Johnson, J. and E. Newport. 1989. Critical period effects in second language learning: The influence of maturational state on the acquisition of English as a second language. *Cognitive Psychology* 21:60–99.

Kenyeres, A. 1938. Comment une petite Hongroise de sept ans apprend le français [How a little seven-year-old Hungarian girl learns French]. *Archives de Psychologie* 26:321–66.

Krashen, S. 1972. Language and the left hemisphere. *Working Papers in Phonetics* 24.

————. 1982. *Principles and practice in second language acquisition.* New York: Pergamon.

Krashen, S., and R. Harshman. 1972. Lateralization and the critical period. *Working Papers in Phonetics* 23.

Krashen, S., M. Long, and R. Scarcella. 1979. Age, rate, and eventual attainment in second language acquisition. *TESOL Quarterly* 13:573–82.

Labov, W. 1969. The study of language in its social context. *Studium Generale* 23:30–87.

Larsen-Freeman, D., and M. Long. 1991. *An introduction to second language acquisition research.* London: Longman.

Lenneberg, E. 1967. *Biological foundations of language.* New York: Wiley.

Loewenthal, K., and D. Bull. 1983. Imitation of foreign sounds: What is the effect of age? *Language and Speech* 27:95–98.

Long, M. H. 1990. Maturational constraints on language development. *Studies in Second Language Acquisition* 12:251–85.

López-Morales, H. 1983. *Estratificación social del español de San Juan de Puerto Rico.* México, DF: Universidad Autónoma de México.

MacDonald, D., G. Yule, and M. Powers. 1994. Attempts to improve English L2 pronunciation: The variable effects of instruction. *Language Learning* 44.1:75–100.

Major, R. C. 1987. A model for interlanguage phonology. In *Interlanguage phonology: The acquisition of a second language sound system,* eds. G. Ioup and S. H. Weinberger, 101–24. Cambridge, MA: Newbury House.

———. 2001. *Foreign accent: The ontogeny and phylogeny of second language phonology.* Hillsdale, NJ: Lawrence Erlbaum.

Major, R., and E. Kim. 1999. The similarity differential rate hypothesis. In *Phonological issues in language learning,* ed. J. Leather, 151–83. Malden, MA: Blackwell.

Mantle-Bromley, C. 1995. Positive attitudes and realistic beliefs: Links to proficiency. *Modern Language Journal* 79:372–86.

Mastreit, C. 1987. Perception et production des sons du français chez les apprenants bilingues [Bilingual learners' perception and production of French sounds]. *Revue de Phonétique Appliquée* 82–83:273–88.

McCandless, P., and H. Winitz. 1986. Test of pronunciation following one year of comprehension instruction in college German. *Modern Language Journal* 70:355–62.

McLaughlin, B. 1987. *Theories of second-language learning.* London: Edward Arnold.

McLaughlin, B., T. Rossman, and B. McLeod. 1983. Second language learning: An information processing perspective. *Language Learning* 33:135–59.

Modern Language Association. 1973. *Modern Spanish.* New York: Harcourt, Brace, Jovanovich.

Moyer, A. 1999. Ultimate attainment in L2 phonology: The critical factors of age, motivation and instruction. *Studies in Second Language Acquisition* 21:81–108.

Murakawa, H. 1981. Teaching English pronunciation to Japanese adults. Ph.D. diss., University of Texas at Austin.

Nathan, G. S. 1987. On the acquisition of voiced stops. *Journal of Phonetics* 15:313–22.

Nemser, W. 1971a. Approximative systems of foreign language learners. *International Review of Applied Linguistics* 9:115–23.

———. 1971b. *An experimental study of phonological interference in the English of Hungarians.* Indiana University Series in Uralic and Altaic Studies 105.

Nespor, M., and I. Vogel. 1986. *Prosodic phonology.* Dordrecht: Foris.

Neufeld, G. 1977. Language learning ability in adults: A study on the acquisition of prosodic and articulatory features. *Working Papers in Bilingualism* 12:45–60.

————. 1978. On the acquisition of prosodic and articulatory features in adult language learning. *Canadian Modern Language Review* 34:163–74.

Neufeld, G., and E. Schneiderman, E. 1980. Prosodic and articulatory features in adult language learning. In *Research in second language acquisition,* eds. R. C. Scarcella and S. D. Krashen, 105–9. Rowley, MA: Newbury House.

Olson, L. L., and J. S. Samuels. 1973. The relationship between age and accuracy of foreign language pronunciation. *Journal of Educational Research* 66.6:263–68.

Oyama, S. 1976. A sensitive period in the acquisition of a non-native phonological system. *Journal of Psycholinguistic Research* 5:261–85.

————. 1982. A sensitive period for the acquisition of a nonnative phonological system. In *Child-adult differences in SLA,* eds. S. Krashen, R. Scarcella, and M. Long, 20–38. Rowley, MA: Newbury House.

Patkowski, M. 1980. The sensitive period for the acquisition of syntax in a second language. *Language Learning* 30:449–72.

————. 1990. Age and accent in a second language: A reply to James Emil Flege. *Applied Linguistics* 11:73–89.

Penfield, W., and L. Roberts. 1959. *Speech and brain mechanisms.* Princeton: Princeton University Press.

Pennington, M., and J. Richards. 1986. Pronunciation revisited. *TESOL Quarterly* 20.2:207–25.

Pimsleur, P. 1963. Discrimination training in the teaching of French pronunciation. *Modern Language Journal* 47:199–203.

Prince, A. S., and P. Smolensky. 1993. *Optimality theory: Constraint interaction in generative grammar.* Piscataway, NJ: Rutgers University Cognitive Sciences Center.

Reeder, J. T. 1997. Mimephonic ability and phonological performance in adult learners of Spanish. In *Contemporary perspectives on the acquisition of Spanish,* vol. 2, *Production, processing, and comprehension,* eds. W. R. Glass and A. T. Pérez-Leroux, 77–90. Somerville, MA: Cascadilla Press.

Rosenmann, A. A. 1987. The relationship between auditory discrimination and oral production of Spanish sounds in children and adults. *Journal of Psycholinguistic Research* 16.6:517–34.

Schulz, R. A., and P. Elliott. 2000. Learning Spanish as an older adult. *Hispania* 83.1:107–19.

Scovel, T. 1969. Foreign accents, language acquisition and cerebral dominance. *Language Learning* 19:245–54.

————. 1981. The recognition of foreign accents in English and its implications for psycholinguistic theories of language acquisition. In *Proceedings of the 5th Congress of AILA,* eds. J-G. Savard and L. Laforge, 389–401. Laval: University of Laval Press.

————. 1988. *A time to speak: A psycholinguistic inquiry into the critical period for human speech.* Rowley, MA: Newbury House.

Seliger, H. 1978. Implications of a multiple critical period hypothesis for second language learning. In *Second language acquisition research: Issues and implications,* ed. W. Ritchie, 11–19. New York: Academic Press.

Selkirk, E. O. 1980. Prosodic domains in phonology. In *Juncture,* eds. M. Aronoff and M-L Kean, 107–29. Saratoga, CA: Anma Libri.

Silva-Corvalán, C. 2001. *Sociolingüística y pragmática del español.* Washington, DC: Georgetown University Press.

Skehan, P. 1989. *Individual difference in second language learning.* London: Edward Arnold.

Snow, C. 1983. Age differences in second language acquisition: Research findings and folk psychology. In *Second language acquisition studies,* eds. K. M. Bailey, M. Long, and S. Peck, 141–50. Rowley, MA: Newbury House.

———. 1987. Relevance of the notion of a critical period to language acquisition. In *Sensitive periods in development: An interdisciplinary perspective,* ed. M. Berstein, 183–209. Hillsdale, NJ: Lawrence Erlbaum.

Snow, C., and M. Hoefnagel-Höhle. 1977. Age differences and the pronunciation of foreign sounds. *Language and Speech* 20:357–65.

Stockwell, R., and J. Bowen. 1965. *The sounds of English and Spanish.* Chicago: University of Chicago Press.

Strozer, J. R. 1994. *Language acquisition after puberty.* Washington, DC: Georgetown University Press.

Suter, R. W. 1976. Predictors of pronunciation accuracy in second language learning. *Language Learning* 26:233–53.

Tahta, S., M. Wood, and K. Loewenthal. 1981. Age changes in the ability to replicate foreign pronunciation and intonation. *Language and Speech* 24:363–72.

Tarone, E. 1978. The phonology of interlanguage. In *Understanding second and foreign language learning,* eds. G. Ioup and S. H. Weinberger, 70–85. Rowley, MA: Newbury House.

———. 1979. Interlanguage as chameleon. *Language Learning.* 29:181–91.

———. 1983. On the variability of interlanguage systems. *Applied Linguistics* 4:142–63.

Terrell, T. D. 1989. Teaching Spanish pronunciation in a communicative approach. In *American Spanish pronunciation: Theoretical and applied perspectives,* eds. P. C. Bjarkman and R. M. Hammond, 196–214. Washington, DC: Georgetown University Press.

Trudgill, P. 1974. *The social differentiation of English in Norwich.* Cambridge: Cambridge University Press.

Tun, P. A., and A. Wingfield. 1997. Language and communication: Fundamentals of speech communication and language processing in old age. *Handbook of human factors and the older adult,* eds. A. D. Fisk and W. A. Rogers, 125–49. San Diego: Academic Press.

Volker, F. 1996. German pronunciation teaching: A course design and preliminary evaluation of its effectiveness. M.A. thesis, Arizona State University.

Walsh, T., and K. Diller. 1981. Neurolinguistic considerations on the optimum age for second language learning. In *Individual differences and universals in language learning aptitude,* ed. K. Diller, 3–21. Rowley, MA: Newbury House.

Weinreich, U. 1953. Languages in contact, findings and problems. The Hague: Mouton.

Weiss, L. 1970. Auditory discrimination and pronunciation of French vowel phonemes. Ph.D. diss., Stanford University.

White, L., and F. Genesee. 1996. How native is near-native? The issue of ultimate attainment in adult second language acquisition. *Second Language Research* 12:233–365.

Williams, J. 1987. Educational treatments for dyslexia at the elementary and secondary levels. In *Intimacy with language: A forgotten basic in teacher education,* ed. W. Ellis, 24–32. Baltimore: Orton Dyslexia Society.

Witkin, H. A., C. A. Moore, D. R. Goodenough, and P. W. Cox. 1977. Field-dependent and field-independent cognitive styles and their educational implications. *Review of Educational Research* 47:1–64.

Wolfram, W. 1969. *A sociolinguistic description of Detroit Negro speech.* Washington, DC: Center for Applied Linguistics.

Zampini, M. L. 1994. The role of native language transfer and task formality in the acquisition of Spanish spirantization. *Hispania* 77:470–81.

———. 1998a. The relationship between the production and perception of L2 Spanish stops. *Texas Papers in Foreign Language Education* 3:85–100.

———. 1998b. L2 Spanish spirantization: A prosodic analysis and pedagogical implications. *Hispanic Linguistics* 10.1:154–88.

2

Tense/Aspect

The Development of Tense/Aspect Morphology in Spanish as a Second Language

SILVINA MONTRUL*   University of Illinois at Urbana-Champaign

RAFAEL SALABERRY   Rice University

1.0   Introduction

The analysis of the acquisition of tense and aspect has become a central topic of research in studies of L2 acquisition in recent years (e.g., Andersen 1986, 1991; Andersen and Shirai 1994, 1996; Bardovi-Harlig 1992, 1994, 1995, 2000; Bergström 1995; Buczowska and Weist 1991; Harley 1989; Hasbún 1995; Housen 1994; Kaplan 1987; Lafford 1996; Liskin-Gasparro 2000; Ramsay 1990; Robison 1990, 1995; Salaberry 1998, 1999, 2000; Shirai and Kurono 1998; Slabakova 2001; Wiberg 1996). This growing interest is motivated by several theoretical and empirical considerations. First, the research on the development of verbal morphology may shed light on how different components of language interact throughout development (i.e., interaction of syntax, semantics, discourse and pragmatics). Second, the comparison of lexical and morphological means to encode temporal and aspectual meanings across languages allows for the analysis of how second language learners learn to map form and meaning. Third, the analysis of the representation of tense and aspect development from its initial stages to its (potential) full acquisition (e.g., Coppieters 1987) leads to the investigation of similar developmental stages in L1 acquisition (e.g., Antinucci and Miller 1976; Wagner 1999), creolization (e.g., Bickerton 1981), or language attrition in bilingualism (e.g., Montrul 2002; Silva-Corvalán 1991). Finally, the acquisition of verbal endings represents a challenge for L2 learners that neither theoretical nor pedagogical accounts have yet adequately addressed (e.g., Schmidt 1995). This chapter provides an overview of the acquisition of tense/aspect as represented in the development of past-tense verbal morphology among adult L2 Spanish classroom learners.

2.0   Aspectual Meaning: Overt and Covert Markers

Tense and aspect are markers of temporality on the verb. *Tense* is a deictic category that places a situation in time with respect to the moment of speech. *Aspect* "concerns the different perspectives which a speaker can take and express with regard to the temporal course of some event, action, process, etc." (Klein 1994:16). Aspect can be expressed lexically by the inherent lexical semantics of the verb and its interaction with direct and indirect arguments and adjuncts (Dowty 1986; Schmitt 1996; Smith 1991; Tenny 1991; Verkuyl 1994). Aspect can also be expressed grammatically through the use of inflectional morphology on the verb. This is termed viewpoint aspect (Smith 1991) because it refers to the partial or full view of a particular situation type, as marked by an overt grammatical morpheme (e.g., the preterit and imperfect in Spanish).

2.1   Lexical Aspect

The notion of different types of verbal predicates (attributed to Aristotle) led Vendler (1967) to classify verbs into four different lexical aspectual categories: *states* (no input of energy), *activities* (arbitrary beginning and endpoint), *accomplishments* (durative and inherent endpoint) and *achievements* (inherent endpoint but no duration). The following examples are representative of the four classes:

> (1) a. statives: *ser* "to be," *tener* "to have," *querer* "to want"
>
> b. activities: *correr* "to run," *caminar* "to walk," *respirar* "to breathe"
>
> c. accomplishments: *escribir una novela* "to write a novel," *construir una casa* "to build a house," *correr una milla* "to run a mile"
>
> d. achievements: *morirse* "to die," *romperse* (intr.) "to break," *notar algo* "to notice something," *darse cuenta de algo* "to realize something"

States are nondynamic predicates, whereas activities, accomplishments and achievements, having input of energy, are dynamic. Within the dynamic classes, accomplishment and achievements are *telic* (i.e., events with inherent endpoints), whereas activities are *atelic* (i.e., events with no inherent endpoint). Telic events differ from each other with respect to durativity: achievements are assumed to be instantaneous, like "John <u>realized</u> he made a mistake," whereas accomplishments are assumed to include the process that leads up to the culmination of the event ("John <u>read the novel</u>"). English and Spanish are both alike with respect to the existence of lexical aspectual classes.

As mentioned, however, the lexical aspectual class of a predicate is not solely determined by the verb. There are other components of the predicate that contribute to its aspectual interpretation: internal and external arguments of the verb and adjuncts. For example, the verb *to run* is typically an activity (atelic) when it is used intransitively:

> (2) *Pedro corrió.*
> "Peter ran."

However, if the object of the verb is indicated (i.e., the distance that Pedro ran), as shown in (3), then *run* is an accomplishment. That is, the grammatical object of the verb establishes an endpoint to the activity thereby making the event telic:

> (3) *Pedro corrió una milla.*
> "Peter ran a mile."

Similarly, the mass/count distinction or the specific/nonspecific features of the internal argument of a given verb change the basic semantic nature of the predicate in essential ways. As shown in (4) and (5), in the absence of other adverbials, the cardinality of the object (whether count or mass noun as in *un artículo* and *artículos,* respectively) can determine whether the activity is interpreted as having an inherent endpoint or not:

> (4) *Pedro leía un artículo.*   (telic)
> "Pedro was reading an article."

> (5) *Pedro leía artículos.*   (atelic)
> "Pedro would read/ used to read articles."

Adjuncts (adverbial phrases) are other basic elements in the composition of the aspectual value of a predicate whose effect on lexical aspectual classes is apparent even in treatments of aspect that rely heavily on verb-level classifications. For instance, Vendler argues that the application of the operational test of aspect modification with the progressive of prototypical stative verbs, such as *to know,* renders an ungrammatical sentence: "*I am knowing." Nevertheless, it is possible to say "Now I know it" or "And then suddenly I knew." In the latter two examples Vendler points out that "to know" is similar to "to get married" (an achievement) rather than "to be married" (a state). In essence, the inceptive point of a state—determined by adverbial phrases (adjuncts)—is considered an achievement in contrast with the state itself (see also Dowty 1986; Dry 1983; Guitart 1978; Smith 1983). Finally, in addition to internal arguments and adjuncts, the nature of the subject of the utterance (the external argument) may affect the inherent semantic aspectual value of the verb as well (e.g., Depraetere 1995; Langacker 1982; Maingueneau 1994). For instance, Maingueneau (1994:71) shows the effect of the external argument on the semantic value of the verbal predicate in French:

> (6) *Luc a franchi le pont toute la matinée.*
> "Luc crossed the bridge all morning long."

> (7) *La foule a franchi le pont toute la matinée.*
> "The crowd crossed the bridge all morning long."

In example (6) one surmises (based on world knowledge) that Luc traversed the bridge several times during the morning—not that it took him the whole morning to cross the bridge. In example (7), in contrast, it is reasonable to assume that it took a whole morning for the crowd to cross the same bridge (this is based on our knowledge about the world; see Klein

1994). The latter case represents the single crossing of many people, and the former many crossings of a single person.

The lexical aspectual class of a given predicate is determined by means of operational tests (i.e., syntactic and semantic tests) that assess the value of the different components that enter into the aspectual calculation of a predicate. Klein (1994) lists three major semantic and syntactic tests to classify lexical aspectual classes: (a) adverb modification, (b) aspect modification, and (c) presuppositions and implications.[1] Entailments are the most consistent of the available operational tests (e.g., Dowty 1979; Hasbún 1995; Shirai 1991). Entailment tests, however, distinguish telic from atelic events only because they are predicated on the notion of an endpoint (telicity). The test of telicity distinguishes telic from atelic verbs by questioning the predicate in the following way: "If you stop in the middle of V-ing, have you done the act of V?" If the answer is affirmative, the verbal predicate is atelic; if the answer is negative, the verbal predicate is telic. For instance, let us compare the verb phrases "to paint" versus "to paint a house." If you stop in the middle of painting, then you have completed the act of painting. Therefore, "to paint" is an atelic predicate (activity). On the other hand, if you stop in the middle of painting the house, then you have not completed the act of painting the house. Thus, "to paint the house" is a telic predicate (accomplishment).

2.2 Grammatical Aspect

Aspect is also expressed morphosyntactically on the verb by inflectional morphemes (e.g., Spanish preterit and imperfect) or periphrastic expressions (e.g., English progressive past tense) to indicate the internal temporal constituency of a situation. At the level of grammatical aspect, languages express several aspectual oppositions, one of the most common ones being the perfective-imperfective opposition. Perfective aspect is concerned with the beginning and end of a situation and is thus "bounded" (it can be inceptive, punctual or completive).

> (8) Mary read a book.

Imperfective aspect, being "unbounded," focuses on the internal structure of the situation instead, viewing it as ongoing, with no specific endpoint (imperfective aspect can be durative or habitual).

> (9) Mary was reading a book.

Notice that grammatical aspect, like lexical aspect, makes reference to complete versus ongoing situations. However, while telicity is used to describe the aspectual nature of events at the lexical level, the notion of "boundedness" (Depraetere 1995), which is also related to endpoints, is relevant to describe the properties of grammatical aspect. Furthermore, viewpoint aspect is not categorical. Comrie (1976:4) points out that "it is quite possible for the same speaker to refer to the same situation once with a perfective form, then with an imperfective, without in any way being self-contradictory." For instance, in (10) (a sentence from Comrie) we can see that *reading* may be used with the progressive or the simple past to refer to the same event:

> (10) John read that book yesterday; while he was reading it, the postman came.[2]

Finally, it is important to point out that verbal morphology (simple past versus progressive, in this case) may override the lexical aspectual value of verb phrases. While telic predicates go well with the preterit and atelic with the imperfect (i.e., prototypical), it is possible for the preterit verbal ending to appear with stative verbs and the imperfect with achievements.

2.3   Spanish and English Past Tense Marking

In Spanish, the perfective/imperfective opposition is grammaticalized with overt tense morphology on the verb. Thus, in the past tense, inflectional morphology indicates both tense (past) and aspect: The preterit (PRET) encodes perfectivity (11) and the imperfect (IMP) tense encodes imperfectivity, as the examples in (12) show:

> (11) a. *En ese momento Julio y Patricia se enamoraron* (PRET).   (inceptive)
>   "At that moment Julio and Patricia fell in love."
>
>   b. *Pedro escribió (PRET) una novela.*   (completive)
>   "Pedro wrote a novel."
>
> (12) a. *María iba (IMP) a la escuela todas las mañanas.*   (habitual)
>   "María would go to school every day."
>
>   b. *Cuando llegamos a la playa, llovía* (IMP).   (continuous)
>   "When we got to the beach it was raining."

Although the progressive/nonprogressive distinction is marked in both English and Spanish (*to be* + *V-ing* and *estar* + *V-ndo,* respectively), English does not make an overt grammatical (inflectional) distinction between preterit/imperfect in the past tense because it has a more impoverished inflectional system (Giorgi and Pianesi 1997). The aspectual distinction marked with preterit and imperfect in Spanish may possibly be conveyed with the simple past and the past progressive in English, when the imperfect describes an action in progress. This is shown in (13).

> (13) a. *Juan durmió* (PRET) = "John slept." (S. PAST)
>   b. *Juan dormía* (IMP) = "John was sleeping." (PAST PROG)[3]
>   c. *Juan pensó* (PRET) *en María* = "Juan thought (S. PAST) about María."
>   d. *Juan pensaba* (IMP) *en María* = "Juan was thinking (PAST PROG) about María."

However, because the progressive in English expresses an action in progress, it cannot be used to express the meaning of habituality that the imperfect expresses in Spanish, as (14) shows. Instead, English lexicalizes habitual aspect in the past with the use of verbs such as "would" or "used to":

> (14) *Cuando era* (IMP) *niño jugaba* (IMP) *con mis vecinos.*
>   *"When I was (S. PAST) a child I was playing (PAST PROG) with my neighbors."
>   "When I was a child I <u>would/used to</u> play/played (S. PAST) with my neighbors."

The simple past in English usually corresponds to the Spanish preterit when the verbs are eventive (nonstative):

> (15) *María fue* (PRET) *a la playa.*
>
> "Mary went (S. PAST) to the beach."

> (16) *Juan compró* (PRET) *un auto.*
>
> "John bought (S. PAST) a car."

However, with stative verbs, the simple past in English is ambiguous or neutral as to the perfective/imperfective distinction, and can be translated into the Spanish preterit or imperfect, depending on the situation:

> (17)   a. *María estaba* (IMP) *enferma y todavía lo está.*
>
>   "Mary was (S. PAST) sick and she is still sick."   (imperfective)
>
>   b. *María estuvo* (PRET) *enferma pero ya no lo está más.*
>
>   "Mary was sick (S. PAST) but she is no longer sick."   (perfective)

Summarizing, the preterit/imperfect contrast in Spanish (represented obligatorily in verbal endings) is a morphological manifestation of grammatical aspect. Unlike Spanish, English does not require such obligatory marking of temporality with inflectional morphology and lacks an inflected tense analogous to the Spanish imperfect. English, however, can convey the meanings expressed by the Spanish imperfect by using the progressive tense to express continuity ("Mary was reading a book"), or verbs like "used to" for habituals ("Mary would read a book/used to read a book").

3.0 Theoretical Perspectives on the Development of Tense/Aspect Morphology

Several empirical studies have analyzed the development of past tense verbal morphology in L2 acquisition of Spanish. These studies have tested specific theoretical hypotheses that have been advanced to provide an explanatory account of how learners approach the task of marking tense/aspect by means of inflectional endings. In this section we present a brief summary of the recent published body of research on the development of tense/aspect phenomena.[4]

3.1 Lexical Semantics Perspectives

Andersen (1986, 1991) used the classification of lexical aspectual classes as the theoretical framework for the analysis of the development of verbal morphology among second language learners. Out of this research emerged the Lexical Aspect Hypothesis,[5] which attempts to explain the observed correlation between tense/aspect morphemes and lexical aspectual classes according to the Relevance Principle (aspect is more relevant to the meaning of the verb than tense, mood, or agreement) and the Congruence Principle (learners choose

Table 2.1
Developmental Stages (based on Andersen 1986)

Stages	States	Activities	Accomplishments	Achievements
1	Present	Present	Present	Present
2	Present	Present	Present	Preterit
3	Imperfect	Present	Present	Preterit
4	Imperfect	Imperfect	Preterit	Preterit
5	Imperfect	Imperfect	Pret/Imperf	Preterit
6	Imperfect	Pret/Imperf	Pret/Imperf	Preterit
7	Imperfect	Pret/Imperf	Pret/Imperf	Pret/Imperf
8	Pret/Imperf	Pret/Imperf	Pret/Imperf	Pret/Imperf

the morpheme whose aspectual meaning is most congruent with the aspectual meaning of the verb). Andersen's Lexical Aspect Hypothesis states that, in early stages of acquisition, verbal morphology encodes only inherent aspectual distinctions (i.e., it does not encode tense or grammatical aspect).

The Lexical Aspect Hypothesis finds its roots in arguments initially made for the evolution of linguistic systems across time and the development of L1 acquisition. For instance, Bybee (1985), Bybee and Dahl (1989), and Frawley (1992) observe that in emergent linguistic systems, aspect markers precede the appearance of tense markers. Further evidence for this developmental trend comes from L1 acquisition studies carried out during the 1970s and 1980s (e.g., Antinucci and Miller 1976; Bloom, Lifter, and Hafitz 1980; Bronckart and Sinclair 1973; Brown 1973; Rispoli and Bloom 1985; Smith and Weist 1987). Andersen proposed a sequence of eight developmental stages for the acquisition of Spanish as a second language, as illustrated in table 2.1.[6]

In essence, the use of perfective markers appears first and spreads from punctual verbs (achievement in stage 2) to stative verbs (but not until stage 8), whereas the use of imperfective markers appears later and spreads from stative verbs (stage 3) to punctual verbs (stage 5 onward, starting with accomplishments).[7] Since its inception, the Lexical Aspect Hypothesis has generated an important body of research in a variety of second languages (for a more comprehensive overview see Bardovi-Harlig 2000). In what follows we concentrate on the analysis of studies that tested this hypothesis with data from Spanish as a second language.[8]

Ramsay (1990) analyzed guided oral production of narratives of thirty English-speaking learners of Spanish. Her subjects were classified into five groups (stages) according to their overall linguistic proficiency (including the appropriate use of verbal endings). As elicitation procedure, Ramsay used a story from a children's book (Disney's *The Magic Stick*), which she presented to the students as a series of ten episodes (pictures) with captions. The text associated with each picture included blank spaces that students had to complete with text.[9] Results revealed that, at stage 2, learners marked 25 percent of all telic verbs with the preterit, and that at stage 3, they marked about 60 percent of telic verbs with the preterit. No telic verb was marked with the imperfect during stages 2 or 3. In contrast, learners marked statives (mostly) with the imperfect at stage 3. Additionally, Ramsay's data revealed that (a) neither native speakers nor nonnative speakers used verbs of the activity type very often, and (b) the distribution of verbal endings was similar for accomplishments and achievements. In short, Ramsay's study appears to offer support for the Lexical Aspect Hypothesis, with the caveat that such sequential development was represented only in the states versus telic events dichotomy.

In contrast to Ramsay's study, Hasbún's (1995) findings cast some doubts on the validity of the Lexical Aspect Hypothesis. Hasbún (1995) analyzed written data from eighty L1 English speakers enrolled in four different levels of Spanish instruction (first to fourth year). Students watched an excerpt from the film *Modern Times* twice and were later asked to narrate the video in writing, by starting with the phrase *Había una vez* . . . "Once upon a time . . ." to avoid the use of the historical present (especially by advanced learners and native speakers). Native speakers, however, were less affected by the instructions and used the historical present to a larger extent than advanced nonnative speakers. As was the case with Ramsay's data, the results showed that among native and nonnative speakers, the distribution of preterit-imperfect with accomplishments and achievements remained proportional. More important, the data did not show a spread of past tense marking (preterit) from telic (achievements and accomplishments) to atelic events (activity verbs) and later to stative verbs. In fact, the marking of tense distinction occurred in group 2 across all categories of aspectual classes. Furthermore, the first uses of past tense marking (in group 1) did not occur with achievements, but mostly with statives (followed by accomplishments and activities).

Lafford (1996) asked thirteen L2 Spanish students from three different levels of proficiency (based on the ACTFL-oral proficiency scale) to do an oral retelling of a ten-minute silent video (*The Sorcerer's Apprentice* from Disney). Results showed that: (a) the majority of verbs used by the subjects were atelic verbs (across all levels), (b) among the subjects from the intermediate low and intermediate mid levels the use of past tense was represented largely by the preterit, (c) the only uses of the imperfect among the students in the intermediate high level were associated with atelic verbs conveying background information, and (d) the proportion of past tense-present tense was higher for telic verbs across all levels. In sum, Lafford's data raised more questions about the relevance of lexical aspect for the development of Spanish past tense markers during the preliminary stages of acquisition. More important, this study suggests that the preterit may be used as a default marker of past tense (i.e., it emerges with both telic and atelic classes initially).

Further support for the finding that the preterit appears with both telic and atelic classes in Spanish was provided by Salaberry (1999). This study analyzed the use of L2 Spanish past tense verbal morphology among twenty college-level adult native speakers of English. The informants were divided into five proficiency levels that were correlated to course placement. To minimize potential problems associated with inaccurate procedures for course placement, each proficiency level corresponded to at least two course levels (a minimum of one year of academic study between any two levels). In addition, a group of native speakers participated in the study as a control group. The participants were tested twice, the second time two months after the first meeting. All participants were asked to perform an oral narration of one of two movie clips from the silent film *Modern Times*. The narrative was implemented as a role-play situation to generate increased functional constraints that were intended to minimized monitoring of form—or at least to make it as realistic as possible.

The results of the study revealed that the number of verb tokens was unequally distributed across lexical aspectual classes irrespective of level, and that the second-semester students (the lowest level represented) did not use the imperfect at all. The latter result occurred despite the fact that the students at that level had reviewed the uses of the imperfect during the weeks before the test. Moreover, the same students used the preterit with statives (nonprototypical). On the other hand, there was a gradual increase from time 1 to time 2 in the use of the preterit with telic verbs and the use of the imperfect with statives. The latter trend was maintained across time and levels. In sum, the data from Salaberry's study may be regarded as evidence in favor of the argument that the preterit is functioning as a default marker for the less proficient learners; thereby, contradicting one of the basic tenets of the Lexical Aspect Hypothesis. Yet, a study from Salaberry (2000) raises questions about the role of the preterit as the only default given that the imperfect may be used as a default as well but in personal narratives. At the same time, the data from the 1999 study provide evidence for an increasing effect of lexical aspectual class with more proficient learners. The latter is in keeping with the prediction of the Lexical Aspect Hypothesis.

In a forthcoming study, Salaberry (2003) investigates the effect of lexical aspectual classes on the use of past tense verbal morphology in a written task. This procedure, although less spontaneous than the oral narratives, allowed for the use of more powerful statistical procedures. The main participants in this study were students from two college-level Spanish language courses: twenty-five students from a third-semester course and twenty-four students from a sixth-semester course. Thirty-two monolingual native speakers of Spanish residing in their native country acted as a control group. All subjects completed a cloze-type fill-in-the-blank task that contained a total of forty-one target items. The data from the advanced students revealed a clear relationship between lexical aspectual classes and past tense verbal endings: the use of imperfect was associated with stative verbs (63 percent) and the use of preterit with the telic event category (82 percent). In contrast, the morphological marking of verbs among the intermediate learners was not necessarily correlated with lexical aspectual types: the use of the preterit was represented in all lexical aspectual categories (a default marker of past tense across lexical aspectual categories). In sum, these data, based on a written task, provide supporting evidence for the claim advanced by Salaberry (1999), the latter based on the analysis of oral data. Thus, the effect of tense appears to be stronger than lexical aspect during the early stages of acquisition of L2 Spanish among English-speaking adult classroom learners. The effect of lexical aspect, however, appears to increase with level of experience in the target language.

Other more recent studies have looked at data from more advanced learners. In an innovative study, Liskin-Gasparro (2000) analyzed oral movie and personal narratives as well as immediate retrospective protocols of eight advanced nonnative speakers of Spanish. According to the ACTFL proficiency scale, the proficiency levels of the eight subjects she interviewed were distributed as follows: Intermediate High (3), Advanced (3), Advanced High (1), and Superior (1). The introspections based on the speakers' personal and movie narratives were used to analyze the conscious processing strategies of learners. Based on the data from the retrospective protocols, Liskin-Gasparro argued that the choice of verbal morphology is influenced by various factors: lexical semantics, discursive constraints, instructional effects, type of narrative task, use of individual processing strategies, and, most important, *the use of the preterit as a default marker of past tense.* Interestingly, the influence of lexical semantics in the selection of verbal morphology for some of these advanced students appears to be categorical. Liskin-Gasparro mentions the case of Jason's "default settings": "for state verbs—he opted for the imperfect" (836), and Rick's "safety things": "certain verbs are always to be encoded in the imperfect, and others in the preterit" (837). In sum, Liskin-Gasparro's study provides evidence for the argument that the role of lexical aspectual categories may be more limited than previously argued by the Lexical Aspect Hypothesis.[10]

3.2 Generative Perspectives

Recent developments within the generative framework (Chomsky 1995) suggest that aspectual phenomena could be explained in syntactic terms and fall within the realm of Universal Grammar. Within this framework, a principled distinction is made between lexical and functional categories: lexical categories contribute the basic semantic content of a sentence (noun, verb, adjective, adverb, and prepositions), while functional categories add referential and grammatical meaning to a sentence (e.g., determiner, number, gender, agreement, tense, aspect, mood, negation). Recent developments in linguistic theory, particularly Chomsky (1995), conceive of functional categories and their features as the locus of all cross-linguistic differences. That is, lexical and functional categories form part of the inventory of Universal Grammar, but different languages may choose different functional categories. For example, it is believed that the functional category tense is not instantiated in Chinese, but it is in English and in Spanish. In addition, languages may have a given functional category, but such category may have different features or feature values in different languages, thus exhibiting different semantic and syntactic effects. This approach has important implications for language acquisition. The general assumption is that if learners have acquired a specific functional category, they will have knowledge both of the inflectional morphology and its syntactic and semantic properties.

Within the generative perspective,[11] grammatical aspect is represented as functional category AspP that varies cross-linguistically (Giorgi and Pianesi 1997; Schmitt 1996; Slabakova 2001; Tenny 1991; Travis 1991; Zagona 1994). However, lexical and grammatical aspect have been argued to be located in different positions within the clause structure, as the tree in (18) shows (irrelevant details omitted).

(18) CP [± wh]

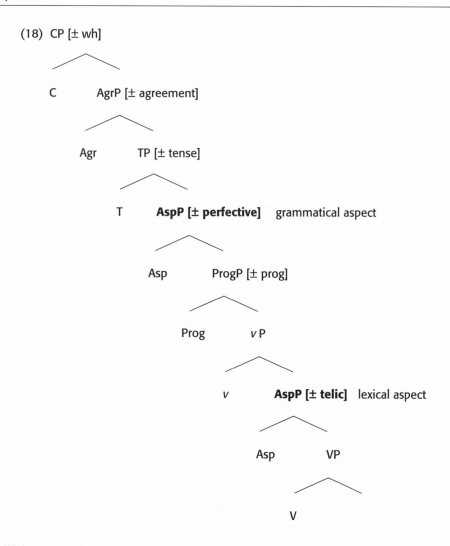

Simplifying somewhat, lexical aspect is represented in the lower functional category AspP, closer to the VP (where the lexical verb is). In this category, the semantic features [± telic] are checked. Grammatical aspect (also called IP or sentential aspect) is in the higher AspP phrase, above the verb phrase and below the tense phrase. Here, the features [± perfective] are checked, through overt tense/aspect morphology (i.e., preterit and imperfect in Spanish). While some authors argue that in Spanish and English the perfective/imperfective distinction is encoded in the higher AspP (Giorgi and Pianesi 1997), these languages vary with respect to the features associated with the functional category and with the morphological manifestation of those features. Spanish has the features [+ perfective] and [− perfective] associated with preterit and imperfect tense morphology, respectively, whereas English only has the feature [+ perfective], usually associated with the simple past verb form. Several studies have analyzed possible access to UG in second language acquisition by focusing on the acquisition of the functional category aspect and the subtle semantic interpretations of the preterit and imperfect tenses in Spanish.[12]

Slabakova and Montrul (2002) tested fifty-seven English-speaking learners of Spanish: intermediate (n = 30) and advanced (n = 27) with a sentence conjunction judgment task, in which subjects had to judge the combinatorial felicity of two conjoined clauses. The purpose was to know whether learners were aware of the semantic implications (logical entailments) of the past tense form (preterit or imperfect) of the verb in the first clause. The example in (19a) shows that the imperfect in the first clause is compatible with a negation of the event as expressed in the second clause, since the event is not viewed as bounded. However, in (19b) the preterit in the first clause turns the combination contradictory:

(19) a. Los González *vendían* la casa pero nadie la compró. (logical)
"The Gonzálezes sold (IMPF) their house but nobody bought it."
b. #Los González *vendieron* la casa pero nadie la compró. (contradictory)
"The Gonzálezes sold (PRET) their house but nobody bought it."

It was hypothesized that if learners already distinguished between the preterit and imperfect forms, then they should also know the semantic implications of these tenses and would successfully recognize logical and contradictory sentences involving these two aspectual forms. A second conjecture was that if the lexical aspect hypothesis extended to the interpretive domain, then learners would be more accurate recognizing that the preterit was illogical with accomplishments and achievements, and only later would they learn that it was illogical with states as well. Similar predictions were made for the imperfect tense: learners would be more accurate with states than with the eventive classes. Having established that the learners had knowledge of the preterit/imperfect morphology through the use of a pretest, group results of the sentence conjunction judgment task showed a statistically significant difference between the preterit and imperfect with accomplishment, achievement, and stative predicates for all the groups (native, advanced, and intermediate).[13] These group results were taken to mean that L2 learners knew the morphology and the semantic entailments associated with each verbal form. On the other hand, there was no evidence in the intermediate learners' data of an asymmetry of responses consistent with the predictions of the lexical aspect hypothesis. That is, it was not the case that states in the imperfect tense and achievement and accomplishments in the preterit were judged more acceptable than the opposite combinations.[14]

Montrul and Slabakova (2002) used the same test instruments as the previous study to investigate whether knowledge of preterit/imperfect morphology correlated with the acquisition of the bounded/unbounded semantic opposition of the features [± perfective] of the functional category outer AspP shown in (18). Subjects were seventy-one intermediate and advanced English-speaking learners and a control group of twenty-three Spanish native speakers. Results of a morphology recognition task showed that twenty-four intermediate learners and one advanced learner scored below 75 percent accuracy, while the remaining eighteen intermediate and twenty-eight advanced learners scored well above 75 percent accuracy. Thus, the intermediate group was split into two subgroups: those with knowledge of the preterit/imperfect morphological distinction (n = 18), and those without reliable knowledge of the morphology (n = 24). For the learners who did not know the morphology there was a statistically significant contrast in the test of semantic interpretations between preterit and imperfect with accomplishment predicates, but no contrast with achievements and states. Most learners who scored above 75 percent in the morphology recognition task discriminated semantically between preterit and imperfect with the three aspectual classes tested, although individual results showed that some of these learners had not acquired the semantic entailments yet. These results suggest that at least in instructional settings, correct morphology is acquired *before* the semantic entailments of these tenses, and that there appears to be a strong relationship between acquisition of morphology and the semantics associated with preterit and imperfect.

Montrul and Slabakova (2000) used a truth value judgment task to investigate other aspects of the semantic entailments of preterit and imperfect: (a) change-of-meaning preterits (*saber, poder*), e.g., *Pedro sabía la verdad* "Pedro knew the truth" versus *Pedro supo la verdad* "Pedro found out the truth"; (b) one-time versus habitual actions in the past, e.g., *Mario robó en el autobús* "Mario stole in the bus" versus *Mario robaba en el autobús* "Mario used to steal in the bus"; and (c) the interpretation of the subject with generic pronouns, e.g., *Se comía bien en este restaurante* "One/we ate/used to eat well in this restaurant" versus *Se comió bien en este restaurante* "We ate well in this restaurant" (see de Miguel 1992). Participants had to indicate whether a sentence with the verb in the preterit or imperfect was true or false in the context provided by a written story. Forty-two intermediate and twenty-seven advanced English-speaking learners of Spanish participated in the experiment, as well as a control group of eighteen Spanish native speakers. Results showed that intermediate learners were (a) more accurate with the imperfect than with the preterit tense with change-of-meaning preterits, (b) more accurate with the preterit than with the imperfect with the condition testing one-time vs. habitual events, and (c) more accurate with the interpretations of the preterit (as specific "we" and never generic "one") and less accurate with the interpretations of the imperfect (both specific and generic). The results of the third test, in particular (i.e., specific "we" or generic "one" use of aspectual *se*), suggest that L2 learners may be able to learn properties of the grammar that are not explicitly taught in language classrooms. Most important, these learners were equally accurate with the three conditions. In contrast, the advanced learners behaved more like the control group. The authors interpret these results as supporting access to Universal Grammar in the semantic domain: learners can learn morphological and semantic properties associated with the aspect phrase. However, because there is an interesting developmental trend in the results, it is also possible that learners acquired these properties by extensive exposure to Spanish and utilizing other inductive, problem-solving procedures, but further research should tease these possibilities apart.

As we have already mentioned, it has been suggested that tense and aspect distributions are very difficult to learn in a second language, are prone to fossilize universally, and their interpretative properties are subject to a critical period (Coppieters, 1987). Montrul and Slabakova (2003) focused on the acquisition of the semantic implications of the Preterite/Imperfect contrast in Spanish by English-speaking individuals of very advanced proficiency in Spanish who were not living in a Spanish-speaking country. Assuming the same theoretical approach and methodology as Slabakova and Montrul (2002), Montrul and Slabakova (2000) and Montrul and Slabakova (2002), this study asked whether ultimate attainment in the aspectual domain is possible, and whether features of functional categories not selected in early childhood are subject to a critical period, as Hawkins and Chan's (1997) Failed Formal Features Hypothesis states.

Based on two independent measures of proficiency to establish near-nativeness, the L2 speakers in Montrul and Slabakova (2003) were divided into three experimental groups: near natives (n = 17), superior (n = 23) and advanced (n = 24). The results of this study showed converging empirical evidence on the performance of the near-native subjects, and established that near-native competence in the domain of aspectual interpretations is attainable, even in individuals who are not totally immersed in the language, or in individuals that might not have arrived at endstate. Many learners (almost 30 percent) in the total subject pool (including advanced to near-native speakers) and 70 percent of the near-native group performed like native speakers on all sentence types in all tasks. While aspect is certainly a difficult area to master, particularly because the meanings of the Imperfect are acquired quite late, L2 learners are clearly able to overcome the parametric options of their L1. The authors concluded that the acquisition of tense/aspect distributions are not universally subject to a critical period. In current generative linguistic terms, this means that universal features of functional categories not selected by a given language in early childhood remain accessible in adulthood when learning a second language. More specifically, the Failed Formal Features Hypothesis was not supported with [+ interpretable] features.

Although the results obtained are consistent with the interpretation that Universal Grammar is still active in this domain, one could argue that other cognitive or problem-solving strategies as proposed by Bley-Vroman's (1989) Fundamental Difference Hypothesis could also be responsible for the results obtained, but the authors do not elaborate on this point. Furthermore, the results are limited in a number of ways. First, a single L1 group was tested on one specific grammatical domain. Second, the near-native subjects were mostly Spanish language teachers and advanced students of Spanish. As the authors admit, these factors limit the generalizability of the results beyond the sample of speakers tested. Whether or not nonnative speakers from other language backgrounds, who are not language teachers, and who have mainly learnt Spanish naturalistically, can also perform in these aspect interpretation tasks like native speakers remains an open question. Leaving aside the issue of whether or not there is a critical period in second language acquisition, this study is still a valuable contribution to the field. Given that the greatest bulk of research on tense and aspect in Spanish has focused on the early and intermediate stages, this study is the first one to address whether the subtlety of the Spanish aspectual forms is eventually acquired in very advanced L2 speakers.

3.3   Context-Based Perspectives: Grounding and Distributional Biases

As an alternative to strictly semantic or syntactic accounts, some researchers have proposed that the choice of verbal morphology is highly influenced by contextual factors such as the structure of narrative discourse or text type. For instance, Hopper (1982:16) argues that the nature of aspectual distinctions cannot be characterized by semantics in a consistent way; the adequate reference may only come from a *global discourse function*. (For additional arguments on the correlation of aspectual differences and perceptual contrasts associated with figure and ground, see Givón 1982; Reid 1980; and Wallace 1982). It is important to note, however, that there is an inherent overlap in the prediction offered by the account based on the lexical semantic value of the predicate and the discourse-based approach (e.g., Bardovi-Harlig 1995; Lafford 1996; Reinhart 1984). Indeed, Reinhart (1984) lists the temporal and textual criteria that mark the notion of foreground: narrativity (only textual/narrative units can serve as foreground), punctuality (punctual events serve more easily as foreground), and completeness (completed events serve more easily as foreground). Bardovi-Harlig (1995) also considers the feature of *newness* (new information is more relevant for the foreground). The similarities that underlie the criteria distinguishing foreground and background information and the classification of verbs according to inherent semantic value are remarkable (i.e., telic and atelic events are correlated with the foreground and background of a story, respectively). Not surprisingly, Bardovi-Harlig claims that the distinction of the predictions of each approach "may be too fine-grained for a study of interlanguage" (Bardovi-Harlig 1995:286.) The studies investigating the role of narrative structure in the acquisition of tense/aspect morphology have been undertaken in a variety of L2s (for an overview and relevant references see Bardovi-Harlig 2000). The only available study on Spanish is the one by Lafford (1996) reviewed in the previous section. Indeed, Lafford found an effect for narrative grounding, although such effect was apparent only among the more proficient learners (i.e., intermediate-high on the ACTFL proficiency scale).

Apart from the above-mentioned effect of narrative grounding, different discursive contexts also bring about distributional weights that generate biases in the marking of tense and aspect morphology. For instance, Andersen (1994) and Andersen and Shirai (1994, 1996) claimed that the correlations of aspect/tense markers and lexical class revealed in interlanguage grammars may reflect the distributional bias manifested in the input they receive from native speakers: the Distributional Bias Hypothesis. For instance, native speakers of American English use more *–ing* endings with activity verbs and more simple past tense forms with achievement and accomplishment verbs. Based on these frequency patterns, Andersen and Shirai argue that L2 learners perceive the activity-progressive and accomplishment/achievement-perfective association as absolute. We should also note that distributional biases may not necessarily be associated with specific contexts of use of the language, but rather with specific cultural conventions. Smith (1991:12) argues that "the conventions involve standard and marked choices, shared information between speaker and receiver, and other pragmatic considerations. The conventions are principles for language use rather than rules." In essence, we may assume that native speakers will conventionally prefer certain marked choices of verbal morphology to unmarked ones. The effect of distributional biases in L2 development has been analyzed in data from L2 Spanish natural acquisition (e.g., Andersen 1994), and L2 French development (e.g., Coppieters 1987; Salaberry 1998). No empirical studies, however, have directly analyzed the effect of distributional biases in classroom Spanish L2 acquisition.

The study from Salaberry, however, is quite revealing for the purpose of our review because the perfective-imperfective contrast in French is analogous to the preterit-imperfect contrast in Spanish. To some extent, Salaberry's data on the use of the *passé composé* and *imparfait* among second-semester French students seem to show that by the end of two semesters of language instruction L2 French learners reached stage 4 in Andersen's developmental sequences. A more detailed analysis, however, revealed some confounding of data when unmarked versus marked choices were teased out (prototypical versus nonprototypical). The net effect was that classroom students present a very different profile from native speakers in the selection of the marked (nonprototypical) use of the *passé composé* with statives (the contrast analyzed in this study). In turn, the data from natural language learners such as Anthony (Andersen, 1986, 1991) show a gradual spread of the prototypical forms towards the nonprototypical ones because natural learners are building the system of past tense aspect in a (highly) contextualized linguistic environment. Classroom students, on the other hand, do not have enough access to the type of (extended) non-classroom discourse that may help them recognize when to reject the prototypical marker of aspect in favor of the nonprototypical one (see also Coppieters, 1987).

3.4 Communicative Perspectives

The distinction between conventional and unmarked choices leads eventually to the analysis of the interaction of aspectual notions with pragmatics or other situation-specific factors. Few studies, however, have investigated how the linguistic notion of lexical aspectual classes or grammatical aspect relate to how tense and aspect markers are perceived and categorized when we consider the totality of a speech act. For this, we must distinguish between a situation with its associated properties and the linguistic expression that makes explicit those properties. For instance, if we compare a typical activity verb (a process) such as "to sleep" and a telic event such as "to leave the room," we readily think of the notion of boundary (telicity) as the discriminating semantic feature that distinguishes these two predicates. The assumption that sleeping has no boundaries, or that the process of sleeping is more homogeneous (a defining feature of activity verbs) than leaving a room (cf. Klein 1994), however, is open to question. Thus, the selective description of the situation will be primarily determined by what "the speaker finds useful and appropriate for his/her communicative purposes" (Smith 1991:11). Klein (1994:75) proposes two maxims to account for the amount of information conveyed by lexical means: maxim of minimality (put as little as possible into the lexical content) and maxim of contrast (add some feature to the lexical content if otherwise the expression cannot be distinguished in lexical content from some other expression). In other words, most temporal information will not be part of lexical content, but part of world knowledge (unless the maxim of contrast forces us to be more specific).

Along the same lines, Olsen (1999), following Grice (1975), has proposed that a principled distinction be made between semantic meaning and conversational pragmatic implicature, arguing that semantic meaning may not be canceled without contradiction or reinforced without redundancy. To illustrate this contrast, "slowly" is part of the lexical entry (semantic meaning) of the verb "plod," meaning to move or walk heavily or laboriously. Thus, the addition of the adverb slowly makes the sentence in (25) contradictory or redundant:

> (25) a. Mary plodded along, #but not slowly.
>   b. Mary plodded along, #slowly.

However, if somebody plods, it is because they are usually tired, a conversational pragmatic implicature. Therefore, the notion of "tiredness" can be cancelled or reinforced because it is not part of the semantics of the verb:

(26) a. Mary plodded along, although she wasn't tired.

b. Mary plodded along; she was very tired.

Olsen (1999) extends this difference between semantic meaning and pragmatic implicature to the aspectual domain. She argues that telicity expresses semantic meaning and is universal, whereas atelicity is derived from conversational implicature and is thus pragmatic. This distinction would explain why the atelicity of activities can be canceled with the addition of an object, whereas telic predicates cannot become atelic. We point out, however, that this theoretical position is controversial (e.g., states may become dynamic with the addition of adverbs), but as such, it represents an interesting option to be explored in future studies. To the best of our knowledge, no empirical study on adult L2 acquisition has been carried out along this particular line of inquiry.

3.5 Cognitive-Perceptual Perspectives

Finally, another factor that may be considered a major contributor to the development of verbal morphology is the role of the perceptual saliency and frequency of verbal endings (i.e., regular-irregular morphology) in past tense marking (e.g., Bayley 1994; Klein, Dietrich, and Noyau 1995; Lafford 1996; Salaberry 2000; Wolfram 1985). For instance, Klein, Dietrich, and Noyau claim that "irregular verbs are typically frequent and the morphological differences are perceptually salient, compared to a regular ending such as -ed, which may be hard to process for many learners" (1995:271). Wolfram (1985) argued that both tense and lexical aspect may be considered to be *higher order factors* (related to discourse level) in contrast with *surface constraints*. Surface constraints are represented by (a) regular versus irregular morphology; (b) type of irregular formation (e.g., suppletive form, internal vowel changes, internal vowel changes plus suffix, final consonant replacement); (c) frequency of the verb (usually irregulars such as "be," "have," "do," "come," "go"); (d) phonetic shape of the suffix on the regular verb (/t/, /d/ and /id/), and (e) the phonological environment that follows the verb (e.g., cluster reduction—with subsequent deletion of the past tense suffix—is favored when following vowel is preceded by a consonant). In essence, the prediction is that the more frequent and irregular the verb the more likely it will appear first in the development of past marking of adult instructed L2 learners—irrespective of the lexical semantic value of the verb phrase (e.g., statives versus telic events). For Spanish in particular, Lafford (1996:16) proposed the saliency-foregrounding hypothesis: "phonologically salient verb forms are used to reflect salient (foregrounded) actions in L2 narrative discourse."[15] Although several of the empirical studies mentioned earlier have made indirect or preliminary reference to the possible effect of perceptual saliency, there are studies in other languages and other environments than the academic that warrant a more systematic look at the above mentioned effect in the development of Spanish past tense verbal morphology (see Dietrich, Klein, and Noyau 1995).

4.0 Methodological Factors

By this stage the reader is already aware of a substantial amount of conflicting evidence regarding the development of tense/aspect markers among L2 Spanish classroom learners. We suspect that some of the discrepancies among studies may reflect theoretical as well as methodological factors. Having discussed the most prevalent hypotheses in the previous paragraphs it is worth discussing in more detail methodological factors in order to provide for a better understanding of the state of the science of this topic at the moment. Various methodological factors should be taken into account in the analysis of findings from empirical studies. We would like to discuss in detail the following: (a) type of data and data collection procedures, (b) selection and use of operational tests to determine lexical aspectual classes, (c) language-specific characteristics of tense-aspectual contrasts, (d) the effect of learning environment, and (e) types of input.

A factor that may qualify the results of several studies in significant ways is that lower-level learners appear to respond differently to task instructions from advanced learners or native speakers. This outcome may have important effects on the type of data elicited for further analysis. For instance, the studies of Hasbún (1995) and Salaberry (1999) revealed that native speakers and advanced nonnatives used the historical present even when explicitly asked to use past tense marking.[16] In addition, less advanced learners appear to focus more on the accurate use of inflectional morphology, whereas advanced learners and native speakers concentrate more on the functional demands of the experimental task (Salaberry 1999). Therefore, when participants behave so differently, these response patterns have the potential to skew severely the data collected, and they should be taken into account in the analysis.

Similarly, the type of data collected for analysis has an impact on the findings (e.g., oral versus written data, comprehension versus production data, discourse-based versus sentence-based data). For instance, although production data are appropriate to investigate when morphological markers are first used, they are limited to draw conclusions about what meaning learners assign to morphological forms, simply because it is unlikely that all possible forms will appear in all possible semantic contexts. Production data can indirectly indicate knowledge of a certain form, but the opposite assumption—that failure to produce a certain form entails lack of knowledge—cannot be supported. That is, L2 learners have been shown to have abstract knowledge of inflectional morphology as evidenced from their behavior with other syntactic phenomena associated with such morphology, even when their production of morphology is still quite random (Lardiere 2000; Prévost and White 1999).

Extending these observations to the acquisition of tense/aspect morphology, it is possible to assume that if learners do not produce preterit with stative verbs initially it does not necessarily mean that learners cannot interpret stative verbs as being telic, or that they do not know the difference between a state in the present and a state in the past. The ideal situation would be studies combining both production and judgment or comprehension data, studies in which results of different tasks and methodologies could show converging trends. In short, only by expanding the existing research design options can we acquire a more complete understanding of the acquisition of the tense and aspect system.[17]

Another major source of discrepancies among studies may be attributed to the inconsistent or inaccurate use of operational tests to classify lexical aspectual classes. As we have shown in section 2, verbal predicates have variable behavior, depending on the syntactic context in which they appear (*correr* versus *correr una milla*). Not all studies have reported on the operational tests used to classify verbs, but even when they are reported, it is clear that differences in criteria may bring about differences in the analysis of data. For instance, in general, the inception of a state (more accurately, a telic event) has been regarded as a nonprototypical state (e.g., Hasbún 1995; Ramsay 1990). In contrast, Salaberry (1999) classified verbs such as *saber* as statives *or* telic events depending on factors such as adverbials, arguments, adjuncts, and the like (see also Montrul and Slabakova 2000). The importance of this methodological classification cannot be overlooked, inasmuch as any claim about the role of lexical semantics on the development of verbal morphology is inherently dependent on how verb types are categorized.

Language-specific factors may also bring about conflicting interpretations of data. For instance, because in Spanish tense and aspect are morphologically fused, it is difficult to establish clearly whether learners are using verbal morphology to encode tense or to encode aspect. Thus, it may be argued that the learners from Ramsay (1990) were marking both tense (i.e., past versus present) and aspectual distinctions (i.e., inherent lexical aspect) at the same time. In fact, Shirai and Andersen (1995:759) argue that it is difficult to claim that *early past morphology* encodes tense or aspect only.[18] In essence, the representation of information about both tense and aspect in verbal morphology limits the extent to which one can claim that lexical aspectual classes have an effect on the development of verbal endings.

The potential effect of the learning context—natural interactional settings versus classroom-only settings—may also play an important role in the analysis of developmental data. In general, L2 learners who receive classroom instruction are immediately concerned about the analysis of verbal endings and their associated nuances of aspectual, tense and mode meaning (e.g., Bardovi-Harlig 1992, 1994; Bergström 1995; Hasbún 1995; Kaplan 1987; Montrul and Slabakova 2002; Ramsay 1990). In contrast, it has been documented that untutored learners do not focus on morphological endings to mark tense and aspect, but rely instead on the use of discursive and pragmatic means such as calendric reference, interlocutor scaffolding, and adverbial marking (e.g., Dietrich, Klein, and Noyau 1995; Perdue and Klein 1992; Schumann 1987; Trévise 1987). In essence, classroom learners and untutored learners use different markers of temporality due to differences of language input, formal and functional requirements, and interactional frameworks (see Paradis 1994; Schmidt 1995). Given that most of the studies reviewed in the previous section involved instructed learners, it is not clear to what extent such findings can be extended to natural settings.

Finally, another factor that should be taken into account is the type of input that learners have access to in instructed settings. Many studies assume that classroom interaction relies on the instructional sequences embedded in lesson plans or textbook materials, without empirically verifying such expected exposure to L2 data. For instance, studies on classroom talk in French instruction have documented that the *passé composé* (perfective) is more frequent than the *imparfait* (imperfective) (Kaplan 1987). Although there are no empirical verifications of classroom input in Spanish, it may turn out that the use of the preterit is more extended than the use of the imperfect in classroom talk in Spanish. This finding may account for the attested phenomenon that the preterit emerges first in instructed second language learners (used as a default tense), as Lafford (1996), Liskin-Gasparro (2000), Salaberry (1999), and others have proposed.[19]

5.0 Conclusion

The studies conducted to date have gathered some information on how the marking of Spanish past tense morphology emerges in early interlanguages of instructed learners, how such verbal morphology relates to the lexical aspectual class of different predicates, and how the semantic entailments of the tenses develop at intermediate and advanced levels of proficiency. A variety of issues remain to be investigated that have not yet been pursued. In the previous section, within the scope of theoretical and methodological issues that are worthy of additional study, we pointed to several broad areas of inquiry that deserve future attention and, in concluding, we mention three more.

Conspicuously absent from studies on tense and aspect in Spanish is the issue of transfer; that is, the role of the first language on the acquisition of a second language. All of the studies reported here have looked at only English-speaking learners of Spanish. It would be fruitful to see whether the availability of preterit and imperfect morphology in the learners' L1 has an effect on how this morphology emerges in the L2, and whether learners of Spanish who speak other Romance languages or Slavic or Asian languages follow the same developmental routes as English-speaking learners. In addition, we believe that it would be fruitful to undertake comparative studies of the emergence of tense/aspect morphology in children learning Spanish as L1, children learning Spanish as L2, as well as adults learning Spanish as L2 in naturalistic settings, to establish how children and adult second language learners' development are different from each other (the issue of age) and how they differ from children learning Spanish as L1. If adult L2 learners pass through a basic variety in which they use only lexical means to encode aspect (Perdue and Klein 1992), is this basic variety true of children as well?

Finally, studies of bilingual individuals in language contact situations could also inform the development and loss of the aspectual system in Spanish. Primary language attrition is the loss of aspects of previously fully acquired primary language as a result of the acquisition of another language (Seliger 1996). Although this phenomenon can be represented in several ways (dysfluency, inability to judge certain grammatical forms, difficulty retrieving words, code-switching, etc.) and in different aspects of grammar, a common manifestation is the erosion of morphological forms, as speakers lose the ability to correctly inflect morphology (Silva-Corvalán 1991). Studies by Silva-Corvalán (1991), Zentella (1997), and Montrul (2002) suggest that in Spanish-English contact situations (Los Angeles, New York City, and Chicago, respectively) subjects tend to use the imperfect tense in contexts where the preterit is appropriate and vice versa. Therefore, studies establishing links between different situations of acquisition and loss and with different populations can provide a better picture of how aspectual phenomena develop.

The study of Spanish second language acquisition has come a long way in the last twenty years or so. The state of the science of studies that focus on the development of inflectional morphology is indicative of such progress. We hope that we have been able to show the current status and further promise of this particular area of studies. Furthermore, we believe that, stemming from the analysis of the theoretical relevance of this topic as discussed above, future studies in this area of inquiry will have much to contribute to the development of any cogent hypothesis having to do with Spanish second language development.

NOTES

*The authors are listed in alphabetical order. Both contributed equally to the writing of this chapter.

1. See chapter 2 in Salaberry (2000) for a more extended analysis of lexical aspect in the context of L2 acquisition studies.

2. Mourelatos (1981, 195) mentions another good example that he obtained from a live TV broadcast: "I can't wait to see what he's been doing (activity) when he's done it (accomplishment)."

3. In fact, *Juan dormía* may also be translated as "John slept." As Guitart (1978) points out, the latter is the most common option (default past tense)—unless one contrasts two co-occurring events.

> **El teléfono sonó (PRET) mientras Juan dormía. (IMP)**
> **"The phone rang while John was sleeping."**

4. For a more extended analysis of the outcome of these studies, see chapter 4 in Salaberry (2000).

5. A number of other labels have been used to refer to the same hypothesis such as the Primacy of Aspect Hypothesis (e.g., Robison 1990, 1995) or the Redundant Marking Hypothesis (e.g., Shirai and Kurono 1998). To the best of our knowledge, no principled difference distinguishes these hypotheses.

6. Andersen based his claim on the analysis of data from two native English speakers learning Spanish (adolescents in an untutored setting).

7. Andersen found empirical support only for four of the eight stages, namely, stages 2, 4, 6 and 8.

8. See also Andersen (2002) for a more recent update on the relevance of the Lexical Aspect Hypothesis.

9. The inclusion of text with each picture was used to prevent students and native speakers from using the 'historical present' in their narratives (e.g., Klein 1994:133–41; Silva-Corvalán 1984). The implementation of the data collection procedure proved to be successful because native speakers never used present tense. In other studies (e.g., Salaberry 1999), however, native speakers rarely used past tense to narrate sequenced events of the type exemplified in the Disney story (see discussion section).

10. See also Wiberg (1996) for the proposal of the unmarked past tense hypothesis.

11. See chapter 7 of this volume for a general discussion of generative perspectives on Spanish L2 acquisition. However, no further discussion of tense/aspect issues will be found there.

12. One can distinguish three main positions on UG availability for L2 learners: "full access," "partial access," and "no access." For the first position, full acquisition of new functional

categories and their associated features is feasible (Epstein, Flynn, and Martohardjono 1996; Schwartz and Sprouse 1996; Vainikka and Young-Scholten 1996). "Partial access" suggests that access to functional categories, features, and feature values is severely restricted, either because L2 learners can only have access to L1 features (Hawkins and Chan 1997; Smith and Tsimpli 1995), or because L2 learners suffer from a "local deficit" and features remain permanently "valueless" (Beck 1998; Eubank et al. 1997). The third position is represented by Meisel (1997) who claims that L2 learners never acquire functional categories or features because L2 acquisition is not constrained by UG.

13. The test did not include activities because sentences with activities were illogical with preterit and imperfect. This response pattern did not fit the overall design of the test.

14. A possible drawback of this study, which the authors acknowledge, is that the learners tested were already too advanced to detect effects of lexical aspect. So, in fact these results do not necessarily contradict the Lexical Aspect Hypothesis.

15. In terms of phonological saliency, both Spanish past-tense regular preterits with final stress and irregular preterits with internal vowel changes stand out phonologically in comparison with verbs that carry penultimate stress and that have only three irregular forms (i.e., the imperfect).

16. See Fleischman (1989, 1990); Klein (1994) and Sebastian and Slobin (1994) for similar findings in other languages.

17. For an insightful analysis along these lines see Bardovi-Harlig (2002).

18. Even though Shirai and Andersen's argument refers to L1 acquisition, the dilemma concerning which factor to consider more important in the early marking of past-tense verbal endings is also relevant for L2 acquisition studies.

19. Alternatively, the effect of language input may be assessed through analysis of the language used in textbooks, as Hasbún (1995) has done. She analyzed the textbook used by the level 1 learners from her study: *Arriba* (Zayas-Bazán, Bacon, and Fernández). The preterit was introduced in lesson 7 and the imperfect in lesson 8 along with a comparison of both past tense markers.

WORKS CITED

Andersen, R. 1986. El desarrollo de la morfología verbal en el español como segundo idioma. In *Adquisición del lenguaje/Aquisição da linguagem,* ed. J. Meisel, 115–38. Frankfurt: Vervuert.

———. 1991. Developmental sequences: The emergence of aspect marking in second language acquisition. In *Crosscurrents in second language acquisition and linguistic theories,* eds. T. Huebner and C. A. Ferguson, 305–24. Amsterdam: John Benjamins.

———. 1994. The insider's advantage. In *Italiano lingua seconda/lingua straniera,* eds. A. Giacalone-Ramat and M. Vedovelli, 1–26. Roma: Bulzoni.

———. 2002. The dimensions of pastness. In *The L2 acquisition of tense-aspect morphology,* eds. R. Salaberry and Y. Shirai, 79–105. Amsterdam: John Benjamins.

Andersen, R., and Y. Shirai. 1994. Discourse motivations for some cognitive acquisition principles. *Studies in Second Language Acquisition* 16:133–56.

————. 1996. The primacy of aspect in first and second language acquisition: The pidgin-creole connection. In *Handbook of second language acquisition,* eds. R. Bhatia and W. Ritchie, 527–70. Malden, NJ: Academic Press.

Antinucci, F., and R. Miller. 1976. How children talk about what happened. *Journal of Child Language* 3:169–89.

Bardovi-Harlig, K. 1992. The relationship of form and meaning: A cross sectional study of tense and aspect in the interlanguage of learners of English as a second language. *Applied Psycholinguistics* 13:253–78.

————. 1994. Anecdote or evidence? Evaluating support for hypotheses concerning the development of tense and aspect. In *Research methodology in second-language acquisition,* eds. E. Tarone, S. Gass, and A. Cohen, 41–61. Hillsdale, NJ: Lawrence Erlbaum.

————. 1995. A narrative perspective on the development of the tense/aspect system in second language acquisition. *Studies in Second Language Acquisition* 17:263–89.

————. 2000. *Tense and aspect in second language acquisition: Form, meaning, and use.* Oxford: Blackwell.

————. 2002. Analyzing aspect. In *The L2 acquisition of tense- aspect morphology,* eds. R. Salaberry and Y. Shirai, 129–54. Amsterdam: John Benjamins.

Bayley, R. 1994. Interlanguage variation and the quantitative paradigm: Past tense marking in Chinese-English. In *Research methodology in second language acquisition,* eds. E. Tarone, S. Gass, and A. Cohen, 157–81. Hillsdale, NJ: Lawrence Erlbaum.

Beck, M. L. 1998. L2 acquisition and obligatory head movement: English-speaking learners of German and the local impairment hypothesis. *Studies in Second Language Acquisition* 20: 311–48.

Bergström, A. 1995. The expression of past temporal reference by English-speaking learners of French. Ph.D. diss., Pennsylvania State University.

Bickerton, D. 1981. *Roots of language.* Ann Arbor, MI: Karoma.

Bley-Vroman, R. 1989. What is the logical problem of foreign-language learning? In *Linguistic perspectives on second language acquisition,* eds. S. Gass and J. Schacter, 41–68. Cambridge: Cambridge University Press.

Bloom, L., K. Lifter, and J. Hafitz. 1980. Semantics of verbs and the development of verb inflection in child language. *Language* 56:386–412.

Bronckart, J. P., and H. Sinclair. 1973. Time, tense, and aspect. *Cognition* 2:107–30.

Brown, R. 1973. *A first language: The early stages.* Cambridge, MA: Harvard University Press.

Buczowska, E., and R. Weist. 1991. The effects of formal instruction on the second language acquisition of temporal location. *Language Learning* 41:535–54.

Bybee, J. 1985. *Morphology: A study of the relation between meaning and form.* Amsterdam: John Benjamins.

Bybee, J. L., and O. Dahl. 1989. The creation of tense and aspect systems in the languages of the world. *Studies in Language* 13:51–103.

Chomsky, N. 1995. *The minimalist program.* Cambridge, MA: MIT Press.

Comrie, B. 1976. *Aspect.* Cambridge: Cambridge University Press.

Coppieters, R. 1987. Competence differences between native and near-native speakers. *Language* 63:544–73.

de Miguel, E. 1992. *El aspecto en la sintaxis del español: Perfectividad e imperfectividad.* Madrid: Ediciones de la Universidad Autónoma de Madrid.

Depraetere, I. 1995. On the necessity of distinguishing between (un)boundedness and (a)telicity. *Linguistics and Philosophy* 18:1–19.

Dietrich, R., W. Klein, and C. Noyau. 1995. *The acquisition of temporality in a second language.* Amsterdam: John Benjamins.

Dowty, D. 1979. *Word meaning and Montague grammar.* Dordrecht: D. Reidel.

———. 1986. The effects of aspectual class on the temporal structure of discourse: Semantics or pragmatics? *Linguistics and Philosophy* 9:37–61.

Dry, H. 1983. The movement of narrative time. *Journal of Literary Semantics* 12:19–53.

Epstein, S., S. Flynn, and G. Martohardjono. 1996. Second language acquisition: Theoretical and experimental issues in contemporary research. *Brain and Behavioral Sciences* 19:677–758.

Eubank, L., J. Bischof, A. Huffstutler, P. Leek, and C. West. 1997. Tom eats slowly cooked eggs: Thematic verb-raising in L2 knowledge. *Language Acquisition* 6:171–99.

Fleischman, S. 1989. Temporal distance: A basic linguistic metaphor. *Studies in Language* 13:1–50.

———. 1990. *Tense and narrativity.* London: Routledge.

Frawley, W. 1992. *Linguistic semantics.* Hillsdale, NJ: Lawrence Erlbaum.

Giorgi, A., and F. Pianesi. 1997. *Tense and aspect: From semantics to morphosyntax.* Oxford: Oxford University Press.

Givón, T. 1982. Tense-aspect-modality: The Creole prototype and beyond. In *Tense-aspect: Between semantics and pragmatics,* eds. P. J. Hopper, 115–63. Amsterdam: John Benjamins.

Grice, P. 1975. Logic and conversation. In *Syntax and semantics: Speech acts,* vol. 3, eds. P. Cole and J. Morgan, 76–88. New York: Seminar Press.

Guitart, J. 1978. Aspects of Spanish aspect: A new look at the preterit/imperfect distinction. In *Contemporary studies in Romance linguistics,* ed. M. Suñer, 132–68.Washington, DC: Georgetown University Press.

Harley, B. 1989. Functional grammar in French immersion: A classroom experiment. *Applied Linguistics* 10:331–59.

Hasbún, L. 1995. The role of lexical aspect in the acquisition of the tense/aspect system in L2 Spanish. Ph.D. diss., Indiana University.

Hawkins, R., and C. Chan. 1997. The partial availability of Universal Grammar in second language acquisition: The "failed functional features hypothesis." *Second Language Research* 13.3:187–226.

Hopper, P., ed. 1982. *Tense-aspect: Between syntax and pragmatics.* Amsterdam: John Benjamins.

Housen, A. 1994. Tense and aspect in second language learning: The Dutch interlanguage of a native speaker of English. In *Tense and aspect in discourse,* eds. C. Vet and C. Vetters, 257–91. Berlin: Mouton de Gruyter.

Kaplan, M. 1987. Developmental patterns of past tense acquisition among foreign language learners of French. In *Foreign language learning: A research perspective,* ed. B. VanPatten, 52–60. Rowley, MA: Newbury House.

Klein, W. 1994. *Time in language.* London: Routledge.

Klein, W., R. Dietrich, and C. Noyau. 1995. Conclusions. In *The acquisition of temporality in a second language,* eds. R. Dietrich, W. Klein, and C. Noyau, 261–80. Amsterdam: John Benjamins.

Lafford, B. 1996. The development of tense/aspect relations in L2 Spanish narratives: Evidence to test competing theories. Paper presented at the Second Language Research Forum 96, Tucson, Arizona.

Langacker, R. 1982. Remarks on English aspect. In *Tense-aspect: Between syntax and pragmatics,* ed. P. Hopper, 265–304. Amsterdam: John Benjamins.

Lardiere, D. 2000. Mapping features to forms in second language acquisition. In *Second language acquisition and linguistic theory,* ed. J. Archibald, 102–29. Malden, MA: Blackwell.

Liskin-Gasparro, J. 2000. The acquisition of temporality in Spanish oral narratives: Exploring learners' perceptions. *Hispania* 83.4:830–44.

Maingueneau, D. 1994. *L'énonciation en linguistique française.* Paris: Hachette.

Meisel, J. 1997. The acquisition of the syntax of negation in French and German: Contrasting first and second language acquisition. *Second Language Research* 13:227–63.

Montrul, S. 2002. Incomplete acquisition and attrition of Spanish tense/aspect distinctions in adult bilinguals. *Bilingualism: Language and Cognition* 5.1:39–68.

Montrul, S., and R. Slabakova. 2000. Acquiring semantic properties of aspectual tenses in L2 Spanish. *Proceedings of the 24th Annual Boston University Conference on Language Development.* 534–45. Somerville, MA: Cascadilla Press.

———. 2002. Acquiring morphosyntactic and semantic properties of aspectual tenses in L2 Spanish. In *The acquisition of Spanish morphosyntax: The L1/L2 connection,* eds. A.-T. Pérez-Léroux and J. Liceras, 131–49. Dordrecht: Kluwer.

———. 2003. Competence similarities between native and near-native speakers: An investigation of the Preterite/Imperfect contrast in Spanish. *Studies in Second Language Acquisition* 25:3.

Mourelatos, A. 1981. Events, processes, and states. In *Syntax and semantics,* vol. 14, *Tense and aspect,* eds. P. Tedeschi and A. Zaenen, 415–34. New York: Academic Press.

Olsen, M. 1999. *A semantic and pragmatic model of lexical and grammatical aspect.* New York: Garland.

Paradis, M. 1994. Neurolinguistic aspects of implicit and explicit memory: Implications for bilingualism and SLA. In *Implicit and explicit learning of languages,* ed. N. Ellis, 393–419. London: Academic Press.

Perdue, C., and W. Klein. 1992. Why does the production of some learners not grammaticalize? *Studies in Second Language Acquisition* 14:259–72.

Prévost, P., and L. White. 1999. Accounting for morphological variation in L2 acquisition: Truncation or missing inflection? In *The acquisition of syntax: Issues in comparative developmental linguistics,* eds. M. A. Friedemann and L. Rizzi, 202–35. London: Longman.

Ramsay, V. 1990. Developmental stages in the acquisition of the perfective and the imperfective aspects by classroom L2 learners of Spanish. Ph.D. diss., University of Oregon.

Reid, W. 1980. Meaning and narrative structure. *Columbia University Working Papers in Linguistics* 5:12–20.

Reinhart, T. 1984. Principles of Gestalt perception in the temporal organization of narrative texts. *Linguistics* 22:779–809.

Rispoli, M., and L. Bloom. 1985. Incomplete and continuing: Theoretical issues in the acquisition of tense and aspect. *Journal of Child Language* 12:471–74.

Robison, R. 1990. The primacy of aspect: Aspectual marking in English interlanguage. *Studies in Second Language Acquisition* 12:315–30.

———. 1995. The aspect hypothesis revisited: A cross sectional study of tense and aspect marking in interlanguage. *Applied Linguistics* 16:344–71.

Salaberry, R. 1998. The development of aspectual distinctions in classroom L2 French. *Canadian Modern Language Review* 54.4:504–42.

———. 1999. The development of past tense verbal morphology in classroom L2 Spanish. *Applied Linguistics* 20:151–78.

———. 2000. *Spanish past tense aspect: L2 development in a tutored setting.* Amsterdam: John Benjamins.

———. 2002. Tense and aspect in the selection of Spanish past tense verbal morphology. In *The L2 acquisition of tense-aspect morphology,* eds. R. Salaberry and Y. Shirai, 397–415. Amsterdam: John Benjamins.

———. 2003. An analysis of the selection of past tense endings in personal and fictional narratives in L2 Spanish. *Hispania.*

Schmidt, R. 1995. Consciousness and foreign language learning: A tutorial on the role of attention and awareness in learning. In *Attention and awareness in foreign language learning,* ed. R. Schmidt, 1–63. Honolulu: University of Hawaii Press.

Schmitt, C. 1996. Aspect and the syntax of noun phrases. Ph.D. diss., University of Maryland.

Schumann, J. 1987. The expression of temporality in basilang speech. *Studies in Second Language Acquisition* 9:21–41.

Schwartz, B., and R. Sprouse. 1996. L2 cognitive states and the full transfer/full access model. *Second Language Research* 12:40–72.

Sebastian, E., and D. Slobin. 1994. Development of linguistic forms: Spanish. In *Relating events in narrative,* eds. R. Berman and D. Slobin, 239–84. Hillsdale, NJ: Laurence Erlbaum.

Seliger, H. 1996. Primary language attrition in the context of bilingualism. In *Handbook of second language acquisition,* eds. C. Ritchie and T. Bhatia, 605–26. San Diego: Academic Press.

Shirai, Y. 1991. Primacy of aspect in language acquisition: Simplified input and prototype. Ph.D. diss., University of California, Los Angeles.

Shirai, Y., and A. Kurono. 1998. The acquisition of tense-aspect marking in Japanese as a second language. *Language Learning* 48.2:245–79.

Shirai, Y., and R. Andersen. 1995. The acquisition of tense-aspect morphology: A prototype account. *Language* 71.4:743–62.

Silva-Corvalán, C. 1984. A speech event analysis of tense and aspect in Spanish. In *Papers from the Twelfth Linguistic Symposium on Romance Languages,* ed. R. Baldi-Philip, 229–51. Amsterdam: John Benjamins.

————. 1991. Spanish language attrition in a contact situation with English. In *First language attrition,* eds. H. Seliger and R. Vago, 151–74. Cambridge: Cambridge University Press.

Slabakova, R. 2001. *Telicity in the second language.* Amsterdam: John Benjamins.

Slabakova, R., and S. Montrul. 2002. Aspectual tenses in L2 Spanish: A UG perspective. In *Tense-aspect morphology in L2 acquisition,* eds. R. Salaberry and Y. Shirai, 359–91. Philadelphia: John Benjamins.

Smith, C. S. 1983. A theory of aspectual choice. *Language* 59:479–501.

————. 1991. *The parameter of aspect.* Dordrecht: Kluwer Academic.

Smith, C. S., and R. M. Weist. 1987. On the temporal contour of child language: A reply to Rispoli and Bloom. *Journal of Child Language* 14:387–92.

Smith, N., and I. Tsimpli. 1995. *The mind of a savant: Language learning and modularity.* Oxford: Blackwell.

Tenny, C. 1991. *Aspectual roles and the syntax-semantics interface.* Dordrecht: Kluwer Academic.

Travis, L. 1992. Inner aspect and the structure of VP. In *Proceedings from the Second Annual Lexical-Syntactic Relations Workshop,* eds. Mariette Champagne and Sylvie Ratté, 130–46. Montreal: University of Quebec.

Trévise, A. 1987. Toward an analysis of the (inter)language activity of referring to time in narratives. In *First and second language acquisition processes,* ed. C. Pfaff, 225–51. Cambridge, MA: Newbury House.

Vainikka, A., and M. Young-Scholten. 1996. Gradual development of L2 phrase structure. *Second Language Research* 12:7–39.

Vendler, Z. 1967. *Linguistics in philosophy.* Ithaca, NY: Cornell University Press.

Verkuyl, H. 1994. A theory of aspectuality: The interaction between temporal and atemporal structure. Cambridge: Cambridge University Press.

Wagner, L. 1999. Applying completion entailments to affected objects: Advanced problems in the acquisition of the imperfective. Paper presented at the 24th Annual Boston University Conference on Language Development, Boston.

Wallace, S. 1982. Figure and ground: The interrelationships of linguistic categories. In *Tense-aspect: Between syntax and pragmatics,* ed. P. Hopper, 201–33. Amsterdam: John Benjamins.

Wiberg, E. 1996. Reference to past events in bilingual Italian-Swedish children of school age. *Linguistics* 34:1087–1114.

Wolfram, W. 1985. Variability in tense marking: A case for the obvious. *Language Learning* 35.2:229–53.

Zagona, K. 1994. Compositionality of aspect: Evidence from Spanish aspectual *se.* In *Aspects of Romance linguistics: Selected papers from the LSRL XXI,* eds. C. Parodi, C. Quicoli, M. Saltarelli, and M. Zubizarreta, 473–88. Washington, DC: Georgetown University Press.

Zentella, A. C. 1997. *Growing up bilingual.* Malden, MA: Blackwell.

3

Subjunctive/Syntax

The Development of Subjunctive and Complex-Syntactic Abilities among Foreign Language Learners of Spanish

JOSEPH G. COLLENTINE   Northern Arizona University

1.0   Introduction

For many foreign-language (FL) learners of Spanish, one of the most unique grammatical constructs of the Spanish language is the subjunctive. Because the subjunctive is not highly productive in English (e.g., "If I <u>were</u> you"), students have almost no first-language (L1) models with which to formulate hypotheses about its use in Spanish. This challenge is augmented by the subjunctive's complexities, being a morpheme that denotes abstract concepts (e.g., marking *irrealis* events and states) with a syntactic distribution largely limited to subordinate clauses. This chapter critically examines almost thirty years of research aimed at understanding the processes through which learners pass in the development of subjunctive abilities and the factors that interact with those processes.

Although the primary purpose of this chapter is to provide an understanding of Spanish subjunctive acquisition in FL contexts, it contextualizes this foray with an analysis of important studies on subjunctive acquisition in first-language (L1) and bilingual contexts. Subsequently, the author examines the factors that affect subjunctive development in FL contexts as well as the variables influencing the development of abilities for processing complex syntax. Finally, the chapter outlines experimental design issues that limit the generalization of the conclusions that these L1, bilingual, and FL studies have offered.

Researchers have examined the roles of both *internal* and *external factors*. In this article, internal factors fall into two categories: (1) Developmental: the processes within the learner's grammatical competence that convert FL data into representations (i.e., long-term knowledge for the FL) and those that restructure existing knowledge structures in accordance with these new representations; (2) Processing: the attentional resources and the short-term memory stores (e.g., phonological, episodic, working) that allow the learner to analyze FL data. External factors are mechanisms that determine where or when a grammatical phenomenon appears in the input. These mechanisms include (1) the distributional features of the subjunctive, such as associations between the morpheme and certain lexical phenomena (e.g., *quiero que* "I want," *para que* "so that") and its frequent occurrence in dependent clauses; (2) institutional variables (e.g., education) that lead to a decline in the frequency with which one is exposed to the subjunctive; and (3) the communicative value of the subjunctive, or the amount of semantic import it contributes to a sentence's message.

2.0 The Development of Subjunctive Abilities in L1 and Bilingual Contexts

In bilingual contexts, investigators concentrating on internal factors have sought to explain how psycholinguistic mechanisms and maturational constraints account for the developmental stages that children exhibit. Investigators focusing on external factors have studied the effects of input (i.e., data) and sociolinguistic factors (e.g., institutional variables) on the development of subjunctive abilities.

2.1 L1 Acquisition of the Subjunctive

Gili Gaya (1972) examines the acquisition of the subjunctive by preschool (three to five years) and school-age (five to ten years) children in Puerto Rico. Gili Gaya posits that preschool children employ what amounts to a lexical-cue strategy of sorts.[1] For instance, he notes that children use subjunctive forms with lexical phenomena that appear most frequently with the subjunctive (e.g., after *querer que* and *para que*). School-age children, however, adopt a semantic strategy by generalizing the subjunctive to directives, volitives, and adverbial clauses with future time reference. Spanish speakers do not master mood selection until adolescence, when sociolinguistic factors (e.g., scholastic institutions) pressure them to conform to adult NS linguistic norms.

Blake (1983, 1985) examines the subjunctive development of Spanish natives aged 4 to 12 (n = 134). His data confirm that school-age children largely employ a semantic strategy, limiting the subjunctive's function to "events that are not yet realized" (1985:167), such as nominal clauses involving volition (e.g., *Quiero que me hagas un favor* "I want you to do me a favor"), adjectival clauses (e.g., *Quiero jugar con el equipo que sea mejor* "I want to play with the team that is better") and adverbial clauses entailing the future (e.g., *Voy a hacer la tarea cuando vuelva a casa* "I am going to do the homework when I return home"). Up to age ten this semantic strategy competes with a lexical-cue strategy, which is especially robust in nominal clauses. Blake accounts for this with a cue-strength hypothesis of sorts. Specifically, adults demonstrate a great amount of variability in their use of the subjunctive in nominal clauses; consequently, children employ the subjunctive with those lexical phenomena that are reliably associated with the subjunctive in the input they receive (e.g., *¡Es bueno que hayan venido!* "It is good that they have come").

Pérez-Leroux (1998) studies the effects of maturational factors on subjunctive development. Her data suggest that certain subjunctive functions (i.e., in adjectival clauses such as *La cocinera busca una gallina que ponga huevos* "The cook is looking for a hen that lays eggs") emerge only once a child can distinguish between their own beliefs and reality. Given that cognitive maturation mediates grammatical development, Pérez-Leroux concludes that children initially map deontic functions—when language reflects or affects changes within one's environment, such as in directives (see Palmer 1986)—onto the subjunctive. As they begin to distinguish between reality and belief, children assign it epistemic functions, which indicate the degree to which the child is committed to the truth value of a given proposition (e.g., *No creo que sea cierto* "I do not believe it is true"; *Quiero una bola que sea grande* "I want a ball that is big"; see Palmer 1986).

2.2 Subjunctive Development in Bilingual Contexts

Dialectologists studying U.S. Spanish have provided insights into the factors that interact with subjunctive development in bilingual contexts (e.g., García and Terrell 1977; Hensey 1973, 1976; Sánchez 1972; Solé 1977). Floyd (1983) summarizes the results of these studies, essentially proposing a *syntactic deficiency hypothesis* to account for the underdeveloped mood-selection abilities of a group of Spanish/English bilinguals she studied in the early 1980s. She surmises that institutional prohibitions on the use of Spanish in public forums (e.g., in public schools) contributed to a delay in many bilinguals' syntactic development, which may in turn have hindered the development of subjunctive abilities.

Guitart (1982) tests an English-interference hypothesis: "The more a Spanish-English bilingual is influenced by English in his use of Spanish, the less he will use the subjunctive. . . . [This hypothesis] is based on the fact that there is no mood contrast in such sentences in English" (61). He compares the subjunctive abilities of three groups of bilingual adults (n = 43), all of which differed in terms of their years of length of U.S. residency. The data Guitart presents support his hypothesis, suggesting a negative correlation between residency in the United States and subjunctive abilities.

Among other verbal phenomena, Silva-Corvalán (1994) examines the use of the subjunctive across five categories of Spanish speakers in Los Angeles, who range from those who emigrated as Mexican nationals to those who were U.S. nationals that speak both Spanish and English. She observes that bilinguals with many or all of their years residing in the United States simplify their Spanish grammatical system to a greater extent than those enjoying the reverse profile. One consequence is that these individuals are much more likely to eliminate the subjunctive from their grammatical repertoire, allowing (1) the present indicative to assume the functions once enjoyed by the present subjunctive and (2) the imperfect indicative (and at times the preterit) to assume functions that the imperfect subjunctive carried out. Indeed, Silva-Corvalán presents evidence suggesting that the subjunctive is one of the first grammatical structures to disappear in the inventory of Spanish-English bilinguals (where Spanish is the subordinate language).

Lynch (2000) employs Silva-Corvalán's methodology to examine subjunctive use in three generations of Cuban Americans in Miami, ranging from first- to third-generation bilinguals. Lynch observed the same simplification processes that Silva-Corvalán did. Yet, the simplification process was not as accelerated in Miami bilinguals as it was in those from Los Angeles. Lynch also observed simplifications that conspired to eliminate the conditional, which effectively increased the expansion of the imperfect subjunctive (e.g., *Si fuera rico, comprara una casa grande* "If s/he were rich, s/he would buy me a big house").

Zentella (1997) examines the mood-selection abilities of school-age females (n = 5) speaking a Puerto Rican variety of Spanish in New York. Similar to Silva-Corvalán, Zentella argues that the late acquisition of the subjunctive (relative to other grammatical constructs such as tense) makes the subjunctive vulnerable to loss especially when the variety of Spanish that the bilingual speaks is stigmatized, as is often the case with Puerto Rican Spanish.

2.3   Summary of Subjunctive Development in L1 and Bilingual Contexts

This review indicates that researchers have focused their study of subjunctive development in L1 and bilingual contexts on both internal and external factors. Concerning internal factors, Pérez-Leroux's (1998) study indicates that the subjunctive's denotation—or range of connotations—is so abstract that acquisition is mediated by maturational constraints for a number of years. Still, even if a preschool child uses only a single semantic strategy when using the subjunctive, this strategy probably coexists with a lexical-cue strategy throughout childhood (see Blake 1983, 1985; Gili Gaya 1972).

Regarding external factors, the subjunctive's distributional characteristics in the input that children receive appear to have important ramifications. Both Gili Gaya (1972) and Blake (1985) suggest that the strength of the association between the subjunctive and certain lexical items explains many developmental patterns. Yet, it is unclear whether cue frequency (the regularity with which children hear particular matrix-clause verbs in conjunction with the subjunctive) or cue strength (the reliability with which the subjunctive co-occurs with certain matrix-clause verbs) better accounts for behaviors observed.

Another important external factor is the strength of the institutional support for Spanish in the social contexts in which children develop (Floyd 1983; Gili Gaya 1972; Guitart 1982). Studies indicate that, where there is institutional support, acquisition of the subjunctive nonetheless does not solidify until adolescence. Additionally, when one uses Spanish where numerous first-generation speakers reside, the elimination of the subjunctive from the grammatical repertoire is less likely to occur (Lynch 2000). Conversely, the stigmatization of a bilingual's variety of Spanish may accelerate the subjunctive-simplification process documented by Silva-Corvalán (see Zentella 1997). As a whole, these observations imply that, apart from any semantic/pragmatic function, the existence of the subjunctive in the Spanish language is largely determined by numerous sociolinguistic forces.

Silva-Corvalán explains the loss of the subjunctive among English-dominant and/or long-time U.S. resident bilinguals by essentially arguing that certain external factors motivate an acceleration of internal processes that conspire to eliminate the subjunctive from the bilingual's grammatical competence. Specifically, Silva-Corvalán argues that paradigms such as the subjunctive have little semantic transparency; its denotation as a *relative* "tense" (e.g., its futuritive function) does not make its meaning and role in the grammar evident. Bilinguals are likely to eliminate those structures in the subordinate language that entail the processing of cognitively complex features because they are less proficient overall in the subordinate language. As a result, the subjunctive becomes a perfect candidate for elimination.

3.0   The Subjunctive and Foreign Language Acquisition

Investigators studying internal factors affecting the acquisition of the subjunctive by FL learners have sought to account for developmental patterns within certain theories of second-language (L2) acquisition (e.g., the Monitor Model; Krashen 1982). Those interested in external factors have not examined the effects of sociolinguistic factors on L2 development, as has been the case in L1 and bilingual studies; rather, they have sought to gauge the conditions that promote subjunctive acquisition in an input-rich learning environment.

3.1   Internal Factors Affecting FL Subjunctive Development

Terrell, Baycroft, and Perrone (1987) describe the subjunctive abilities of students completing one year of university-level studies (n = 70) from the perspective of Krashen's (1982) Monitor Model. The learners' curriculum was based on a "cognitive approach" (Terrell, Baycroft, and Perrone 1987:21), in which grammar explanations were followed by guided drills and practice as well as guided conversations. In a writing task, the participants employed the subjunctive with 92 percent accuracy. However, in an oral (conversational) task, the learners' subjunctive accuracy averaged only 12.3 percent. It is also important to note that in the oral task, the subjects produced few mood-selection contexts, or the pragmatic and syntactic conditions (i.e., subordinate clauses) that would necessitate the use of the subjunctive.[2] Because the learners seemed limited to generating the subjunctive where they could monitor their performance (i.e., the writing task), Terrell, Baycroft, and Perrone (1987) conclude that their subjects had "learned" but not "acquired" the subjunctive.

Stokes (1988) and Stokes and Krashen (1990) also attempt to account for subjunctive acquisition within the Monitor Model, wondering whether "acquired knowledge" can result from classroom instruction. The participants were advanced university-level students of Spanish, possessing varying amounts of formal Spanish study and time living in Spanish-speaking countries (n = 27). For the study, the learners completed a sentence-completion task, which required them to repeat a matrix-clause (e.g., *Mis padres quieren que yo—* "My parents want me to—") and complete that clause with an original statement (e.g., *Mis padres quieren que yo estudie italiano* "My parents want me to study Italian"). The learners completed the task before and after "a week-long lesson on the subjunctive" (Stokes 1988:706). (He provides no description of the materials or the methodological approach of the training component.) Stokes and Krashen (1990) examine the correlations between the participants' scores on the task, their number of semesters of classroom time, and their years of foreign residence. The analysis suggests that foreign residence correlates significantly with subjunctive abilities, but classroom instruction does not. Stokes and Krashen found the same correlations even after the subjects completed the week-long subjunctive lesson. They conclude that "classroom instruction does not bring students far enough along to acquire the subjunctive" (Stokes and Krashen 1990:806).

Collentine (1995) attempts to describe and account for the subjunctive abilities of learners completing the second year (i.e., the intermediate level) of university-level Spanish FL instruction (n = 78) within Givón's (1979) Pidginization Hypothesis. The learners' curriculum was proficiency-oriented. Analyzing two oral-production tasks (i.e., one involving spontaneous speech and the other planned speech), Collentine suggests that most learners completing the intermediate level exhibit behaviors typical of the presyntactic stage[3] of development, employing morphology unreliably and exhibiting poor subjunctive abilities even when they have a generous amount of time to produce utterances. Collentine (like Floyd 1983) employs a syntactic-deficiency hypothesis to explain the difficulties that these learners face with learning the subjunctive. Specifically, he posits that these learners are not yet at the syntactic stage where they can process in short-term memory both complex syntax and the semantic/pragmatic relationships (e.g., volition, doubt/denial) existing between two clauses.

3.2   External Factors Affecting FL Subjunctive Development

The literature contains two types of studies that provide insight into the external factors favoring subjunctive acquisition. The first set of studies is concerned with the question of focus on form,[4] and they examine the extent to which learners attend to the subjunctive in input. The second set of studies seeks to assess the efficacy of particular classroom methodologies for promoting subjunctive acquisition.

Lee (1987) is the first to study the focus-on-form issue with the subjunctive. He assesses the tenability of the premise that learners need early exposure to the subjunctive before they can comprehend reading passages containing forms such as *tenga* "X has" and *compre* "X buys." Two groups of FL learners of Spanish read a passage containing numerous subjunctive forms: a first-semester group (n = 90) without prior subjunctive instruction and a second-semester group (n = 90) with prior instruction. Lee (1987) finds that prior exposure to the subjunctive did not predict comprehension, inasmuch as both groups understood the reading's content equally well.

Lee and Rodríguez (1997) provide insights into the effects of various factors on learners' propensity to attend to the subjunctive in input, studying the interaction between three linguistic variables and reading comprehension: (1) mood, exposing intermediate-level learners of Spanish (n = 120) to a passage with either proper uses of the subjunctive or with (erroneous) indicative forms (e.g., *Es importante que se *prepara/prepare* "It is important that one prepare"); (2) subordination, having subjects read a passage containing either subordinate or nonfinite clauses (e.g., *Es necesario que lo hagan/*hacerlo* "It is necessary that they do it"); and (3) vocabulary, having the learners read subjunctive and/or subordinate clauses with either known vocabulary or nonce terms. Lee and Rodríguez present data from both comprehension and recognition tests. Passages containing subjunctive forms and/or complex syntax were no more difficult to comprehend than those containing simpler morphology and syntax. Nonetheless, the authors argue that subjunctive forms became intake less frequently than indicative forms, implying that the morphological differences between the present indicative and the present subjunctive are not perceptually salient to learners at the intermediate level. Interestingly, the learners were more likely to attend to the subjunctive and subordinate-clause syntax when the vocabulary items encoding or associated with such grammatical information were familiar.

Leow (1993) asks whether simplified input (i.e., a simulated-authentic passage as opposed to an authentic one) facilitates the intake of verbal morphology at the first and second years of university study. Two groups of first-semester learners of Spanish (n = 49) and two fourth-semester groups (n = 88) read either a simplified or an authentic passage containing either the present perfect or the present subjunctive. The fourth-semester groups had previous exposure to both structures. Leow operationalized intake with a pretest/ posttest recognition test. Simplified input did not facilitate intake at either level of proficiency, although the fourth-semester learners experienced significantly more intake of the targeted structures. Leow conjectures that advanced learners intake more grammatical information because they can dedicate more attentional resources to such phenomena than less advanced learners, who are primarily concerned with processing input for lexical content (i.e., for meaning). That is, Leow assumes that learners must establish a particular grammatical foundation before they will intake morphological paradigms like the subjunctive. Leow (1995) replicates his 1993 study in the aural mode. Again, proficiency level rather than simplification accounted for intake. However, Leow reveals that FL learners of Spanish are less likely to intake the subjunctive than they are the present perfect in aural passages. Leow essentially argues that the (synthetic) phonological properties of the subjunctive are less salient to learners than the (analytic) features of the present perfect.

Following Leow (1995), Collentine (1997) asks whether learners are more likely to attend to so-called irregular subjunctive forms (e.g., *sea* "X is," *sepa* "X knows," *tenga* "X has," *vaya* "X goes") than regular subjunctive forms (e.g., *compare* "X compares," *beba* "X drinks," *viva* "X lives"). As verbal stimuli go, the former are perceptually more "novel" (Cowan 1995). Intermediate-level learners of Spanish (n = 30) utilized a computer application that measured whether irregular forms required more time to process and whether they interfered with comprehension, behaviors that VanPatten (1990) views as indications that attention to grammatical form has occurred. Collentine observed both behaviors, concluding that irregular subjunctive forms are more likely to attract learners' attention than regular forms in input tasks.

Research examining the efficacy of instructional methodologies on subjunctive learning has primarily investigated whether "structured input" promotes acquisition. Structured-input tasks expose learners to sentences containing exemplars of a targeted structure. Intake of the targeted structure is likely to occur if the task is designed in such a way that the proper interpretation of a sentence's message largely depends on properly interpreting the connotation of that structure. For instance, in a lesson on indirect-object pronouns, a student might somehow indicate whether first-person singular or second-person singular is the recipient in *Te doy mi suéter favorito* "I'm giving you my favorite sweater."

Collentine (1997) conjectures that, because structured-input tasks prompt learners to interpret sentences in a way in which accurate interpretation depends on accurately deciphering the meaning of a targeted structure, structured-input tasks cannot promote subjunctive intake in nominal clauses. While Collentine provides no empirical support for this prediction, he observes that in nominal clauses, the modality that the subjunctive connotes is invariably encoded lexically into the main-clause verb phrase (e.g., _Quiero_ que me _hagas_ un favor "I want you to do me a favor," _Dudo_ que _tengan_ suficiente "I doubt they have enough"). However, Pereira's (1996) work implies that Collentine's prediction is erroneous. Third-semester FL learners of Spanish (n = 68) participated in Pereira's study, which—among other things— assessed the potential of structured input to promote subjunctive development in nominal clauses. The learners had no prior subjunctive instruction. A pretest, a posttest, and a delayed posttest entailing grammaticality judgments and a dialogue-completion exercise confirmed the efficacy of structured input in promoting subjunctive knowledge.

Woodson (1997) compares the efficacy of Processing Instruction (PI) (VanPatten 1993)—a methodology that employs structured input—to what she terms Interactive Processing Instruction (IPI) for promoting subjunctive acquisition. IPI incorporates principles of the Interactionist Hypothesis and cooperative learning (Gass and Varonis 1994; Pica and Doughty 1985; Pica, Young, and Doughty 1987; Mackey 1999). IPI prompts learners to focus on a structure's form and meaning in tasks where they share their interpretations of aural and written input with other learners. Whereas PI focuses on providing learners with meaningful opportunities to process a targeted structure in input (VanPatten 2002), IPI focuses on output, that is, the production of a targeted structure. In IPI, learners problem-solve in the target language (e.g., in jigsaw activities) in tasks where they must write or generate orally the targeted phenomenon. High school-level FL learners of Spanish (n = 48) without prior subjunctive instruction participated in the study. Assessment entailed two written and two oral tasks. Woodson found PI and IPI to be equally effective.

Collentine (1998) compares the efficacy of PI and an output-oriented approach to grammar instruction on subjunctive development in adjectival clauses. The output-oriented instruction involved learners in meaningful speaking and writing tasks where they were prompted to produce the subjunctive. Second-semester FL learners of Spanish without prior subjunctive instruction participated in the study (n = 54). Utilizing a pretest/posttest paradigm, an interpretation task (where learners identified whether particular uses of the subjunctive were appropriate given contextual clues) and a written production task assessed the treatments' effects. As Woodson (1997) found, Collentine's analysis indicated that the input-oriented PI and the output-oriented approaches are equally effective at promoting subjunctive on both the interpretation and the production tasks.

Farley (2001) raises concerns about the internal validity and generalizability of Collentine's (1998) PI study. Farley surmises that the PI treatment in Collentine (1998) does not actually consider how learners will process subjunctive forms in input. In response, to provide an example of "authentic" subjunctive PI, Farley (2001) presents the results of his own experiment (n = 60) in which he compares the efficacy of PI and an output-oriented approach to subjunctive instruction involving nominal clauses with matrices of doubt. Interestingly, like Collentine (1998), Farley's data suggest that subjunctive PI is equally as effective as subjunctive output-oriented instruction.[5]

3.3   Summary of Internal and External Factors Affecting FL Subjunctive Development

The research investigating internal factors (Collentine 1995; Terrell, Baycroft, and Perrone 1987; Stokes 1988; Stokes and Krashen 1990) concentrate on the status of the learners' L2 knowledge at particular points in their development. All told, the research describes the status of classroom learners' subjunctive knowledge that might account for their deficiencies with this structure. Terrell, Baycroft, and Perrone (1987) as well as Stokes (1988) and Stokes and Krashen (1990) detail the abilities of learners who appear to possess only learned

knowledge for the subjunctive, that is, knowledge that cannot be utilized in most spontaneous situations because its use requires monitoring. These researchers maintain that the
lack of exposure to comprehensible input fostering subjunctive knowledge accounts for this
state of affairs. Collentine (1995) argues that because the Spanish grammatical competence
of most learners completing their FL studies is still at a presyntactic stage, they cannot benefit from traditional methodologies for promoting subjunctive acquisition.

Yet, the most important generalization to extrapolate from the research on subjunctive
acquisition in FL environments stems from the investigations providing insights into the external factors that have the potential to affect subjunctive acquisition. By and large, this research indicates that the subjunctive will elude the attention of learners in meaningful input
tasks.

Indeed, though it is encouraging that subjunctive instruction is apparently not a prerequisite to understanding subjunctive forms (and their surrounding co-text), Lee's (1987)
findings ultimately imply that learners do not notice the subjunctive. Following VanPatten
(1990), grammatical constructs place varying demands on one's short-term memory and attentional capacity, both of which are limited in capacity at any given moment. If learners
attend to exemplars of a grammatical structure for which they have little background
knowledge, they have fewer processing resources to dedicate to the comprehension of the
meaning of the sentence/passage surrounding those exemplars. Thus, if a new grammatical structure is associated with a decrease in comprehension, attentional resources have
been dedicated to that form. If the subjunctive forms in Lee (1987) had received a significant amount of cognitive attention by the less-proficient participants, the learners would
have exhibited a decrease in comprehension.

Additionally, Lee and Rodríguez (1997) report that FL learners of Spanish intake significantly fewer subjunctive than indicative forms. The literature provides three explanations. First, the subjunctive is not phonologically salient (Collentine 1997; Leow 1995). Many
present-subjunctive forms do not differ significantly from their present indicative counterparts, possessing the same stems (e.g., _canto_ "I sing" [indicative] versus _cante_ "I sing" [sub-
junctive]) and inflections that learners already associate with the (present) indicative (e.g.,
bebe "X drinks" [indicative] versus _cante_ "X sings" [subjunctive]). Second, the subjunctive's
overall lack of communicative value creates a situation in which learners in an input-rich
classroom do not need to attend to the subjunctive to achieve comprehension (Collentine
1997). Third, Leow's work (1995) implies that regardless of the teaching methodology, the
learner's overall proficiency mediates whether he or she will attend to it in input, perhaps
indicating that a certain linguistic foundation must be in place before subjunctive intake will
occur reliably. Interestingly, Collentine (1995), Pereira (1996), as well as Terrell, Baycroft, and
Perrone (1987) conjecture that subjunctive instruction will only be beneficial once a learner
can process complex syntax. Indeed, recall that Floyd (1983) explains the underdeveloped
subjunctive abilities of the bilinguals in her study by essentially implying that their inability to generate complex syntax interacted with the acquisition of their subjunctive abilities.

The research reviewed above also reveals that, regarding the efficacy of subjunctive instruction, there exist viable and effective teaching strategies to the traditional skills-getting
and skills-using classroom. First, Lee and Rodríguez (1997) as well as Collentine (1997) suggest that tasks promoting comprehensible input targeting learners' subjunctive knowledge

must consider the type of subjunctive forms that they will include. So-called high frequency verbs (i.e., the most common verbs, which also tend to be the most irregular) possess some feature(s) (either semantic or phonological) that partially offset(s) the factors that make it nonsalient. Second, while input-oriented techniques, such as those involving structured input, may be important facilitators in promoting subjunctive development (VanPatten 1993), they are probably not sufficient (Pica and Doughty 1985; Gass and Varonis 1994; see also Swain 1985; Swain and Lapkin 1995). Indeed, the research to date on the acquisition of the subjunctive provides important support for a postulate that is gaining increasing momentum, namely, that (relatively) complete acquisition of most grammatical phenomena require both input and output oriented instruction (VanPatten 2002).

4.0 The Development of Abilities to Process Complex Syntax and Their Relationship to the Acquisition of Verbal Inflectional Abilities

The following discussion reviews the tenability of the *syntactic-foundation hypothesis* (Collentine 2000) namely, that the acquisition of the ability to process complex syntax establishes certain prerequisite developmental conditions for the acquisition of the subjunctive. There have been three approaches to studying this hypothesis: (1) general structuralist approaches, apparently informed by European functionalist perspectives on language use; (2) formalist approaches that study the role of Universal Grammar (UG); and (3) cognitive approaches.

4.1 General Structuralist Approaches to Understanding the Relationship Between Syntactic and Morphological Development in SLA

The 1970s and 1980s saw a plethora of studies detailing the order in which learners acquire various grammatical entities, including morphology and syntax. R. Ellis (1987) summarized the findings of these studies, surmising that learners generally progress through four sequential stages: (1) the development of basic syntactic knowledge, such as SVO in English; (2) the acquisition of variant word order, such as knowing that subject-verb inversion equates to question formation; (3) the development of morphological knowledge; and, (4) the acquisition of knowledge relating to complex sentence structure.

Bardovi-Harlig and Bofman (1989) specifically studied the relationship between the acquisition of interlanguage (IL) morphology and syntax. They compared the syntactic and morphological errors of advanced learners of English, concluding that these learners committed fewer syntactic than morphological errors. Bardovi-Harlig and Bofman (1989) reasoned that, when the L1 and the L2 are Indo-European languages such as English, German, and Spanish, syntax develops before morphology because syntax enjoys greater cross-linguistic "stability" than morphology. That is, there are greater syntactic similarities between Indo-European languages than morphological similarities, which may give the acquisition of syntax an advantage.

Skiba and Dittmar (1992) study syntactic and morphological development from the earliest stages of German L2 acquisition from a "grammaticalization" perspective. Skiba and Dittmar observe that learners' sensitivity to certain morphological features follows an important advancement in their syntactic abilities, namely, after they abandon the basic TOPIC-COMMENT word order (e.g., *Juan . . . listo y simpático* "Juan . . . smart and nice") in favor of a SUBJECT-PREDICATE strategy (e.g., *Juan es listo y simpático* "Juan is smart and nice"). It is only once learners enter the SUBJECT-PREDICATE stage that they "try to modify verb forms morphologically" (339). Skiba and Dittmar posit that morphological systems develop out of the assignment of syntactic features to individual lexical items, such as the assignment of $[+N, -V]$ to terms such as *casa* "house" and $[-N, +V]$ to *trabaja* "X works."

As discussed previously, Collentine (1995) assesses the syntactic abilities of intermediate-level learners of Spanish by measuring their development according to Givón's pidginization hypothesis. The hypothesis predicts that morphosyntactic abilities progress from a presyntactic to a syntactic stage. In the presyntactic stage, which is pidginlike, the emergence of any morphology is generally unintended or formulaic. Furthermore, bipropositional utterances here normally take the form of parataxis (e.g., *Juan dijo . . . no me gusta* "Juan said . . . I don't like it") or coordination (e.g., *María no viene y no me gusta* "María is not coming and I don't like it"). As learners approach the syntactic stage, they employ morphology purposefully and can readily generate subordinate structures. Collentine notes that, in tasks involving both unplanned and planned speech, his participants generated few subordinate clauses (e.g., *Marcos sabe que la fiesta es mañana* "Marcos knows that the party is tomorrow"), favoring instead parataxis (e.g., *Marcos sabe . . . [pause] . . . la fiesta es mañana* "Marcos knows . . . the party is tomorrow") and coordination (e.g., *La fiesta es mañana y Marcos sabe* "The party is tomorrow and Marcos knows"). Collentine conjectures that these learners are too taxed by their processing of complex syntax to attend fully to (and so improve their procedural knowledge for) complex morphemes such as the subjunctive.

Similarly, Silva-Corvalán (1994), who examines the syntactic complexity of Mexican-Spanish bilinguals in Los Angeles across varying levels of Spanish proficiency, asserts that the simplification processes that erode the subjunctive from the Spanish competence of less-proficient bilinguals ultimately conspires to make the production of complex syntax a cognitively burdensome task, and so less-proficient bilinguals rarely generate subordination. Silva-Corvalán goes further than Collentine, detailing that the Spanish discourse of less-proficient bilinguals is more assertive (i.e., matter-of-fact), and thus less hypothetical and evaluative, than that of more proficient bilinguals.

Collentine et al. (in press) reports the work of the only researchers to date to test the tenability of the syntactic-foundation hypothesis in a classroom setting. Three groups of intermediate-level, FL learners of Spanish (n = 69) participated in the study. One group received instruction fostering knowledge of complex Spanish syntax (i.e., how verb and noun complements can be either lexical or clausal—e.g., *María ve agua/que se van* "María sees water/that they are going"; *Juan tiene un coche viejo/que va lento* "Juan has an old car/a car that goes slowly") followed by (morphological) instruction on the subjunctive in adjectival clauses (e.g., *María busca una casa que esté en el campo* "María is looking for a house that is in the country"). Another group received a placebo treatment (involving indirect-object pronouns) and the same subjunctive instruction. A control group received the placebo and the syntactic instruction. All treatments were CALL-based (i.e., the lessons were computer-based and multi-media in design); methodologically speaking, the treatments entailed consciousness-raising tasks and structured input. The researchers tested the efficacy of the treatment combinations with pretests and posttests involving recognition and production tasks.

The results reported in Collentine et al. (in press) indicate that both the syntax-subjunctive group and the subjunctive-only group were significantly better than the control group at identifying when the subjunctive was necessary, although neither enjoyed an advantage. However, the data also indicated that the syntax-subjunctive group was significantly more adept than the subjunctive-only group at identifying the syntactic contexts in which the subjunctive was not permissible: the syntax-subjunctive group rarely produced subjunctive forms in the main clauses of sentences (e.g., *Carlos tiene / *tenga un coche que va lento* "Carlos has a car that goes slowly") and in subordinate-clauses requiring the indicative (e.g., *María tiene una casa que es / *sea elegante* "María has a house that is elegant"), whereas the subjunctive-only group did so significantly. All in all, then, the syntax instruction did have a facilitative effect on subjunctive acquisition.

4.2 Universal Grammar Perspectives on the Relationship Between the Development of Syntax and Morphology

UG predicts that syntactic knowledge will outpace morphological knowledge in some aspects of IL development (Cook 1994).[6] First, syntactic knowledge resides at the core of UG, whereas morphological knowledge resides at the periphery. Thus, if UG is accessible to the adult acquiring a FL, he or she possesses a more powerful set of developmental principles for syntax than for morphology. Second, a central tenet of UG is the *structure dependency* principle: one does not combine morphemes (and so words) with great freedom; instead, their usage is limited to particular syntactic environments (e.g., *campo* "field/countryside" cannot serve as a verb). Accordingly, if a learner has not developed the syntactic knowledge that surrounds the use of a given morpheme (e.g., gender agreement often depends on an understanding of how one forms a noun phrase in the target language), the learner may attend to it marginally in the input or he or she may not contemplate using that morpheme in production.

SLA research informed by UG predicts that one's IL grammar will not generate verbal morphology until it can generate certain phrase-structure constituents. The Gradual Development Hypothesis (Vainikka and Young-Scholten 1994, 1996) posits that learners do not initially generate functional projections such as IP, that is, a constituent that carries information such as person, tense, and mood. Consequently, one cannot expect a learner's competence to intentionally produce certain morphology (i.e., which is not the case when one generates a formulaic chunk; *Me gusta estudiar español* "I like to study Spanish") until the IL starts to encode utterances with the requisite syntactic structure.

The principal syntactic problem that subjunctive learners face is that they need to develop knowledge for generating and parsing sentences with complex syntax. Students must expand their complementation strategies: while nominal and adjectival complements can simply be lexical phrases (e.g., *Juan sabe* [NP *la verdad*] "Juan knows [NP the truth]"; *María tiene amigos* [AP *fieles*] "María has loyal friends"), they can also be functional phrases representing an entire clause (e.g., *Juan sabe* [CP *que Paco lo hizo*] "Juan knows [CP that Paco did it]"; *María tiene amigos* [CP *que son buenos*] "María has friends [CP that are good]"). In terms of underlying syntactic structure, a complement containing a subjunctive form is reportedly much more integrated into the main clause of its sentence than is an indicative complement (Rochette 1988). Consequently, the morphosyntactic behaviors of subjunctive complements are, in a sense, much more influenced by the grammatical configuration of the main clause they modify than are the behaviors of indicative complements.

Specifically, Rochette (1988) compares subjunctive behaviors in a number of Romance languages from a Principles and Parameters perspective, arguing that whereas indicative complements project all the way up to a CP structure (e.g., *Juan sabe* [CP *que* [IP *la boda es mañana*]] "Juan knows [CP that [IP the wedding is tomorrow]]"), subjunctive complements only project up to an IP structure (e.g., *Juan desea que* [IP *la boda sea mañana*] "Juan wants [IP the wedding to be tomorrow]").[7] Kempchinsky (1986) reasons that volitional and directive predicates represent a type of embedded imperative. She explains that an abstract imperative operator resides in the head of these subjunctive CPs, which causes the properties responsible for inflecting verbs to move to the COMP position at Logical Form.[8] Under both of these analyses of subjunctive complements, while an indicative complement is opaque with respect to its main clause, a subjunctive complement is transparent; that is, the "local domain" of subjunctive complements is the main clause, whereas indicative complements constitute their own local domain. If a learner were to generate subjunctive and indicative complements equally, their IL would not place the same distributional restrictions on subjunctive complements that the competence of native speakers does.

What are some of the restrictions resulting from the underlying structural differences between indicative and subjunctive complements? One is what Rochette (1988) and Kempchinsky (1986) refer to as the obviate phenomenon. Students must learn that indicative complements enjoy no subject co-reference restrictions, while many are placed on subjunctive complements. For instance, if a learner processed the syntax of indicative and subjunctive complements differentially, he or she would know that, while the subject of a subjunctive complement cannot normally be co-referential to its main-clause subject (e.g., *Juan*{i} *quiere que él*{*i,j} *prepare la cena* "Juan wants him(self) [Juan] to prepare the dinner"), such restrictions are not placed on indicative complements (e.g., *Juan*{i} *sabe que él*{i,j} *preparará la cena* "Juan knows that he [Juan] will prepare the dinner"). Furthermore, the expanded local domain of subjunctive complements affects interclausal tense dependencies (Rochette 1988).[9] Tense operators can only be present in complements with C(OMP) as their head, implying that subjunctive complements must inherit tense from the main clause (Rochette 1988:253–57).

Another consequence of the structural differences between these two complements is stylistic inversion (Kayne 1994), which refers to the fact that subjunctive complements readily invert their subjects and verbs (e.g., *Juan quiere que hable Pablo* "Juan wants Pablo to talk"). Although there is much controversy over what licenses stylistic inversion, Jones (1999) argues that the presence of a mood phrase/projection (MP) in subjunctive clauses essentially creates the conditions for the embedded-clause verb to raise to the SPEC of IP (or, more specifically, of TP).[10]

Bruhn de Garavito (1993) sought to determine whether advanced learners of Spanish as a FL (n = 27) observe the co-reference restrictions placed on main- and subordinate-clause subjects in sentences containing subjunctive complements. The participants read a passage whose content was thought to encourage them to accept (ungrammatical) co-reference in sentences such as **Juan* {i} *quiere que* [pro{i}] *prepare la cena* "Juan wants him(self) [Juan] to prepare the dinner."[11] Some of the subjects, indeed, accepted co-reference. Bruhn de Garavito reasons that these learners did not possess the type of morphological knowledge that would allow them to readily determine a verb's mood. A handful of learners did, however, reject co-reference, an observation that Bruhn de Garavito interprets to lend support to the notion that advanced learners eventually process complex syntax in the manner that native speakers do.

4.3 Cognitive Perspectives on the Relationship Between the Development of Syntax and Morphology

Cognitive perspectives on SLA suggest that syntax need not necessarily outpace morphology during IL development.[12] Connectionism—a theory of learning with roots in the field of cognitive psychology—posits that generalized principles of learning rather than innate, language-specific principles (e.g., UG) account for acquisition (N. Ellis 1999). The connectionist perspective currently makes two principal predictions about SLA. First, because knowledge domains (e.g., the L1, the L2, knowledge of syntax, knowledge of morphology) are not modularized, the influence of one domain over another is likely during the learning process (i.e., transfer) (MacWhinney 1996). Second, where the L1 does not provide good models, the learner's working- and phonological-memory stores play a central role in processing utterances and building an L2 grammatical system (N. Ellis 1996).

Initially, for the native English speaker, because Spanish and English share many syntactic and few morphological features, syntactic development in Spanish will be accelerated whereas morphological development will be slow. The Competition Model (MacWhinney 1996), which outlines learning principles that account for why some grammatical forms develop from generalizations (e.g., so-called regular conjugations of verbs) and others from rote memorization (e.g., so-called irregular conjugations, such as *sea*), posits that the superficial syntactic similarities between English and Spanish (e.g., both are SVO languages) will cause the learner to use English word-order strategies while processing Spanish. The Competition Model also predicts that L1–L2 connections will weaken (and so L2 specific strategies will strengthen) when the learner encounters sufficient evidence (e.g., from input, corrective feedback) that English syntactic frames are not entirely reliable models for Spanish (e.g., *Te quiero llamar mañana* does not mean "I want you to call tomorrow"). At this point, the connectionist perspective appears to predict, in contradistinction to UG, that knowledge of target-language morphology establishes conditions for the acquisition of complex syntactic knowledge (e.g., knowledge of how to form a dependent clause in the target language), in that determining that a given string represents a syntactic frame depends on one's ability to parse the string's lexical and morphological features: "It is difficult to separate the acquisition of formal marking systems [i.e., morphology] from the overall syntactic system of a language. Perhaps the easiest way to think of the relation is to realize that syntax uses both local morphological markings and non-local word order or configurational patterns to express a variety of underlying concepts and meanings"[13] (MacWhinney 1996:311).[14]

Connectionist accounts of SLA predict that certain types of short-term memory (STM) play especially critical roles in the development of knowledge of syntactic and nonlocal morphological structures. An important mechanism in the development of both syntactic and verbal morphological knowledge is phonological short-term memory (PSTM). Learners analyze and compare PSTM chunks to chunks stored in long-term memory (LTM) in order to extrapolate generalizations about the target language's grammatical system (N. Ellis 1996; MacWhinney 1982). One's ability to maintain and operate on information in working memory is also crucial for the acquisition of verbal morphology (King and Just 1991), as the referents for person/number morphemes are often only retrievable upon an examination of a given discourse's so-called thematic nodes, or slots in episodic memory that represent the actors/objects in a discourse (Givón 1990). These STM stores, whose capacity increases as the chunks of information that one can store there increase in size, is particularly important to consider in the acquisition of Spanish as a FL, as Spanish verbal morphology places "heavy demands on working memory and phonological rehearsal" (MacWhinney 1996:311–12).

Collentine (2000) investigates, from both a structural and a cognitive perspective, whether there is a positive, linear relationship between the syntactic and morphological abilities of FL learners of Spanish. Advanced-level learners at least a semester beyond the intermediate level (n = 30) participated in a study gauging their abilities to utilize syntactic and morphological cues to interpret aural passages. Although the analysis indicated that increasing syntactic abilities correlate positively with increasing morphological abilities, it did not confirm that the learners' syntactic abilities were superior to their morphological abilities. Furthermore, the most robust predictor of both syntactic and morphological behavior was the extent to which a learner could process long-distance dependencies (i.e., referential morphology, such as person and number, and inter-clausal syntactic relationships, such as subordination). Collentine conjectures that although enhanced syntactic abilities may support the development of mood-selection abilities, researchers may need to consider whether the principal factor that impedes subjunctive development is neither syntactic nor morphological in nature; instead, both abilities may improve in tandem as learners' general abilities to process long-distance dependencies in short-term and working memory improve (Ellis and Schmidt 1997).

4.4   Summary of the Development of Syntactic Abilities and Their Relationship to the Acquisition of Verbal Inflectional Abilities

The available SLA literature documents that syntactic abilities tend to outpace morphological abilities during IL development, at least when the L1 and the L2/FL are Indo-European in origin (Bardovi-Harlig and Bofman 1989; R. Ellis 1987). Indeed, Collentine (1995) reveals that at the same time that FL learners of Spanish are struggling to process the subjunctive, they are also struggling to generate the complex syntax that encompasses this morpheme. UG theory and its SLA students argue unequivocally that some syntactic knowledge is a prerequisite for the processing, and so development of, verbal morphology (Skiba and Dittmar 1992; Vainikka and Young-Scholten 1994, 1996). Yet, the syntactic foundation hypothesis is still a tentative postulate, as only one study to date has provided evidence that subjunctive instruction enhanced with syntactic instruction offers learners of Spanish an advantage in their development of mood-selection abilities (Collentine et al. in press). Nonetheless, from the onset of acquisition, learners are hard pressed to process large phonetic chunks and long-distance dependencies in short-term memory, which may interact with one's capacity for processing and storing both complex syntax and morphological structures such as the subjunctive (Ellis 1996; MacWhinney 1996).[15] Of course, support for this explanation is essentially theoretical, with only one study—(Collentine 2000)—providing empirical considerations.

5.0 Methodological Limitations and Considerations

Any comprehensive review of a body of research necessitates a consideration of the experimental design and the analytical tools supporting that research's findings. This section delineates general issues that future researchers must consider in interpreting the studies reviewed here and upon undertaking future studies. It is, however, essential to bear in mind that the field of applied linguistics has shifted in the past thirty years from favoring ethnographic approaches to research design and analysis to favoring decidedly experimental protocols. Thus, it is not entirely fair to expect that the tight controls placed on experiments today should have been applied to studies when the field was in its infancy.

The legitimacy of the conclusions extrapolated from any experiment is invariably mediated by the extent to which investigators control for variables and how they operationalize research questions. Researchers have tended to treat the subjunctive as a monolithic phenomenon (Blake, personal communication). This approach undoubtedly masks a range of developmental patterns that might be uncovered if, for instance, investigators were to compare developmental patterns of the subjunctive in nominal, adjectival, and adverbial clauses.

Collentine (1998) suggests that experiments fostering subjunctive semantic knowledge should gauge both pretreatment subjunctive semantic knowledge and pretreatment subjunctive morphological knowledge. Knowing the subjunctive conjugation is one matter; knowing the semantic and pragmatic conditions under which those forms are employed (e.g., doubt, coercion, indefinite referents) is another. Collentine (1998) notes that within Spanish's system of verb morphology, the subjunctive is aprototypical because it derives from a conjugated form (e.g., *tengo > tengamos* "I have > we have," etc.) instead of an infinitive (e.g., *tener > tenemos* "to have > we have"). He therefore argues that subjunctive acquisition involves two important processes—namely, knowledge of the subjunctive's formal properties and knowledge of the subjunctive's meaning(s)—and experimenters should not conflate them when measuring subjunctive acquisition. Pereira (1996) and Woodson (1997) do not measure their subjects' pretreatment knowledge of the subjunctive's formal properties. It is not unreasonable to conjecture that if group A possessed greater subjunctive morphology knowledge than group B, regardless of the treatment type (e.g., traditional, input-oriented), mere exposure to information about the subjunctive's semantic properties would cause group A to possess greater overall subjunctive abilities. Collentine (1998) and Collentine et al. (in press) are the only experiments to use pretreatment data isolating participants' knowledge of the morphology of the subjunctive as a covariate in pretest/posttest comparisons. Controlling for participants' prior knowledge of grammatical phenomena such as the subjunctive is especially important given that subjunctive development may interact with the development of one's overall grammatical abilities.

The legitimacy of any conclusion also depends on how investigators operationalize their research questions. First, the studies investigating the internal factors that account for subjunctive development routinely treat instruction as a monolithic phenomenon (Collentine 1995; Terrell, Baycroft, and Perrone 1987; Stokes 1988; Stokes and Krashen 1990). That is, they do not account for the external factors interacting with the internal mechanisms on which these researchers focus. By all accounts, these studies sampled student populations that learned Spanish in curricula characterized by traditional form-focused instructional strategies, and so their conclusions potentially misrepresent the effects of meaning-focused curricula, such as those that employ the Natural Approach or Processing Instruction. Second, assessment-task measures are often problematic, in that there is no consensus about which testing format(s) assess the current status of a learner's subjunctive knowledge with the greatest reliability and validity. The most notable design flaw in the studies reviewed here is found in Stokes (1988) and Stokes and Krashen (1990), who attempt to assess learners' acquired knowledge for mood selection with a sentence-completion task. Such a task is not naturalistic, and so it is unclear how their subjects' performance exhibits the types of cognitive processes and behaviors manifested in spontaneous language use (e.g., conversational tasks). Third, the research on L1 subjunctive development purports to account for the stages children experience (e.g., Blake 1983, 1985; Gili Gaya 1972; Pérez-Leroux 1998). Yet, the design of these studies was not longitudinal but rather cross-sectional, which paints an oversimplistic picture of one's developmental status at any given point (Ellis 1987).

SLA researchers tend to operationalize narrowly how they measure behaviors, infrequently conducting multivariate studies. Consequently, researchers should be especially mindful of the threat of instrument sensitivity (i.e., the extent to which a pretest task constitutes an opportunity to learn the phenomenon targeted in the treatment). For instance, Leow (1993, 1995), who measures subjunctive intake by comparing pretest and posttest recognition tasks, does not employ a control group. It would be useful to know if or how much the pretest primed the subjects for the treatment and/or whether the pretest led to inflated posttest results. Interestingly, Leow (1999) comments on the limitations of SLA investigations for operationalizing constructs; he encourages researchers to include online assessment measures (i.e., data gathered during a treatment such as think-aloud protocols) to provide insights into the relationship between the learners' behaviors during a treatment and their subsequent performance on immediate off-line assessment measures (i.e., data gathered after a treatment).

The appropriateness of any study's statistical analyses is a crucial consideration upon contemplating the legitimacy of one's conclusions. Such analytical rigor is absent in the research conducted on subjunctive development in L1 and bilingual contexts as well as in much of the research on the internal factors that promote subjunctive development in a FL context. (See Stokes 1988 and Stokes and Krashen 1990 for notable exceptions.) Studies such as Collentine (1995) claim certain significant differences between FL learners' indicative and subjunctive abilities; yet, Collentine (1995) employs only nonparametric analyses, thus raising concerns about the generalizability of his conclusions to the student population as a whole. The best statistical strategies for future investigations are present in the research on the external variables accounting for FL subjunctive development (e.g., Collentine 1998; Lee and Rodríguez 1997; Leow 1993, 1995; Pereira 1996) as well as in the analyses employed by Pérez-Leroux (1998).

6.0   Concluding Remarks

Researchers are only beginning to understand the multitude of factors that subjunctive acquisition entails. While the summaries given above infer many avenues of new research, there are broader questions that researchers would do well to address. Future research must be particularly careful to develop robust research designs and to submit data to careful statistical analysis. We still know little about the effects of instruction on subjunctive development, and so researchers should be cautious about extolling the virtues of recently developed instructional techniques, which tend to advocate either a largely input- or a largely output-oriented approach to instruction. Many subjunctive forms appear to elude intake. In addition, evidence exists that production-oriented learning tasks are equally effective at promoting subjunctive development as input-oriented tasks. Indeed, as several SLA scholars (e.g., Salaberry 1997 and VanPatten 2002) note, relatively complete acquisition of any grammatical phenomenon may require both input- and output-oriented teaching strategies; perhaps the research on the subjunctive is the strongest *cohesive* body of empirical evidence supporting this growing acceptance within SLA.[16] Finally, if subjunctive development interacts with various developmental processes, researchers will ultimately need to tease out how the array of developmental factors interact with different teaching techniques.

Of course, it is possible to argue that investigating subjunctive development focuses an extraordinary amount of resources on the acquisition of one grammatical phenomenon at the expense of studying phenomena whose developmental patterns are more generalizable (e.g., the acquisition of one's overall inflectional abilities). Yet, as the preceding review indicates, subjunctive research provides insight into the multifarious nature of L2 development. That said, it is not unreasonable to expect that this very line of research provides a different sort of generalized view of Spanish FL acquisition.

NOTES

1. Cognitively speaking, a "cue" is a morphological or syntactic pattern that evokes a particular idea (e.g., NP VP might evoke a declarative sentence whereas VP NP, an interrogative) or a pattern that frequently co-occurs with some grammatical phenomenon in input, such as *querer que* and the subjunctive (see Ellis and Schmidt 1997).

2. According to Collentine (1995, 1997), from the perspective of a FL learner of Spanish, the syntactic distribution of the subjunctive is largely limited to dependent clauses. Thus, for all intents and purposes, it is reasonable to conjecture that a learner confronts mood selection once he or she generates a nominal (e.g., *Es obvio/Pido que traes/traigas fruta buena* "It is obvious/I

ask that you bring me good fruit"), adjectival (e.g., *Busco un restaurante que sirve/sirva comida marrueca* "I am looking for a restaurant that serves Moroccan food"), or an adverbial clause (e.g., *Me llama cuando tiene/tenga tiempo* "Call me when you have time").

3. See Collentine (1995), table 1, for a comparison of Givón's presyntactic and syntactic stages of development.

4. Long (1991) distinguishes between an instructional *focus on forms,* the traditional systematic attention to grammatical aspects of the second language, and a *focus on form,* instruction that attempts to draw attention to formal properties of the target language within communicative interactions in meaningful contexts. Focus-on-form research addresses the concerns of many pedagogues that simply providing comprehensible input does not guarantee that learners will acquire grammatical knowledge (see Lee and Valdman 1999). Focus-on-form studies essentially ask two questions: Does focusing learners' attention on the formal properties of grammatical phenomena facilitate grammatical development within a curriculum that is input rich? If so, what input conditions encourage learners to attend to grammatical features? (See Larsen-Freeman and Long 1991; Lee and VanPatten 1995; Schmidt 1990; and VanPatten 1993, 1997.)

5. Collentine (2002) responds to Farley's concerns and Farley (2002) responds to Collentine in the December 2002 issue of *Hispania.*

6. See chapter 7 of this volume for a general discussion of generative perspectives on Spanish L2 acquisition. However, no further discussion of the Spanish subjunctive is found there.

7. One important argument supporting this assertion is termed the obviate phenomenon. Specifically, the subject of a subjunctive clause behaves like an anaphor: its referent must not reside in its governing domain. Thus, the argument goes, since a subjunctive subject cannot co-refer to its main-clause subject (e.g., **Dudamos que lo hagamos bien* "We doubt that we do it well"), while an indicative-complement subject can (e.g., *Creemos que lo hacemos bien* "We think that we do it well"), the governing domain of a subjunctive complement must be its main clause. By extension, because CP clauses must constitute their own governing domain, subjunctive clauses cannot project up to CP (i.e., there could not be an intervening CP between the main and subordinate clauses). Another important argument involves tense restrictions. The IP node of a subordinate clause receives its tense features from the main clause IP when there is no intervening CP; when there is an intervening CP, each IP is free to select tense features. This ostensibly accounts for the observation that, whereas subjunctive complements must agree in tense with their main-clause verb (e.g., *Me gustaría que me *ayudes/ayudaras más tarde* "I would like you to help me later"), indicative complements do not (e.g., *Dirían que eso es aceptable* "They would say that that is acceptable").

8. Within a minimalist framework, Kempchinksy (1998) has similarly argued that subjunctive complements contain an intervening MP (Mood Phrase) node below CP yet above IP/TP, which also causes the binding domain of such complements to be the main clause. Indicative complements do not, however, contain the additional functional syntactic constituent MP that compromises the independence of the subjunctive complement.

9. It is important to note that Kempchinsky (1986, personal communication) argues that this sequence-of-tenses phenomenon in subjunctive contexts is not as robust as textbooks would imply. She notes that the *Ezbozo de la gramática de la RAE* recognizes relaxations of this stipulation (e.g., *Mandé que vaya/fuera* "I ordered X to go"). According to Kempchinsky, such re-

laxations are attributable to the fact that tense is licensed by a semantic referential expression rather than by a syntactic operator.

10. Interestingly, as VanPatten (1997) has argued, one of the key psycholinguistic principles that interacts with the acquisition of Spanish morphosyntax is the First Noun Strategy (i.e., learners interpret the first noun of a sentence—and so, perhaps, of a clause as well—as its subject; e.g., *Lo compra mañana* "He > (lo) buys tomorrow."). Thus, it is not unreasonable to suspect that the First Noun Strategy coupled with the high probability that many subjunctive complements contain subject-verb inversion in input interacts with the learner's acquisition of the subjunctive and his or her hypotheses as to the syntactic configuration that subjunctive utterances should possess.

11. Bruhn de Garavito gathered native-speaker, baseline data [n = 12] to corroborate her assumptions about the grammaticality of her test sentences.

12. See chapter 8 of this volume for a more complete discussion of cognitive issues in Spanish SLA. Chapter 5 also contains further discussion of the connectionist model.

13. Local dependencies refers to the linguistic distance between syntactic constituents and the referents of morphemes. Nonlocal word order involves syntactic structures that include three or more lexical items, such as a simple, two-argument proposition (e.g., *María compró chocolate* "María bought chocolate"). Nonlocal morphology entails displaced inflectional dependencies, such as when a subject appears earlier in discourse (e.g., *Juan es bajo y, por eso, pensábamos que no estaba presente en la fiesta* "Juan is short and, for that reason, we thought that he was not present at the party") or it is inferable from the situation in which it is uttered.

14. The difficulty in separating syntactic from morphological abilities reflects the connectionist assumption that syntax and morphology are not strictly modularized, neurologically speaking. That is, linguistic knowledge is stored in associative neurological networks. Thus, while nativist perspectives such as UG posit that syntactic knowledge is encapsulated (i.e., the processing of syntax is not affected by one's knowledge of morphology; cf. Fodor 1983), connectionists predict that any meaningful clustering of linguistic knowledge is possible, such that it is plausible to posit that syntactic and morphological knowledge for comprehending and generating complex utterances is neurologically localized.

15. Recall that the subjunctive often redundantly marks pragmatic information that is "recoverable" in the main clause of a sentence in which it appears: *Queremos que nos hagas un favor* "We want you to do us a favor."

16. See chapter 10 of this volume for a general discussion of the effects of input- and output-oriented teaching strategies.

WORKS CITED

Bardovi-Harlig, K., and T. Bofman. 1989. Attainment of syntactic and morphological accuracy by advanced language learners. *Studies in Second Language Acquisition* 11:17–34.

Blake, R. 1983. Mood selection among Spanish speaking children, ages 4 to 12. *Bilingual Review* 10:21–32.

———. 1985. From research to the classroom. *Hispania* 68:166–73.

Bruhn de Garavito, J. 1993. L2 acquisition of verb complementation and binding principle B. *McGill Working Papers in Linguistics* 9:102–20.

Collentine, J. 1995. The development of complex syntax and mood-selection abilities by intermediate-level learners of Spanish. *Hispania* 78:122–35.

———. 1997. Irregular verbs and noticing the Spanish subjunctive. *Spanish Applied Linguistics* 1:3–23.

———. 1998. Processing instruction and the subjunctive. *Hispania* 81:576–87.

———. 2000. The relationship between syntactic and morphological abilities in FL learners of Spanish. In *Spanish applied linguistics at the turn of the millennium,* eds. R. Leow and C. Sanz, 20–35. Somerville, MA: Cascadilla Press.

———. 2002. On the acquisition of the subjunctive and authentic processing instruction: A response to Farley. *Hispania* 85.4:879–88.

Collentine, J., K. Collentine, V. Clark, and E. Fruginal. In press. Subjunctive instruction enhanced with syntactic instruction. Proceedings of the *4th Hispanic Linguistics Symposium,* ed. S. Montrul. Somerville, MA: Cascadilla Press.

Cook, V. 1994. Universal Grammar and the learning and teaching of second languages. In *Perspectives on pedagogical grammar,* ed. T. Odlin, 25–48. Cambridge: Cambridge University Press.

Cowan, N. 1995. *Attention and memory: An integrated framework.* New York: Oxford University Press.

Ellis, N. 1996. Sequencing in SLA: Phonological memory, chunking, and points of order. *Studies in Second Language Acquisition* 18:91–126.

———. 1999. Cognitive approaches to SLA. *Annual Review of Applied Linguistics* 19:22–42.

Ellis, N., and R. Schmidt. 1997. Morphology and longer-distance dependencies: Laboratory research illuminating the A in SLA. *Studies in Second Language Acquisition* 19:145–72.

Ellis, R. 1987. *Second language acquisition in context.* Englewood Cliffs: Prentice Hall.

Farley, A. 2001. Authentic processing instruction and the Spanish subjunctive. *Hispania* 84:289–99.

———. 2002. Processing instruction, communicative value and ecological validity: A response to Collentine. *Hispania* 85.4:889–95.

Floyd, M. B. 1983. Language acquisition and use of the subjunctive in Southwest Spanish. In *Spanish and Portuguese in social context,* eds. J. Bergen and G. Bills, 31–41. Washington, DC: Georgetown University Press.

Fodor, J. D. 1983. *The modularity of the mind: An essay on faculty psychology.* Cambridge, MA: MIT Press.

García, M. E., and T. Terrell. 1977. Is mood in Spanish subject to variable constraints? In *Studies in Romance linguistics,* ed. M. Hagiwara, 214–26. Rowley, MA: Newbury House.

Gass, S., and E. Varonis. 1994. Input, interaction, and second language production. *Studies in Second Language Acquisition* 16:283–302.

Gili Gaya, S. 1972. *Estudios de lenguaje infantil.* Barcelona: Bibliograf.

Givón, T. 1979. *On understanding grammar.* New York: Academic Press.

Guitart, J. 1982. On the use of the Spanish subjunctive among Spanish-English bilinguals. *Word* 33:59–67.

————. 1990. *Syntax: A functional-typological introduction,* vol. 2. Amsterdam: John Benjamins.

Hensey, F. 1973. Grammatical variation in southwestern American Spanish. *Linguistics* 108:5–26.

————. 1976. Toward a grammatical analysis of southwest Spanish. In *Studies in Southwest Spanish,* eds. J. Bowen and J. Orstein, 29–44. Rowley, MA: Newbury House.

Jones, M. 1999. Subject-clitic inversion and inflectional hierarchies. *Journal of French Language Studies* 9:181–209.

Kayne, R. 1994. *The antisymmetry of syntax.* Cambridge, MA: MIT Press.

Kempchinsky, P. 1986. Romance subjunctive clauses and logical form. Ph.D. diss., University of California, Los Angeles.

————. 1998. Mood phrase, case checking and obviation. In *Linguistic Symposium on Romance Languages XXVII,* eds. A. Schwegler, B. Tranel, and M. Uribe-Etxebarria, 143–54. Amsterdam: John Benjamins.

King, J., and M. Just. 1991. Individual differences in syntactic processing: The role of working memory. *Journal of Memory and Language* 30:580–602.

Krashen, S. 1982. *Principles and practice in second language acquisition.* Oxford: Pergamon.

Larsen-Freeman, D., and M. Long. 1991. *An introduction to second language acquisition research.* London: Longman.

Lee, J. F. 1987. Comprehending the Spanish subjunctive: An information processing perspective. *Modern Language Journal* 71:50–57.

Lee, J. F., and R. Rodríguez. 1997. The effects of lexemic and morphosyntactic modifications on L2 reading comprehension and input processing. In *Contemporary perspectives on the acquisition of Spanish,* eds. W. Glass and A. Pérez-Leroux, 2:135–57. Somerville, MA: Cascadilla Press.

Lee, J. F., and A. Valdman. 1999. *Form and meaning: Multiple perspectives.* Boston: Heinle and Heinle.

Lee, J. F., and B. VanPatten. 1995. *Making communicative language teaching happen.* New York: McGraw-Hill.

Leow, R. 1993. To simplify or not to simplify: A look at intake. *Studies in Second Language Acquisition* 15:333–56.

————. 1995. Modality and intake in second language acquisition. *Studies in Second Language Acquisition* 17:79–90.

————. 1999. Attention, awareness, and focus on form research: A critical overview. *Form and meaning: Multiple perspectives,* eds. J. F. Lee and A. Valdman, 69–96. Boston: Heinle and Heinle.

Long, M. 1991. Focus on form: A design feature in language teaching methodology. In *Foreign language research in cross-cultural perspective,* eds. K. De Bot, R. Ginsberg, and C. Kramsch, 39–52. Amsterdam: John Benjamins.

Lynch, A. E. 2000. The subjunctive in Miami Cuban Spanish: Bilingualism, contact, and language variability. Ph.D. diss., University of Minnesota.

Mackey, A. 1999. Input, interaction, and second language development: An empirical study of question formation in ESL. *Studies in Second Language Acquisition* 21:557–87.

MacWhinney, B. 1982. Basic syntactic processes. *Language acquisition,* vol. 1, *Syntax and semantics,* ed. S. Kuczaj, 73–136. Hillsdale, NJ: Lawrence Erlbaum.

———. 1996. Language specific prediction in foreign language learning. *Language Testing* 12:292–320.

Palmer, F. R. 1986. *Mood and modality.* Cambridge: Cambridge University Press.

Pereira, I. 1996. Markedness and instructed SLA: An experiment in teaching the Spanish subjunctive. Ph.D. diss., University of Illinois, Urbana-Champaign.

Pérez-Leroux, A. 1998. The acquisition of mood selection in Spanish relative clauses. *Journal of Child Language* 25:585–604.

Pica, T., and C. Doughty. 1985. The role of group work in classroom second language acquisition. *Studies in Second Language Acquisition* 7:233–49.

Pica, T., R. Young, and C. Doughty. 1987. The impact of interaction on comprehension. *TESOL Quarterly* 21:737–58.

Rochette, A. 1988. Semantic and syntactic aspects of Romance sentential complementation. Ph.D. diss., Massachusetts Institute of Technology.

Salaberry, R. 1997. The role of input and output practice in second language acquisition. *Canadian Modern Language Review* 53:422–51.

Sánchez, R. 1972. Nuestra circunstancia lingüística. *El grito* 6:45–74.

Schmidt, R. 1990. The role of consciousness in second language learning. *Applied Linguistics* 11:127–58.

Silva-Corvalán, C. 1994. *Language contact and change: Spanish in Los Angeles.* New York: Oxford University Press.

Skiba, R., and N. Dittmar. 1992. Pragmatic, semantic, and syntactic constraints and grammaticalization: A longitudinal perspective. *Studies in Second Language Acquisition* 14:323–50.

Solé, Y. 1977. Continuidad/descontinuidad idiomática en el español tejano. *Bilingual Review/Revista Bilingüe* 4:188–99.

Stokes, J. 1988. Some factors in the acquisition of the present subjunctive in Spanish. *Hispania* 71:705–10.

Stokes, J., and S. Krashen. 1990. Some factors in the acquisition of the present subjunctive in Spanish: A re-analysis. *Hispania* 73:805–6.

Swain, M. 1985. Communicative competence: Some roles of comprehensible input and comprehensible output in its development. In *Input in second language acquisition,* eds. S. Gass and C. Madden, 235–53. Rowley, MA: Newbury House.

Swain, M., and S. Lapkin. 1995. Problems in output and the cognitive processes they generate: A step towards second language learning. *Applied Linguistics* 16:371–91.

Terrell, T., B. Baycroft, and C. Perrone. 1987. The subjunctive in Spanish interlanguage: Accuracy and comprehensibility. In *Foreign language learning: A research perspective,* eds. B. VanPatten, T. Dvorak, and J. F. Lee, 23–48. Cambridge: Cambridge University Press.

Vainikka, A., and M. Young-Scholten. 1994. Direct access to 'X'-theory: Evidence from Korean and Turkish adults learning German. In *Language acquisition studies in generative grammar,* eds. T. Hoekstra and B. Schwartz, 265–316. Amsterdam: John Benjamins.

————. 1996. Gradual development of L2 phrase structure. *Second Language Research* 12:7–39.

VanPatten, B. 1990. Attending to content and form in the input: An experiment in consciousness. *Studies in Second Language Acquisition* 12:287–301.

————. 1993. Grammar teaching for the acquisition rich classroom. *Foreign Language Annals* 26:435–50.

————. 1997. The relevance of input processing to second language theory and second language teaching. In *Contemporary perspectives on the acquisition of Spanish*, eds. W. Glass and A. Pérez-Leroux, 2:93–108. Somerville, MA: Cascadilla Press.

————. 2002. Processing instruction: An update. *Language Learning* 52.4:755–803.

Woodson, K. 1997. Learner-centered input processing: Bridging the gap between foreign language teachers and SLA researchers. Ph.D. diss., Georgetown University.

Zentella, A. 1997. *Growing up bilingual: Puerto Rican children in New York*. Oxford: Blackwell.

4

Clitics

Cognitive and Linguistic Perspectives on the Acquisition of Object Pronouns in Spanish as a Second Language

JAMES F. LEE   Indiana University

1.0   Introduction

Object pronouns (clitics) in Spanish are good examples of language that has both form and meaning, and they have been well researched in the acquisition literature for this reason. Clitics have syntactic properties in that their placement is restricted vis-à-vis the verb. In preverbal position, object-verb, they violate canonical subject-verb-object word order. In addition to their syntactic properties, object pronouns in Spanish are morphologically varied, in that some forms are inflected for person, number and case whereas other forms are inflected only for person and number. Learners' developing linguistic systems must eventually incorporate all these features. Finally, discourse constrains the use of object pronouns. Once a referent is established in discourse, all future unambiguous references should occur in pronominalized form. Whether intrasentential or intersentential, discourse constraints require language learners to process language across clause boundaries.[1]

In this chapter I primarily review the empirical research on the acquisition of object pronouns (clitics) by classroom learners of Spanish as a second language.[2] The work in this area falls under two rubrics: processing incoming information (decoding meaning) and producing language samples (encoding meaning). Under the rubric of processing, I review the extensive data on the First Noun Strategy, which is the tendency of learners to assign subject role to the first noun they encounter in a string even if that noun is a grammatical object. Under the rubric of production I review the database that traces learners' use of clitics when expressing themselves. This data is limited to a case study comparison of a naturalistic and classroom learner. The final part of the chapter examines the research carried out within generative theories of syntax. This research is at times processing-oriented and at other times production-oriented. Its purpose is to explain language competence according to a particular theory.[3]

2.0   The First Noun Strategy: Decoding Meaning

The fundamental characteristic of language learners, be they children acquiring their first language, children acquiring a second language, or adults acquiring a second language, is that they possess an incomplete linguistic system. Their grammars do not include all the elements of the code that linguistically mature speakers use to encode or decode meaning. Linguistically mature speakers, depending on the language, utilize a variety of syntactic constructions, morphological configurations, and semantic and pragmatic features to encode their intended meanings. Given their incomplete linguistic systems, learners must utilize the resources at their disposal to interpret the meaning of utterances they hear or read. The variety of resources available to linguistically mature speakers is unavailable to language learners for either encoding or decoding meaning, and so they must rely on and make do with fewer linguistic resources. One such resource is word order. In order to assign meaning, learners must assign grammatical and semantic roles to words in the input. When processing the meaning of incoming information, learners utilize the order of the words as cues to assign grammatical roles such as agent and object.

A well-documented phenomenon in the first and second language acquisition literature is that of the First Noun Strategy, also referred to as SVO processing. When processing incoming information for meaning, language learners tend to interpret the first noun they hear or read as the grammatical subject of the sentence, in effect, processing the string of words as subject-verb-object. The importance of the pervasiveness of the first noun strategy cannot be underestimated in second language acquisition because it delivers incorrect intake data to learners' developing systems. A preverbally placed *lo,* for example, does not mean *he* but *him.* Interpreting a preverbally placed *lo* as a subject pronoun has consequences for the internal grammar learners are constructing for Spanish. VanPatten (1996:89) hypothesizes that the first noun processing strategy alone may contribute to a host of learner production errors including misuse of object and reflexive pronouns as subjects, use of *gustar* "to be pleasing to/to like" as a transitive verb, overreliance on subject pronouns, nonuse of the object case marker *a,* overreliance on SVO word order in language production, and a delay in the acquisition of person-number verbal morphology.

LoCoco (1987) compared the processing strategies of 151 first-year learners of Spanish and German on three types of sentences presented either aurally or visually (in writing). I will report here only on the Spanish data. The first type (Type I) of sentence paired SVO and OVS sentences in which the object was marked with the case marker *a.* There were no semantic constraints on subject and object in that either entity could possibly perform the action of the verb. Research on the acquisition of word order has established OVS sentences as the last-acquired word order pattern among children acquiring Spanish as their L1 (Echevarría 1978) and among adult learners of Spanish (González 1997).

> *El muchacho empuja al camión.*
> "The boy pushes the truck."
>
> *Al camión empuja el muchacho.*
> "The truck-pushes-the boy" = "The boy pushes the truck."

La ballena jala al bote.
"The whale pulls the boat."

Al bote jala la ballena.
"The boat-pulls-the whale" = "The whale pulls the boat."

Subjects performed a picture-matching task, selecting the picture that matched their interpretation of what they either heard or read. Results revealed that the Type 1 OVS Spanish sentences were interpreted as SVO between 42 percent and 57 percent when presented orally and between 31 percent and 42 percent when presented in writing.

The second type (Type 2) of sentence involved indirect object pronouns accompanied by the full indirect object noun phrase and full noun phrase direct objects (IOVDOS). The direct objects were semantically constrained from performing the action of the verb.

El muchacho le trae la cerveza a la muchacha.
"The boy brings the girl beer."

A la muchacha le trae la cerveza el muchacho.
"To the girl-to her-brings-beer-the boy" = "The boy brings the girl beer."

El muchacho le da las flores a la niña.
"The boy gives flowers to the girl."

A la niña le da las flores el muchacho.
"To the girl-to her-gives-flowers-the boy" = "The boy gives flowers to the girl."

Results of the picture-matching task revealed that the Type 2 IOVDOS Spanish sentences were interpreted as SVO between 22 percent and 72 percent when presented orally and between 32 percent and 40 percent when presented in writing. The direct object in Type 2 sentences was never interpreted as the grammatical subject because it was semantically constrained from doing so, but when the indirect object preceded the grammatical subject, it was interpreted as the grammatical subject to varying degrees.

The third type (Type 3) of sentence included subjects, direct objects, and objects of prepositions (O_{prep}VDOS). There were no semantic constraints on subject and object such that any of the three nouns in the sentence could perform the action of the verb.

La madre empuja al niño hacia el padre.
"The mother pushes the boy toward the father."

Hacia el padre empuja al niño la madre.
"Toward the father-pushes-the boy-the mother" = "The mother pushes the boy toward the father."

El señor lleva al niño hacia la abuela.
"The man carries the boy toward the grandmother."

Hacia la abuela lleva al niño el señor.

"Toward the grandmother-carries-the boy-the man" = "The man carries the boy toward the grandmother."

Results of the picture-matching task revealed that the preverbally placed object of the preposition was interpreted as the subject between 7 percent and 30 percent when presented orally but was never misinterpreted when presented in writing. As LoCoco's results clearly demonstrate, word order is a very powerful cue for native speakers of English learning Spanish especially when processing oral input.

LoCoco, González, and Echevarría used full noun phrases in their research on the acquisition of word order, but what happens to learners' processing strategies when noun phrases are pronominalized in this late-acquired word order pattern?

2.1 Processing Object Pronouns in Sentences

As the following review of the literature indicates, SVO processing occurs despite several permutations in word order and the linguistic characteristics of the preverbal element (e.g., case, number, and gender markings).

VanPatten (1984) examined the processing strategies of fifty-nine first- and second-semester learners of Spanish when presented with OVS sentences in which the objects were both direct and indirect object pronouns. The target sentences follow.

Direct Objects

Los invita él al cine.
them-invites-he-to the movies
"He invites them to the movies."

Lo visita la muchacha.
him-visits-the girl
"The girl visits him."

Lo invitan ellos al cine.
him-invite-they-to the movies
"They invite him to the movies."

La visita el chico.
her-visits-the boy
"The boy visits her."

Los invita el chico al cine.
them-invites-the boy-to the movies
"The boy invites them to the movies."

Indirect Objects

Les da él dinero.
to them-gives-he-money
"He gives them money."

Les pregunta la muchacha, '¿qué hora es?'
to them-asks-the girl-what time is it?
"The girl asks them, 'What time is it?'"

Le dan dinero ellos.
to him/her-give-money-they
"They give him/her money."

Le pregunta el chico, '¿qué hora es?'
to him/her-asks-the boy-what time is it?
"The boy asks him/her 'What time is it?'"

Les da dinero el chico.
to them-gives-money-the boy
"The boy gives them money."

Al chico lo invitan los chicos al cine.
the boy- him-invite-the boys-to the movies
"The boys invite the boy to the movies."

Al chico le dan dinero ellos.
the boy-to him-give-money-they
"They give money to the boy."

Lo invitan los chicos al cine.
him-invite-the boys-to the movies
"The boys invite him to the movies."

Le dan dinero los chicos.
to him/her-give-money-the boys
"The boys give money to him/her."

Subjects were shown four pictures, heard a target sentence, and then chose the picture that matched their interpretation of the sentence. Overall, his results showed that learners interpreted OVS sentences as SVO sentences between 35 percent and 70 percent of the time indicating a robust use of the First Noun Strategy during input processing.[4] VanPatten found no significant difference between first- and second-semester learners. He also found that subjects misinterpreted the first noun as a subject significantly more often when the pronoun referred to a direct object than when it referred to an indirect object. He attributed the difference between direct and indirect object pronouns as one of multiple functions; *lo, los, la,* and *las* have multiple meanings, whereas *le* and *les* do not. Andersen (1990 and elsewhere) indicates that early stage language learners operate on a One-to-One Principle; learners assign one meaning to a form no matter if the form has multiple meanings. Moreover, as reported in VanPatten (1983), no significant differences in performance were found across singular/plural paired verb forms, that is, *invita/invitan* and *da/dan*.

Lee (1987) examined the processing strategies of twenty-two first-year learners of Spanish who were presented with eight cojoined sentences in which the gender of the nouns and pronouns varied systematically across pairs of sentences. Number was also examined in the study. In contrast to other studies, the direct object pronouns all occurred in sentence internal position, never in sentence initial position as the following sample sentences demonstrate.

Roberto piensa ir al laboratorio de lenguas con el trabajo de español porque lo entrega mañana. [singular, genders-same]

"Robert plans to go to the language laboratory with the Spanish homework because (he) will turn it in tomorrow."

Teresa piensa ir al laboratorio de lenguas con el trabajo de español porque lo entrega mañana. [singular, genders-different]

"Teresa plans to go to the language laboratory with the Spanish homework because (she) will turn it in tomorrow."

Como son estudiosos, Pablo y David compran muchos libros y los leen durante las vacaciones. [plural, genders-same]

"Because they are studious, Paul and David buy many books and (they) read them on their vacations."

Como son estudiosas, Juana y Virginia compran muchos libros y los leen durante las vacaciones. [plural, genders-different]

"Because they are studious, Jane and Virginia buy many books and (they) read them on their vacations."

Subjects were presented the sentences individually in written form with the direct object pronoun underlined. They were given ten seconds to read each one, and respond to the question, "What does *lo/la/las/los* refer to?" (The form of the pronoun in the question matched the form in the input sentence.) Results revealed that the direct object pronouns were interpreted as subjects between 27 percent and 73 percent of the time. Statistical analyses indicated that plural object pronouns were interpreted as subjects significantly more often than singular pronouns (66 percent versus 38 percent, respectively). There was no significant difference in performance between sentences in which the genders of the nouns were the same and those in which they were different (58 percent versus 46 percent, respectively). There was an interaction between gender and number such that within singular sentences, the object pronouns in the gender-same sentences were interpreted as subjects significantly more often than those in the gender-different sentences (46 percent versus 30 percent, respectively). No such difference was found between the plural sentences (70 percent SVO processing for the gender-same sentences versus 61 percent for the gender-different sentences). These results demonstrate the influence that morphological factors have on promoting or attenuating the use of the First Noun Strategy. One of Slobin's (1973) operating principles for language acquisition is "Pay attention to the ends of words," and these learners did. The gender marker appears at the end of the word in singular sentences and so it attenuated SVO processing only under those conditions. When the gender marker was obscured by a number marker, learners did not process it. In essence, then, the plural marker promoted SVO processing.

Houston (1997) examined the role of background knowledge (a type of extrasentential context) in the use of the First Noun Strategy by fourth-semester learners of Spanish. All twenty-eight subjects were enrolled in courses which utilized the *Destinos* video series. He created two matching sets of ten sentences, all with OVS word order. In one set, the target sentences all referred to events in the *Destinos* series, whereas in the other set fictitious names were used. Note the following examples.

Destinos	*Fictitious*
A Raquel la contrata don Pedro.	*A Silvia la contrata Ricardo.*
Raquel-her-hires-don Pedro	Sylvia-her-hires-Richard
"Don Pedro hires Raquel."	"Richard hires Sylvia."

Before listening to the target sentences, all subjects performed a task on the characters from *Destinos*. This task ensured not only that subjects possessed appropriate background knowledge but also that it was activated for the sentence interpretation task. Subjects were given ten seconds in which they heard a sentence and then had to interpret it. The interpretation task consisted of a verb, in English, with two blank lines on each side of it which subjects were to fill in with names. All subjects heard both the *Destinos*-based sentences as well as the fictitious person sentences.

Results revealed a significant effect for background knowledge that showed that background knowledge attenuated the First Noun Strategy, although not completely. Only 28 percent of the background knowledge sentences were misinterpreted, whereas 48 percent of the fictitious sentences were misinterpreted by using a First Noun Strategy. Whereas previous research had used primarily first-year learners, Houston demonstrated the pervasiveness of the First Noun Strategy in second-year learners. He also demonstrated a specific type of pragmatic constraint on learners' use of word order-based processing strategies.

VanPatten and Houston (1998) examined the effects of sentence-internal context on forty-six fourth-semester learners' processing strategies. They created ten target sentences containing OVS word order in which a clause preceding the object pronoun provided contextual information. The target sentences were paired with ten sentences that contained a preceding clause that did not provide a contextual cue. The target sentences were constructed with the verbs *attacked, insulted, rejected, greeted,* and *kissed.* Note the following examples.

Context

Ricardo está enojado porque lo insultó Susana en la reunión.
"Richard is angry because Susanna insulted him in the meeting."

Roberto está en el hospital porque lo atacó María con un cuchillo.
"Robert is in the hospital because Mary attacked him with a knife."

No Context

Ricardo me dice que lo insultó Susana en la reunión.
"Richard tells me that Susanna insulted him in the meeting."

Gloria contó a sus amigas que la atacó Ramón en su casa.
"Gloria told her friends that Ramón attacked her in her house."

Subjects performed a sentence interpretation task in which they were given a verb, in English, with two blanks on each side of it that they were to fill in with names. Results revealed that sentence-internal context attenuated the use of the First Noun Strategy in interpreting sentences. In the context condition, only 59 percent of the sentences were misinterpreted, whereas 84 percent were misinterpreted in the no-context condition. VanPatten and Houston also found a significant effect for verb in that subjects performed better on sentences with *attacked, insulted* and *rejected* than they did with *kissed* and *greeted.* A significant interaction between verb and condition was found and attributed to differing performance on the *kissed* sentences across the context conditions. They removed these sentences from the data and the subsequent ANOVA revealed, once again, main effects for condition and verb, but no significant interaction.

2.2 Summary of the Research on Sentence Processing

The First Noun Strategy applies to full noun phrases (LoCoco 1987) as well as to object pronouns (Houston 1997; Lee 1987; VanPatten 1984; VanPatten and Houston 1998). Its use is certainly pervasive among first- and second-year language learners who employ it both when listening and reading, on simple and complex sentences, and on object pronouns in sentence initial and sentence internal positions. Its use is not, however, absolute but variable, occurring with first-year learners between 35 percent and 70 percent of the time on simple OVS sentences (VanPatten 1984), with second year learners between 28 percent and 48 percent of the time with these same sentence types (Houston 1997), between 27 percent and 73 percent of the time on cojoined SVO+OVS sentences (Lee 1987), and between 59 percent and 84 percent of the time on complex sentences in which the object pronoun is sentence internal (VanPatten and Houston 1998). Not only is the use of the First Noun Strategy naturally variable, but it is also systematically variable in that its use is attenuated semantically by nouns that cannot perform the action of the verb (LoCoco 1987), pragmatically by extrasentential background knowledge (Houston 1997), morphologically by number and gender markings (Lee 1987), and contextually by intersentential discourse (VanPatten and Houston 1998). In that the use of the First Noun Strategy is both naturally and systematically variable has consequences for learners' developing systems. The data they take into the system is inconsistent and so the system is not stable; *lo* sometimes means *him* and other times, *he*. Likewise, *las* sometimes means *them* and other times, *they* or *the*.

2.3 Possible Directions for Future Research on Sentence Processing

Perhaps the most notable lacuna in the database is the lack of L1 linguistic diversity of the subject population we have to date examined. The second language learners who have been examined have all been adult native speakers of English whose L1 prefers the use of SVO word order. Is the First Noun Strategy as pervasive among native speakers of Japanese learning Spanish as a second language? In other words, to what extent does L1 transfer contribute to the use of the First Noun Strategy? Addressing these questions would be fruitful directions for future research.

Another lacuna in the data base is the direct comparison of native speaker performance with that of nonnatives.[5] Do native Spanish-speaking children employ a First Noun Strategy to interpret preverbal object pronouns? If they do, until what age do they do so? If they do, do they employ the First Noun Strategy in the same contexts and to the same degree as native English-speaking learners of Spanish, be they adults or children?

Another lacuna to point out is the narrow empirical focus on third-person direct object pronouns. While third-person pronouns provide formal consistency (*lo-los* "him"-"them" [m.], *la-las* "her"-"them" [f.]) and others do not (*me-nos* "me"-"us," *te-os* "you" [fam. sg.]-"you" [fam. pl.-Spain], *te-los* "you" [fam. sg.]-"you" [fam. and formal pl]) experimental conditions could be established to examine a greater variety of pronouns. Are other object pronouns, for example *me, te,* and *nos,* ever assigned the grammatical role of subject? Do other object pronouns contribute to or inhibit the use of the First Noun Strategy? If they do, in what contexts do they do so? Anecdotally, given how learners misinterpret sentences such as *Me gusta el chocolate* to me-is pleasing-chocolate = "I like chocolate," a detailed examination of how learners process the pronoun *me* could provide many interesting insights into second language acquisition. Given the formal similarity between English *me* and Spanish *me,* future research might include subjects other than native-speakers of English.

The final possible direction for future research I will suggest is to combine the foci of different studies into one. Do pragmatic factors such as background knowledge (Houston 1997) influence (i.e., attenuate or promote) the role morphological factors (Lee 1987) play in learners' use of the First Noun Strategy? Likewise, does intrasentential context (VanPatten and Houston 1998) influence the role morphological factors (Lee 1987) play in learners' use of the First Noun Strategy?

2.4   Processing Instruction: Attenuating the Effects of the First Noun Strategy

Given the pervasiveness of the First Noun Strategy[6] and the problem its use creates for providing accurate information to learners' developing linguistic systems, can learners be explicitly taught not to employ it? To determine whether instruction could be directed toward altering the first noun processing strategy, VanPatten developed what he termed Processing Instruction, which was incorporated into VanPatten et al. (1992) and explicated in Lee and VanPatten (1995) and VanPatten (1996). The goal of Processing Instruction is to alter the way learners perceive and process linguistic data in the input. In the specific case of object pronouns, the goal of instruction is to have learners perceive, process, and then assign the grammatical role of object (not subject) to a preverbally placed object pronoun.

VanPatten and Cadierno (1993) compared the effects of processing instruction with traditional instruction and a no-instruction control group. All 129 subjects were first-semester learners of Spanish who scored below 60 percent on the pretest. Processing instruction involved the explanation of third-person object pronouns and information about learners' processing strategies, specifically, the tendency of learners to employ the First Noun Strategy. Subjects then practiced correctly interpreting sentences that contained object pronouns. Traditional instruction involved the explanation of the full paradigm of direct object pronouns followed by oral practices that required subjects to manipulate object pronouns in a series of mechanical, meaningful, and communicative practices. At no time did the processing group produce an object pronoun, nor did the traditional group interpret the meaning of a sentence containing an object pronoun.

VanPatten and Cadierno used a pretest/posttest design in which the test consisted of two formats, both of which employed visual cues, a ten-sentence interpretation task and a five-item object pronoun production task. For the interpretation task, subjects heard a sentence and selected the picture that matched their interpretation. For example, subjects heard *A la chica la abraza la mamá* the girl-her-embraces-the mother = "The mother embraces the girl" and selected either a picture of a woman hugging a child who does not hug back or of a child hugging a woman who does not hug back. For the production task, subjects were given a two-part drawing and an incomplete sentence that they were to complete according to the picture. For example, subjects were given *El chico piensa en la chica y entonces* ___ "The boy thinks about the girl and then ___." The visuals showed a boy thinking about a girl in the first drawing and the boy calling the girl on the phone in the second. The desired written response was *la llama* her-he calls = "(he) calls her," because discourse constraints would dictate the use of an object pronoun.

Subjects were tested before instruction, immediately after instruction, one week later, and then again one month later. VanPatten and Cadierno found that the processing group improved significantly on the interpretation task, moving from a score of less than 2 on the pretest to a score of more than 8 on the first posttest, and sustained this level of improvement over the next two posttests. The traditional group did not, however, significantly improve on the interpretation posttests, scoring less than 2 on the pretest and between 3 and 4 on the posttests. The traditional group's performance on the production test was as expected. It significantly improved from the pretest to the first posttest, moving from a score of less than 3 to a score of more than 8, and sustained this level of improvement across the next two posttests. The surprise finding of this study (and all other studies involving processing instruction) was that the processing group also improved significantly on the production posttests. The group moved from a score of just more than 2 to a score of more than 8 on the first production posttest and sustained this level of performance on the next two posttests. The two groups' scores on production tests were not significantly different from each other. The control group did not improve significantly on either the interpretation or production task on any of the posttests. VanPatten and Cadierno demonstrated that through focused instruction the First Noun Strategy, which other research has shown to be pervasive among even fourth-semester learners, could almost be eliminated in first-semester learners.

VanPatten and Oikkenon (1996) partially replicated VanPatten and Cadierno (1993) to assess whether fifty-nine learners receiving processing instruction benefited most from (1) the explanation of object pronouns (word order and case markings) and processing strategies; (2) carrying out structured input activities that required them to interpret the meanings of object pronouns; or (3) a combination of the two, which is processing instruction as VanPatten and Cadierno (1993) carried it out. VanPatten and Oikkenon used a pretest/posttest format using the same materials as VanPatten and Cadierno. The results on the sentence interpretation posttest revealed that both the processing-instruction and structured input-activities groups performed significantly better than the explanation-only group and that the processing-instruction and structured input-activities groups performed equally. The results on the production posttest were similar but not identical. The processing-instruction group performed significantly better than the explanation-only group, but not better than the structured input-activities group. There was no significant difference between the scores of the explanation-only and structured input-activities groups, although the latter were higher. VanPatten and Oikkenon concluded that within processing instruction, the critical factor is carrying out structured input activities, not overt explanation.

VanPatten and Sanz (1995) examined the effects of processing instruction on more communicative and discourse-oriented language use. They compared processing instruction on objects pronouns (identical to that in VanPatten and Cadierno) with no instruction for forty-four third-semester learners of Spanish who scored less than 60 percent on an interpretation pretest containing twenty target items. Each subject also completed an interpretation posttest immediately following instruction. They also completed three different kinds of production tests in both oral and written modes as pretests and posttests: an eight-item sentence completion task based on VanPatten and Cadierno (1993), a structured interview for which learners answered an average of eleven questions about seven pictures, and a video narration for which subjects described what they had just watched twice on a video. The four different videos depicted seven connected events. One, for example, involved a man who comes home with groceries and then prepares a potato for eating. He washes it, cuts it, fries it, and finally eats it. The posttests were administered immediately after instruction; no delayed posttesting took place.

Given the different number of target items across tasks, VanPatten and Sanz calculated percentages of correct pronoun use and then transformed the means in their statistical analyses. They found that as a result of processing instruction, subjects significantly improved on the interpretation test and the three production tests. On the production tests, mode was a significant factor affecting subjects' performance on the sentence-completion and video-narration tests. Mean scores for correct pronoun use during the structured interview were very low in both written and oral modes, even though processing instruction did significantly improve performance.

With reference specifically to the written mode, VanPatten and Sanz found that the processing group improved significantly from pretest to posttest, whereas the control group did not. The processing group significantly outperformed the control group on all posttests. They also found that the scores for sentence completion were significantly higher than those for video narration. With reference specifically to the oral mode, VanPatten and Sanz found that the processing group improved significantly from pretest to posttest on the sentence completion task but not on the video narration task. The control group did not improve on either task. Overall, their results indicated that processing instruction had a significant impact on altering learners' use of the First Noun Strategy in both writing and speaking (especially in controlled contexts) as well as across a variety of discourse-based tests.

2.5 Summary

Processing Instruction is one example of how classroom learning can work with acquisitional processes rather than against them. By focusing on a specific problematic aspect of the pronominal system, by informing learners about processing strategies, and importantly, by providing learners structured input activities VanPatten, Cadierno, Sanz, and Oikkenon helped learners to feed accurate input into their developing systems. Their research has examined the effects of processing instruction using several different tasks: written and oral fill-in-the-blank production tests, picture-identification interpretation tests, structured oral interview based on picture description, structured written picture description, and an oral and written video narration task. There are task effects as well as mode effects, and yet the processing groups significantly improved from pretest to posttest on all tasks but the oral video narration task. The effects of processing instruction are, then, evident at both sentential and discourse levels, in oral and written modes, and in structured and communicative tasks.[7]

2.6 Possible Directions for Future Research

A lacuna in the database on processing instruction is an examination of the long-term effects of using different tasks to measure the impact of processing instruction. Are the effects of processing instruction stable over time with discourse-level and communicative tasks as they are with sentence-level and structured tasks?

A possible direction in which to explore further the effects of processing instruction involves examining closely what aspects of the instructional treatment are beneficial. Processing instruction involves grammatical explanation, an explanation of processing strategies, and practice activities with structured input. VanPatten and Oikkenon's (1996) results suggest that performing structured input activities is more beneficial to processing temporal reference than is the grammatical explanation. What do learners benefit most from in terms of learning object pronouns: grammatical explanation, an explanation of processing strategies, practice activities with structured input, or a combination of these?

In all the research on processing instruction the instructional treatment occurs at only one point; it is a single exposure. What would the effects be of multiple exposures to the instructional treatment for a processing group, traditional group and a control group?

Perhaps the most important research yet to be carried out is that which examines the long- and short-term impact of processing instruction versus traditional instruction on the areas in which VanPatten (1996) hypothesizes that the First Noun Strategy affects. Does processing instruction affect the misuse of object and reflexive pronouns as subjects, use of *gustar* as a transitive verb, overreliance on subject pronouns, nonuse of the object case marker *a,* overreliance on SVO word order in language production, and the delay in the acquisition of person-number verbal morphology? In other words, are there as yet undiscovered effects and/or noneffects of processing instruction on language development?

2.7 Processing Object Pronouns in Written Discourse: Interpreting Subject/Object Relations

In all the studies reviewed so far, the learners had received some form of formal instruction on object pronouns prior to participating in the studies. What happens when learners encounter object pronouns for the first time? What meaning(s) do they assign to these words?

Lee (2000) examined the relationship between reading comprehension and input processing in twenty-seven first-semester learners of Spanish. Learners who had never formally studied Spanish object pronouns read a passage that contained six instances of third-person singular direct object pronouns. Their reading of the passage constituted their initial exposure to the targeted linguistic item. Lee created three orientations to the task of reading the passage. One-third of the subjects were told before reading that the passage contained the words *lo* and *la* and that they should try to figure out what these words meant as they encountered them in the passage. These words appeared in the passage in bold, underlined type. Another third were given multiple choice comprehension questions that contained the subject-object relations in full noun phrases that in the passage were encoded with object pronouns. This group was told that they should guess at answers to the questions in order to get an idea of the passage's content and then, as they read, determine if they were right or wrong. The object pronouns appeared in the passage in regular typeface. A third group was told to read the passage for comprehension (the neutral condition). The object pronouns appeared in the passage in regular typeface. Half the subjects read a passage about a male protagonist and the other half read the same passage but with the male protagonist replaced by a female.

Lee assessed comprehension of the relations encoded by object pronouns using multiple-choice questions written in English, the subjects' native language, and used full noun phrases not object pronouns in the questions. He assessed input processing using a sentence recognition task. With regard to comprehension, he found significant effects for passage and orienting condition. Comprehension of the male protagonist passage was higher than that of the female protagonist passage (75 percent versus 62 percent, respectively). Learners who were told to figure out the meaning of *lo* and *la* outperformed the others (77 percent). The lowest comprehension score was in the neutral condition (58 percent) while those who received comprehension questions as a prereading aid scored in the middle (67 percent). (Note that although there was a main effect for orienting condition, there were no significant differences found between the three means given above.) Even though these subjects had never been exposed to object pronouns in Spanish, they could comprehend the relationships between subject and object between 58 percent and 77 percent of the time.

To measure input processing or attention to form, Lee presented subjects a list of sentences in Spanish and asked them to check off the sentences that appeared in the passage they had read. He found no significant effects for passage or orienting condition for the sentence recognition data (although the interaction of the two approached a level of significance). Scores on the input processing data were lower than those on the comprehension data. For the male protagonist passage, learners recognized 50 percent of the sentences containing object pronouns, whereas they recognized only 40 percent from the female protagonist passage. Recognition of sentences containing object pronouns by orienting condition varied from 33 percent in the neutral condition to 46 percent in the *lo/la* condition to 50 percent in the comprehension questions condition. Even though the highest score is only 50 percent (i.e., performing at chance level), it is notable that the learners did, to some degree, attend to the forms in the input. Finally, Lee correlated the comprehension and input-processing scores but the correlation between the two was not significant. He concluded that the good comprehender was not necessarily the good input processor, and, conversely, that the poor comprehender was not necessarily the poor input processor. Overall, the results were encouraging. Learners at the most initial stage of language development can correctly assign meaning to object pronouns embedded in written discourse as well as recognize that they did attend to specific forms in the input.

2.8   Possible Directions for Future Research

The greatest limitation on generalizing the findings of Lee (2000) is the linguistic background of the subjects. All but a few had studied languages other than Spanish and so cannot be considered naive language learners. In order to examine the effects of learners' initial exposure to object pronouns in text, naive language learners would be needed. Do naive language learners process the meaning of object pronouns and identify them as having been in the input?

With language acquisition research in general, we often find that the type of task we use to elicit data affects our findings. As seen above, such was the case with processing instruction (VanPatten and Sanz 1997). Future research that examines how learners process object pronouns in discourse could explore task effects. Comprehension can be measured with free recall, cued recall and/or the type of test VanPatten and Houston (1998) and Houston (1997) used, specifically, providing learners a verb with two blanks on either side of it and asking them to fill in the names of people involved in the action of the verb. Input processing could be measured with a simpler task than sentence recognition, such as having learners select a form to fill in a blank from a choice of four forms. Are there tasks that more effectively allow learners to demonstrate the knowledge they gain from their exposure to object pronouns in written input?

Another direction in which to explore further how learners process object pronouns would be to determine if learners could produce an object pronoun after their initial exposure to them in written input. Possible production tests include a modified cloze passage or a structured fill in the blank test. Can learners who are exposed to object pronouns in written input produce the forms to which they were exposed?

A final direction I will suggest for further exploring processing object pronouns in discourse is to examine factors we know affect sentence processing: morphological factors, background knowledge, and context. What factors promote processing object pronouns as pronouns and not subjects in written discourse? What factors promote the use of the first noun strategy in written discourse?

3.0   Acquisition in Instructed and Noninstructed Contexts: Encoding Meaning

Case study research places specific individuals, who are selected for particular characteristics, under a microscope. The benefit of this type of research is its level of detailed analysis. We are able to examine language development in such a way as to hypothesize which elements of learner performance are idiosyncratic and/or generalizable. Idiosyncratic performance allows us to develop models of individual differences whereas generalizable performance allows us to determine universals of language acquisition.

In a series of publications, Andersen described and explained the interlanguage development of Anthony (a pseudonym) who lived in Puerto Rico for four years from ages ten to fourteen. Anthony and his parents lived in a mixed middle-class and working-class neighborhood where only one other English-speaking family lived. The school Anthony attended provided instruction in both English and Spanish, although Spanish was only a medium of instruction, not a school subject. Anthony's social network consisted mainly of Spanish-speaking children who lived in his neighborhood. He is, then, an example of someone who acquired a language in a noninstructed, natural context. Andersen (1983) provided an account of Anthony's acquisition of clitic pronouns when Anthony was fourteen years old.

VanPatten (1990) provided a comparative case study of the acquisition of clitic pronouns by Andersen's Anthony and David, a twenty-year-old American college student. David was described as a very good student who began Spanish language instruction in college and had not studied another language. He is, then, an example of someone who acquired Spanish in an instructed, classroom setting. The type of instruction David received would be what VanPatten and Cadierno (1993) termed traditional, that is, explanation followed by a variety of oral practices.

Whereas Andersen's data came from a single interview, VanPatten's were collected every two weeks over a period of three months during the second semester of David's formal study of Spanish. VanPatten's comparison of the two learners involved both quantitative (correct suppliance of pronouns) and qualitative analyses (contexts of usage, knowledge of forms, and placement or position of pronouns).

To compare data gathered in different ways across different subjects was not an easy task. Anthony correctly supplied pronouns in twenty-one of twenty-nine (72 percent) obligatory contexts for OV word order patterns. He correctly supplied pronouns in five of ten (50 percent) obligatory contexts for VO word order patterns. David correctly supplied pronouns in fifty-eight of seventy (79 percent) obligatory contexts for OV word order patterns and six of nine (67 percent) contexts for VO word order patterns. VanPatten made two points about the quantitative data. First, David supplied an extraordinary number of third-person indirect object pronouns (28 of 29) that elevated his overall score above Anthony's. Removing this one category from the quantitative data would drop David's score to 66 percent, less than Anthony's. Anthony and David performed similarly with high scores for first person *me* (88 percent and 93 percent, respectively) and low scores for third-person direct object pronouns (0 percent and 20 percent, respectively).

In comparing the contexts in which Anthony and David used clitics, VanPatten noted more differences than similarities. Both relied heavily on SVO word order configurations but while Anthony produced OproV patterns (but only with *me*), David did not. He never produced an utterance without including an explicit marker of all underlying semantic information regarding agents, objects, datives and patients. Anthony, by contrast, would occasionally omit a direct object clitic. David would use the wrong person, whereas Anthony never did, and David would repeat full noun-phrase complements instead of supplying an object pronoun.

Regarding knowledge of forms, Anthony and David did not use all forms in all contexts, that is, using *me, te,* and *nos* as indirect, direct, and reflexive pronouns. David used all forms but *la(s)* in at least one obligatory context, whereas Anthony used all forms but *te.* Anthony and David shared difficulties with third-person clitics; sometimes they were absent in obligatory contexts, other times only under partial control.

As VanPatten stated, instruction may have had both beneficial and retarding effects on acquisition (1990:131). The retarding effects were apparently due to the limited range of language experiences that the typical classroom learner is exposed to. David experienced an hour of classroom contact per day, whereas Anthony lived, played, and was educated in a Spanish-language medium. As a result of his analysis, VanPatten proposed the following hypotheses regarding the acquisition of clitics in instructed and noninstructed contexts.

1. Instruction does not impact overall difficulty of learning nor order of acquisition.

2. Regardless of context, *me* is the easiest pronoun to acquire while third person directs are the most difficult.

3. SVO word order is somehow maintained.

4. A one-form, one-function strategy obtains in all learning contexts.

5. Instruction impacts upon omission. Classroom learners tend not to omit surface realizations of underlying verbal arguments.

6. Naturalistic learners begin the acquisition of reflexive *se* through the process of chunking phrases. Classroom learners begin the acquisition of reflexive *se* through its association with a set of marked lexical items.

7. Classroom learners begin the acquisition of third-person indirect object pronouns via lexical items, i.e., verbs that are prototypical three-argument verbs and are frequent in classroom discourse.

8. Differences in performance patterns between classroom and naturalistic learners are not due to a change in underlying processes which govern the creation of a linguistic system. Differences are attributable to quantity and quality of input received by the learner. (VanPatten 1990:131)

3.1   Possible Directions for Future Research

Given that the database consists of two case studies, we can recommend several directions for future research that examines learners' use of clitics when expressing themselves. Certainly, the database would benefit from examining a greater number of language learners. To what extent is Anthony's and David's use of clitics idiosyncratic or is their pattern of performance generalizable to a wider population?

The comparison of Anthony's and David's use of clitics was made indirectly, meaning that the data were not gathered in the same way using identical data elicitation procedures. Future research could continue to compare the longitudinal development of naturalistic and instructed learners, but systematically and directly by having them perform the same tasks at periodic intervals in their development. Do the same developmental patterns characterize the acquisition of clitics in both naturalistic and instructed contexts? Does the context of acquisition affect the rate of development? This line of investigation would also allow us to address task effects in learner performance such as those VanPatten and Sanz (1995) found. Do learners perform similarly across different tasks such as an oral interview, video narration, and picture description?

Given how limited the database is, cross-sectional investigations would also be extremely informative. Because David was a first-year language learner we can naturally ask the question, What patterns of clitic use characterize second-, third-, and fourth-year learners of Spanish? Cross-linguistic investigations would also be informative. These studies could compare the performance of speakers whose native language allows preverbal placement of clitics with those whose native language does not. What are the effects of learners' L1 on the L2 acquisition of Spanish clitics?

Andersen used the data he gathered on Anthony and other data to develop seven cognitive operating principles of second language acquisition, which he hypothesized as applicable to both naturalistic and instructed contexts. These principles and their supporting evidence are summarized in Andersen (1990), along with Andersen's proposals for future research. To my knowledge no one has pursued his suggestions although it would appear from David's data (VanPatten 1990) that Andersen's principles might indeed explain the acquisition of Spanish clitics. Do Andersen's cognitive operating principles account for instructed second language acquisition?[8]

4.0   Generative Theories of Syntax

The studies reviewed above all approach second language development from a cognitivist perspective. That is, they represent attempts to account for the principles, processes, and strategies guiding how learners perceive input and produce output. We want to characterize the learners' internal (mental) grammar for the second language. We want to know how they relate the forms they find in the input to their intended meanings, as well as the forms they use in their output to their intended meanings and then map the progression toward nativelike performance. The types of errors learners make are important to cognitivists. The studies reviewed below examine learner language for what it can tell us about theories of syntax. That is, they represent attempts to contribute to an abstract representation of the restrictions a particular language places on the order of words and the forms of words as they perform particular functions.

Characterizing the learners' internal grammar is not as important as comparing/contrasting that grammar to the abstract representation found in the theory of syntax. We want to know if language learners order words like native speakers do; if so, then we know what part of the theory of syntax is operational in learners. What language learners do correctly is important to syntacticians.

Behaviorist theory dominated thought for more than half the twentieth century. According to behaviorism, language was a set of habits that resulted from associating particular stimuli and responses. Habits were formed and hence, language was acquired, through the processes of imitation and repetition of input (i.e., stimuli). Children acquiring their native language supposedly imitated and repeated the language in their environment. Serious flaws in the theory were revealed when researchers discovered that although some children did (and do) imitate and repeat elements found in their linguistic environment, most of their utterances were novel; they could not be traced to input. For example, do children ever hear *goed* from their caretakers? The input was, moreover, found to be impoverished or underdetermined in that children produced or generated language structures beyond what they were exposed to. From these observations generative theories of language were developed. Children must possess an innate language faculty (language acquisition device—LAD) that responds to and interacts with the input in the linguistic environment in order to generate, not recreate, a grammar of the language. For behaviorists, the relationship between input and output or stimulus/response was a direct 1-to-1 matching. For generativists, the relationship is best characterized, metaphorically speaking, as 1-to-20.

Theories of generative grammar have shifted and evolved since Chomsky first proposed the idea with the most recent formulations being Government and Binding, Universal Grammar, and the Minimalist Program. Among the issues facing a generative theory are: Is Universal Grammar accessible to adult second language learners, or is access shut off after puberty? Is a second language acquired through access to Universal Grammar or through general learning and problem-solving strategies? If Universal Grammar (UG) is accessible, then what is the initial state for second language acquisition, UG or L1 transfer? Whereas the theory describes native language competence, can it adequately describe second language (or interlanguage) competence given that learner language is inherently variable and dynamic (evolving)?

Approaches to addressing these questions include comparing child L1 developmental patterns to adult L2 patterns. If they coincide, then we can conclude that UG is accessible. Also, we can compare L2 developmental patterns for adults whose native languages are typologically different. If the L2 developmental patterns coincide, then UG must be operating not (just) first language transfer or general learning strategies. Finally, we can compare language learners with adult native speakers to determine which elements of interlanguage are nativelike and which are not.

According to the theory (Chomsky 1981), Universal Grammar is made up of principles (universal truths for all languages) and parameters (set according to language-specific data). Particular combinations of values form clusters of properties associated with language specific parameters. Second language acquisition of some of these language-specific properties is said to involve resetting the parametric values assigned in the L1 acquisition process. Of interest to the present review is the acquisition of the Pro-drop Parameter (also referred to as the Null Subject Parameter). Spanish, for example, is a pro-drop language because it allows constructions in which no overt subject is present in the surface syntax, whereas French and English obligatorily fill in the subject in surface syntax.[9] The syntactic behavior of clitic pronouns varies between pro-drop and non-pro-drop languages.

Focusing on the status of clitics in learner language, Liceras (1985) examined the Spanish interlanguage development of thirty subjects whose native, dominant, and most-used language was English and thirty whose native, dominant, and most-used language was French. (These data were reported again in Liceras 1986, 1996; the latter is the reference for the present work.)[10] All subjects were enrolled in university-level Spanish courses (beyond those commonly referred to as basic language instruction) and had studied Spanish for three or four years before the study. Data were collected using two tasks. In the first, subjects saw images projected on a screen and were asked to write a story or dialogue narrating what they saw. Because the images repeated characters, objects, and situations, learners were strongly and overtly encouraged not to repeat nouns but to use object pronouns. The second task consisted of highly structured, substitution exercises one would find in a grammar-driven language textbook. Five native speakers of Spanish acted as a control group.

The data from both the narrative and structured tasks revealed nativelike placement of object pronouns for both groups of subjects: before a conjugated verb, after an infinitive, before a periphrastic verb phrase, and clitic doubling. These data supported the interpretation that clitics are affixed elements in grammars of nonnative Spanish speakers. Liceras noted three nonnative uses in the narrations and substitution exercises: omission of an obligatory clitic but the presence of pronominal reduplication (among English speakers only), clitics following conjugated verbs, and clitics placed in the middle of periphrastic verb phrases. The substitution exercise data had many more examples of clitic placement between verbs than the narration data, especially among the French speakers. The latter data supported an interpretation that clitics appear as words in the syntax in the grammars of nonnative speakers of Spanish.

It should be noted that these learners never produced utterances in which a word was placed between the clitic and a verb, as was possible in Old Spanish. Such constructions would have lent the greatest support to the words/syntax hypothesis. Liceras argued that the two types of data supported the idea that interlanguage is permeable with respect to the process of cliticization; clitics are generated from nonargument positions as lexicalized affixes and from argument positions as words in the syntax. It seems, then, that as far as language learners are concerned, clitics are not one or the other type of item; they can be both.

As a follow-up, Liceras et al. (1997) examined the interlanguage development of very early stage learners of Spanish. They gathered spontaneous speech and sentence repetition data from five secondary school and six university students. Although the subjects were beginning their study of Spanish, they were all "French dominant, bilingual with French as one of the languages, bilingual with Arabic, Italian, Greek, or Portuguese as one of the languages or proficient second language speakers of French" (Liceras et al. 1997:117). Even though the subjects could be considered beginning learners of Spanish, they certainly could not be considered naive language learners. Data were collected at three points in time: after fifty, sixty-five, and eighty hours of instruction. Subjects were interviewed individually for thirty minutes during which they were asked questions on personal topics and questions based on pictures. They were also given a sentence repetition task at each of these three times (details of the task were not provided).

Liceras et al. (1997) examined four types of clitics: reflexives, experiencers, direct objects, and indirect objects.[11] As seen in table 4.1, spontaneous production of clitics was very low considering that the results combined the three data gathering sessions. There were no instances of double object pronouns (i.e., indirect plus direct). What I find notable in the data is the extreme individual variation in production across learners. Whereas all eleven subjects produced reflexive and experiencer clitics, only nine produced direct object clitics, and only seven produced indirect object clitics. The percentages for nativelike uses ranged from 36 percent to 100 percent for reflexives, 0 percent to 100 percent for experiencers, 67 percent to 100 percent for those nine who produced direct object pronouns, and from 0 percent to 100 percent for those seven who produced indirect object pronouns. They also found that the beginning learners did not have a set of pronouns in their nonnative grammars that correlated to the native one and showed variable use of casemarked forms (e.g., *se* for *le* and *nos* for *nosotros*). In other words, these learners, similar to Anthony (Andersen 1983) and David (VanPatten 1990), had clitic function, but not necessarily the appropriate clitic form in their interlanguage.

From a theoretical perspective, the number of clitics produced is not as important as whether they are nativelike or not in their placement. As table 4.2 shows, many nativelike instances of clitics were found in all categories, most notably with direct objects. Viewing the data another way, we can say that many nonnativelike instances were also found most notably with indirect objects. Liceras et al. stated that the nonnativelike reflexive clitics were a reflection of a morphological shortcoming (the nature of which was not made explicit in the article) that did not have syntactic consequences. They were more concerned with the large percentage of nativelike occurrences of direct object pronouns because the finding contrasted with Liceras's 1985 findings. These beginning learners did not place a clitic after a conjugated verb nor between a conjugated verb and an infinitive as Liceras's more advanced subjects did, and so it was difficult for Liceras et al. to conclude that clitics had multiple values in nonnative grammars.[12]

The other task Liceras et al. used was a sentence repetition task administered at each of the three interviews. The target sentences contained clitics. Failure to repeat exactly an input sentence is indicative, psycholinguistically, of an incomplete linguistic system or underdeveloped psycholinguistic mechanisms. As table 4.3 indicates, the subjects varied in their success in repeating the clitic pronouns they heard in the input sentences.

Individual variation once again characterized learner performance in that the secondary students' scores ranged from 18 percent to 69 percent correct repetition and the university subjects' from 32 percent to 53 percent. As the authors stated, "all subjects had problems repeating the clitics, especially in the case of the IO + DO sequences. They produce clitics, but they substitute dative *les* for *los, las, le, nos,* etc. In other words, they fill in the clitic but are far from mastering the agreement features" (Liceras et al. 1997:125).

Overall, these multilingual learners of Spanish did not spontaneously produce very many clitics to analyze. Given the rather extraordinary previous language experience of

Table 4.1

Total Instances of Spontaneous Production of Clitics

Participants	Reflexive (n = 11)[a]	Experiencer (n = 11)	Direct (n = 9)	Indirect (n = 7)
Secondary (n = 5)	41	8	19	4
University (n = 6)	43	36	5	8

[a]Number of participants who produced a clitic. Maximum number is 11.
Source: Liceras et al. 1997.

Table 4.2

Average Percentage of Nativelike Spontaneous Production of Clitics

Participants	Reflexive (n = 11) (%)	Experiencer (n = 11) (%)	Direct (n = 9) (%)	Indirect (n = 7) (%)
Secondary (n = 5)	68 28/41	62.5 5/8	84 16/19	50 2/4
University (n = 6)	51 22/43	58 21/36	100 5/5	63 5/8

Note: Liceras et al. (1997) reported responses as overall percentages. In order to describe these data in aggregate terms more accurately, I had to derive the number of tokens represented by these percentages and then calculate averages. This process revealed either inconsistencies or typographical errors in the original report. I have corrected them in my calculations.
Source: Liceras et al. 1997.

Table 4.3

Average Percentage of Nativelike Repeated Production of Clitics

	Interview 1 (n = 10)[a] (%)	Interview 2 (n = 10) (%)	Interview 3 (n = 11) (%)
Secondary (n = 5)	68	34	34
University (n = 6)	46	49	42

[a]Number of participants in repetition tasks. A number less than 11 signifies that a participant missed the given interview.
Note: Raw data for these percentages was not provided.
Source: Liceras et al. 1997.

these early stage learners of Spanish, Liceras et al. could not corroborate the findings from Liceras (1985) that clitics have mixed properties in nonnative grammars. The data supported the conclusions that these learners had a clitic slot in their interlanguage syntax but that they did not yet have the full set of appropriately casemarked pronouns.

Sanchez and Al-Kasey (1999) examined the acquisition of direct object clitic pronouns for twelve first- and second-year university-level learners of Spanish, who were placed into three groups based on syntactic indicators of proficiency, such as producing correct subject-verb agreement and correct copula use in progressive and copular constructions. The learners' data were compared with those of six monolingual native speakers of Spanish. All subjects performed two tasks: an oral narrative from a series of pictures (in both the L1 as well as the L2 for the learners) and a sentence-picture matching task containing fourteen pictures. The sentence-matching task required subjects to select from a set of choices the sentence that described a picture. Sentences varied in word order, animacy of the object, and presence or absence of a clitic. Examples follow.

> *La niña abre la puerta.*   SVO
> the girl-opens-the door
> "The girl opens the door."
>
> *La puerta la niña abre.*   OSV
> the door-the girl-opens
> "The girl opens the door."
>
> *La niña la puerta abre.*   SOV
> the girl-the door-opens
> "The girl opens the door."
>
> *La niña la abre la puerta.*   SVO
> the girl-it-opens-the door.
> "The girl opens (it) the door."
>
> *La puerta la niña la abre.*   OSV
> the door-the girl-it-opens
> "The girl opens the door."
>
> *La niña la puerta la abre.*   SOV
> the girl-the door-it-opens
> "The girl opens the door."

These sentences tested sensitivity to noncanonical word order as well as, in the last two, recognition of the clitic as a syntactic licenser of fronting. They also included sentences with clitic-doubling as in the following sentences.

> *Un carro lo lava un hombre.*   OVS
> a car-it-washes-a man
> "A man washes a car."

Un hombre lo lava un carro.　　　SVO
a man-it-washes-a car
"A man washes a car."

Un hombre un carro lo lava.　　　SOV
a man-a car-it-washes
"A man washes a car."

The oral narrative data revealed that the L2 subjects treated clitics differently than the native speakers did. They produced many fewer clitics (by percentage), many more overt direct objects, and no instances of clitic-left dislocation constructions, preferring instead SclVO order. These data are consistent with those of Andersen (1983) for Anthony and VanPatten (1990) for David. The use of overt direct objects instead of clitics is also consistent with the oral narration data reported in VanPatten and Sanz (1995). Table 4.4 shows some of the differences between native and nonnative speakers' distribution of direct object types in their narratives. (DP stands for determiner phrase, the syntactic unit that contains the direct object.) As Sanchez and Al-Kasey pointed out, their data indicated that avoidance, which they defined as the incorrect use of overt DPs (determiner phrases) that had immediate antecedents in the discourse, is much more frequent than clitics. Only two of the more advanced learners produced clitic doubling, no learners produced clitic left dislocation, and the only clitic construction present in the data is $SO_{pro}V$. These learners, in contrast to the intermediate and advanced learners in Liceras (1985) or the beginning learners in Liceras et al. (1997), did not produce the full range of nativelike syntactic configurations.

The data for the sentence-picture matching task follow in table 4.5. Clearly, all subjects, in the absence of clitics preferred canonical word order. When clitics were present the data diverged in that the native speakers accepted far fewer SVO word order configurations than the nonnative speakers. This finding indicated that nonnative speakers did not readily identify clitics as licensers of fronted direct objects. Learners showed a preference for clitic doubling with [-def, -anim] objects, whereas the native speakers preferred the instances in which the clitic could be interpreted as clitic left dislocation. Sanchez and Al-Kasey stated that they believed the learners were selecting the clitic doubling constructions as a reflection of SVO preference and not to an overgeneralization of clitic doubling.

As Sanchez and Al-Kasey explained and explained well, recent developments in syntactic theory, specifically Chomsky's Minimalist Program (1995), conceive of cross-linguistic differences as the result of differences in the feature specification of syntactic categories, both lexical categories such as noun, verb, and adjective, and functional categories such as tense and agreement. Differences in feature specifications of functional categories trigger differences in feature-checking operations and in syntactic movement. From this perspective, the process of L2 syntax acquisition is dependent to a large extent on the acquisition of functional categories and their feature specification. With specific regard to the acquisition of the Spanish direct object pronominal system, Sanchez and Al-Kasey pointed out that direct object pronouns and clitics are viewed now as nominal elements whose identification and checking properties are closely related to the functional category Agreement Objects

Table 4.4

Distribution of Direct Object Types

Subject	Correct Overt DP (%)	Incorrect Overt DP (%)	Percent of Clitics (%)	No. of Clitics (%)
Group 1 n = 4	65	29	4	63
Group 2 n = 4	76	19	4	135
Group 3 n = 4	51	28	13	145
Native speakers n = 6	58	0	42	113

Source: Sanchez and Al-Kasey 1999.

Table 4.5

Clitic Preferences

Subject	SVO No clitic	S cl VO	S cl [-def, -anim] O	S cl DO IO
Group 1	12/12 100%	11/12 92%	3/4 75%	3/4 75%
Group 2	12/12 100%	8/12 67%	3/4 75%	3/4 75%
Group 3	12/12 100%	12/12 100%	4/4 100%	4/4 100%
Native speakers	17/18 94%	7/18 39%	1/6 17%	6/6 100%

Source: Sanchez and Al-Kasey 1999.

(AgrO°) and to its feature specification. They argued that their data pointed toward the early stage of acquisition of clitics as one that only partially specifies the values of AgrO. (Even though Chomsky [1995] eliminated AgrO as a functional category, other scholars have not and so they continue to work with it.)

Three theories account for how functional categories work in second language acquisition. The Minimal Trees Model claims that only lexical projections transfer from the L1 and that functional projections develop and mature in the L2 only gradually (Vainnika and Young-Scholten 1996). The Valueless Features Hypothesis maintains that the features of functional categories are not specified in early stage L2 acquisition or are specified for an inactive or inert value because the overt inflectional morphology of functional categories does not transfer (Eubank 1993); it cannot transfer because the L1 and L2 morphology are different. The Full Transfer/Full Access Hypothesis holds that functional categories are present in initial L2 acquisition with their L1 specifications, which, over time, are replaced by the L2 feature values (Schwartz and Sprouse (1996).

Sanchez and Al-Kasey claimed that if the Minimal Trees Hypothesis is correct, then it applies only at the very earliest stages of acquisition, because all the subjects in their study had clitics of some sort in their interlanguage. Lack of strong pronouns indicated that subjects were also beyond the Full Transfer stage. All three hypotheses were supported in that the subjects did not recognize clitics as licensers of left dislocation. In that two of the more syntactically advanced learners produced clitic doubling indicated that they were attempting a more complex specification of the conditions under which AgrO° and D° are spelled out.

Montrul (1997) examined the acquisition of dative experiencers, which, in Spanish, have both subject and object properties in the syntax, and occur with a class of psych verbs that includes *gustar*. For this class of psych verbs the experiencer appears to be in subject position but has dative case marking. The verb triggers agreement on the theme, which appears to remain in object position. A property unique to this class of psych verbs is that either one of the two arguments can appear in preverbal or postverbal position:

> *A Juan le gusta María.*
> to John-to him-is pleasing Mary
> "John likes Mary."

> *María le gusta a Juan.*
> Mary-to him-is pleasing-to John
> "John likes Mary."

The dative experiencer is common in non-psych verb unaccusative predicates like the "no fault" *se* construction.

> *A los niños se les ocurrió una idea.*
> to the children-to them-occurred-an idea
> "An idea occurred to the children."

Another class of psych verbs is straightforward transitive constructions in which the experiencer appears in subject position and the theme, a lower argument, appears in object position.

> *Juan teme el futuro.*
> "John fears the future."

For the other class of pysch verbs the experiencer appears in object position and the theme is in subject position.

> *Juan asusta a María.*
> "John frightens Mary."

Dative experiencers in Spanish are marked with dative case like a typical indirect object pronoun but obligatorily take clitic doubling whereas it is optional for indirect objects. Their subject properties include control over pronominalization in adjunct clauses as in the following.

> *Sin saber por qué, a Juan le gusta María.*
> "Without knowing why, John likes Mary."

They have this control because they are the most prominent argument. If second language learners have access to Universal Grammar, then they should recognize that agents are more prominent than themes and goals in agentive predicates and that experiencers are more prominent in psych predicates. In other words, they should perform according to the thematic hierarchy (agent/theme/goal).

Montrul examined the acquisition of dative experiencers by comparing two groups of low intermediate learners with a native-speaker control group. The learners were nineteen native speakers of English and seventeen native speakers of French who possessed varying levels of knowledge of English. The nonnative subjects all scored similarly on the MLA Placement Test and so were considered to be of equivalent Spanish proficiency. Subjects were asked to perform an interpretation task. Target sentences consisted of a main clause with two animate arguments and an infinitival adjunct clause, which was ambiguous in that it could be attributed to either animate argument in the main clause.

The interpretation tasks consisted of twenty-eight sentences of four main types that varied in thematic roles and syntactic positions.

1. Agent-active verb-accusative theme
   Al bajar del tren, la mujer abrazó al niño.
   "Upon getting off the train, the woman embraced the child."

2a. Dative experiencer-psych verb-nominative theme
    Sin saber por qué, a Juan le cae mal María.
    "Without knowing why, John does not like Mary."

2b. Dative experiencer-unaccusative *se* verb-nominative theme
    Al bajar del tren, a María se le escapó el perro.
    "Upon getting off the train, the dog escaped from Mary."

3a. Nominative experiencer-psych verb-accusative theme
    Sin saber por qué, Juan odia a Pedro.
    "Without knowing why, John hates Peter."

3b. Nominative *theme*-psych verb-accusative experiencer
    Al bajar del tren, María sorprendió a Juan.
    "Upon getting off the train, Mary surprised John."

4. Agent-ditransitive verb-dative goal

Pedro les escribió a mis padres antes de salir de viaje.

"Peter wrote my parents before leaving on a trip."

Subjects read the target sentence, underneath which appeared a question, followed by three possible answers.

Prompt: *A Juan le gusta María sin saber por qué.*

"John likes Mary without knowing why."

Question: *¿Quién no sabe por qué?*

"Who does not know why?"

Options: a. *Juan*   John

b. *María*   Mary

c. *Cualquier de los dos*   either one of the two

In half the sentences, the adjunct clause appeared in initial position and in the other half in final position. Subjects performed the interpretation task three times, in October, January, and April.

Overall results revealed that the language learners were at least 70 percent accurate in selecting the appropriate referent and perform in accordance with the thematic hierarchy. Both French and English speakers performed significantly differently than the control group at each of the three data gathering times. English-speaking and French-speaking subjects performed significantly differently from each other at times 1 and 3, with the French speakers outperforming the English speakers. Results on active versus psych verbs revealed that English speakers were significantly different from the control group on both active and psych verbs at each of the three times. The French speakers were significantly different from the control group on pysch verbs at each of the three times, but not on active verbs. Although Montrul had predicted no difference on active versus psych verbs, the latter presented the greater challenge for nonnative speakers. Accuracy in responses ranged from 65 percent to 84 percent for psych verbs and from 78 percent to 92 percent for active verbs. The English speakers performed significantly different from the control group on all sentence types except active agent. The French speakers performed significantly different from the control group and from the English speakers only on one sentence type, accusative psych verbs. No other significant differences between the French and English groups emerged. Based on these results, Montrul argued that these learners of Spanish still had access to Universal Grammar, that they did not entirely rely on their native languages to interpret the test sentences, and that they were sensitive to the different sentence types.

4.1 Summary of Research on Generative Theories of Syntax

Liceras et al. (1997) show us that L2 learners whose native language is French have a clitic slot in their interlanguage syntax but do not have a full set of casemarked pronouns to insert in that slot. Liceras (1985) showed that the value of clitics in interlanguage of L1 English and L1 French speakers is permeable: meaning that learners place clitics in both native and nonnative ways.[13] These data support two different theories of clitics, one being that clitics are generated from argument positions and the other that they are not.

Sanchez and Al-Kasey (1999) show us that the percentage of clitics in Spanish L2 learner speech is lower than in native speech. In contrast to natives, learners produce more overt direct objects for antecedents already established in discourse. Nonnatives produce no instances of left dislocation. Their data showed that in the early stages of L2 acquisition, L2 learners only partially specify the values of the functional category AgrO (Agreement Objects). Their data support three different theories of how functional categories operate in second language acquisition.

Montrul shows us that adult second language learners probably still have access to Universal Grammar to guide their acquisition of syntactic properties of the second language. Although she found that some learners are not misled by dative case marking and appropriately assign agents on all sentence types on the interpretation task, there was great individual variation in the data.[14]

4.2   Possible Directions for Future Research

The studies we have that examine object pronouns from a linguistic perspective demonstrate that learner data are an important source of information for supporting and refining generative theories of syntax. Taken as a group, these studies indicate the need for a longitudinal examination of the acquisition of object pronouns. The analyses might continue along the lines of Liceras's work and examine the emergent value of clitics in learner language or along those of Sanchez and Al-Kasey and examine how functional categories emerge in learner language to become more and more specified. Moreover, cognitively oriented research has shown us little about indirect object pronouns (VanPatten 1983) while linguistically oriented research shows us many nonnative uses of indirect object pronouns (Liceras et al. 1997).

The studies reviewed above offer us the instrumentation for the recommended longitudinal study. I would recommend the use of a sentence repetition task (Liceras et al. 1997); it is an easy way to gather data on a wide variety of syntactic patterns. In addition to analyzing the repetition of target elements, future research could also measure processing time, specifically, the time lag between when a target sentence is heard and the onset of learner speech. The picture-matching task enjoys a long history in cognitive and linguistic research (Sanchez and Al-Kasey 1999). Montrul's interpretation task, however, allows us to provide learners complex syntactic patterns, in particular, patterns that would be difficult to represent visually. The recommended longitudinal study should also combine processing and production data (Sanchez and Al-Kasey 1999). Finally, comparing the Spanish L2 clitic acquisition of monolingual English speakers with that of bilingual French/English speakers will not be as useful as research that exerts greater restrictions on the linguistic background of the French-speaking subjects. The question "Is third language learning the same as second language learning?" will always plague any generalization of the findings from these investigations.

5.0 Conclusion

By way of conclusion, I will offer a few general statements regarding the acquisition of object pronouns by classroom learners of Spanish as a second language, which will incorporate findings from both processing and production data as well as from cognitive and linguistic perspectives:

1. The use of the First Noun Strategy to assign grammatical roles and producing full noun phrases instead of object pronouns are probably related linguistic and cognitive phenomena. As a result of the First Noun Strategy, learners' developing systems are fed faulty data. Forms that are marked for accusative case are fed into the developing system as nominatives. The system would not necessarily contain a form for accusative case that it could access. Some would say that learners avoid using direct object pronouns and prefer to use full noun phrases even though the discourse would require a pronoun. Because "avoidance" sounds like a conscious performance strategy, I prefer to say that object pronominalization is acquisitionally delayed until the use of the First Noun Strategy is attenuated and the developing system is fed intake data that recognize accusative forms. To that end, processing instruction offers us a promising picture. The data consistently demonstrate that learners can be taught not to use the First Noun Strategy when they are given information on processing strategies and are provided structured input activities to practice making agent/object distinctions.

2. The value of object pronouns in learner language is permeable in that they may have both subject and object properties. Even fourth-semester learners of Spanish assign nominative, as well as accusative, case to object pronouns when processing sentences, indicating that they perceive these forms as having multiple values. It is likely then that when learners access their developing systems in order to produce an object pronoun, they assign it multiple values and do not restrict its placement in a completely nativelike manner. In this regard we may see distinctions between classroom and naturalistic learners. Andersen's 1983 data demonstrated that his naturalistic learner began the acquisition of object pronouns by restricting their form/function distribution. For example, the form *la* in native Spanish is both a direct object pronoun and a definite article. His subject, however, never used *la* as an object pronoun, only as a definite article; in fact, *la* was the only form of the definite article he used. Classroom learners, perhaps because instruction provides them paradigms and inventories of multiple forms, use the same form in multiple ways (e.g., *le* for *lo, nos* for *nosotros*). Whereas naturalistic learners must extract forms they perceive in the input, classroom learners must appropriately distribute the plethora of forms they are presented.

3. Object pronouns are a late acquired feature of nonnative Spanish. Even fourth-semester learners of Spanish employ the First Noun Strategy and learners enrolled in advanced courses show nonnative use of clitics: placement of a clitic after a conjugated verb, omission of a clitic but presence of nominal reduplication, and placement of a clitic in the middle of periphrastic verb phrases. Because object pronouns are late-acquired and involve syntax, morphology, and discourse semantics, they are an ideal linguistic item to examine longitudinally.

Several questions present themselves beyond the obvious one: What are the stages of development that characterize the acquisition of object pronouns by second language learners of Spanish? For instance, are there cognitive and/or linguistic prerequisites to object pronoun development? Are there cognitive and/or linguistic correlates of object pronoun development? Is object pronoun development a cognitive and/or linguistic prerequisite for the acquisition of some other feature of Spanish? With these important questions outstanding, it is obvious the case is not closed on the acquisition of object pronouns in Spanish as a second language.

ACKNOWLEDGMENT

I thank my colleague Kimberly Geeslin for providing feedback on an earlier version of this chapter. Her comments on generative theories were extremely helpful.

NOTES

1. Throughout this review of previous research I have tried to report findings in a consistent manner. Because different authors reported data in different ways, I have taken the liberty of reporting their findings my own way. For example, many studies reported data as individual performance, whereas I report it in aggregate terms. Some authors only provided raw numbers whereas I report percentages. I have done this only for the sake of consistency.

2. The fullest version of the present review would contain a section on the acquisition of various word order patterns, of which OproVS is only one pattern. Length constraints as well as a desire to maintain a coherent focus led to the decision to exclude such a section. For L1 acquisition, the reader is directed to González (1997), who cites Echevarría's work on Chilean children. González's work would also be included as an example of an L2 study on the acquisition of various word orders, as would Glisan (1985) and Sagarra (2001).

3. I have purposefully excluded from this review work on object pronouns carried out in language contact situations such as Spanish/Quechua, Spanish/English, or Spanish/Catalan. Perhaps the issues are similar, perhaps not. My decision was one of maintaining a coherent focus in this work on classroom language learners.

4. In later publications (e.g., 1996), VanPatten refers to the First Noun Strategy as a universal default processing strategy that characterizes early stage language acquisition.

5. González only indirectly relates her work on nonnatives with Echevarría's work with native speakers.

6. See chapter 10 of this volume for further discussion of Processing Instruction.

7. Salaberry (1997) is purposefully not included in this section on Processing Instruction because, in part, his research is not framed by the First Noun Strategy, which is the organizing principle of my review of the literature. Sanz and VanPatten's (1998) response to his article clearly points out, among other problematic aspects, how his study confuses input processing and meaning interpretation tasks with comprehension. My specific critique of Salaberry (1997) is that the goal of processing instruction on object pronouns is to affect learners' use of the First Noun Strategy for interpreting sentences with preverbal object pronouns. Salaberry never mentions the First Noun Strategy. Processing Instruction would overtly address learners' use of the First Noun Strategy, a focus that is clearly not a feature of the sample exercise Salaberry (1997, 449) provided: *¿Tienes el bronceador? Sí, aquí (yo/tú/lo/la) tengo.* "Do you have the tanning lotion?

Yes, here (I) have (I, you, it [m], it [f])." To assess the effect of Processing Instruction with an input-based task would require a researcher to determine if learners' use of the First Noun Strategy had been attenuated. Salaberry's assessment task, which is similar to his instructional activity, failed to do so. This pronoun-selection task does not require learners to interpret the meaning of object pronouns, that is, to assign the pronoun the grammatical role of object, not subject.

8. An anonymous reviewer suggested that I address the impoverished quality of the input classroom learners are exposed to as a factor to explain their lack of development with object pronouns. Because this chapter is a review of empirical works, I cannot do so, for it would only be anecdotal evidence I would cite. To my knowledge no study has directly related teacher talk to the acquisition of object pronouns.

9. Newer versions of generative theories do not refer to surface structure. Instead, they refer to "spell out" and would say that pronouns are present in pro-drop languages in the logical/semantic structure but are not then phonetically realized.

10. Liceras (1985), the original study, was conducted under a Government and Binding Framework and predated the Minimalist Program. In her 1996 work, Liceras attempts to update the 1985 Government and Binding discussion to a 1996 Minimalist Program discussion. The issues uniquely relevant to each get a bit confused.

11. Montrul (1997:191–93) provides a thorough discussion of dative experiencers.

12. Although Liceras et al. (1997) do not consider it, I believe we must consider the tremendous language experience of the subjects they examined.

13. See chapter 7 of this volume for further discussion of the study of the acquisition of Spanish L2 clitics within a generative framework.

14. An anonymous reviewer suggested that I include the research conducted on the acquisition of null subjects. Although I believe this work is related to the acquisition of clitics, reviewing it would be beyond the scope of the present work.

WORKS CITED

Andersen, R. W. 1983. Transfer to somewhere. In *Language transfer in language learning,* eds. S. M. Gass and L. Selinker, 177–201. Rowley, MA: Newbury House.

———. 1990. Models, processes, principles and strategies: Acquisition inside and outside the classroom. In *Second language acquisition-foreign language learning,* eds. B. VanPatten and J. F. Lee, 45–68. Clevedon: Multilingual Matters.

Chomsky, N. 1981. *Lectures on government and binding.* Dordrecht: Foris.

———. 1995. *The minimalist program.* Cambridge, MA: MIT Press.

Echevarría, M. S. 1978. *Desarrollo de la comprensión infantil de la sintaxis española.* Concepción, Chile: Universidad de Concepción.

Eubank, L. 1993. On the transfer of parametric values in L2 development. *Language Acquisition* 3:183–208.

Glisan, E. 1985. The effect of word order on oral comprehension in learners of L2 Spanish. *Language Learning* 35:443–72.

González, N. 1997. A parametric study of L2 acquisition: Interpretation of Spanish word order. In *Contemporary perspectives on the acquisition of Spanish,* vol. 1, *Developing grammars,* eds. A. T. Pérez-Leroux and W. R. Glass, 133–48. Somerville, MA: Cascadilla Press.

Houston, T. 1997. Sentence processing in Spanish as a second language: A study of word order and background knowledge. In *Contemporary perspectives on the acquisition of Spanish,* vol. 2, *Production, processing and comprehension,* eds. W. R. Glass and A. T. Pérez-Leroux, 123–34. Somerville, MA: Cascadilla Press.

Lee, J. F. 1987. Morphological factors influencing pronominal reference assignment by learners of Spanish. In *Language and language use: Studies in Spanish,* eds. T. Morgan, J. F. Lee, and B. VanPatten, 221–32. Lanham, MD: University Press of America.

———. 2000. Comprehending subject-object relations while processing object pronouns in written input. In *Spanish applied linguistics at the turn of the millennium: Papers from the 1999 conference on the L1 & L2 acquisition of Spanish and Portuguese*, eds. R. P. Leow and C. Sanz, 119–40. Somerville, MA: Cascadilla Press.

Lee, J. F., and B. VanPatten. 1995. *Making communicative language teaching happen.* New York: McGraw-Hill.

Liceras, J. 1985. The value of clitics in non-native Spanish. *Second Language Research* 1:151–86.

———. 1986. *Linguistic theory and second language acquisition: The Spanish non-native grammar of English speakers.* Tübingen: Gunter Narr.

———. 1996. *La adquisición de las lenguas segundas y la gramática universal.* Madrid: Editorial Síntesis.

Liceras, J. M., D. Maxwell, B. Laguardia, Z. Fernández, R. Fernández, and L. Díaz. 1997. A longitudinal study of Spanish non-native grammars: Beyond parameters. In *Contemporary perspectives on the acquisition of Spanish,* vol. 1, *Developing grammars,* eds. A. T. Pérez-Leroux and W. R. Glass, 99–132. Somerville, MA: Cascadilla Press.

LoCoco, V. 1987. Learner comprehension of oral and written sentences in German and Spanish: The importance of word order. In *Foreign language learning: A research perspective,* eds. B. VanPatten, T. R. Dvorak, and J. F. Lee, 119–29. Cambridge, MA: Newbury House.

Montrul, S. A. 1997. Spanish *gustar* psych verbs and the unaccusative *se* construction: The case of dative experiencers in SLA. In *Contemporary perspectives on the acquisition of Spanish,* vol. 1, *Developing grammars,* eds. A. T. Pérez-Leroux and W. R. Glass, 189–207. Somerville, MA: Cascadilla Press.

Sagarra, N. 2001. The role of syntactic modifications on L2 oral comprehension. In *Romance syntax, semantics and L2 acquisition,* eds. J. Camps and C. Wiltshire, 197–210. Amsterdam: John Benjamins.

Salaberry, M. R. 1997. The role of input and output practice in second language acquisition. *Canadian Modern Language Review* 53:422–51.

Sanchez, L., and T. Al-Kasey. 1999. L2 acquisition of Spanish direct objects. *Spanish Applied Linguistics* 3:1–32.

Sanz, C., and B. VanPatten. 1998. On input processing, processing instruction, and the nature of replication tasks: A response to Salaberry. *Canadian Modern Language Review* 54:263–73.

Schwartz, B., and R. Sprouse. 1996. L2 cognitive states and the full transfer/full access model. *Second Language Research* 12:40–72.

Slobin, D. 1973. Cognitive prerequisites for the development of grammar. In *Studies of child language development,* eds. D. Slobin and C. Ferguson, 175–276. Hillsdale, NJ: Lawrence Erlbaum.

Vainnika, A., and M. Young-Scholten. 1996. The early stages in adult L2 syntax: Additional evidence from Romance speakers. *Second Language Research* 12:7–39.

VanPatten, B. 1983. Processing strategies in second language acquisition. Ph.D. diss., University of Texas at Austin.

———. 1984. Learners' comprehension of clitic pronouns: More evidence for a word order strategy. *Hispanic Linguistics* 1:57–67.

———. 1990. The acquisition of clitic pronouns in Spanish: Two case studies. In *Second language acquisition-foreign language learning,* eds. B. VanPatten and J. F. Lee, 118–39. Clevedon: Multilingual Matters.

———. 1996. *Input processing and grammar instruction: Theory and research.* Norwood, NJ: Ablex.

VanPatten, B., and T. Cadierno. 1993. Explicit instruction and input processing. *Studies in Second Language Acquisition* 15:225–43.

VanPatten, B., and T. Houston. 1998. Contextual effects in processing L2 input sentences. *Spanish Applied Linguistics* 2:53–70.

VanPatten, B., J. F. Lee, W. R. Glass, and D. Binkowski. 1992. *Manual que acompaña ¿Sabías que . . . ?* New York: McGraw-Hill.

VanPatten, B., and S. Oikkenon. 1996. Explanation versus structured input in processing instruction. *Studies in Second Language Acquisition* 18:495–510.

VanPatten, B., and C. Sanz. 1995. From input to output: Processing instruction and communicative tasks. In *Second language acquisition theory and pedagogy,* eds. F. R. Eckman, D. Highland, P. W. Lee, J. Mileham, and R. R. Weber, 169–85. Hillsdale, NJ: Lawrence Erlbaum.

5
Lexicon

The Acquisition of Lexical Meaning by Second Language Learners: An Analysis of General Research Trends with Evidence from Spanish

BARBARA A. LAFFORD   Arizona State University

JOSEPH G. COLLENTINE   Northern Arizona University

ADAM S. KARP   American River College

1.0   Introduction

After a period of relative neglect vis-à-vis other aspects of second language learning (phonology, grammar and discourse issues), the study of L2 vocabulary acquisition has gained momentum in the last fifteen years. Long and Richards (1997:ix) note that since the mid-1980s there has been "a growing body of empirically based studies of such issues as the nature of the bilingual lexicon, vocabulary acquisition, lexical storage, lexical retrieval, and the use of vocabulary by second language learners." However, most of this research has been carried out on data gathered from learners of languages other than Spanish.[1]

This chapter will present an overview of important issues involved in the study of the acquisition of a second language lexicon by focusing on several key points:

- The importance of the study of second language vocabulary
- The composition of the L2 lexicon
- The organization of the L2 lexicon
- The determination of lexical competence
- The facilitation of L2 vocabulary acquisition

A review of studies of L2 lexical acquisition carried out on data gathered from learners of Spanish as a second/foreign language will be included in the general discussion of these issues. The chapter will conclude with a discussion of the limitations of the existing Spanish L2 lexical research and an agenda for future L2 vocabulary acquisition studies.

2.0 Issues Involved in L2 Vocabulary Acquisition Studies

2.1 The Importance of the Study of Second Language Vocabulary

The importance of the study of L2 vocabulary is evident from research findings cited by Gass and Selinker (2001:372): (1) lexical errors constitute most L2 errors and (2) both learners and native speakers view lexical errors as the most serious and disruptive obstacles to communication. Levelt (1989:181) even asserts that the L1 lexicon is the "driving force in sentence production" inasmuch as it mediates conceptualization and the encoding of grammar and phonology. Gass and Selinker (2001) extend this idea to L2 contexts by stating, "In general, there is good reason to believe that the lexicon is an important factor, if not the most important factor, in accounting for the bulk of second language data, in that the lexicon mediates language production" (373). In addition, recent research supports a positive relationship between lexical knowledge and reading comprehension (Hawas 1990; Koda 1989; Laufer 1992; Mecartty 2000) as well as listening comprehension (Kelly 1991; Mecartty 2000).

2.2 The Composition of the L2 Lexicon

Many scholars seem to agree that L1 and L2 lexicons are composed of codified lexical items at the word level or higher. According to Schmitt and McCarthy (1997) a lexical item, or a lexeme, is "an item which functions as a single meaning unit, regardless of the number or orthographical words it contains. *Fly, pain-induced,* and *put your nose to the grindstone* are all lexical items" (329). That is, the lexicon stores semantic units as both single- and multi-word items (e.g., phrases, idioms, proverbs). Ellis (1997) asserts that among the first items acquired by L2 learners are formulaic utterances ("lexical phrases"), which are later analyzed by segmentation (e.g., *buenos días* "good morning," *por favor* "please," *no sé* "I don't know"). Similarly, Terrell's (1986) Binding Access framework asserts that unanalyzed phonological chunks are first "bound" to a general meaning and are later reanalyzed into lexical stems and grammatical properties, for example, *teng-o* "I have" (*-o* is an inflectional morpheme indicating a first-person singular subject of the verb *tener* "to have").

2.3 The Organization of the L2 Lexicon

Meara (1997) points out that the lack of tradition of using formal organizational models in applied linguistics literature has prevented much fruitful communication between psycholinguistics and applied linguistics. Meara, therefore, advocates more model-based research on L2 vocabulary acquisition to facilitate communication between applied linguistics research and other model-based disciplines asking similar research questions about the acquisition of the lexicon. It is therefore proper to ask how formal and cognitive theories of language envision the organization of the lexicon and its interaction with other levels of linguistic representation such as morphology, syntax, and phonology.

2.3.1 Universal Grammar's View of the Lexicon

The Principles and Parameters perspective envisions the lexicon as a dictionary (Cook 1988), containing words subcategorized for a variety of syntactic, grammatical, and semantic features.

beber	"to drink"	[−noun,+verb], subject=agent, [+transitive]
bebida	"drink"	[+noun,−verb], [+inanimate]

In this model, the lexicon resides in one's peripheral grammar, receiving little assistance from innate (core), universal principles of language. This makes the development of lexical idiosyncrasies a more difficult task than the development of syntactic knowledge (Cook 1988). The *structure dependency principle* (Chomsky 1988; Cook 1994) has an important effect on the nature of the lexicon, stipulating that any grammatical operation (e.g., movement, lexical insertion) must consider the syntactic environment at hand. Thus, a learner's lexicon would dictate that *bebida* (a noun) rather than *beber* (a verb) could combine with [*tengo* [. . .]] "I have."

The Minimalist Program (Chomsky 1990, 1995) posits that *all* linguistic idiosyncrasies reside in the lexicon. In addition to dictionary entries, the lexicon stores derivational, inflectional, and free grammatical morphemes. For instance, Principles and Parameters predicts that learners of an L2 must reset certain parameters. Spanish students might need to learn that the clause is a binding domain; independently, students would learn the reflexive pronouns. On the other hand, minimalism posits that one learns individual parameters for individual words.

2.3.2 Connectionist View of the Lexicon

Connectionism aims to model the neural organization and processes of language (see MacWhinney 1997; Ellis 1999). Connectionists assume that the brain stores information in networks of nodes, or relatively discrete knowledge structures. The process of creating (binding) form-meaning relationships occurs when neural networks are strengthened over time as the learner frequently encounters the item in the input. The connectionist perspective predicts that although different levels of representation are localized (neurologically speaking), there is no strict modularization.

Connectionism also views linguistic knowledge to be integrated with academic knowledge (i.e., what we know about the world), be it concrete or abstract (Ellis 1999; Alexander, Schallert, and Hare 1991). For instance, Universal Grammar (UG) predicts that vocabulary errors result from erroneous lexical entries or performance factors (see Levelt 1989). A connectionist would view an error as an insight into the organization of lexical knowledge and that knowledge's relationship to other knowledge sources. The connectionist perspective recognizes that the words that learners use are quite sensitive to so-called priming effects, or the processing of one node simply because a related node (i.e., one that is semantically or structurally related) has been activated. For example, in an activity relating to food, a learner may be hard-pressed to generate in the foreign language a term relating to medicine even if the term is fully acquired, because the learner's present cognitive activity does not require the activation of medical terms.

The connectionist view not only recognizes the existence of codified multiword chunks in the lexicon, but some theoreticians also propose a central role for them during production. Crick (1979) asserts that the mind has a vast storage capacity but a limited processing capacity (see Ellis 1997:230). Fluency, he asserts, is the use of prefabricated and memorized lexical phrases rather than the employment of syntactic rules. That is, connectionists believe that language production is "the retrieval of larger phrase units from memory" rather than being rule governed (Zimmerman 1997:17).

Whereas the UG perspective views lexical development as an accumulation of entities, Connectionism posits that such entities must also be organized into efficient (neurological) networks (Elman et al. 1996). At the moment a learner is discussing (or reading about) foods, he or she should be able to activate culinary terms much more quickly than terms relating to computer technologies.

Ellis (1996) provides an overview of sequencing in SLA and proposes that much of the acquisition of language is due to learning of sequences. While acquiring vocabulary, the L2 learner becomes familiar with the phonological units of the target language and their phonotactic sequences. In order to create L2 discourse, the learner acquires lexical units and knowledge of their placement and sequences within clauses. According to Ellis (1996), "the resultant long-term knowledge base of language sequences serves as the database for the acquisition of language grammar" (91). One of the major factors that determine the ability of an individual to learn a language is the capacity of his/her short-term memory (STM), "the ability to remember simple verbal strings in order" (92). Interaction between STM and long-term memory allows chunking and fine-tuning of L2 systems to reflect structural information for particular languages. The article concludes with a very insightful comparison of Connectionist and UG theories, in which Ellis (1996) points out not only how the two models differ, but how they can complement each other in the quest for understanding of the acquisition of L2 lexicons.

2.4 The Determination of Lexical Competence

Meara (1996) proposes that lexical competence is measured by both the size (breadth) of a learner's store of lexical items and the organization of those items.

2.4.1 Size

The size of a learner's vocabulary predicts well a learner's reading and writing abilities (Nation and Waring 1997; Laufer 1998). According to Laufer (1997), vocabulary size better predicts reading success than syntax and general reading ability, and Wittrock, Marks, and Doctorow (1975) even suggest that a lack of knowledge of a single word can impede comprehension. Laufer (1997) conjectures that good L1 readers need a "threshold vocabulary" of about three thousand word "families" (24)—e.g., *lengua* "a specific language," *lenguas* "languages," *lenguaje* "language ability"—to interpret an authentic text. Most scholars agree that extensive reading, which promotes incidental learning, advances lexical development after the attainment of the threshold (Huckin and Coady 1999:182).[2] Still, students need strategies for learning less frequent vocabulary after reaching the threshold (Nation 1990).

Read (2000) describes a pioneering initiative in the area of vocabulary size assessment carried out by Paribahkt and Wesche (1997, 1999), which proposes the use of the Vocabulary Knowledge Scale (VKS) for use in research on incidental vocabulary acquisition. The graduated five-point scale invites learners to indicate their level of familiarity with a particular lexeme. Joe's (1995, 1998) studies modified the VKS by adding another category and also asked learners to retell orally information read in a reading task. Joe found that the act of retelling the information led to significant gains in depth of knowledge of key content words, especially when the subjects were encouraged by the researcher to exert greater mental effort in processing the information.

Karp's (2002) study (N = 80) further expanded the depth of vocabulary knowledge assessed by the VKS by prompting learners of Spanish to demonstrate awareness of words semantically related to the target items and to write additional sentences using inflectionally or derivationally related words. However, contrary to the expected outcome, Karp found that glossary use did not significantly predict greater depth of vocabulary knowledge. This suggests that the complexity of modifications made to the simpler five-point graduated scale of the original VKS may have diminished the effectiveness of this instrument.

These refinements of the VKS instrument, which lead to gains in depth of knowledge of vocabulary items in Joe's study, begin to address the concern that several researchers (Meara 1996; Read 1993, 1997; Wesche and Paribahkt 1999; Karp 2002) have expressed about the need for further research on ways to assess aspects of vocabulary knowledge other than size (e.g., organization of the vocabulary items in the lexicon and depth of knowledge of individual words). It is through the development of such rigorous instruments that more insights can be gained into the stages of vocabulary acquisition, as form-meaning connections are incrementally made (bound) and stored in a learner's lexicon.

2.4.2   Organization: What Does It Mean to Know a Word?

Knowledge of a word requires an understanding of its spoken and written form, frequency, grammatical patterns and collocations, semantic, pragmatic, stylistic and register constraints, sociolinguistic aspects, and connotations as well as its associations with other related words (Nation 1990; Nation and Waring 1997).[3] Indeed, Meara (1996) proposes that a learner's ability to make connections between words is what distinguishes a true vocabulary from a mere list of words.

Laufer (1997) discusses factors that make a word hard or easy to learn, such as pronounceability, orthography, morphology, synformy,[4] and semantic features (e.g., abstractness, register restriction, multiple meanings). Other factors that may facilitate or inhibit a learner's ability to acquire the target language include (1) the orthographic distance between the L1 and L2: a L2 learner who already speaks a L1 written with an alphabet (Koda 1989; A. Ryan 1997); (2) the transparency (shallowness) or opacity of the L2 orthography: transparent (shallow) orthographies have a clear phoneme/grapheme correspondence with only a few exceptions (e.g., Spanish) while opaque orthographies match several different orthographic strings to one phonological realization (e.g., English) (Jiménez González and Hernández Valle 2000); (3) *neighborhood effects*: a word's physical relationship to other words, for example, "flight" differs only by a single letter from the target word "fright" (Andrews 1997; Carreiras, Perea, and Grainer 1997); (4) the ability to transfer knowledge from their L1 to understanding of the L2 and improve L2 reading proficiency (e.g., conscious recognition of cognates) (Koda 1989, 1994; Jiménez, García, and Pearson 1996). However, because no study of these issues has been carried out using adult L2 learners of Spanish, these aspects of L2 vocabulary acquisition will not be explored in detail here.

Henricksen (1999), building on the work of Aitchison (1994) and Meara (1996), offers a microconnectionist view of the L2 lexicon that expands Ellis's (1994) macro model. Henricksen distinguishes between three types of knowledge of a word: partial/precise knowledge; depth of knowledge about the word; and receptive/productive dimension.

2.4.2.1 Partial-precise knowledge dimension

Lexical development involves the incremental *mapping* of various features onto an item. Two processes are involved in mapping: *semantization/labeling* and *packaging*. The terms *semantization/labeling* refer to Saussurian (Saussure 1916) *intrasign* relations, or the mapping of meaning *(signatum)* onto form *(signans)*. This process is also known as *binding* (Terrell 1986) or, from a connectionist perspective, the strengthening and amplification of related nodes. This process is longitudinally dynamic. A student of Spanish initially might associate *galleta* with "cracker" and later extend it to "cookie," or a learner might overgeneralize the extension of *pescado* to both food and live fish.

The other component of mapping, *packaging* (adding features to a lexical item, e.g., pragmatic, sociolinguistic, contextual/dialectic, and metaphoric features), requires extensive reading and listening as well as interaction with a native speaker (e.g., a lengthy stay in the target culture on a study-abroad program). Packaging is an arduous process, because learners often make naive assumptions about the relationship between the native and target languages, for example, that words have exact equivalents in different languages (Naïve Lexical Hypothesis, see Guntermann 1992a:184). Upon noticing that their original hypotheses are too simplistic, learners look for other potential meanings of the target form in the input (see Andersen's Multifunctionality Principle, Andersen 1990). Relationships between L1 and L2 lexical forms (cognates) or between similar L2 forms (synforms) can delay packaging. Although true cognates are helpful to the L2 learner, false cognates such as *embarazada* "pregnant" are not. The packaging process may also be negatively affected by the teaching of similar L2 forms (synforms) at the same time, such as "affect/ effect" (see Laufer 1997).

As mentioned, formulaic chunks (e.g., *meter la nariz* "to stick one's nose into someone's business") also behave as discrete lexical items during development. According to Moon (1997) formal errors may result from learner's failure to recognize that the string of words is noncompositional (e.g., ESL learners produce "the smallest" for "at least") or from using a calque of a L1 multiword unit (e.g., Spanish speakers learning English might use "to pull one's hair" [*tomarle el pelo a alguien*] for "to pull one's leg"). Pragmatic errors may arise when learners misunderstand or misuse multiword units in a given discursive context, such as *¡Con permiso!* "Excuse me!" (instead of the more appropriate *perdón*) after stepping on someone's toe. Stylistic errors may occur "through use of an excessively marked multi-word item—very rare, dated or over-informal, or in an inappropriate genre" (Moon 1997:60) (e.g., using *Erase una vez* "Once upon a time" in a scholarly historical essay). All of these errors are often exacerbated by the learner's lack of relevant sociocultural background knowledge (e.g., having to know about the Christian reconquest of Moorish Spain in order to understand the phrase *Hay moros en la costa* "There are Moors on the coast" = "The walls have ears").

2.4.2.2   Partial-precise dimension research using Spanish L2 data

Spanish L2 research examining the partial-precise dimension has examined mapping (semantization/labeling and packaging), in the acquisition of the two copula verbs *(ser/estar)* and the prepositions *por/para*.

2.4.2.2.1   Stages of acquisition of Spanish lexical items: *Ser* versus *estar*[5]   The 1970s morpheme order studies explored the sequential development of different grammatical morphemes by child and adult learners of English (see Dulay and Burt 1974; Bailey, Madden, and Krashen 1974) and found general parallel orders of acquisition for these groups. In the early 1980s Spanish L1 and L2 researchers (see Van Naerssen 1980, 1986) investigated the acquisition of the Spanish copula *(ser/estar)* relative to other grammatical structures (e.g., various past tense forms). Yet, by comparing these verbs with inflectional morphemes, scholars did not treat the copulas as lexical phenomena. Nevertheless, Lafford (1986) asserts that abstract semantic features (primarily relational features, with *estar* being more marked than *ser*) still distinguish the two.

Van Naerssen (1980) used oral data to study copula acquisition and revealed that students (N = 15) had good control (73.7 percent accuracy) after a year of study using the Natural Approach. However, the accuracy rates for *ser* and *estar* were averaged into one category "copula," so it is impossible to tell which copula was used more accurately. Smith (1980), whose seventy-seven subjects were at the beginning level, also found good "copula" control in compositions; however, these scores may be inflated because the participants could monitor their written production.

In the late 1970s and early 1980s scholars shifted their attention from orders of acquisition (recognizing the limitations of the "accumulated entities assumption"; see Dulay, Burt, and Krashen 1982) to stages of acquisition of particular structures (e.g., negation; Schumann 1979). Van Patten (1985, 1987) investigated the stages of acquisition of *ser* and *estar*. His 1985 study involved six adults learning Spanish as a foreign language in a communicatively based first-year university-level classroom. Tasks involved conversations and picture-descriptive storytelling. The 1987 study added a grammaticality judgment task with a different group of learners (with one to two and a half years of study) and classroom observation data. VanPatten (1987) posits five—largely sequential—stages in the packaging of these copulas.

1. Absence of copula in learner speech
   Juan alto. *"John tall."

2. Selection of *ser* to perform most copula functions
   Juan es alto. "John is tall."
   Juan es enfermo. "John is sick."
   Juan es estudiando. "John is studying."

3. Appearance of *estar* with progressive
   Juan está estudiando. "John is studying."

4. Appearance of *estar* with locatives
   Juan está en la clase. "John is in the classroom."

5. Appearance of *estar* with adjectives of condition
   Juan está enfermo. "John is sick."

VanPatten (1987) proposes that the interaction of four developmental processes accounts for these stages: (1) Communicative value—both copulas are "meaningless functors" in terms of propositional content; (2) Simplification—in stage 2, the learners used only one of the copulas (*ser*). Additionally, the noncontrastive uses appear (e.g., *estar* + progressive) before the contrastive uses (e.g., *ser/estar* + locatives, *estar* + adjectives); (3) Transfer—English-speaking learners tend to linger in stage 2 because English has only one copula (see Andersen's Transfer to Somewhere Principle; Andersen 1983); (4) frequency in input—learners hear and read fewer *estar* forms.

Other scholars have investigated the acquisition of the copulas in a study-abroad context. For instance, DeKeyser (1990) showed that the classroom development of the copulas differs from their study-abroad development and that *ser* is used more accurately than *estar* during this process. In addition, Ryan and Lafford (1992) examined the stages of *ser* and *estar* in a study-abroad context. Sixteen students in an intensive beginning-level, study abroad program participated in a series of oral interviews. Ryan and Lafford defined "acquisition" as 90 percent accuracy on the use of a copula in a given function on at least one of the interviews. Like VanPatten, they found *ser* used consistently more correctly than *estar; ser* accuracy hovered around 90 percent throughout the data-collection period, while *estar* generally never reached that level. The study-abroad data from Ryan and Lafford's (1992) study partially contradict VanPatten's classroom findings: *estar* is acquired in conditional before locative contexts. Ryan and Lafford also observed a protracted use of zero copula in conditional contexts calling for *estar.*

Guntermann (1992b) investigated *ser* and *estar* stages, examining conversational data (Oral Proficiency Interviews) from nine Peace Corps volunteers who studied Spanish in both the classroom and abroad. For each informant, two conversations were analyzed: one recorded at the completion of the experience abroad and another a year later. Guntermann's findings were partially consistent with VanPatten (1985, 1987) and Ryan and Lafford (1992), but she added a stage: the late acquisition of the *ser* passive construction. Guntermann also provides a functional perspective, discussing the discursive roles of certain formulaic expressions (e.g., *es muy mal* "It's very bad" as a topic closer).

Finnemann (1990) investigated the interaction of markedness relations between *ser* (unmarked) and *estar* (marked), and learning styles (form- or meaning-oriented) and copula development. He charted the copula development of three university-level foreign language learners; at the inception of the study, none had any knowledge of Spanish. Based on oral data, Finnemann argued that learning style interacted with how these learners employed the two copulas.

Recent work on the acquisition of the copulas *ser* and *estar* has been carried out by Geeslin (2000, 2001), who points out the need to study the acquisition of the copula without judging SLA data against prescriptive normative use of these verbs (an approach that was characteristic of the aforementioned studies). Geeslin (2000) proposes a new approach to the study of the structure [copula + adjective] that takes into account the interaction of contextual features such as frame of reference (class versus individual), susceptibility to change, adjective class (age, size, color, physical appearance), modality (the degree to which the adjective changes its meaning with *ser* or *estar*), dynamicity, perfectivity, grammatical accuracy, task, and the like. Her study of seventy-seven high school students of Spanish from four different levels involved eliciting the copulas in three tasks: oral interview, picture description, and contextualized questionnaire. The results show that different contextual features play significant roles at the various levels of acquisition of *estar*. Thus, Geeslin has paved the way for further research into the ways in which context at the sentence and discourse levels influences the selection of certain lexical items.

Geeslin (2001) looks at how the variability of native speaker norms of copula usage poses a challenge to SLA researchers who wish to measure the accuracy of learners' copula choice. In this study, ten educated native speakers of Spanish from five Spanish-speaking countries (Mexico, Spain, Chile, Peru, and Guatemala) were asked to fill out a fifteen-item contextualized questionnaire in which three copula contexts were tested: "Those in which only *ser* is allowed by native speakers, those where only *estar* is allowed by native speakers, and those where native speakers disagree, despite the fact that the discourse context is specified" (37). The participants in this study were taken from the same pool as those of Geeslin (2000). The results showed that the *estar*-only (allowed) contexts were the only accurate predictors of learners' accurate copula choice. Geeslin hypothesizes that the learners' tendency to overgeneralize *ser* in the beginning stages of development may account for the lack of this copula's consistent predictive ability regarding the accuracy of copula choice at the various levels.

Both of Geeslin's studies constitute a qualitative step forward in the analysis of the acquisition of Spanish copulas, inasmuch as they point out the need to look at SLA data on its own terms and to judge learner progress in the acquisition of lexical or grammatical items only in those contexts in which there is native speaker agreement on their usage. Geeslin notes that researchers must be cautious when comparing learner interlanguage systems to native speaker norms for lexical and grammatical usage, which, in and of themselves, may be variable and in the process of renegotiating the boundaries of their semantic and/or syntactic territories.[6] Because of the small sample size (especially of the native speakers involved in Geeslin 2001), these results call for further investigation of the various lines of research proposed in both these innovative studies.

2.4.2.2.2   Stages of acquisition of Spanish lexical items: *Por* versus *para*[7]   Guntermann (1992a) used the same methodology as Guntermann (1992b) to investigate the acquisition (packaging) of the prepositions *por* and *para*. Lunn (1978) informed the data codification (with some modifications). Excluding formulaic utterances (e.g., *por ejemplo* "for example"), subjects were significantly more accurate with *para* (73 percent) than with *por* (32 percent); *para* was also targeted more frequently than *por.* Guntermann (1992a) offers several explanations: (1) the Naive Lexical Hypothesis, or every L1 word has an L2 equivalent, causes learners to equate L1 "for" with L2 *por;* (2) *para* is less marked than *por* (see Beale 1978); and (3), similar to VanPatten's (1985) communicative value hypothesis, *para* seems to be more essential for communication from the beginning. Furthermore, similar to Finnemann (1990), individual learners tend to favor one preposition, with *por* being favored by less proficient learners.

Lafford and Ryan (1995) investigated the correct suppliance of *por* and *para* and over-generalizations used by Spanish L2 learners abroad. The data were collected from ACTFL-style oral interviews conducted with nine learners three times throughout one semester; two native speakers corroborated the analysis. Their study's results concurred for the most part with those of Guntermann (1992a); *para* is generally targeted more often and more correctly than *por* across proficiency levels. Lafford and Ryan (1995) also propose a relative order of acquisition (packaging) of various functions of *por* and *para* based on the correct ("canonical") uses of these prepositions prescribed by Lunn (1978). However, these authors also go a step further and carry out a detailed analysis of the incorrect ("non-canonical") uses of the prepositions: the substitution of these two prepositions for each other and for conjunctions, the systematic variability in the use of *por* and *para* in time expressions, and the use of both prepositions (especially *para*) as deictic markers of topicalization.

2.4.2.2.3   The acquisition of Spanish multiword utterances   Liontas (1999, 2003) are the only studies to date to investigate the acquisition of Spanish L2 multiword utterances. Liontas (1999, 2003) examined the comprehension and interpretation of *vivid phrasal idioms,* whose meaning is not transparent based on its elements (e.g., *le falta un tornillo* = "he has a screw loose"; *cuando las ranas críen pelo* "when frogs grow hair" = "when pigs fly"). Eighty English-speaking foreign-language learners of French, German, and Spanish, all enrolled in third-level university classes, participated in this study. Experimental and qualitative data indicated that a learner's lack of background and cultural knowledge interacts with the interpretation of the vivid phrasal idiom to affect comprehension: "The degree of difficulty associated with the comprehension and interpretation of the TL [target language] idiom corresponds to the degree of distance associated with the semantic/imagery distance between TL and NL idioms" (1999:119).

2.4.2.3   *Depth of knowledge dimension*

The least studied aspect of the learner's lexicon is the depth-of-knowledge dimension (Henriksen 1999; Haastrup and Henriksen 2000), or the structure of the student's lexical knowledge, that is, how different lexical items relate to one another. Learners need optimal neurological networks to access lexical items efficiently, achieved through the creation of "intentional links" and "sense relations" between lexemes (see Aitchison 1994). For example, *ardiente* "burning" might be linked to *caliente* "hot" via a synonymous connection, *despierto* "awake" and *dormido* "asleep" via antonymy, and *fresco* "cool" and *frío* "cold" as a gradation. Markedness relations also influence the network-construction process. Early on, errors and word-association tasks indicate that the intrasign connections between synforms, or phonologically similar signs (e.g., *hombre* "man" versus *hambre* "hungry"), have the most robust influence on performance (see Meara 1978; Gass and Selinker 2001).

In addition, Schmitt and Meara (1997) showed that grammatical knowledge and word-association knowledge are related and have an important impact on performance. For instance, Lafford and Collentine (1987) report that third-year foreign language learners regularly commit errors involving derivationally related items, e.g., the use of *Voy a la <u>universitaria</u>* "I am going to the (pertaining to the) university" (adjectival meaning) instead of *universidad* "university" (noun form). Learners apparently are quick to incorporate a new term into their networks that might fill some perceived gap (Brown, Sagers, and LaPorte 1999). In the absence of a known candidate, students often employ an L1 word or create neologisms based on L1 or L2 morphological rules, e.g., the use of *tení* for *tuve* "I had" (Lafford and Collentine 1987).

2.4.2.3.1   Depth of knowledge dimension researched using Spanish L2 data   Lafford and Collentine (1987) analyzed lexical oral-production data from nineteen third-year, university-level students of Spanish enrolled in a proficiency-based program. Using a Jakobsonian semantic framework (Jakobson 1957; Waugh 1982), Lafford and Collentine (1987) outline intersign relationships that may exist in a learner's interlanguage, assuming that signs are interconnected through four basic relationships involving *similarity* (involving the notion of resemblance, e.g., simile, metaphor) and *contiguity* (entailing temporal or spatial adjacency, cause/effect, part/whole).

1. *Formal partners*: signs related only via similarity relations among *signantia* (Laufer's 1988 "synforms") with no obvious semantic similarity or contiguity connections (e.g., *sentar* "sit" versus *sentir* "feel").

2. *Grammatical paradigms*: signs that constitute a grammatical category and are related primarily through similarity relations of markedness among grammatical features in the *signata* of different signs, e.g., the morpheme indicating number in the determiners *los* and *las* (the definite articles for masculine and feminine plural, respectively).

3. *Lexical/derivational constellations*: signs related by similarity relations among the *signantia* and among lexical features in the *signata*, e.g., *universitaria* "university-related" (adjective) versus *universidad* "university" (noun).

4. *Semantic schemata*: groups (semantic fields) of grammatical paradigms and lexical/derivational constellations whose *signata* are related through relations of similarity and contiguity, e.g., all terms related to "writing" such as *carta* "letter," *pluma* "pen," *papel* "paper," *escribir* "to write," *escritura* "writing," *escribo* "I write."

The assertions made by Lafford and Collentine (1987) about *intersign* relations are also quite consonant with the current connectionist view of the lexicon.

In addition, Lafford and Collentine (1987) propose that some of the L2 acquisition data analyzed in their study of third-year, university-level learners of Spanish could be explained using a markedness framework, which focuses on the asymmetrical relationship among various linguistic signs; for example, *ser,* the unmarked copula, is often used in early stages of acquisition as a substitute for the more marked copula *estar.*[8]

Ife, Vives Boix, and Meara (2000), asking whether greater proficiency correlates with greater vocabulary learning abroad, studied the development of intersign relationships among thirty-six L2 Spanish learners in study-abroad context. University-level learners participated in a word-association task and a translation task before and after their study-abroad experience (four to eight months); although results were not statistically significant, trends appeared indicating possible gains in both size and lexical organization for *both* intermediate and advanced learners. Gains in lexical organization were especially noted in the advanced learners who stayed abroad for a longer period (two semesters = eight months).

2.4.2.4   *Receptive/productive dimension*

Henriksen's (1999) third dimension is consonant with the assumption that lexical knowledge is best conceptualized as a continuum between the ability to recognize the meaning of a lexical item and the ability to use it productively (Gass 1988; Melka 1997), effectively rejecting the popular conception that one possesses distinct receptive and productive sets of vocabulary items. To increase the likelihood that a term will be available for production, learners must practice retrieving L2 items; this retrieval process strengthens and automatizes so-called I/O (input/output) channels (i.e., knowledge for decoding and encoding structural properties; Ellis 1994). Bialystok and Sharwood Smith (1985) contend that learners need "control" over—as opposed to mere "knowledge" of—a lexeme's use for it to appear in output. Laufer and Paribakht (1998) investigate what they term passive, controlled active and free active vocabulary knowledge. Each develops at a different rate: passive is fastest, free active is slowest and controlled active occupies an intermediate position between these two. To these authors' knowledge, no research has been conducted to date on the receptive/productive dimension in Spanish L2 contexts.

2.4.2.5   *Cross-linguistic influence*

Other developmental factors that have not been fully discussed in the Spanish L2 investigations to date surely interact with all three of Henriksen's dimensions. First, research on "cross-linguistic influence," which amounts to a resurgence in the interest in what has been termed "transfer," indicates that the L1 is an important factor in the development of L2 vocabulary (see Kellerman and Sharwood Smith 1986; Swan 1997). Stockwell, Bowen, and Martin's (1965) behavioristically based Hierarchy of Difficulty predicts that substantial problems will occur when the L2 contains two semantic categories for which the L1 has just one form. Thus, this hierarchy predicts that native speakers of English will often have trouble distinguishing the copulas *ser/estar* or the prepositions *por/para* because both pairs can mean "to be" or "for," respectively.

Additionally, the L1 conspires to keep learners in a certain stage of acquisition of the L2 morpheme. For instance, English-speaking students may continue to rely on *ser* for most copula functions for a long period because *es* (third person singular form of *ser*) is so similar to English "is." In addition, Major's (2001) Similarity-Difference Rate Hypothesis states that it is easier to acquire L2 forms that are truly different from each other. Therefore, the pairs *ser/estar* and *por/para* are harder to acquire because the members of each pair are so similar in form and meaning to each other, not because they are so different.

2.5   The Facilitation of L2 Vocabulary Acquisition

Little is known about the acquisition of L2 vocabulary (and much less Spanish vocabulary, to which the previous section testifies), and clear-cut principles with which to approach the teaching of vocabulary are scant. In her review of historical trends in L2 vocabulary instruction, Zimmerman (1997) states: "Although the lexicon is arguably central to language acquisition and use, vocabulary instruction has not been a priority in second language acquisition research or methodology" (17). Some of the most substantive help that instruction received in the past were the efforts of scholars to collate word-frequency lists. Yet, scholars now recognize that instruction has generally assumed that vocabulary acquisition proceeds "implicitly" (see Ellis 1994) or incidentally (Gass 1999).

However, Ellis (1994) affirms that vocabulary learning is greatly enhanced by explicit instructional intervention,[9] or techniques that promote the deep processing of terms (i.e., using and processing a term in a variety of contexts to better incorporate it into the learner's lexical network). As more nodes are activated during the learning process, the item becomes embedded within a network of nodes instead of residing as a (relatively) isolated node among the learner's L2 knowledge store (see Haastrup and Henricksen 2000). Leow (1998) found that multiple exposures to Spanish morphological forms significantly affected their recognition, production, and retention by L2 learners. Chun and Plass (1996a) note the need for repetition and manipulation of the new L2 items in order for them to be acquired.[10]

In addition, using the Vocabulary Knowledge Scale as a research tool, Paribakht and Wesche (1997) found that an experimental treatment involving reading plus vocabulary instruction led to greater progress in vocabulary acquisition. In later studies (Paribakht and Wesche 1999; Wesche and Paribakht 2000) these authors gathered introspective data that helped to confirm the 1997 findings. The 1999 and 2000 studies showed that learners found more vocabulary learning advantages in using a variety of text-based vocabulary exercises together with a reading test than in using only multiple reading texts containing the same vocabulary items. The results of Wesche and Paribakht (2000) also supported a view of vocabulary acquisition as an elaborate, reiterative process, in which multiple exposures to a new lexical item in several different tasks promoted the strengthening of various aspects of word knowledge. Thus, research into the effectiveness of various vocabulary-learning strategies is beginning to provide a plethora of techniques and assumptions for pedagogues and materials designers to consider.

2.5.1   Word Frequency Lists

Word frequency lists contain "core vocabulary which L2 teachers are recommended to use to decide which words and meanings should be taught first" (Ellis 1994:212).[11] With the arrival of more communicative teaching methods, the use of frequency lists has recently been criticized by some scholars (see Zimmerman 1997:14 for a review of this research), although some still find them useful for curriculum design (Nation and Waring 1997:17–18). In recent years, computer-based programs to aid acquisition of core vocabulary and word families have been utilized (Cobb and Horst 2001; Groot 2000; Ghadirian 2002).

2.5.1.1   Core vocabulary studies using Spanish L2 data

Buchanan (1927) and Keniston (1941) created word lists for curriculum designers and teachers of Spanish. However, Bull (1950) questioned the lists' reliability, wondering whether the same lists would arise from samples of a variety of materials. He argued that there was very little predictive power in Keniston's list outside of pedagogical texts, since the words were rare in a set of authentic literary texts that Bull and his assistants sampled. Because scholars have found that written discourse evidences a greater variety of lexical items than oral discourse (Chafe and Danielwicz 1987; Biber 1988, 1995), it is possible that frequency lists based on transcriptions of oral data would yield very different results.

2.5.2   Vocabulary Learning Strategies

Ellis (1994) contends that mapping form to meaning is the result of cognitive mediation, which depends on explicit learning processes, for example, mnemonics or semantic or imagery mediation between the FL word (or a keyword approximation) and the L1 translation. Fraser (1999:226) found positive results for the teaching of so-called lexical processing strategies (LPS).

Coady (1997) identified four major positions toward the use of strategies for vocabulary instruction: (1) No formal strategy use: vocabulary acquisition occurs incidentally in context as the learner engages in extensive reading (Krashen 1989); (2) Strategy instruction: formal instruction in the use of vocabulary learning strategies is essential to learning items in context (Oxford and Scarcella 1994); (3) Development plus explicit instruction: a combination of formal instruction and vocabulary learning strategies is needed (Paribakht and Wesche 1997; Zimmerman 1994); (4) Classroom activities: this approach advocates the teaching of vocabulary along traditional lines, often using handbooks which emphasize practical activities (see Allen 1983).[12]

The following five subsections review the research done on selected learning strategies using Spanish data: guessing from context, inferring meaning from glosses, and using dictionaries, multimedia cues, and semantic mapping.

2.5.2.1   Guessing from context

A common L2 vocabulary learning strategy involves inferring a lexeme's meaning from its oral or written context (Haastrup 1991). Inferring involves the consideration of graphomorphemic (orthographic), morphological (e.g., roots, stems, and affixes), syntactic and semantic qualities; it also entails the use of one's background knowledge (Lee and Wolf 1997). The research suggests that beginning L2 readers rely on graphomorphemic correspondences, a bottom-up strategy[13] (Coady 1997; Lee and Wolf 1997). Higher-level learners may be more effective guessers because they possess a larger lexicon, which in turn allows them to employ both bottom-up and top-down strategies. Interestingly, however, Mondria and Wit-de Boer (1991) hypothesize that if context makes meaning too clear, lexical retention diminishes.

2.5.2.1.1   Spanish L2 studies on inferencing strategies   Lee and Wolf (1997) examined lexical inferencing strategies used during reading by twenty-eight Spanish native speakers and university-level native English-speaking learners of Spanish at beginning, intermediate and advanced levels. They employed a retrospective think-aloud protocol, asking participants to describe how they guessed the meanings of certain words. The results indicate that inferences increase with greater proficiency and that less proficient learners favor "bottom-up" strategies while advanced learners (and natives) favor "top-down" strategies.

Pulido (2000) looked at the impact of topic familiarity, reading proficiency, sight vocabulary (i.e., one's overall knowledge of Spanish vocabulary in the task), and level of instruction (beginning, intermediate and advanced university-level study) on incidental vocabulary gain through reading by ninety Spanish L2 learners. Results showed that L2 reading proficiency was the strongest predictor of vocabulary gain, followed by topic familiarity. However, results were not as compelling for the variable of L2 passage sight vocabulary.

2.5.2.2 Inferring meaning from glosses

Foreign language reading materials have long glossed texts largely with English translations and paraphrases/definitions in the target language. However, research that has examined the actual effects of glosses on comprehension or retention has been inconclusive (see Lomicka 1998; Roby 1999).

Nevertheless, Hulstijn, Hollander, and Greidanus (1996) did find that marginal glosses were more effective than dictionary use in preparing students for a productive vocabulary test. In addition, Hulstijn (1992) found that the mental effort associated with a multiple-choice gloss (e.g., selecting one translation from a series of four) best predicted comprehension. Thus, his study supports the Mental Effort Hypothesis, which predicts that if the meaning of a word must be inferred by the learner (i.e., high mental effort) it will be retained longer. Watanabe (1997) concluded that single-word or multiple-choice glosses are more effective than providing appositive definitions or no glosses at all. Nagata (1999) followed the line of research initiated by Hulstijn (1992) and Watanabe (1997) and found that multiple-choice glosses are more effective than single glosses for recalling the target vocabulary and grammatical items.

2.5.2.2.1   Spanish L2 studies on inferring meaning from glosses   Blake (1992) investigated the types of glosses chosen by university-level students of Spanish to understand a reading passage. He found that first-year learners mostly looked up nouns, and that beginning and advanced learners had difficulty with Spanish-English cognates and inferring the meaning of past participles.

More recently, Jacobs, Dufon, and Hong (1994) investigated the effects of glossing on recall and retention with a written recall protocol and a translation task. Eighty-five university-level, native speakers of English at various levels of proficiency studying Spanish as a foreign language participated, reading a text either with no glosses, English glosses, or Spanish glosses. The recall data suggested that glossing affected recall only at higher levels of proficiency. In addition, the language of the gloss (English/Spanish) made no significant difference on the posttest of reading comprehension. Participants reading the glossed text outperformed other learners on the translation task, although this difference was not sustained over time. Bell and Le Blanc (2000) (N = 40) discovered that students with access to English glosses accessed almost twice as many words as the Spanish gloss group. However, like Jacobs, Dufon, and Hong (1994), they found no significant difference between the two gloss groups on a posttest of reading comprehension.

Roby (1991) examined dictionaries and glosses used by ninety-five American students of Spanish in book and electronic formats. He found that students who had a dictionary and glosses available to them read the passage given to them in significantly less time than those who only used a dictionary. He also found that students using computers looked up significantly more words than students using books. Although there were no differences detected between the groups on the comprehension measure, qualitative data from a postexperimental questionnaire indicated that students using the online format were more satisfied with the semantic support available to them than were students using books. As Roby (1999) notes, there are two important implications to these findings. First, that subjects were able to read passages much quicker with the help of glosses is strong support for their inclusion in both print and online materials. Second, future research is needed to address the issue of controlling for students' unnecessary overuse of online glosses due to their novelty. As such, the online provision of comprehension aids would appear to lessen the disruption of the reading process caused by conventional dictionary look-ups.

2.5.2.3   The use of dictionaries

Researchers have wondered whether dictionary use during reading tasks affects vocabulary learning. Luppescu and Day (1993) report that dictionary use contributes to L2 vocabulary learning although it does slow reading and may cause confusion when an entry has more than one definition.

The studies examining the effects of dictionary use on vocabulary learning have involved bilingual rather than monolingual dictionaries. Harmann (1983) found that learners at all levels prefer bilingual dictionaries, although monolingual ones are common at advanced levels. Nonetheless, Baxter (1980) and Atkins (1985) conjecture that continued use of a bilingual dictionary may impede the advancement of L2 proficiency because it makes fewer demands on learners than do monolingual dictionaries.

Two investigators have compared dictionary use to alternative means for defining potentially indeterminable lexemes. Hulstijn, Hollander, and Greidanus (1996) found that incidental vocabulary learning is much higher when L2 readers have access to the meanings of words through marginal glosses than through a dictionary. This discovery has implications not only for the type of gloss made available to learners (i.e., marginal gloss versus dictionary), but also for the degree to which the word look-up assistance disrupts or distracts learners from the reading process. Additionally, Fraser's (1999) study states that inference tasks followed by dictionary use positively affect vocabulary learning.

2.5.2.3.1   Spanish L2 studies on the use of a dictionary   Lantolf, Labarca, and den Tuinder (1985) examined the dictionary accessing skills of eighty-nine university students at three levels in Spanish. Their results demonstrated that bilingual dictionaries are of pedagogical use only to students at a self-regulatory (the most advanced, in Vygotskian terms) stage of development. The researchers admit, however, that using the dictionary may result in slower reading speed, and it may be confusing for students when multiple definitions are given for the same lexical item.

Knight (1994) reports on an experiment that looked at the effects of intermediate level (second year) Spanish learners' (N = 105) verbal ability level (based on ACT scores) and bilingual dictionary (specifically, an electronic, online dictionary) use on incidental vocabulary learning and reading comprehension. The researcher controlled for dictionary use and the subjects' overall verbal ability. All told, the students learned more vocabulary when using a dictionary, and high verbal ability students learned more words than low verbal ability students. Additionally, access to the dictionary allowed low level students to gain receptive knowledge of almost as many words as the high level students. Moreover, those who used a dictionary achieved higher scores on measures of reading comprehension than those who had to infer meanings from context.

2.5.2.4   Multimedia cues

The increasing availability of computers and electronic corpora in recent years has facilitated the creation of new types of tools, such as online dictionaries (http://espanol.dir.yahoo.com/Materiales_de_consulta/Diccionarios/Espanol/) and even inverse dictionaries (Teschner 1996). Multimedia programs for teaching foreign languages often use glosses in the form of the L1 equivalent of a synonymous L2 word, with pictures, images, sound, or video to accompany the L2 word.

One of the major advantages of multimedia cues is that they provide opportunities for meeting the needs of students with various learning styles (e.g., aural, visual). Recognizing that students learn using different cognitive styles, Chun and Plass (1996a, 1996b) investigated the effects of different multimedia modalities on incidental vocabulary learning by native English-speaking learners of German. Their studies partially support the "dual-coding effect": a word annotated or coded with combined textual + visual or audio + visual modes of information will be learned better than a word coded with only the textual or audio mode (Paivio 1986). In addition, Al-Seghayer (2001) found that video clips are more effective than a still picture for teaching unknown vocabulary to ESL students through multimedia annotations. Lomicka (1998) and Laufer and Hill (2000) also confirmed the advantages of multimedia glosses and dictionaries on textual comprehension and vocabulary knowledge.

2.5.2.4.1   Spanish L2 research on the use of multimedia cues   Abraham (2001) investigated the effects of various types of multimedia annotations (glosses) in the form of video, photographs, Spanish definitions, and English definitions on acquiring new vocabulary and comprehending an authentic story in Spanish (N = 102). Results show that those learners who had access to multimedia annotations performed better on measures of vocabulary learning and reading comprehension than those without such access.

Karp's (2002) study (N = 80) investigated the effects of single versus multiple-choice textual glosses and single multimedia (i.e., text plus picture) versus multiple-choice multimedia cues on the depth of knowledge (i.e., word meaning, grammatical knowledge and word associations) acquired through reading. The results showed that students in the definition-only group used the glossary more frequently than any other group, in agreement with Lomicka (1998), although no single gloss type was statistically linked to higher vocabulary posttest scores. Contrary to expectations derived from prior research studies, apparently learners did not want to be bothered with the elaborate multimedia or multiple-choice offerings, as evidenced by the infrequent number of words they looked up in the online glossary. This pattern was even more pronounced among more advanced learners, who clicked on far fewer glossed words in the texts than did lower-level learners. Despite these results for gloss type, further analysis indicated that initial vocabulary size was the best predictor of foreign language vocabulary learning in this study. Nevertheless, this lack of an effect for dual-coded glosses is not unique to Karp's study. Chun and Plass (2001, 2002) reports that while learners tended to favor multimedia glosses in the mid-1990s (when multimedia applications were a novelty), the recent trend is that learners prefer text-only glosses containing L1 definitions.

2.5.2.5   Semantic mapping

Semantic mapping involves the building of diagrammatic maps that illustrate how certain word clusters are associated with a key word, idea, or concept. The clusterings are based on semantic and syntactic similarities (e.g., apricot, peach, plum, nectarine, pear, apple). This technique was originally developed by Johnson and Pearson (1978) to teach vocabulary to children learning to read in their native language.[14]

2.5.2.5.1   Spanish L2 research on semantic mapping   Morin and Goebel (2001) study the effects of semantic mapping on the acquisition of Spanish L2 vocabulary by English-speaking college students. A control group (N = 31) employed a set of vocabulary items in communicative tasks (e.g., small group and pair assignments). An experimental group (N = 31) participated in the same tasks, but only the experimental group was taught semantic mapping strategies. The results show that although both groups knew approximately the same amount of vocabulary (providing L1 definitions for a list of L2 words), the semantic mapping group remembered having heard more words on the list provided to them, implying that semantic mapping initially helps to emphasize the creation of "acoustic images" (phonological forms) onto which meaning is then mapped. The study also indicates that the semantic mapping group significantly outperformed the vocabulary activities group in meaning recall and in their ability to organize L2 vocabulary according to thematic relations to other words.

3.0   Limitations of the Existing L2 Lexical Research

Investigation into vocabulary learning is just beginning to form an important part of the SLA research agenda. As in any new area of study, wide-ranging discrepancies in research design make it difficult to make sweeping generalizations about the potential implications of this research for the classroom. It is important to note that many of the researchers cited in this chapter do, in fact, acknowledge these shortcomings.

Three methodological shortcomings limit the extent to which findings are generalizable to the population of Spanish students as a whole. First, a recurrent flaw of the studies reported here stems from the restricted number of tasks and the small pool of subjects sampled (e.g., Finnemann 1990; Guntermann 1992b; Ife, Vives Boix, and Meara 2000; Lee and Wolf 1997; Ryan and Lafford 1992; Lafford and Ryan 1995; VanPatten 1985, 1987). Notable exceptions are DeKeyser (1990) and Karp (2002), each of which employed three data collection tasks. Second, the proposals that learners advance through certain stages (Guntermann

1992b; Ryan and Lafford 1992; Lafford and Ryan 1995; VanPatten 1985, 1987) certainly requires longitudinal corroboration, either with a highly qualitative study of a small sample
or a cross-sectional study realized over an extended period of time. Another approach to
this dilemma could entail a cross-sectional multivariate study (examining a number of variables with a relatively large sample) and submitting the data to a path analysis (a statistical exploratory technique). Third, conclusions drawn from a single data-collection technique
naturally demand tenuous interpretations about the status of the learner's development; any
task places particular processing demands on the learner which in turn influences performance (Guntermann 1992b; Ryan and Lafford 1992, Lafford and Ryan 1995; VanPatten
1985, 1987). For instance, different orders may have been revealed in the *ser/estar* and
por/para stage studies if written composition data had been used instead of oral data. Recall protocol studies are hard pressed to reveal subconscious processes, masking any implicit learning that may have occurred.

Future investigations should pay closer attention to the construct validity of their
methodologies—that is, does the instrument effectively measure the theoretical construct it
targets? Such validity can be corroborated with more explicit descriptions of one's data
analysis. For instance, neither VanPatten (1985, 1987) nor Ryan and Lafford (1992) clearly
operationalizes "obligatory" contexts for the use of *ser/estar.* Notable exceptions are Guntermann (1992b), clearly delineating a theoretical thesis for her data analysis, and Lafford
and Ryan (1995), who recruited native speakers for corroboration.

Other shortcomings in the cited research relate to nature and the number of instruments employed. First a major limitation noted of Jacobs, Dufon, and Hong (1994) concerns
the fact that the Spanish glosses were not pilot-tested to see whether the students could understand them. Second, Ife, Vives Boix, and Meara (2000) employed no control group, such
that it is unclear the extent to which the subjects simply improved in terms of their ability
to complete the data-collection task. Finally, both Knight (1994) and Morin and Goebel (2001)
designed studies in which the treatment groups simply received more time on task, which
may significantly account for their findings.

Although dictionary use has been shown to facilitate vocabulary learning (Knight
1994), students encounter difficulty when pressed to decipher or process extraneous lexical
information contained in dictionary entries (Luppescu and Day 1993). As a result, textual
glossing seems to offer a more secure way for learners to access definitions or translations
for unfamiliar vocabulary items (Hulstijn, Hollander, and Greidanus 1996). However, there
is conflicting evidence in terms of L1 or L2 glossing. Although L2 glossing averts inter-
rupting the text flow, learners typically favor glosses in the form of L1 translations. Tap-
ping into the benefits espoused by dual-coding theory, research has shown evidence supporting the use of multimedia glosses (Chun and Plass 1996a, 1996b; Al-Seghayer 2001).
However, despite these successful findings, "multimedia" is a vague descriptor. As a result,
it is difficult to make comparisons across the pertinent studies that fall under this umbrella
category, in that they represent approaches that have looked at various combinations of
glosses in the form of text, pictures, audio, and video. Moreover, current research suggests
that multimedia glosses are not as effective for vocabulary learning as previously reported
in the mid-1990s (Chun 2001, 2002; Karp 2002).

Positive results stem from employing the inferring method for vocabulary learning (Hulstijn 1992; Watanabe 1997; Nagata 1999), yet the pervasive problem with multiple-choice glossing is the danger that learners make incorrect inferences, select the wrong multiple-choice options, and return to the reading passage having gained little or no vocabulary assistance and, possibly worse, been misled into learning incorrect meanings of words. A notable exception is Karp's (2002) study, in which learners in the multiple-choice groups received feedback through the computer until they arrived at the correct meaning of glossed words.

Finally, a common theme in all SLA research is the extent to which a study measures comprehension or intake; that is, are observed gains long-term? These are clearly separate issues, and their consideration has an important impact on pedagogical recommendations.

4.0   Agenda for Future Research in L2 Vocabulary Studies

Approaches to the analysis of L2 vocabulary data have been varied. Most L2 lexical studies to date have been based on written data, but some studies have been carried out using oral data.[15] Some scholars have preferred carrying out quantitative studies (e.g., Nation and Waring 1997) to establish a core L2 vocabulary based on calculating the most frequent words used in the L2, while others have taken a more qualitative approach to see how words are learned. (e.g., Parry 1997; Altman 1997; Grabe and Stoller 1997). Paribahkt and Wesche (1999) used talk-aloud protocols and retrospective protocols to get at learners' strategies to acquire L2 vocabulary.

Based on this review of the literature, it is clear that there are several issues regarding L2 vocabulary acquisition that still need to be addressed. Under the Minimalist Program, the lexicon is considered to be a store of *all* idiosyncratic L2 information, lexical and grammatical. Additionally, researchers approach the acquisition of Spanish phenomena with varying assumptions about the grammatical and / or lexical status of phenomena such as *ser/estar* and *por/para*. Clearly, then, the most important issues for researchers to address now are the following:

- What are the limitations of the theoretical models delineated here?
- Do certain heretofore assumed grammatical phenomena behave more like lexical phenomena during development (i.e., their incorporation into the learner's interlanguage)?
- To what extent do the theories of lexical development and organization detailed above account for overall L2 development better than theories of grammatical development?

At some point, an extensive proposal for key design features of vocabulary instruction will be welcomed by instructors and materials designers. These design features should provide as much predictive power as those that aim at the development of grammatical knowledge (e.g., focus on form). The effectiveness of the use of computer-based technology should also be explored in greater depth to see to what extent it facilitates vocabulary acquisition. Researchers also would do well to examine the acquisition of other apparent lexical obstacles for learners of Spanish, such as *saber/conocer.* Such studies would provide further insights into the factors that interact with the processes of mapping (labeling and packaging) and acquiring depth of knowledge (including markedness relations). Clearly, a better under-standing of the receptive/productive dimension as it relates to the acquisition of Spanish is necessary as well.

Additional research questions may include the following: What are the relative effects of different types of input modifications on vocabulary learning through inferred meaning? That is, how effective are particular types of glosses, cues, or tasks for allowing learners to infer the meaning of unknown words without running the risk of making incorrect infer-ences? Furthermore, does the interaction associated with computer-mediated tasks lead to an increase in depth of word knowledge and retention of meaning without distracting learners from comprehending what they read? Finally, a benchmark is needed for how much vocabulary knowledge changes over time in advanced Spanish students with respect to var-ious types of glosses, cues, and tasks.

Although there has been an advantage in exploring various ways to describe and measure L2 vocabulary acquisition, the lack of a coherent research agenda has prevented the field from developing at a faster rate. As stated earlier, Meara (1997) proposes that fu-ture research in vocabulary acquisition should involve the use of common models and more communication with researchers in other disciplines. He also advocates for researchers ask-ing the same questions, rather than having each one follow a different line of research, with no replication of studies or accumulation of knowledge in given areas. As the twenty-first century dawns, L2 research scholars need to answer this call for more rigor and system-aticity in the study of the acquisition of second language lexicons.

NOTES

1. For an extensive bibliography of recent work in vocabulary acquisition, see the Vocabu-lary Acquisition Research Group Archive (VARGA) maintained by Paul Meara (www.swan.ac.uk/cals/calres/varga). This archive contains work published on vocabulary acquisition in many lan-guages other than English (e.g., French, German, Dutch). Works written in Spanish include Sego-viano (1996) and a recent article by Suarez and Meara (2000).

2. Wesche and Paribakht (1999) define *incidental* learning of vocabulary as that which takes place when "learners are focused on comprehending meaning rather than on the explicit goal of learning new words." (176). An extensive review of the concept of incidental learning goes beyond the scope of this paper. See *Studies in Second Language Acquisition* (1999), vol. 21.2, for a detailed review of recent research on incidental vocabulary learning.

3. The following discussion of the organization of the lexicon relates only to the struc-ture of the L2 lexicon. Readers who wish to familiarize themselves with the literature on the or-ganization of bilingual lexicons are referred to all chapters in Schreuder and Weltens (1993), Meara (1999), and Libben (2000) and relevant studies they cite.

4. Laufer (1988) uses synform to refer to pairs or groups of words in the same language that are similar in form (e.g., *sentir* "to feel" and *sentar* "to sit"). Lafford and Collentine (1987) em-ploy the term *formal partners* for this phenomenon.

5. See chapter 8 of this volume for a discussion of the cognitive aspects of the L2 ac-quisition of these Spanish copulas.

6. Lafford and Ryan (1995) also noted variation in native speaker usage of *por* and *para* and called for more research in this area before learners' systems are compared to NS norms.

7. See chapter 8 of this volume for a discussion of the cognitive aspects of the L2 acquisition of these Spanish prepositions.

8. Waugh and Lafford (1994, 2000) provide overviews of the concept of markedness and state that a marked term (e.g., woman) is more specialized, more precise, more constrained, less general and more complex than its unmarked counterpart (e.g., man), and that unmarked elements (e.g., present tense) are generally acquired before marked ones (e.g., past tense) in first and second language acquisition.

9. See chapter 10 of this volume for a general discussion of the effects of various types of instruction on Spanish L2 acquisition.

10. Research on the effects of semantic elaboration (tasks in which a learner's processing resources are directed at the semantic properties [referential, meaning-based properties] of items during input processing) to aid vocabulary acquisition have produced conflicting results (see Barcroft 2000 for discussion of these studies).

11. West's (1953) list of high frequency words in English is still used in spite of more current lists created through computer technology (Meara 1980); see also Nation (1984) and Coxhead (2000).

12. Nation (1990), Schmitt (1997), and Coady (1997) provide extensive reviews of lexical strategies and their utility.

13. Barnett (1989) categorized reading models as top-down and bottom-up. In top-down (reader-driven) models, a learner's prior schemata contribute to the comprehension of the text. In bottom-up (text-driven) models learners start a reading by decoding letters, words, phrases, and sentences and build their comprehension of the text based on their understanding of these elements.

14. Hague (1987) proposes various strategies for teaching foreign language vocabulary with semantic mapping.

15. See Brown, Sagers, and LaPorte (1999) and McCarthy and Carter (1997) for a discussion of the differences between oral and written data for lexical studies.

WORKS CITED

Abraham, L. 2001. The effects of multimedia on second language vocabulary learning and reading comprehension. Ph.D. diss., University of New Mexico.

Aitchison, J. 1994. *Words in the mind: An introduction to the mental lexicon.* 2d ed. Oxford: Blackwell.

Alexander, P., D. Schallert, and V. Hare. 1991. Coming to terms: How researchers in learning and literacy talk about knowledge. *Review of Educational Research* 61:315–43.

Allen, V.F. 1983. *Techniques in teaching vocabulary.* Oxford: Oxford University Press.

Al-Seghayer, K. 2001. The effect of multimedia annotation modes on L2 vocabulary acquisition: A comparative study. *Language Learning & Technology* 5.1:202–32.

Altman, R. 1997. Oral production of vocabulary: A case study. In *Second language vocabulary acquisition,* eds. J. Coady and T. Huckin, 68–97. Cambridge: Cambridge University Press.

Andersen, R. 1983. Transfer to somewhere. In *Language transfer in language learning,* eds. S. Gass and L. Selinker, 177–201. Rowley, MA: Newbury House.

———. 1990. Models, processes, principles and strategies: Second language acquisition inside and outside of the classroom. In *Second language acquisition-foreign language learning,* eds. B. VanPatten and J. F. Lee, 45–68. Clevedon: Multilingual Matters.

Andrews, S. 1997. The effect of orthographic similarity on lexical retrieval: Resolving neighborhood conflicts. *Psychonomic Bulletin and Review: A Journal of the Psychonomic Society* 4.4:439–61.

Atkins, B. T. 1985. Monolingual and bilingual learners' dictionaries: A comparison. In *Dictionaries, lexicography and language learning,* ed. R. Ilson, 15–24. Oxford: Pergamon.

Bailey, N., C. Madden, and S. Krashen. 1974. Is there a "natural sequence" in adult second language learning? *Language Learning* 24:235–43.

Barcroft, J. 2000. The effects of sentence writing as semantic elaboration on the allocation of processing resources and second language lexical acquisition. Ph.D. diss., University of Illinois, Urbana-Champaign.

Barnett, M.A. 1989. More than meets the eye: Foreign language reading. *Language in education theory and practice,* no. 73. Englewood Cliffs, NJ: Prentice Hall.

Baxter, J. 1980. The dictionary and vocabulary behavior: A single word or a handful? *TESOL Quarterly* 14.3:325–36.

Beale, L. 1978. Lexical analysis of the preposition in Spanish: Semantics and perception. Ph.D. diss., Cornell University.

Bell, F. L., and L. B. LeBlanc. 2000 The language of glosses in L2 reading on computer: Learners' preferences. *Hispania* 83:274–85.

Bialystok, E., and M. Sharwood Smith. 1985. Interlanguage is not a state of mind: An evaluation of the construct for second language acquisition. *Applied Linguistics* 6.3:101–17.

Biber, D. 1988. *Variation across speech and writing.* New York: Cambridge University Press.

———. 1995. *Dimensions of register variation: A cross-linguistic comparison.* New York: Cambridge University Press.

Blake, R. 1992. Second language reading on the computer. *ADFL Bulletin* 24:17–22.

Brown, C., S. L. Sagers, and C. LaPorte. 1999. Incidental vocabulary acquisition from oral and written dialogue journals. *Studies in Second Language Acquisition* 21.2:259–83.

Buchanan, M. A. 1927. *A graded Spanish word book.* Toronto: University of Toronto Press.

Bull, W. 1950. Spanish word counts: Theory and practice. *Modern Language Journal* 43:18–26.

Carreiras, M., M. Perea, and J. Grainer. 1997. Effects of orthographic neighborhood in visual word recognition: Cross-task comparisons. *Journal of Experimental Psychology: Learning, Memory, and Cognition* 23.4: 857–71.

Chafe, W., and J. Danielwicz. 1987. Properties of spoken and written language (TechRep No. 5, Report No. CS 210 519). Center for the Study of Writing, University of California, Berkeley.

Chomsky, N. 1988. *Language and problems of knowledge: The Managua lectures.* Cambridge, MA: MIT Press.

————. 1990. Language and mind. In *Ways of communicating: The Darwin College lectures,* ed. D. H. Mellor, 56–80. Cambridge: Cambridge University Press.

————. 1995. *The minimalist program.* Cambridge, MA: MIT Press.

Chun, D., and J. Plass. 1996a. Effects of multimedia annotations on vocabulary acquisition. *Modern Language Journal* 80:183–98.

————. 1996b. Facilitating reading comprehension with multimedia. *System* 24.4:503–19.

————. 2001. A longitudinal study of user behavior and L2 reading comprehension in a multimedia CALL environment. Paper presented at the Annual Meeting of American Association of Applied Linguistics, St. Louis, Missouri.

————. 2002. L2 reading comprehension with CALL: A decade of data. Paper presented at the Annual Meeting of Computer Assisted Language Instruction Consortium, Davis, California.

Coady, J. 1997. L2 vocabulary acquisition: A synthesis of the research. In *Second language vocabulary acquisition,* eds. J. Coady and T. Huckin, 273–90. Cambridge: Cambridge University Press.

Cobb, T., and M. Horst 2001. Reading academic English: Carrying learners across the lexical threshold. In *Research perspectives on English for academic purposes,* eds. J. Flowerdew and M. Peacock, 315–29. Cambridge: Cambridge University Press.

Cook, V. 1988. *Chomsky's Universal Grammar: An introduction.* Oxford: Blackwell.

————. 1994. Universal Grammar and the learning and teaching of second languages. In *Perspectives on pedagogical grammar,* ed. Terence Odlin, 25–48. Cambridge: Cambridge University Press.

Coxhead, A. 2000. A new academic word list. *TESOL Quarterly* 34.2:213–38.

Crick, F. H. C. 1979. Thinking about the brain. *Scientific American* 241.3:181–88.

DeKeyser, R. M. 1990. From learning to acquisition: Monitoring in the classroom and abroad. *Hispania* 73.1:238–47.

Dulay, H., and M. Burt. 1974. Natural sequences in child second language acquisition. *Language Learning* 24.1:37–53.

Dulay, H., M. Burt, and S. Krashen. 1982. *Language two.* New York: Oxford University Press.

Ellis, N. 1994. Vocabulary acquisition: The implicit ins and outs of explicit cognitive mediation. In *Implicit and explicit learning of languages,* ed. N. Ellis, 211–82. New York: Academic Press.

————. 1996. Phonological memory, chunking and points of order. *Studies in Second Language Acquisition* 18:91–126.

————. 1997. Vocabulary acquisition: Word structure, collocation, word-class, and meaning. In *Vocabulary: Description, acquisition and pedagogy,* eds. N. Schmitt and M. McCarthy, 122–39. Cambridge: Cambridge University Press.

————. 1999. Cognitive approaches to SLA. *Annual Review of Applied Linguistics* 19:22–42.

Elman, J. L., E. A. Bates, M. H. Johnson, A. Karmiloff Smith, A. P. Domenico, and K. Plunkett. 1996. *Rethinking innateness: A connectionist perspective on development.* Cambridge, MA: MIT Press.

Finnemann, M. 1990. Markedness and learner strategy: Form and meaning oriented learners in the foreign language context. *Modern Language Journal* 74.2:176–87.

Fraser, C.A. 1999. Lexical processing strategy use and vocabulary learning through reading. *Studies in Second Language Acquisition* 21.2:225–41.

Gass, S. 1988. Second language vocabulary acquisition. *Annual Review of Applied Linguistics* 9:92–106.

———. 1999. Incidental vocabulary learning. *Studies in Second Language Acquisition* 21.2:319–33.

Gass, S., and L. Selinker. 2001. *Second language acquisition: An introductory course*. 2d ed. Mahwah, NJ: Lawrence Erlbaum.

Geeslin, K. 2000. A new approach to the study of the SLA of copula choice. In *Spanish applied linguistics at the turn of the millennium,* eds. R. P. Leow and C. Sanz, 50–66. Somerville, MA: Cascadilla Press.

———. 2001. Changing norms, moving targets and the SLA of copula choice. *Spanish Applied Linguistics* 5.1–2:29–55.

Ghadirian, S. 2002. Providing controlled exposure to target vocabulary through the screening and arranging of texts. *Language Learning and Technology* 6.1:147–64.

Grabe, B., and F. L. Stoller. 1997. Reading and vocabulary development in a second language: A case study. In *Second language vocabulary acquisition,* eds. J. Coady and T. Huckin, 98–122. Cambridge: Cambridge University Press.

Groot, P. J. M. 2000. Computer assisted second language vocabulary acquisition. *Language Learning & Technology* 4.1:60–81.

Guntermann, G. 1992a. An analysis of interlanguage development over time: Part I: *POR* and *PARA*. *Hispania* 75.1:177–87.

———. 1992b. An analysis of interlanguage development over time: Part II, *SER* and *ESTAR*. *Hispania* 75.5:1294–303.

Haastrup, K. 1991. *Lexical inferencing procedures or talking about words*. Tübingen: Gunter Narr.

Haastrup K., and B. Henriksen. 2000. Vocabulary acquisition: Acquiring depth of knowledge through network building. *International Journal of Applied Linguistics* 10.2:221–40.

Hague, S.A. 1987. Vocabulary instruction: What L2 learners can learn from L1. *Foreign Language Annals* 20.3:217–25.

Harmann, R. R. K. 1983. The bilingual learner's dictionary and its uses. *Multilingual* 2:195–201.

Hawas, H. M. 1990. Vocabulary and reading comprehension: An experimental study. *International Review of Applied Linguistics* 87–88:43–65.

Henriksen, B. 1999. Three dimensions of vocabulary development. *Studies in Second Language Acquisition* 21.2:303–18.

Huckin, T., and J. Coady. 1999. Incidental vocabulary acquisition in a second language: A review. *Studies in Second Language Acquisition* 21.2:181–93.

Hulstijn, J. H. 1992. Retention of inferred and given word meanings: Experiments in incidental vocabulary learning. In *Vocabulary and applied linguistics,* eds. P. Arnaud and H. Bénoint, 113–25. London: Macmillan.

Hulstijn, J. H., M. Hollander, and T. Greidanus. 1996. Incidental vocabulary learning by advanced foreign language students: The influence of marginal glosses, dictionary use and reoccurrence of unknown words. *Modern Language Journal* 80:327–39.

Ife, A., G. Vives Boix, and P. Meara. 2000. The impact of study abroad on the vocabulary development of different proficiency groups. *Spanish Applied Linguistics* 4.1:55–84.

Jacobs, G. M., P. Dufon, and F. C. Hong. 1994. L1 and L2 vocabulary glosses in L2 reading passages: Their effectiveness for increasing comprehension and vocabulary knowledge. *Journal of Research in Reading* 17.1:19–28.

Jakobson, R. 1957. The cardinal dichotomy of language. In *Language: An enquiry into its meaning and function,* ed. R. Anschen, 155–78. New York: Harper.

Jimenez, R. T., G. E. Garcia, and P. D. Pearson, 1996. The reading strategies of bilingual latina/o students who are successful English readers: Opportunities and obstacles. *Reading Research Quarterly* 31.1:90–112.

Jiménez González, J., and I. Hernández Valle. 2000. Word identification and reading disorders in the Spanish language. *Journal of Learning Disabilities* 33.1:44–60.

Joe, A. 1995. Text-based tasks and incidental vocabulary learning. *Second Language Research* 11:149–58.

———. 1998. What effects do text-based tasks promoting generation have on incidental vocabulary acquisition? *Applied Linguistics* 19:357–77.

Johnson, D., and P. D. Pearson. 1978. *Teaching reading vocabulary.* New York: Holt, Rinehart, and Winston.

Karp, A. 2002. Modification of glosses and its effect on incidental L2 vocabulary learning in Spanish. Ph.D. diss., University of California, Davis.

Kellerman, E., and M. Sharwood Smith, eds. 1986. *Cross-linguistic influence in second language acquisition.* Elmsford, NY: Pergamon.

Kelly, P. 1991. Lexical ignorance: The main obstacle to listening comprehension with advanced foreign language learners. *International Review of Applied Linguistics* 29:135–49.

Keniston, H. 1941. *A standard list of Spanish words and idioms.* Lexington, MA: D. C. Heath.

Knight, S. 1994. Dictionary use while reading: The effects on comprehension and vocabulary acquisition for students of different verbal abilities. *Modern Language Journal* 78:285–99.

Koda, K. 1989. The effects of transferred vocabulary knowledge on the development of L2 reading proficiency. *Foreign Language Annals* 22:529–42.

———. 1994. Second language reading research: Problems and possibilities. *Applied Psycholinguistics* 15.1:1–28.

Krashen, S. 1989. We acquire vocabulary and spelling by reading: Additional evidence for the input hypothesis. *Modern Language Journal* 73.4:440–64.

Lafford, B., and J. G. Collentine. 1987. Lexical and grammatical access errors in the speech of intermediate/advanced level students of Spanish. *Lenguas Modernas* 14:87–112.

Lafford, B., and J. Ryan. 1995. The acquisition of lexical meaning in a study abroad context: The Spanish prepositions *por* and *para. Hispania* 75.3:528–47.

Lantolf, J., A. Labarca, and J. den Tuinder. 1985. Strategies for accessing bilingual dictionaries: A question of regulation. *Hispania* 68:858–64.

Laufer, B. 1988. The concept of "synforms" (similar lexical forms) in L2 learning. *Language and Education* 2:113–32.

———. 1992. Reading in a foreign language: How does L2 lexical knowledge interact with readers' general academic ability? *Journal of Research in Reading* 15:95–103.

———. 1997. The lexical plight in second language reading: Words you don't know, words you think you know and words you can't guess. In *Second language vocabulary acquisition,* eds. J. Coady and T. Huckin, 20–34. Cambridge: Cambridge University Press.

———. 1998. The development of passive and active vocabulary in a second language: Same or different? *Applied Linguistics* 19.2:255–71.

Laufer, B., and M. Hill. 2000. What lexical information do L2 learners select in a CALL dictionary and how does it affect word retention? *Language Learning & Technology* 3.2:58–76.

Laufer, B., and S. Peribakht. 1998. The relationship between passive and active vocabularies: Effects of language learning context. *Language Learning* 48:365–91.

Lee, J. F., and D. F. Wolf. 1997. A quantitative and qualitative analysis of the word-meaning inferencing strategies of L1 and L2 readers. *Spanish Applied Linguistics* 1.1:24–64.

Leow, R. 1998. The effects of amount and type of exposure on adult learners' L2 development in SLA. *Modern Language Journal* 82.1:49–68.

Levelt, W. 1989. *Speaking: From intention to articulation.* Cambridge, MA: MIT Press.

Libben, G. 2000. Representation and processing in the second language lexicon: The homogeneity hypothesis. In *Second language acquisition and linguistic theory,* ed. J. Archibald, 228–48. Oxford: Blackwell.

Liontas, J. I. 1999. Developing a pragmatic methodology of idiomaticity: The comprehension and interpretation of SL vivid phrasal idioms during reading. Ph.D. diss., University of Arizona.

———. 2003. Killing two birds with one stone: Understanding Spanish VP idioms in and out of context. *Hispania* 86.2:900–913.

Lomicka, L. 1998. To gloss or not to gloss: An investigation of reading comprehension online. *Language Learning & Technology* 1.2:41–50.

Long, M., and Richards, J. C. 1997. Series editors' preface. In *Second language vocabulary acquisition,* eds. J. Coady and T. Huckin, ix–x. Cambridge: Cambridge University Press.

Lunn, P. 1978. *The semantics of* por *and* para. Bloomington: Indiana University Linguistics Club.

Luppescu, S., and R. Day. 1993. Reading, dictionaries and vocabulary learning. *Language Learning* 43:263–87.

MacWhinney, B. 1997. Second language acquisition and the competition model. In *Tutorial in bilingualism: Psycholinguistic perspectives,* eds. A. de Groot and J. Kroll, 113–42. Mahwah, NJ: Lawrence Erlbaum.

Major, R. 2001. *Foreign accent: The ontogeny and phylogeny of second language phonology.* Mahwah, NJ: Lawrence Erlbaum.

McCarthy, M., and R. Carter. 1997. Written and spoken vocabulary. In *Vocabulary: Description, acquisition and pedagogy,* eds. N. Schmitt and M. McCarthy, 20–39. Cambridge: Cambridge University Press.

Meara, P. 1978. Learners' word associations in French. *Interlanguage Studies Bulletin* 43: 192–211.

————. 1980. Vocabulary acquisition: A neglected aspect of language learning. In *Language teaching and linguistics: Abstracts,* 221–46. New York: Newbury House.

————. 1996. The dimensions of lexical competence. In *Performance and competence in second language acquisition,* eds. G. Brown, K. Malmkjaer, and J. Williams, 35–53. Tampere, Finland: Publications de l'Association Finlandaise de Linguistique Appliquée.

————. 1997. Towards a new approach to modeling vocabulary acquisition. In *Vocabulary: Description, acquisition and pedagogy,* eds. N. Schmitt and M. McCarthy, 109–21. Cambridge: Cambridge University Press.

————. 1999. Self organization in bilingual lexicons. In *Language and thought in development,* ed. S. P. Broeder and J. Murre, 127–44. Tübingen: Gunter Narr.

Mecartty, F. 2000. Lexical and grammatical knowledge in reading and listening comprehension by foreign language learners of Spanish. *Applied Language Learning* 11.2:323–48.

Melka, F. 1997. Receptive vs. productive aspects of vocabulary. In *Vocabulary: Description, acquisition and pedagogy,* eds. N. Schmitt and M. McCarthy, 84–102. Cambridge: Cambridge University Press.

Mondria, J., and M. Wit-de Boer. 1991. The effects of contextual richness on the guessability and the retention of words in a foreign language. *Applied Linguistics* 12.3:249–67.

Moon, R. 1997. Vocabulary connections: Multi-word items in English. In *Vocabulary: Description, acquisition and pedagogy,* eds. N. Schmitt and M. McCarthy, 40–63. Cambridge: Cambridge University Press.

Morin, R., and J. Goebel. 2001. Basic vocabulary instruction: Teaching strategies or teaching words. *Foreign Language Annals* 34.1:8–17.

Nagata, N. 1999. The effectiveness of computer-assisted interactive glosses. *Foreign Language Annals* 32.4:469–79.

Nation, I. S. P., ed. 1984. *Vocabulary lists, word, affixes and stems.* Wellington: English Language Institute, Victoria University at Wellington.

————. 1990. *Teaching and learning vocabulary.* New York: Newbury House/Harper & Row.

Nation, P., and R. Waring. 1997. Vocabulary size, text coverage and word lists. In *Vocabulary: Description, acquisition and pedagogy,* eds. N. Schmitt and M. McCarthy, 6–19. Cambridge: Cambridge University Press.

Oxford, R. L., and R. C. Scarcella. 1994. Second language vocabulary learning among adults: State of the art in vocabulary instruction. *System* 22:231–43.

Paivio, A. 1986. *Mental representation: A dual-coding approach.* New York: Oxford University Press.

Paribakht, T. S., and M. Wesche. 1997. Vocabulary enhancement activities and reading for meaning in second language vocabulary acquisition. In *Second language vocabulary acquisition,* eds. J. Coady and T. Huckin, 174–200. Cambridge: Cambridge University Press.

————. 1999. Reading and "incidental" L2 vocabulary acquisition: An introspective study of lexical inferencing. *Studies in Second Language Acquisition* 21.2:195–224.

Parry, K. 1997. Vocabulary comprehension: Two portraits. In *Second language vocabulary acquisition,* eds. J. Coady and T. Huckin, 55–68. Cambridge: Cambridge University Press.

Pulido, D. 2000. The impact of topic familiarity, L2 reading proficiency, and L2 passage sight vocabulary on incidental vocabulary gain through reading for adult learners of Spanish as a foreign language. Ph.D. diss., University of Illinois, Urbana-Champaign.

Read, J. 1993. The development of a new measure of L2 vocabulary knowledge. *Language Testing* 10:355–71.

———. 1997. Vocabulary and testing. In *Vocabulary description, acquisition and pedagogy,* eds. N. Schmitt and M. McCarthy, 303–20. Cambridge: Cambridge University Press.

———. 2000. *Assessing vocabulary.* Cambridge: Cambridge University Press.

Roby. W. B. 1991. Glosses and dictionaries in paper and computer formats as adjunct aids to the reading of Spanish texts by university students. Ph.D. diss., University of Kansas.

———. 1999. What's in a gloss? *Language Learning & Technology* 2:94–101.

Ryan, A. 1997. Learning the orthographical form of L2 vocabulary—a receptive and a productive process. In *Vocabulary: Description, acquisition and pedagogy,* eds. N. Schmitt and M. McCarthy, 181–98. Cambridge: Cambridge University Press.

Ryan, J., and B. Lafford. 1992. Acquisition of lexical meaning in a study abroad environment: *SER* and *ESTAR* and the Granada experience. *Hispania* 75.3:714–22.

Saussure, F. de. 1916. *Cours de linguistique générale.* Lausanne and Paris: Payot.

Schmitt, N. 1997. Vocabulary learning strategies. In *Vocabulary: Description, acquisition and pedagogy,* eds. N. Schmitt and M. McCarthy, 199–227. Cambridge: Cambridge University Press.

Schmitt, N., and M. McCarthy. 1997. Glossary. In *Vocabulary: Description, acquisition and pedagogy,* eds. N. Schmitt and M. McCarthy, 327–31. Cambridge: Cambridge University Press.

Schmitt, N., and P. Meara. 1997. Researching vocabulary through a word knowledge framework: Word associations and verbal suffixes. *Studies in Second Language Acquisition* 19:17–36.

Schreuder, R., and B. Weltens, eds. 1993. *The bilingual lexicon.* Amsterdam: John Benjamins.

Schumann, J. 1979. The acquisition of English negation by speakers of Spanish: A review of the literature. In *The acquisition and use of Spanish and English as first and second languages,* ed. R. Andersen, 3–32. Washington, DC: Teachers of English to Speakers of Other Languages.

Segoviano, C. 1996. *La enseñanza del léxico español como lengua extranjera.* Madrid: Iberoamericana.

Smith, K. 1980. Common errors in the compositions of students of Spanish as a foreign language. Ph.D. diss., University of Texas at Austin.

Stockwell, R., J. Bowen, and J. Martin. 1965. *The grammatical structures of English and Spanish.* Chicago: University of Chicago Press.

Suárez García, J., and P. M. Meara. 2000. Palabras olvidadas. *Vida Hispánica* 22:13–16.

Swan, M. 1997. The influence of the mother tongue on second language vocabulary acquisition and use. In *Vocabulary: Description, acquisition and pedagogy,* eds. N. Schmitt and M. McCarthy, 156–80. Cambridge: Cambridge University Press.

Terrell, T. 1986. Acquisition in the Natural Approach: The binding/access framework. *Modern Language Journal* 70.3:213–27.

Teschner, R. 1996. *El triple diccionario de la lengua española (TRIDIC)/The triple dictionary of the Spanish Language (TRIDIC).* CD-ROM. Hatfield, PA: Star-Byte.

Van Naerssen, M. 1980. How similar are Spanish as a first language and Spanish as a foreign language? In *Research in second language acquisition,* eds. R. C. Scarcella and S. D. Krashen, 146–54. Rowley, MA: Newbury House.

————. 1986. Hipótesis sobre la adquisición de una segunda lengua, consideraciones interlenguaje: Comprobación en el español. *Adquisición de lenguaje/Aquisição de linguagem,* ed. J. Meisel, 139–55. Frankfurt: Vervuert.

VanPatten, B. 1985. The acquisition of *ser* and *estar* by adult learners of Spanish: A preliminary investigation of transitional stages of competence. *Hispania* 68.2:399–406.

————. 1987. Classroom learners' acquisition of SER and ESTAR. In *Foreign language learning: A research perspective,* eds. B. VanPatten, T. Dvorak, and J. F. Lee, 19–32. Cambridge, MA: Newbury House.

Watanabe, Y. 1997. Input, intake, and retention: Effects of increased processing on incidental learning of foreign language vocabulary. *Studies in Second Language Acquisition* 19:287–307.

Waugh, L. R. 1982. *Roman Jakobson's science of language.* Lisse: Peter de Ridder.

Waugh, L. R., and B. A. Lafford. 1994. Markedness. In *The Encyclopedia of Language and Linguistics,* V:2378–383. Oxford: Pergamon.

————. 2000. Markedness. In *Morphologie/Morphology,* eds. G. Booji, C. Lehmann, and J. Mugdan, 1:272–81. New York: Walter de Gruyter.

Wesche, M., and T. S. Paribakht. 1999. Introduction. In *Incidental L2 vocabulary acquisition: Theory, current research, and instructional implications,* eds. M. Wesche and T. S. Paribakht. Special issue of *Studies in Second Language Acquisition* 21.2:175–79.

————. 2000. Reading-based exercises in second language vocabulary learning: An introspective study. *Modern Language Journal* 84.2:196–213.

West, M. 1953. A general service list of English words. London: Longman, Green.

Wittrock, M. C., C. Marks, and M. Doctorow. 1975. Reading as a generative process. *Journal of Educational Psychology* 67.4:484–89.

Zimmerman, C. B. 1994. Self-selected reading and interactive vocabulary instruction: Knowledge and perceptions of word learning among L2 learners. Ph.D. diss., University of Southern California.

————. 1997. Historical trends in second language vocabulary instruction. In *Second language vocabulary acquisition,* eds. J. Coady and T. Huckin, 5–19. Cambridge: Cambridge University Press.

6

Pragmatics/Discourse

Pragmatics and Discourse Analysis in Spanish Second Language Acquisition Research and Pedagogy

DALE A. KOIKE   University of Texas at Austin

LYNN PEARSON   Bowling Green State University

CARYN WITTEN   Southeastern Oklahoma State University

1.0   Introduction

Two related areas of linguistic research that have grown in importance in the last decade are those of pragmatics and discourse analysis. Studies in pragmatics examine language as it is used by speakers interacting in given speech situations and as it is understood by others (Leech 1983; Mey 1993). The focus of pragmatic study is how the meanings of utterances originate in the speaker's intentions in relation to the context in which they occur, how they are communicated, and how they are understood by an addressee. The field of pragmatics has been applied to the second language acquisition (SLA) context to discover ways that learners at different levels of second language (L2) proficiency understand and deal with speech situations in the target language, and how they are able to codify their intents and attitudes. The areas of study in L2 pragmatics include investigations into Spanish learners' interlingual pragmatic knowledge and use of various speech acts (SAs), their sense of politeness in the second language, as well as the application of such techniques to teach pragmatics as metapragmatic discussions, videotaped interactions, and role-play practice.

Discourse analysis is another very broad area of linguistic research that focuses on the text itself as produced by speakers situated within a given context. The text may be as small as a single word or a lengthy discourse by a single speaker or multiple interactants. Studies utilizing discourse analysis have played an increasing role in the understanding of L2 learners' gains in SLA proficiency, corresponding to a shift in focus to learners' performance in communicative interactions. Recent studies utilize perspectives of discourse analysis to approach various topics, including learners' development of such linguistic elements as tense, aspect, definite articles, and discourse markers. They also examine such issues as the syntactic complexity of written texts, types of texts used in reading, the evaluation of learners' performance in communicative contexts, and the discourse of other interactants in the speech event such as the interviewer.

We begin with an overview of the theories that have had great impact on pragmatic and discursive studies. Because any advances toward the target language pragmatics and discourse by the learner and any analyses of cross-cultural and linguistic behavior by the researcher must depart from knowledge of native speaker norms, a brief overview of relevant Spanish first-language (L1) studies is presented first. This chapter also examines several recent studies (generally, in the last decade since 1990) in the areas of Spanish pragmatics and discourse analysis as applied to the context of Spanish SLA. We review the works in terms of their theoretical bases and frameworks, research designs and methodologies of data collection, discussions of the data, conclusions, and contributions to the field of Spanish SLA. Finally, we propose directions of future research in Spanish SLA pragmatics and discourse analysis.

2.0 Pragmatics

Pragmatics concerns the functional use of language within a social, cognitive, and cultural context. Pragmatic study centers on the implicatures of utterances, the strategies that the speaker uses to produce an utterance, and the strategies employed by the addressee to interpret the utterances and reconstruct the speaker's intent. The most commonly recognized areas of pragmatics are speech acts, politeness, implicature, deixis, and presuppposition. In the following sections, we briefly review these terms and the areas in which we find pragmatic research that applies to the Spanish SLA context.

2.1 Speech Acts (SAs)

Perhaps the most popular topic of SLA investigation in pragmatics is the understanding and use of SAs, such as apologies, by L2 learners. Speech act theory, developed by linguistic philosophers Austin (1962) and Searle (1969, 1975, 1976, 1979), was intended to explain how language is used to perform different functions. Austin noted that some utterances could not be classified by their truth value, but instead performed given functions. For example, in (1) the speaker communicates that she wants the addressee to give her the salt and conveys an utterance conventionally recognized as a request:

> 1. Could you pass the salt?

Such an illocutionary act must satisfy certain conditions ("felicity conditions") to be successful. For example, the speaker must be sincere in uttering (1), and the addressee must be able to give her the salt.

2.1.1 Speech Acts, Politeness, and Implicature

Related to SAs and the force that they carry (illocutionary force) are the notions of directness (and indirectness), implicature, and politeness. We focus here on a brief discussion of politeness, since it is most pertinent to the Spanish SLA pragmatic research to date. The best-known model of politeness is that of Brown and Levinson (1987), who propose the concept of an ideal person who is a rational, face-bearing agent. They refer to *face* as one's public self-image; one can save or lose one's own face or do something to protect or damage the face of others. There are two kinds of face in their model: negative and positive. Positive face refers to the notion that one's wants are desired by others, while negative face denotes one's basic claim to territories and rights that should be unimpeded by others.

Following these two concepts of face, tied to the notion of politeness, when a speaker expresses a *face-threatening act* (FTA), or an act that could cause the speaker or the hearer to lose face in an interaction, the speaker has various options to express the act. The choice among options depends largely on the speaker's estimation of the risk of face loss. One can choose to express the FTA or not to express it. If the speaker opts to perform the FTA, it can be done directly (e.g., using an imperative form) or indirectly. Indirect realizations of FTAs contain redressive actions to reduce the threat to face and can be more ambiguous than direct FTAs. Some measures to take redressive action include strategies of positive and negative politeness, which derive from the face types described earlier. Examples of positive politeness include noticing the addressee's interests or wants, using in-group identity markers, avoiding disagreement, or joking, as in

> 2. Come on, Billy, let's clean up this mess before Zeus [referring to mother] gets home. We don't want to see what happens when she gets angry, do we?

The speaker can also choose negative politeness strategies, such as hedging utterances, minimizing the imposition, paying deference, or apologizing, as in

> 3. I'm really sorry to bother you at home but I wanted to ask if you could write just a little letter of recommendation for me by tomorrow. I promise I won't ask for another favor.

These strategies let the addressee know that the speaker recognizes that the request is an imposition that is impeding the addressee's rights and territory. The speaker considers factors of social distance between the speaker and addressee, power relations between them, and the rank of the specific act in terms of the gravity of its imposition when choosing which strategies to use.

The strongest criticism of this model is that it is most applicable to Western cultures and does not seem to account for all the complexities of the politeness systems of, for example, various Asian cultures (Ide 1989, 1993; Wierzbicka 1991). Another model of politeness that may lead to fruitful SLA research is that of Escandell-Vidal (1996, 1998a, 1998b). She proposes a model of politeness based on the Relevance Principle of Sperber and Wilson (1986) that establishes that all communication is assumed to be relevant. Key to this proposition is the notion of *context* as perceived by the hearer, which denotes an internal, cognitive component that determines the relevance of an utterance. Context here refers to a set of assumptions that a hearer uses to interpret given utterances. By using the Relevance Principle as a framework, communicative acts in different cultures can be analyzed for politeness. For example, she points out that an utterance like (1) is heard as an ability question in Slavic languages (cf. Wierzbicka 1991) and not as a polite request as it would be in English or Spanish. Escandell-Vidal suggests that the polite reading of (1) is a consequence of the English- and Spanish-speaking interactants' knowledge of this convention to relay a particular intended force.

Rather than use a speech act approach to politeness, involving notions of directness and indirectness that are expressed in discrete acts, Escandell-Vidal posits that the hearer, guided by the notion that relevance is at play in the exchange, selects the context that will give a relevant interpretation. Therefore, politeness is not linked to inferences but to relevance, which is formed by the knowledge base of each individual. This approach adds a cognitive dimension to the interpretation of speech act behavior beyond Brown and Levinson's largely social construct.

Until recently, very little work has been done in Spanish L1 pragmatics, which could explain, at least in part, the lack of Spanish L2 research. Several studies on Spanish L1 pragmatics that can serve as a baseline for studies in Spanish L2 pragmatics have been published in the last decade, however. Among them we find several Spanish speech act studies (García 1989, 1992, 1993, 1996; Chodorowska 1997; Koike 1998), an investigation of the relationship between politeness in Spanish and use of the conditional mood (Haverkate 1979, 1990), a comparison of perceptions of politeness by speakers of Peninsular Spanish and Mexican (Curcó 1998) and Ecuadorian (Palencia 1996) Spanish, and an early study on the association of deference with linguistic form (Fraser and Nolen 1981). Haverkate's (1994) important book on Spanish politeness and a recent volume on linguistic pragmatics in Spanish (Haverkate, Mulder, and Fraile Maldonado 1998) are noteworthy additions to the body of literature.

Among the studies that contrast Spanish L1 pragmatics with those of other languages, there is research on conventional indirectness in requests in four areas, including Argentine Spanish and Australian English (Blum-Kulka 1989) and on the mitigating effects of negation in Spanish and English suggestions and requests (Koike 1994). A recent study by Márquez-Reiter (2000) compares requests and apologies in British English and Uruguayan Spanish.

2.1.2 Deixis

Deixis, another area of pragmatics, refers to the linguistic system of indexicals that signify relationships, generally from the egocentric perspective of the speaker. There are four kinds of deixis: spatial (e.g., here, there); temporal (e.g., now, then); personal (e.g., I, you); and social (e.g., honorifics [Your Honor], humiliatives [Your Servant]) (Fillmore 1975). Deictics are a pragmatic category because they encode the speaker's attitude toward the referent or proposition being expressed. They are a central part of the language because they indicate a point of reference and a perspective.

There are no published studies on Spanish SLA and deixis, but we find a number of works based on Spanish L1 deixis. For instance, Davidson (1996) studied the pragmatic weight of *tú* "informal you" and *yo* "I." Blas Arroyo (2000) investigated how personal deixis is used in a Spanish presidential debate to examine how politicians manipulate the pronominal system to express (a) certain viewpoints, (b) responsibility for a given act, (c) an ideology or alliance, or (d) to strengthen solidarity. Uber (1999) documents and compares address forms in Latin American countries, and Schwenter (1993) examines dialectal differences in the use of *tú* and *usted* "formal you" in Spain and Mexico. In a contrastive vein, an early study by Jensen (1982) explored the differences in the deictic systems of Spanish and English with respect to the motion verbs <u>come</u> and <u>go</u>.

2.1.3   Presupposition

Presupposition, a third area of pragmatics, refers to the information or knowledge that speakers assume their hearers to have already at the time of the interaction. Several L1 Spanish studies address presupposition. An early study by Terrell and Hooper (1974) examines the Spanish subjunctive mood with respect to presupposition and assertion. They claim that speakers use the indicative mood when they believe that they are asserting the truth value of information:

> 4. *Creo que te vas.*
>   "I think that you are going."

On the other hand, speakers use the subjunctive mood when they do not assert (presuppose) information in order to express desire, disbelief, uncertainty, or some unrealized or not yet realized event:

> 5. *Quiero que te vayas.*
>   "I want you to go."

Mejías-Bikandi (1994) expands on the work by Terrell and Hooper but claims that their model cannot explain all cases of mood, especially those after expressions of emotion (e.g., *Me alegro de que* "I am happy that —"). Based on a definition of assertion drawn from the theories of Austin (1962), Strawson (1970), and Grice (1975), and the semantic framework of Mental Spaces by Fauconnier (1985), Mejías-Bikandi posits that the indicative mood is used in a complement clause when the speaker's intention is to indicate that a proposition is part of an individual's view of reality. The expressions of emotion do not assert this view of reality and truth because the speaker assumes that the listener is familiar with the proposition of the dependent clause; thus, the speaker relies on pragmatic presupposition. Based on this presupposition, it is not necessary to assert that proposition as truth; therefore it is marked with the subjunctive mood:

> 6. *Me alegro de que hayas venido.*
>   "I am happy that you have come."

The research by Mejías-Bikandi (1994) draws a connection between the syntactic and the pragmatic systems.

2.1.4   Pragmatics and Spanish SLA Research

In the area of SLA investigations of SAs in Spanish, researchers have analyzed cross-culturally the ways that learners understand and produce L2 SAs, comparing them to native L1 and the target language SAs. Several studies have examined whether learner behavior is derived from a transfer of L1 pragmatic knowledge to the L2 situation or from their developing pragmatic competence in their interlanguage. All the studies reviewed here are based on Speech Act Theory and rely heavily on Brown and Levinson's (1987) theory of politeness.

For example, Koike's (1989) work on pragmatic competence in interlanguage investigates the notion of a separate component of the interlanguage system that comprises pragmatic knowledge. Her investigation is one of the few to examine the pragmatic competence of lower-level learners. The goal of the study was to determine whether Spanish learners could easily recognize types of SAs in the L2 such as requests and apologies. Also examined were the learners' ability to work within speech act frames to communicate their intents, and if the learners who produced requests demonstrated a pragmatic competence distinct from their grammatical competence.

A series of three experiments was conducted. In the first experiment, which involved listening comprehension, forty second-semester Spanish learners listened to a request, an apology, and a command read by their native Spanish instructor, after which they identified the type of act and the elements (e.g., certain words, intonation) that helped them understand the message. The results show that nearly all of the learners were able to identify correctly the SAs in question, even without the aid of visual information such as gestures and facial expressions. Most of the learners indicated that they could identify the SAs because they perceived similarities in certain L2 formulaic expressions usually associated with those acts in their L1 (e.g., *lo siento* "I'm sorry," *por favor* "please," *rápido* "quickly") in conjunction with familiar intonation patterns.

In a second experiment intended to explore the transfer of L1 speech act knowledge and pragmatic competence, twenty-seven first-semester Spanish learners were asked to write what they would say after hearing a situation described to them. In the first situation, learners had to ask for a glass of water, while in the second they were directed to request that a visitor in their home get out of their father's favorite chair. The data indicate that, since the second situation involves a FTA, a more complicated speech act was needed. There were few request forms, hints, and distractions used to respond to this particular situation, probably because these indirect SA forms are more grammatically difficult and would represent an extra load for the learners beyond expressing their point. The direct commands and assertions, which the learners gave more often, are more efficiently and easily expressed, but they are less polite.

Finally, in a third experiment carried out to gather L1 English baseline data, the same production experiment was administered to twenty-three native English-speaking university students. The data contrast with those of the second experiment, in that nearly every directive was formulated as a request, showing the learners' consciousness of the need for polite SA forms. The author posits that because the L2 grammatical competence does not develop as quickly as the pragmatic concepts require, the expression of the SA conforms to the grammatical level of the learner. It appears that, acknowledging their limited grammatical knowledge, the learners opt for meaning over form in their target language (TL) utterances. As Koike notes, the findings of the study are limited due to the use of a written questionnaire to collect the data instead of eliciting more spontaneous responses from the learners.

LePair (1996) investigated requests by twenty-two advanced Dutch-speaking learners of Spanish and thirty-six native Spanish speakers (NS). The investigator asked informants to respond orally to various situations in a discourse completion task. The requests were analyzed using criteria from the Cross Cultural Speech Act Research Project (CCSARP) on SAs (Blum-Kulka 1989), which specifies nine levels of directness from the most direct formula of the imperative form (e.g., *Limpie el escritorio* "Clean the desk") to the most indirect strategy of a mild hint (e.g., *Parece que has estado muy ocupado* "It seems that you have been very busy"). The analysis focused on the head act of the request itself to determine the requestive strategies used by the participants. The study is the first stage of a larger investigation that includes the examination of Spanish requests by NNSs and their reception by NSs. For this reason, Le Pair did not analyze the external and internal modifications to the request head act, nor did he consider factors such as intonation and prosody.

The results of the study showed that both NSs and learners preferred the "query preparatory" formulas, in which the speaker refers to the hearer's possibility, ability, or willingness to carry out the action. Although direct strategies (e.g., imperatives, statements of need or want) were used by both groups, the NS usage was almost double that of the learners. LePair suggests that the unmitigated imperative forms seem too strong for Dutch speakers, as well as the suggestory formula (e.g., *¿Por qué no vas tú —?* "Why don't you go—?"), which implies irritation and can be interpreted as a complaint from the Dutch perspective. LePair also examined preparatory strategies used before requests, finding that the Dutch learners opted overwhelmingly (88 percent) to employ formulas concerning the addressee's ability or possibility to perform the action (*¿Puedes ayudarme—?* "Can you help me?"). In contrast, NSs also used strategies that addressed the hearer's willingness to do the action (e.g., *¿Quieres ayudarme?* "Do you want to help me?").

LePair concludes that the Spanish NSs are more direct in their request strategies than the Dutch learners, who show an ability to formulate conventional Spanish indirect requests and employ them more often than NSs. The results also indicate that these indirect forms are shared by both cultures. As stated earlier, however, the learners question the hearer's ability to do the action more frequently (*¿Puedes ayudarme?* "Can you help me?"), while the NSs address the hearer's willingness to do the action (*¿Le importaría ayudarme?* "Would you mind helping me?"). The investigator concludes that this willingness strategy may be culturally specific instead of universal and can be verified with a comparison of request data from Dutch NSs that were unavailable at the time the study was published.

Koike (1996a) conducted a study on the transfer of suggestion strategies from L1 English to L2 Spanish in listening comprehension. The suggestion speech act was chosen because, as Koike (1994) points out, many Spanish suggestions are realized differently than in English, seen in (7) to (10) (the English translations of (7) and (9) are provided in (8) and (10), respectively):

7. *¿No has pensado en leer este libro?*

8. "Haven't you thought about reading this book?"

9. *¿Has pensado en leer este libro?*

10. "Have you thought about reading this book?"

To convey the illocutionary force of a suggestion in Spanish, the suggestion must be expressed negatively, as in (7). The utterance without the negation in (9) conveys a simple yes-no information question. To the English speaker, however, the translated equivalent of (7), seen in (8), conveys a much stronger force than its Spanish counterpart, which can come across as a reproach to the native English-speaking listener.

The study utilized a set of videotaped stimuli to which 114 Spanish learners of various levels of proficiency were asked to provide written identification of the seven contextualized SAs heard and to respond to them. The investigator found that approximately 50%–75% of learners assigned the incorrect illocutionary force to the Spanish suggestion forms examined, especially when the forms were not prefaced by formulaic suggestion expressions such as *¿Por qué no ___?* "Why don't you ___?" and *Si fuera tú ___* "If I were you ___." Regarding the suggestion in (1), only a few learners in each of the three groups (between 6% and 9%) thought a rebuke was expressed, showing that most of them did not perceive the negative element in this utterance or they did not associate it with the English interpretation. Many learners could respond to the speech act appropriately or say something that would encourage further interaction and more input from the speaker, which presumably would lead them to understand the original intent.

In general, the data suggest that the more advanced learners are more proficient in understanding and identifying the suggestion SA, but only some of these learners notice the negative element in the interrogative suggestions. Regarding transfer, the data indicate that the transfer strategy is applied by learners at different levels of proficiency, leading to some correct and some incorrect hypotheses about the input. The learners seem to transfer pragmatic knowledge in matching what they can understand of the utterance to the context and other cues such as intonation. The more advanced learners, who can begin to analyze the input more closely, can sometimes make incorrect hypotheses about those details if they transfer matching L1 expressions and their meanings to those of the L2. The researcher suggests that L2 learners be exposed not only to the target language, but also to contextualized, interactive language use through media such as video. A limitation of the study derives from the use of written responses to stimuli, instead of spontaneous, oral responses.

3.0   Discourse Analysis

As stated earlier, discourse analysis covers a broad range of linguistic research, and the central focus is the text itself, which can vary from oral to written modality, and from one word to a long monologue. Research in discourse analysis has ranged from examining the structural elements of the text such as the lexicon, syntax, organization, and turn-taking, to the ideological perspective expressed in the text. For our purposes, we focus on those studies in discourse analysis as applied to Spanish SLA produced since 1990 that study the text itself—its features, organization, and so forth—and also those that use discourse analysis as a means to examine another aspect of learners' L2 competence; for example, to investigate the use of verbal aspect by Spanish learners in the context of a narrative.

The latter strand of studies can be characterized as a discourse approach to the study of lexical and grammatical items. A discourse approach to linguistic study implies a *top-down* perspective, one that can provide a broader context to the elements under scrutiny. Instead of working at the level of the sentence, one works with paragraphs or many exchanges between participants. The greater degree of contextualization allows the researcher to perceive patterns more easily and thoroughly, along with factors that influence them, and to draw meaning at a deeper level from the discourse. In the case of interactions, for example, one can see how the discourse is co-constructed by the interactants.

Discourse analysis studies are based on several frameworks for understanding text, including a functional look at such linguistic elements as revealed in dialogue and how they illustrate a social construction. Arundale (1999), for example, revisits the notion of politeness and proposes not an act-by-act model as that of Brown and Levinson (1987) but rather one in which the politeness emerges throughout the course of the interaction as the participants co-construct their meanings. Researchers may also utilize approaches such as critical discourse analysis (Fairclough 1995) or dialogic frameworks (Linell 1998). Other investigations examine nonlinguistic correlates of discourse, such as gestures, facial expressions, and proxemics (McNeill 1992; Farnell 1999). Many studies employ the microanalytic techniques of Conversation Analysis (CA) (Sacks, Schegloff, and Jefferson 1974) in recording their data, although they may not follow the framework entirely or may focus on such aspects of importance to CA as turn-taking or preference structure. Such a fine description yields details that may indicate hesitancies, self-selection in turn-taking, emotional expressions, paralinguistic, and gestural information that can attenuate or emphasize an utterance, turn overlaps, and the alignment that participants may or may not be working to achieve in their talk.

With so many approaches to discourse analysis, it would be impossible to list all the models that one can employ. We consider certain earlier work, however, to be basic to studies in Spanish SLA discourse analysis. Such research includes Pica (1987), Pica and Doughty (1985), Porter (1986), Long and Porter (1985), Day (1986), Varonis and Gass (1986), and Gass and Varonis (1985) on interaction studies, Sacks, Schegloff, and Jefferson (1974) for conversation analysis, and Kramsch (1982) on discourse analysis. More recent work on interaction can be found in Hall (1993, 1995), Pica (1994, 1998), Young (1999), and Riggenbach (1998). According to van Dijk (1994), discourse studies are also seen to clarify various aspects of language, such as grammar and information structure. We first review some studies that look at grammatical elements as used by Spanish L2 learners in the context of discourse genres like the narrative, followed by studies in Spanish SLA assessment and interaction. These are the three areas in which we find substantial activity in Spanish SLA discourse analysis. Our review of the studies, however, should not be considered comprehensive.

3.1 Discourse Analysis Studies on L1 Spanish Relevant to SLA

To identify areas of discourse analysis of the Spanish language that most influence Spanish SLA is an extremely difficult task. It is clear that more work is needed in L1 Spanish discourse analysis to learn more about the discourse of the language. In the area of Spanish grammar and its interaction with discourse, we find four recent studies. Cameron (1997) examines personal pronominal and null subjects in the light of Ariel's (1988) Accessibility Theory and Givón's (1983) work on topic continuity. Morris (1998) investigates topic-prominence in spontaneous Spanish discourse. Blackwell's (1998, 2000) studies on constraints on Spanish NP anaphora show the connection between syntax and pragmatics and how anaphoric expressions are interpreted successfully in discourse. Other work on Spanish information structure by researchers such as Fant (1984) can inform us about syntax and its function and, in the case of Bolinger (1954), of intonation, syntax, and function. Contreras's (1978) early investigation on word order yields much insightful information. Studies on discourse markers, such as that of De Fina (1997) on the use of *bien* "well, then" to manage transitions between activities and frames in the classroom may lead to other work on discourse and classroom management. This work adds to a growing body of literature on Spanish discourse markers (Busquets, Koike, and Vann 2001; Koike, Vann, and Busquets 2001; Montes 1999; Schwenter 1996; Koike 1996b).

The study of Spanish discourse genres should yield much information on what we can and should expect from learners in their efforts to produce such functions as narratives and opinions to approximate nativelike norms. Thus, such work as Fleischman (1990) on Spanish narrative and research published in such journals as *Oralia: Análisis del discurso oral* and *Spanish in context* can prove extremely useful to Spanish SLA study.

3.2   Discourse and the L2 Acquisition of Spanish Grammar and Rhetoric

Some studies in Spanish SLA employ the context of a lengthy discourse, such as a narrative or exchanges between conversants, to show how learners deal with grammatical elements. For example, Liskin-Gasparro (1996a) and Salaberry (1999) look at the development of past-tense verbal morphology by Spanish learners in the context of personal and movie narratives, using Vendler's (1967) verbal categories as applied by Andersen and Shirai (1994) to the SLA context.[1] The verbal categories are discrete, but are largely context-dependent for their meaning; thus, they must be analyzed within the larger discourse in which they occur.

Westfall and Foerster's (1996) work deals with the preterit-imperfect distinction from a pedagogical perspective. They propose that this aspectual distinction be explained in terms of a discourse model that illustrates how the two forms interact to determine discourse dynamics. They recommend that Spanish L2 teachers explain semantic theories of discourse such as the Discourse Representation Theory (Kamp 1979, 1981; Kamp and Rohrer 1983) to their learners. This model demonstrates how the preterit introduces a new reference time into the discourse with each new event while the imperfect invokes an available past reference time during which the action was occurring. Each form would be taught within its temporal discourse frameworks. Teachers should then show the interaction of the two forms in the discourse, making learners aware of how the preterit advances the story line while the imperfect fills out the story. The study does not contribute a new paradigm for the understanding of the preterit/imperfect distinction; instead, it builds on theoretical research by Bull (1965) and others. It does, however, inform us that Spanish textbooks have not yet incorporated the insights on the aspectual forms that have been developed over the past decades. In the second part of the article, the authors outline useful classroom activities on input and production designed to accompany and further illustrate the framework.

Task, another factor that influences the accuracy of L2 production, was investigated by Salaberry and López-Ortega (1998) in the context of Spanish SLA. They studied the accuracy in different tasks by seventy-four L2 Spanish learners at the third- and sixth-semester levels to see whether communicative pressure, dictated by the demands of the task, is as important as attention to form in determining levels of accuracy, as Tarone and Parrish (1988) claim. They also examined the factors of communicative control, or whether unconstrained choices in the L2 allow learners to avoid problem areas and upgrade their levels of accuracy and competency. They looked at whether advanced learners are affected by attention to form, task demands, and communicative control. The study offers an insightful discussion and critique of the different, and at times contradictory, claims of various SLA researchers. It also provides insights into current controversies concerning L2 development that are accessible to novice readers of SLA research.

The data for the study were collected through completion of two production tasks: a narration task requiring learners to write a story in the past and a grammatical task in the forms of a multiple-choice or fill-in-the-blank cloze test. Focusing on definite and indefinite article use, subject pronouns, and past aspect marked by the preterit or imperfect, the results showed that attention to form was not a singular predictor of accuracy for all three grammatical items. Although there was a difference in performance according to task, the effect of communicative pressure was not found to be statistically significant. Communicative control appears to be a source for variation in accuracy levels because learners improve their performance by using their L2 resources and avoiding gaps in their knowledge. Learners at higher levels gave less varied responses on both task types, suggesting that more advanced L2 proficiency reduces the effect of the task. As noted by Salaberry and López-Ortega, a drawback to this investigation is that it is based only on written discourse. They also note that it is difficult to compare their results to those of others because the components of each study and each experimental treatment are so different.

A study by Montaño-Harmon (1991) examines the discourse features of written Mexican Spanish and how this knowledge can be used in the L2 classroom. She claims that instructors should focus on language at the textual rather than the sentential level, which is the more common practice in the Spanish L2 classroom. Canale and Swain (1988) also describe discourse competence as a component of communicative competence, lending support to her contention.

Montaño-Harmon analyzed compositions written by fourteen- and fifteen-year-old students from four groups for discourse styles and features. One group consisted of Mexican NSs who wrote in Spanish. The other three groups, including Mexican ESL students, Mexican-American students, and Anglo-American students, all wrote in English. On average, the Mexican students writing in Spanish produced longer compositions with fewer but longer sentences. They used more run-on sentences and more synonyms, and consciously often deviated from the theme. Whereas the Anglo-Americans used an enumerative organizational style with connectors such as "first" and "next," none of the Mexican students used this device. The Mexican students generally employed a more flowery, formal, and complex style.

The investigator concluded that the Spanish learner must be made cognizant of the different written discourse styles of the two languages to avoid writing that may seem simplistic and even rude to the NS Spanish reader. A caveat to this conclusion is that learners may not be willing to accommodate to a different rhetorical style than the one they have learned in their L1. It may be feasible to make the average Spanish L2 learner only aware of different rhetorical styles. She also concludes that writing difficulties experienced by the Mexican-American group in writing in Spanish are due more to literacy issues than to L2 interference. A possible problem with this study is that, although the informants are working-class high school students, the investigator extrapolates her findings to be reflective of university L2 learners and instructors. Montaño-Harmon notes that university Spanish instructors often teach learners to write in Spanish using an American rather than a Spanish rhetorical style.

3.3   Discourse and Spanish SLA Assessment

With the current focus on achievement of an overall communicative competence in the L2 and the popular use of the ACTFL Oral Proficiency Interview (OPI) format for proficiency assessment, the testing paradigm has shifted to focus on paragraph-like structures in the context of completing language functions, such as narrating in the past, supporting an opinion, and comparing advantages and disadvantages of given referents. Thus, tests are based on production at the discursive and functional level, rather than at the discrete item and single utterance level. Language proficiency tests like the OPI seek to define language ability based on the learners' performance on various tasks. The model of language ability proposed by Bachman and Palmer (1996) expands on an earlier construct in Bachman (1990). According to these researchers, language ability entails two areas: linguistic knowledge (organizational, grammatical, textual, pragmatic, functional, and sociolinguistic competence), and strategic competence (metacognitive strategies such as goal setting, assessment, and planning). Language ability, therefore, is multicomponential, as learners use these competencies and strategies to "create and interpret discourse, either in responding to tasks on language tests or in non-test language use" (Bachman and Palmer 1996:67).

Research in this area of Spanish SLA analyzes learners' production in testing situations. Some studies look at the discourse of the learners' proficiency levels, seeking to clarify the ACTFL Guidelines that describe the criteria for evaluating a testee's discourse at a given level. An example of this line of inquiry is Bearden (1998), who examines the production of Novice-level Spanish learners in the OPI context in order to elaborate on the very minimal description provided in the Guidelines for this level of proficiency. This article adds an important contribution in that the Novice Level has received little attention in the literature. Bearden provides some interesting data on a proficiency level that is underdescribed in the ACTFL Guidelines, in spite of the many L2 learners who never progress beyond the Novice Level.

Using six audiotaped samples that were previously rated by two independent raters to be at the novice level, Bearden analyzed the data for cohesive devices, use of the L1, interaction strategies (e.g., repetition, expansion, clarification requests), intonation, negotiation, and scaffolding. She also discusses the interviewer's role in the learner's production. She found, for example, that only at the Novice-Mid or High levels did learners make any attempt to initiate topics or take control of the dialogue, and she suggests that teachers implement tasks that would help learners practice these discourse skills. Although she does not compare oral proficiency testing with and without an interviewer, Bearden clarifies the many ways in which the interviewer serves to facilitate the L2 learners' production. Alluding to the problem of objectivity encountered in tests done with live interviewers, she also notes how the differing behaviors of various interviewers can affect the data given by an interviewee and, as a result, affect the learner's score on the OPI. Bearden concludes with proposed revisions for the ACTFL Guidelines for Novice level oral production to yield more precise descriptions of the discourse features of Novice-level speech, such as including commentary on topic initiation and control, negotiation for vocabulary, and cohesive devices. She also proposes that L2 instructors provide explicit instruction in various negotiation techniques in order to improve learners' communicative performance.

Liskin-Gasparro (1996a) examines the interaction between narrative strategies and the development of oral skills by one English-speaking learner of Spanish. She compares the narrative, descriptive, and evaluative structures found in two stories about the same event told by the same person at the Intermediate level and later, after a semester of study in Spain, at the Advanced level of proficiency. The specific narratives were not elicited by the interviewer but instead occurred spontaneously during two separate OPIs. Although the study investigates the discourse of a single learner, Liskin-Gasparro provides an extensive analysis using a narrative methodology based on the work of Labov (1972) and Polanyi (1982). She identifies the three kinds of narrative, durative-descriptive, and evaluative clauses and compares them in the two narratives. The results show that the main story line is contextualized by durative-descriptive clauses and phrases, and contains an evaluation of key propositions in both narratives. The Advanced narrative, however, is longer and more detailed, uses a variety of linguistic resources to provide context, and has almost twice the number of evaluative devices used in a more elaborate and systematic way to draw the listener into the story world. The investigator recommends making learners aware of structural frameworks incorporated in narratives to aid the L2 production of these speech events. One might question, however, whether the same, emotionally charged narrative told several times truly reflects a certain proficiency level or the embellishment of a terrifying experience over time.

Another study by Liskin-Gasparro (1996b) addresses the need for a finer description of the language produced in OPI conditions by Intermediate High (IH) and Advanced (A) speakers. Communication strategies used by seventeen IH and thirteen A learners were examined to discover which strategies were most frequently used by speakers of each level to cope with lexical gaps. The audiotaped OPIs, conducted and independently rated by ACTFL-certified testers, were analyzed for such strategies as borrowing, paraphrase, and avoidance. She found that there seems to be an emerging ability across the IH/A border to rely on the L2 in moments of difficulty, with a greater tendency by A speakers to use strategies based in the L2. Due to the small number of learners in this study, the findings are limited. The author suggests that the ACTFL Guidelines need to define *circumlocution* more carefully so that testers and raters are more aware of the shift from a reliance on L1-based strategies to those based on the L2 at the more advanced proficiency levels.

Koike's (1998) study compares the discourse produced under the OPI context with that produced in the SOPI (Simulated Oral Proficiency Interview), in which the testee listens to a tape-mediated test format instead of a live interviewer and records all answers onto an audiocassette tape. Data provided by ten testees, four at the Intermediate level and six at the Advanced, in OPI and SOPI conditions were compared for the discourse features of pauses, possible turn signals, fillers, turns, self-correction, rising intonation, false starts, switches to English, propositions/supporting statements, quotes, SAs, and uncorrected errors. Results showed that testees in the OPI took significantly more turns, quoted more, used more SAs, and switched into English more often than in the SOPI. On the other hand, in the SOPI they used more fillers but tended to produce more ideas with better organization, and they stayed more focused on the specific task than in the OPI. The results, however, may have been affected by the topics of the elicitation tasks. In general, the OPI results suggest an increased awareness of and response to the presence of a live interviewer and a desire to utilize the linguistic resources of that person. This finding is important, given the fact that in L1 dialogue, interactants often rely on each other's linguistic resources. Thus, it raises the question of how oral proficiency examinations like OPIs are rated as if they were monologic, although they occur within the context of a dialogue.

Koike and Hinojosa (1998) propose a discourse approach to be used to assess oral production in a classroom testing situation, in which the structural elements of the learner's speech are compared to a template of a given function made by learners of the Advanced level. They examine the varying degrees to which 24 Spanish learners at the Intermediate and Advanced levels (not as defined by the ACTFL Guidelines but by the researchers' own adaptation of them in terms of the discourse produced) use paragraph-like structure in their answers to a stimulus requiring a comparison of advantages and disadvantages of two given referents during a SOPI. An analysis reveals that the Advanced learners in the study provide more propositions and supporting statements to complete the paradigm, closely following the template answer in organization. The Intermediate testees provide fewer propositions and supporting statements and either do not complete the paradigm or begin to diverge from their original intent. The less proficient speakers usually work at the level of the single proposition with a single supporting statement and use other strategies to attempt to compensate for their deficiencies. The authors propose that this template discourse approach be used to assess L2 oral proficiency in the classroom, inasmuch as it can reveal more of a global, effective expression of ideas, as opposed to the evaluation of discrete items such as verb conjugation and agreement errors. Some weaknesses of the investigation are due to the lack of validity and reliability of the authors' adaptation of the ACTFL Guidelines, as well as the lack of an extensive review of the literature on which to base their proposals.

We should note that the OPI as a measurement of speaking ability has been criticized by various researchers for its construct validity, use of prescriptive scales as seen in the ACTFL Guidelines, the rating procedures, idealization of the native speaker norm, and a theory of proficiency based solely on the test itself (see Johnson 2001 for a summary).

3.4   Interaction Studies and Spanish SLA

Given the push for communicative activities in the classroom in which learners interact with each other in an effort to negotiate for meaning and to make learning more meaningful overall, researchers have examined the discourse produced under such conditions to see what the quality of the interaction is and if there are certain features of the discourse that promote learning (Brooks 1991). One line of study follows a Vygotskian approach to the study of this interaction.[2] Two such studies are briefly discussed here.

Brooks, Donato, and McGlone (1997) follow Vygotsky's sociocultural theory of speaking and learning in examining various features of learner discourse produced by three pairs of intermediate level college Spanish learners in the completion of information gap activities. Those features include metatalk (learners talking about their own talk), metacognition (talk about how to perform the task), use of L1 English, and whispering to themselves in the L1 and L2 during the task. The researchers view these features as necessary steps for learning as the learners begin to use the L2 to communicate. They posit that the oral communication not only relays messages to listeners, but also serves as a cognitive tool that helps speakers solve problems and perform actions. It allows learners to reflect and control various features of their own L2 abilities. As the learners become accustomed to the format of the task, they produce more Spanish utterances directly related to the goals of the task. Although the findings are limited by the small number of learners, the study has some important implications for the L2 classroom. The learners' discourse shows that the utterances described here, which may be viewed by the instructor as "off-task talk," are instead an important part of the acquisition process.

DiCamilla and Antón (1997) also based their analysis of the role of learner repetition on the Vygotskian concept that sociocultural activity and mental activity are interdependent. Their investigation centered on the repetition, defined as any restatement of content or form of the task, that occurred in the discourse of ten adult beginning Spanish learners working in pairs on writing assignments. In their efforts to produce short texts, the learners used repetition in both their L1 and L2 to mediate their sociocultural activity, which was the collaboration with a partner, and their mental activity, which mediated their cognitive functions. They found that repetition functioned as a scaffolding strategy to hold and extend the externalized knowledge of each participant so that they construct new forms, such as the correct morphological form, and a device to establish and maintain *intersubjectivity*. This term denotes a common view of the task shared by both learners, which leads to the formation of a monologic text. The text is created by the two individuals repeating each other's utterances and adding words or parts of words, thus creating a single voice between the paired learners. The use of repetition in both cases allowed the learners to complete the joint activity by drawing on their shared efforts and knowledge to construct texts on the assigned topics.

Although these conclusions are thought-provoking, a criticism of this study is that it presents data by only ten subjects. Moreover, due to the nature of the task, which was the creation of a common written document, some of the repetition could be classified as either part of the editing process (mental activity) or negotiation for agreement on what to write (sociocultural activity). Both kinds of activities are necessary when two adult speakers collaborate in their L1 on such a task. The interlocutors' repetition may serve to facilitate the completion of a specific task as well as to enhance the SLA process. That is, repetition may simply result from encouraging learners to perform such collaborative tasks rather than from a specific L2 learner strategy, although repetition appears to facilitate SLA.

An article by Jordan (1990) studied the concept of self-selection in turn-taking as defined by Sacks, Schegloff, and Jefferson (1974) and later refined by Allwright (1980). After observing Spanish learners in first-, second-, and third-year classes, Jordan concluded that self-selected turn-taking can be encouraged during all types of instruction, not just during conversation practice. As Lorscher (1982) indicates, it is necessary for the learner to develop strategies to perform this skill in order to be able to function in conversational situations outside of the classroom. To encourage this behavior, instructors must refrain from dominating in the teacher-learner exchange. The investigator noticed that learners used the conjunctions *pero* "but" and *entonces* "so, then" to initiate their turns, showing that the teacher's ability to interest them in a discussion topic motivates them to protest and state their own opinions as well as to summarize various points. She concluded that these kinds of connectors should not only be taught as vocabulary words but also be modeled as pragmatic connectives that facilitate conversation. She claimed that the ultimate goal of the instructor should be to break the strict question-answer format of the classroom and to encourage learners to initiate language so that they may develop a higher level of discourse competence.

A limitation of this study is that it does not consider the differences between classroom and "real world" discourse. Moreover, while Jordan collected her data from learners in classroom situations, she did not experiment with classes in which self-selected turn-taking was modeled and encouraged as she recommends. Her recommendations may also be better suited to classes with small enrollments or in activities requiring small groups.

Lynch (1998) conducted a preliminary study of three Spanish L2 learners in a university immersion program to examine their turn-taking behavior and discourse structure before and after participation in the program. These learners were found to improve in the length of their turns and pauses by the end of the program. In comparison to three native Spanish speakers, however, they appeared to maintain their L1 English norms for turn-taking and discourse structure. The researcher suggests that the learners may be more aware of local elements, such as pauses, as their interlanguage develops, but may need to have elements at the higher discourse-pragmatic level pointed out to them. As the investigator indicates, this study is based on a data sample that is too minimal to draw any solid conclusions, but the findings point to another interesting area of research in Spanish SLA.

In another investigation of discourse functions, Makara (1991) studied the internal structure of an extended turn-at-talk by NS and non-NS graduate Spanish students and non-NS beginning Spanish learners in the context of a personal oral narrative of a silent film. Learners at intermediate levels were not included because the objective was to obtain baseline data from learners at opposite extremes of proficiency. Sixty subjects were asked to retell the researcher all they could remember about this film in their L2, and then retell it in their L1. The audiotaped retellings were double rated and analyzed for ability in a variety of communication tasks, including elaboration, background, circumstance (a subtype of description), restatement (in descriptive tasks), and purpose, evaluation, cause, and meta-communication (in interpretive tasks). She found that the highest significant comparative factors between non-NS graduate and beginning Spanish students were for overall description and circumstance. The highest significant comparative factors between the NS Spanish graduate students in English and the beginning Spanish learners in Spanish were for overall description and overall interpretation. She concluded that personal oral narratives for nonnative learners of both levels are largely in the form of descriptions, and differ from those of NS graduate Spanish students in that the latter can communicate opinions and doubts about events in their L1. She proposed using a series of activities from Galbán, Hawkins, and Hudson (1987) that address the non-NS learners' need for opportunities and contexts that require them to take the floor, generate an extended turn at talk, and produce a variety of descriptive and interpretive metacomments that are important in conversation. Unfortunately, the article lacks examples of discourse to illustrate her findings.

Lafford (1995) examines types of communication strategies used by L2 learners who acquired Spanish during a study abroad experience in Spain (N = 15) or Mexico (N = 13) as compared to those who learned only in a formal classroom in the U.S. (N = 13). In the context of a role-play situation during OPIs, the strategies the learners used to initiate, maintain, develop, and close a conversation during which they obtained directions from an interlocutor were documented.[3] Based on a pre-established taxonomy of communication strategies, a quantitative and qualitative analysis of their discourse showed that the study abroad learners performed better in all phases of the role-play. For example, all study abroad learners initiated the conversation by producing channel-opening signals to get the hearer's attention (e.g., *Perdón* "Excuse me") or appeals for help (*Tengo preguntas para ti* "I have questions for you"). These learners were also able to maintain the conversation with strategies such as fillers (*y* "and" or *entonces* "therefore") and backchannel signals (*¿sí?* "yes?" or *claro* "right") and extend the role-play by adding information not present in the written cues. Moreover, they used various discourse strategies to obtain the necessary information of the location of a museum and end the conversation appropriately. The author concludes that immersion in the L2 through study abroad expands the range of communication strategies of learners and fosters the development of key components of communicative competence and conversation management. The findings of the study are limited, however, by the small number of participants in the study and the task to elicit the learner responses.

4.0   Directions for Future Research in Spanish SLA Pragmatics and Discourse Analysis: Pedagogical Applications

As one can see from the review of existing research in Spanish pragmatics, there is a paucity of published research in Spanish SLA on SAs, politeness, deixis, and especially presupposition and implicature. There are, however, several dissertations that deal with Spanish L1 and L2 speech acts and politeness issues that promise more investigation in these areas in the future.[4]

The pragmatic and discourse analysis studies we have reviewed suffer from methodological problems of data collection. In the pragmatic studies on SAs, while the investigators realize the need to collect spontaneous, oral responses to realistic SA situations, such a format implies the administration of a questionnaire or treatments to individual learners. This procedure is both time-consuming and implies the use of native speaker interaction with each learner outside of the classroom context. Data collection for situations involving implicatures and presuppositions may be even more difficult to present in a natural way.

Many of the discourse analysis studies examine the discourse of very few learners, probably because discourse analysis involves the very time-consuming process of transcription of individual learners' discourse. The limited data sample then compromises the investigator's ability to generalize the findings to a broader population of learners. Technological advances may facilitate the collection of data in the future.

Following investigations of L2 learners' pragmatic competence in interlanguage, the next step is to examine how instruction can improve the learners' performance in this area of language acquisition. As an example, García and Spinelli's (1995) Spanish language textbook *Mejor dicho* has a pragmatic perspective to teaching the language. In this textbook, learners are provided with lists of expressions that can be used to perform various speech acts (*Lo siento* "I'm sorry," *Le pido disculpas* "I beg your pardon") and given situations in which they can apply these SA forms. A criticism of the book, however, may be the listing approach to teaching SAs instead of teaching learners sensitivity to the implicatures of the various SA forms.

García (1996) presents some ideas on teaching SA performance that focus on the invitation SA, based on previous work by Di Pietro (1987) and Olshtain and Cohen (1991).[5] Witten (1999, 2000) applies such techniques as metapragmatic discussion, videotaped interactions, and role-plays to develop *pragmatic competence* (the ability to perform linguistic functions appropriately in various social contexts) in the Spanish L2 classroom. There are also several dissertations that test treatments that may lead learners to acquire a better L2 pragmatic competence.[6]

We believe the fields of pragmatics and discourse analysis as applied to the investigation of Spanish SLA will continue to develop in two broad areas, in keeping with trends in SLA study in general. In pragmatics, the focus will continue to be on the functional use of language, with investigations in different areas of SAs and how they can best be acquired by learners. The focus will shift, however, from isolating SAs to showing how they are co-constructed by speaker and addressee over several turns, thus integrating pragmatics and discourse analysis even further. There will probably be an increasing emphasis placed on the sequentiality of SAs over the course of a conversation to show how they are used by the participants, for example, to keep in alignment with one another. Work in such pragmatic areas as deixis and presupposition should continue to explore the interaction of these two linguistic constructs with Spanish L1 syntax, phonology, and lexicon so that more complete grammatical descriptions can be drawn for learners, along with effective ways to present this material.

Spanish SLA will continue to draw from explorations of discourse in different Spanish L1 contexts and genres (Koike and Biron 1996), for they yield a view into language learning that quantitative models cannot provide. Spanish SLA discourse analysis will provide more information on interactionist models of SLA, utilizing a finer, microanalytic approach. Such studies can show how learners may achieve more nativelike discourse, as well as point out features of L2 discourse that seem to lead to acquisition. The direct connection between those discourse features and acquisition, however, is yet to be drawn.

Discourse features of text associated with the other language skills besides oral production should continue. The features of written text, such as Spanish textbooks, and teacher talk used to provide input to learners should be studied and correlated with gains in proficiency and understanding (Lantolf 1988; Lee and Musumeci 1988). Research needs to continue to work toward a more detailed description of the discourse by and for learners at different levels of proficiency.

We see a real need for work to continue in the area of L2 assessment, refining the description of the learners' talk in different genres and, to the extent possible, in different social contexts, thereby showing a control of various styles and registers. As long as the emphasis in the Spanish L2 classroom is on communicative competence, the fields of pragmatics and discourse analysis will be extremely useful to SLA researchers to show features of language use and organization, two of the most important linguistic aspects of successful communication.

NOTES

1. See chapter 2 of this volume for further discussion of these studies on the development of past tense morphology.

2. See chapters 9 and 10 of this volume for further discussion of Spanish L2 studies carried out within a Vygotskian sociocultural framework.

3. See also DeKeyser (1991) for another study concerning the development of communication strategies by Spanish learners during a semester-abroad experience.

4. Among these dissertations we find Ragone (1998), Hobbs (1990), and Delgado (1994).

5. Kasper (1997) discusses issues related to the teaching of pragmatic competence. She maintains that pragmatic competence, like linguistic competence, cannot be "taught." Language instruction, however, can be formulated to give learners the opportunities to observe and practice target language pragmatics and facilitate the development of pragmatic competence. Rose and Kasper (2001) edited a recent volume on the acquisition of pragmatics in L2 and FL classroom contexts. The studies included therein examine learners' L2 pragmatic competence, informal instruction, the effects of teaching pragmatics, and ways to assess pragmatic competence. See also García (2001) for ways to teach cultures of the Hispanic world through the study of speech acts.

6. For example, Overfield (1996) investigates the effect of consciousness-raising techniques, input from authentic video excerpts and audiotaped dialogues, and role-play practice to teach Spanish requests, apologies, and refusals. Pearson (2001) studies metapragmatic discussions in the classroom and their relationship to learners' pragmatic competence in using expressions of gratitude, apologies, and directives. Witten (2002) examines the effects of enhancing the viewing of a videotaped *telenovela* by a series of worksheets that elicit the reporting of pragmatic features from learners.

WORKS CITED

Allwright, R. L. 1980. Turns, topics, and tasks: Patterns of participation in language learning and teaching. In *Discourse analysis and second language research,* ed. D. Larsen-Freeman, 165–87. Rowley, MA: Newbury House.

Andersen, R., and Y. Shirai. 1994. Discourse motivation for some cognitive acquisition principles. *Studies in Second Language Acquisition* 16:133–56.

Ariel, M. 1988. Referring and accessibility. *Journal of Linguistics* 24:65–87.

Arundale, R. 1999. An alternative model and ideology of communication for an alternative to politeness theory. *Pragmatics* 9:119–53.

Austin, J. 1962. *How to do things with words.* Cambridge, MA: Harvard University Press.

Bachman, L. 1990. *Fundamental considerations in language testing.* Oxford: Oxford University Press.

Bachman, L., and A. Palmer. 1996. *Language testing in practice.* Oxford: Oxford University Press.

Bearden, R. 1998. Discourse features of Spanish oral production at the novice level. In *Perspectives on second language acquisition from Spanish,* eds. D. Koike and M. Carpenter, 1–32. Austin, TX: Center for Foreign Language Education Studies.

Blackwell, S. 1998. Constraints on Spanish NP anaphora: The syntactic versus the pragmatic domain. *Hispania* 81:606–18.

———. 2000. Anaphora interpretations in Spanish utterances and the neo-Gricean pragmatic theory. *Journal of Pragmatics* 32:389–424.

Blas Arroyo, J.L. 2000. *Mire usted Sr. González. . . .* Personal deixis in Spanish political-electoral debate. *Journal of Pragmatics* 32:1–27.

Blum-Kulka, S. 1989. Playing it safe: The role of conventionality in indirectness. In *Cross-cultural pragmatics: Requests and apologies,* eds. S. Blum-Kulka, J. House, and G. Kasper, 37–70. Norwood, NJ: Ablex.

Bolinger, D. 1954. English prosodic stress and Spanish sentence order. *Hispania* 37:152–56.

Brooks, F. 1991. Talking and learning to talk in the Spanish conversation course. *Hispania* 74:1115–123.

Brooks, F., R. Donato, and J. R. McGlone. 1997. When are they going to say 'it' right? Understanding learner talk during pair-work activity. *Foreign Language Annals* 30:524–41.

Brown, P., and S. Levinson. 1987. *Politeness: Some universals in language usage.* Cambridge: Cambridge University Press.

Busquets, J., D. Koike, and R. Vann. 2001. Spanish *no, sí:* Reactive moves to perceived face-threatening acts. Part I. *Journal of Pragmatics* 33.5:701–25.

Bull, W. 1965. *Spanish for teachers: Applied linguistics.* New York: Ronald.

Cameron, R. 1997. Accessibility theory in a variable syntax of Spanish. *Journal of Pragmatics* 28:29–67.

Canale, M., and M. Swain. 1988. Theoretical bases of communicative approaches to second language teaching and testing. *Applied Linguistics* 1:1–47.

Chodorowska, M. 1997. On the polite function of *¿me entiendes?* in Spanish. *Journal of Pragmatics* 28:355–71.

Contreras. H. 1978. *El orden de palabras en español.* Madrid: Ediciones Cátedra.

Curcó, C. 1998. ¿No me harías un favorcito? Reflexiones en torno a la expresión de la cortesía verbal en el español de México y el español peninsular. In *La pragmática lingüística del español,* eds. H. Haverkate, G. Mulder, and C. Fraile Maldonado, 129–72. Amsterdam: Rodopi.

Davidson, B. 1996. "Pragmatic weight" and Spanish subject pronouns: The pragmatic and discourse uses of *"tú"* and *"yo"* in spoken Madrid Spanish. *Journal of Pragmatics* 26:543–65.

Day, R., ed. 1986. *Talking to learn: Conversations in second language acquisition.* Rowley, MA: Newbury House.

De Fina, A. 1997. An analysis of Spanish *bien* as a marker of classroom management in teacher-student interaction. *Journal of Pragmatics* 28:337–54.

DeKeyser, R. 1991. Foreign language development during a semester abroad. In *Foreign language acquisition: Research and the classroom*, ed. B. Freed, 104–110. Lexington, MA: D. C. Heath.

Delgado, V. L.C. 1994. Politeness in language: Directive speech acts in Colombian and Castilian Spanish and United States English. Ph.D. diss., State University of New York at Stony Brook.

DiCamilla, F., and M. Antón. 1997. Repetition in collaborative discourse of L2 learners: A Vygotskian perspective. *Canadian Modern Language Review* 53:609–33.

Di Pietro, R. 1987. *Strategic interaction: Learning languages through scenarios*. Cambridge: Cambridge University Press.

Escandell-Vidal, V. 1996. Towards a cognitive approach to politeness. *Language Sciences* 18:629–50.

———. 1998a. Cortesía y relevancia. In *La pragmática lingüística del español,* eds. H. Haverkate, G. Mulder, and C. Fraile Maldonado, 7–24. Amsterdam: Rodopi.

———. 1998b. Politeness: A relevant issue for relevance theory. *Revista alicantina de estudios ingleses* 11:45–57.

Fairclough, N. 1995. *Critical discourse analysis.* London: Longman.

Fant, L. 1984. *Estructura informativa en español: Estudio sintáctico y entonativo*. Uppsala, Sweden: Acta Universitatis Upsaliensis.

Farnell, B. 1999. Moving bodies, acting selves. *Annual Review of Anthropology* 28:341–73.

Fauconnier, G. 1985. *Mental spaces.* Cambridge, MA: MIT Press.

Fillmore, C. 1975. *Santa Cruz lectures on deixis 1971.* Bloomington: Indiana University Linguistics Club.

Fleischman, S. 1990. *Tense and narrativity: From medieval performance to modern fiction*. Austin: University of Texas Press.

Fraser, B., and W. Nolen. 1981. The association of deference with linguistic form. *International Journal of the Sociology of Language* 27:93–109.

Galbán, J., B. Hawkins, and T. Hudson. 1987. Planning a trip through Spanish-speaking countries. In *Technology in the curriculum: A foreign language resource guide,* 299–312. Sacramento: California State Department of Education.

García, C. 1989. Disagreeing and requesting by Americans and Venezuelans. *Linguistics and Education* 1:299–322.

———. 1992. Refusing an invitation: A case study of Peruvian style. *Hispanic Linguistics* 5:207–43.

———. 1993. Making a request and responding to it: A case study of Peruvian Spanish speakers. *Journal of Pragmatics* 19:127–52.

———. 1996. Teaching speech act performance: Declining an invitation. *Hispania* 79:267–79.

———. 2001. Perspectives in practices: Teaching culture through speech acts. In *Teaching cultures of the Hispanic world: Products and practices in perspective*, ed. V. Galloway, 95–112. Mason, OH: Thomson Learning.

García, C., and E. Spinelli. 1995. *Mejor dicho.* Lexington, MA: D. C. Heath.

Gass, S., and E. Varonis. 1985. Variation in native speaker speech modification to non-native speakers. *Studies in Second Language Acquisition* 7:37–57.

Givón, T. 1983. Topic continuity in discourse: An introduction. In *Topic continuity in discourse: A quantitative cross-language study,* ed. T. Givón, 1–41. Amsterdam: John Benjamins.

Grice, H. P. 1975. Logic and conversation. In *Syntax and semantics,* vol. 3, *Speech acts,* eds. P. Cole and J. Morgan, 41–58. New York: Academic Press.

Hall, J. 1993. The role of oral practices in the accomplishment of our everyday lives: The sociocultural dimension of interaction with implications for the learning of another language. *Applied Linguistics* 14:145–66.

———. 1995. (Re)creating our worlds with words: A sociohistorical perspective of face-to-face interaction. *Applied Linguistics* 16:206–32.

Haverkate, H. 1979. *Impositive sentences in Spanish: Theory and description.* Amsterdam: North Holland.

———. 1990. Politeness and mitigation in Spanish: A morpho-pragmatic analysis. In *Unity in diversity: Papers presented to Simon C. Dik on his fiftieth birthday,* eds. H. Pinkster and I. Genee, 107–31. Dordrecht: Foris.

———. 1994. *La cortesía verbal: Estudio pragmalingüístico.* Madrid: Gredos.

Haverkate, H., G. Mulder, and C. Fraile Maldonado, eds. 1998. *La pragmática lingüística del español: Recientes desarrollos.* Special edition of *Diálogos hispánicos,* vol. 22. Amsterdam: Rodopi.

Hobbs, D. 1990. Gender differences in issuing directives in Mexican Spanish. Ph.D. diss., University of Texas at Austin.

Ide, S. 1989. Formal forms and discernment: Two neglected aspects of universals of linguistic politeness. *Multilingua* 8:223–28.

———. 1993. Preface: The search for integrated universals of linguistic politeness. *Multilingua* 12:7–11.

Jensen, J. 1982. Coming and going in English and Spanish. In *Readings in Spanish and English contrastive linguistics,* vol. 3., eds. R. Nash and D. Belaval, 37–63. San Juan: Inter-American University Press.

Johnson, M. 2001. *The art of non-conversation: A reexamination of the validity of the Oral Proficiency Interview.* New Haven: Yale University Press.

Jordan, I. 1990. Self-selection in turn-taking: An approach to teaching Spanish. *Hispania* 73:1154–57.

Kamp, H. 1979. Events, instants, and temporal reference. In *Semantics from different points of view,* eds. R. Bauerle, U. Egli, and A. von Stechow, 376–417. Berlin: Springer-Verlag.

———. 1981. A theory of truth and semantic representation. In *Formal methods in the study of language,* eds. J. A. G. Groenendijk, T. M. V. Janssen, and M. B. J. Stockhof, 251–69. Berlin: de Gruyter.

Kamp, H., and C. Rohrer. 1983. Tense in texts. In *Meaning, use, and interpretation of language,* eds. R. Bauerle, C. Schwarze, and A. von Stechow, 250–69. Berlin: de Gruyter.

Kasper, G. 1997. Can pragmatic competence be taught? NetWork #6. Honolulu: University of Hawaii Second Language Teaching and Curriculum Center. Available online at www.nflrc.hawaii.edu/NetWorks/NW06.

Koike, D. 1989. Pragmatic competence and adult L2 acquisition: Speech acts and interlanguage. *Modern Language Journal* 73.3:279–89.

———. 1994. Negation in Spanish and English suggestions and requests: Mitigating effects? *Journal of Pragmatics* 21:513–26.

———. 1996a. Transfer of pragmatic competence and suggestions in Spanish foreign language learning. In *Speech acts across cultures,* eds. S. Gass and J. Neu, 257–81. Berlin: Mouton de Gruyter.

———. 1996b. Functions of the adverbial *ya* in Spanish narrative discourse. *Journal of Pragmatics* 25:267–79.

———. 1998. What happens when there's no one to talk to? Spanish foreign language discourse in oral proficiency interviews. In *Language proficiency interviews: A discourse approach,* eds. R. Young and A. He, 69–98. Amsterdam: John Benjamins.

Koike, D., and C. Biron. 1996. Genre as a basis for the advanced Spanish conversation course. *Hispania* 79:289–96.

Koike, D., and F. Hinojosa. 1998. A discourse approach to the assessment of foreign language oral proficiency. *Texas Papers in Foreign Language Education* 3.3:33–50.

Koike, D., R. Vann, and J. Busquets. 2001. Spanish *no, sí:* Reactive moves to perceived face-threatening acts. Part II. *Journal of Pragmatics* 33.6.:879–99.

Kramsch, C. 1982. *Discourse analysis and second language teaching.* Washington, DC: Center for Applied Linguistics.

Labov, W. 1972. *Sociolinguistic patterns.* Philadelphia: University of Pennsylvania.

Lafford, B. 1995. Getting into, through, and out of a simple survival situation: A comparison of communicative strategies used by students studying Spanish—abroad and "at home." In *Second language acquisition in a study abroad context,* ed. B. Freed, 97–121. Amsterdam: John Benjamins.

Lantolf, J. 1988. The syntactic complexity of written texts in Spanish as a foreign language: A markedness perspective. *Hispania* 71:933–40.

Lee, J. F., and D. Musumeci. 1988. On hierarchies of reading skills and text types. *Modern Language Journal* 72:173–87.

Leech, G. 1983. *Principles of pragmatics.* London and New York: Longman.

LePair, R. 1996. Spanish request strategies: A cross-cultural analysis from an intercultural perspective. *Language Sciences* 18:651–70.

Linell, P. 1998. *Approaching dialogue.* Amsterdam: John Benjamins.

Liskin-Gasparro, J. 1996a. Narrative strategies: A case study of developing storytelling skills by a learner of Spanish. *Modern Language Journal* 80:271–86.

———. 1996b. Circumlocution, communication strategies, and the ACTFL proficiency guidelines: An analysis of student discourse. *Foreign Language Annals* 29.3:319–30.

Long, M, and P. Porter. 1985. Group work, interlanguage talk, and second language acquisition. *TESOL Quarterly* 19:207–28.

Lorscher, W. 1982. Conversation analysis and foreign language instruction. *Neusprachliche Mitteilungen aus Wissenschaft und Praxis* 35:211–18.

Lynch, A. 1998. Exploring turn at talk in Spanish: Native and nonnative speaker interactions. *Spanish Applied Linguistics* 2.2:199–228.

Makara, C. 1991. The internal structure of extended turn-at-talk within an academic context: Native graduate Spanish, non-native graduate Spanish, and non-native beginning Spanish speaker data. *Hispania* 74:1110–114.

Márquez-Reiter, R. 2000. *Linguistic politeness in Britain and Uruguay: A contrastive study of requests and apologies*. Amsterdam: John Benjamins.

McNeill, D. 1992. *Hand and mind: What gestures reveal about thought.* Chicago: University of Chicago Press.

Mejías-Bikandi, E. 1994. Assertion and speaker's intention: A pragmatically based account of mood in Spanish. *Hispania* 77.4:892–902.

Mey, J. 1993. *Pragmatics: An introduction.* Oxford: Blackwell.

Montaño-Harmon, M. R. 1991. Discourse features of written Mexican Spanish: Current research in contrastive rhetoric and its implications. *Hispania* 74:417–25.

Montes, R. G. 1999. The development of discourse markers in Spanish: Interjections. *Journal of Pragmatics* 31:1289–1319.

Morris, T. 1998. Topicity vs. thematicity: Topic-prominence in impromptu Spanish discourse. *Journal of Pragmatics* 29:193–203.

Olshtain, E., and A. Cohen. 1991. Teaching speech act behavior to nonnative speakers. In *Teaching English as a second language or a foreign language,* 2d ed., ed. M. Celce-Murcia, 154–65. New York: Newbury House.

Overfield, D. M. 1996. Teaching pragmatic competence: Input, interaction, and consciousness-raising. Ph.D. diss., University of Pittsburgh.

Palencia, M. E. 1996. Pragmatic variation: Ecuadorian Spanish versus Peninsular Spanish. *Spanish Applied Linguistics* 2:71–106.

Pearson, L. 2001. The effect of metapragmatic discussion on the acquisition of expressions of gratitude, apologies, and directives by L2 Spanish learners. Ph.D. diss., University of Texas at Austin.

Pica, T. 1987. Second language acquisition, social interaction, and the classroom. *Applied Linguistics* 8:3–21.

———. 1994. Research on negotiation: What does it reveal about second language learning conditions, processes, and outcomes? *Language Learning* 44.3:493–527.

———. 1998. Second language learning through interaction: Multiple perspectives. In *Contemporary approaches to second language acquisition in social context,* ed. V. Regan, 9–31. Dublin: University College Dublin Press.

Pica, T., and C. Doughty. 1985. Input and interaction in the communicative classroom: A comparison of teacher-fronted and group activities. In *Input in second language acquisition,* eds. S. Gass and C. Madden, 115–32. Rowley, MA: Newbury House.

Polanyi, L. 1982. Linguistic and social constraints on storytelling. *Journal of Pragmatics* 6:509–24.

Porter, P. 1986. How learners talk to one another: Input and interaction in task-centered discussions. In *Talking to learn: Conversation in second language acquisition,* ed. R. Day, 200–222. Rowley, MA: Newbury House.

Ragone, A. 1998. An exploratory study of thanking in French and Spanish: Native norms vs. non-native production. Ph.D. diss., University of Texas at Austin.

Riggenbach, H. 1998. Evaluating learner interactional skills: Conversation at the micro level. In *Talking and testing: Discourse approaches to the assessment of oral proficiency,* eds. R. Young and A. He, 1–24. Amsterdam: John Benjamins.

Rose, K., and G. Kasper. 2001. *Pragmatics and language teaching.* Cambridge: Cambridge University Press.

Sacks, H., E. Schegloff, and G. Jefferson. 1974. A simplest systematics for the organization of turn-taking in conversation. *Language* 50:696–735.

Salaberry, R. 1999. The development of past tense verbal morphology in classroom L2 Spanish. *Applied Linguistics* 20:151–78.

Salaberry, R., and N. López-Ortega. 1998. Accurate L2 production across language tasks: Focus on form, focus on meaning, and communicative control. *Modern Language Journal* 82.4:514–32.

Schwenter, S. 1993. Diferenciación dialectal por medio de pronombres: Una comparación del uso de *tú* y *usted* en España y México. *Nueva revista de filología hispánica* XLI:127–49.

————. 1996. Some reflections on *o sea:* A discourse marker in Spanish. *Journal of Pragmatics* 25:855–74.

Searle, J. 1969. *Speech acts.* Cambridge: Cambridge University Press.

————. 1975. Indirect speech acts. In *Syntax and semantics,* vol. 3, *Speech acts,* eds. P. Cole and J. Morgan, 59–82. New York: Academic Press.

————. 1976. The classification of illocutionary acts. *Language in Society* 5:1–24.

————. 1979. *Expression and meaning.* Cambridge: Cambridge University Press.

Sperber, D., and D. Wilson. 1986. *Relevance: Communication and cognition.* Oxford: Blackwell.

Strawson, P. 1970. *Meaning and truth.* Oxford: Oxford University Press.

Tarone, E., and B. Parrish. 1988. Task-related variation in interlanguage: The case of articles. *Language Learning* 38:21–44.

Terrell, T., and J. Hooper 1974. A semantically based analysis of mood in Spanish. *Hispania* 57:484–94.

Uber, D. R. 1999. Forms of address in the commercial Spanish of five Latin American cities. In *Advances in Hispanic linguistics,* eds. J. Gutiérrez-Rexach and F. Martínez-Gil, 110–18. Somerville, MA: Cascadilla Press.

van Dijk, T., ed. 1994. *Discourse as structure and process.* London: Sage.

Varonis, E., and S. Gass. 1986. Non-native/non-native conversations: A model for negotiation of meaning. *Applied Linguistics* 6:71–90.

Vendler, Z. 1967. *Linguistics in philosophy.* Ithaca, NY: Cornell University Press.

Westfall, R., and S. Foerster. 1996. Beyond aspect: New strategies for teaching the preterit and the imperfect. *Hispania* 79.3:550–60.

Wierzbicka, A. 1991. *Cross-cultural pragmatics: The semantics of human interaction.* Berlin and New York: Mouton de Gruyter.

Witten, C. 1999. Teaching for pragmatic competence in the beginning Spanish L2 classroom: A synopsis of a pilot study. In *Proceedings of the eighth colloquium on Hispanic and Luso-Brazilian literature and romance linguistics,* eds. E. Widener, C. Witten, A. McNair, R. Guadalupe, and A. Fuentes, 153–63. Austin: University of Texas at Austin.

———. 2000. Using video to teach for sociolinguistic competence in the foreign language classroom. *Texas Papers in Foreign Language Education* 5.1:143–76.

———. 2002. The effects of input enhancement and interactive video viewing on the development of pragmatic awareness and use in the beginning Spanish L2 classroom. Ph.D. diss., University of Texas at Austin.

Young, R. 1999. Sociolinguistic approaches to second language acquisition. *Annual Review of Applied Linguistics* 19:105–32.

Part II

Theoretical Perspectives: Processes

7

Generative Perspectives

Current Issues in the Generative Study of Spanish Second Language Syntax

LILIANA SÁNCHEZ   Rutgers University

ALMEIDA JACQUELINE TORIBIO   Pennsylvania State University

1.0   Introduction

In this chapter we review recent developments in the area of Spanish second language acquisition, devoting particular attention to second language syntactic research grounded within the paradigm of Principles and Parameters (or the theory of Universal Grammar) that has emerged over the past decades (see Chomsky's [1981, 1986] Government and Binding Theory and the ensuing [1993, 1995] Minimalist Program for linguistic theory). Section 1 provides an overview of the conceptual and analytical tools of the framework and identifies some of the prevailing themes in generative second language research. Section 2 surveys several issues that have engaged the interests of researchers in adult second language acquisition of Spanish; rather than present an exhaustive and, therefore, cursory survey, the discussion focuses on four prominent properties of Spanish syntax: null elements, clitics, word order, and predicate argument structure, as represented in the recent and current literature. Section 3 enjoins researchers to a consideration of investigations in cognate areas—specifically, language attrition, language variation, and child and adult bilingualism, all addressing grammar change within an individual speaker—as potentially contributing positive and productive insights to the advancement of the fields of second language acquisition in general and Spanish second language acquisition in particular.

2.0   The Generative Study of Second Language Acquisition

With the advancement of the generative enterprise in formal linguistics, research inquiry into adult language learning has emerged as a scientific discipline fully distinct from applied studies and independent of pedagogical aims (Newmeyer and Weinberger 1988; Flynn

1996; Flynn, Martohardjono, and O'Neil 1998). Today the generative framework is perhaps the most privileged paradigm in contemporary second language study: the approach is theory-driven—couched within the theory of Universal Grammar—and the research agenda reflects the changes and shifts in perspectives in generative theorizing. In contextualizing the present study, the discussion in this section references works proffering far-reaching and insightful theoretical proposals on language acquisition and analyses specific to Spanish second language learning.

In linguistic theory (see Chomsky 1981, 1986), Universal Grammar (UG) is put forth, in part, as a solution to the *logical problem of language acquisition* (variously referenced as the *learnability problem, projection problem,* or *poverty of the stimulus*). Briefly stated, the logical problem is the following: the ambient linguistic data available to children underdetermine what they come to know; therefore children must be innately endowed with cognitive structures specific to language.[1] Thus, in taking account of how child learners acquire such linguistic knowledge (and in characterizing the adult competence), proponents of UG argue for universal principles, which hold true of all languages, with differences between languages reduced to a small number of open parameters (e.g., the verb-movement parameter) that are fixed by experience.[2] The theory is further bolstered by consideration of the developmental problem of acquisition: UG is observed to be implemented in incremental stages, restricting the linguistic hypotheses that children contemplate in the course of language acquisition. Thus, in addition to explaining what linguistic competence consists of, researchers have sought to understand how the child's cognitive abilities interact with the ambient language samples in the course of acquisition.

Similar issues have constituted the basis for generative investigations of second language competence: Does the input from the target-language environment underdetermine the knowledge-state that adult learners achieve? Does domain-specific knowledge (universal principles and parameters of UG) guide second language acquisition and constrain representations of interlanguage grammars?[3] Indeed, the study of second language acquisition invites a reexamination of the logical and developmental problems of acquisition.[4] To date, the question that has dominated much of the debate in the published literature surrounds the issue of attainment. In particular, researchers have explored what adults' overall capacity for language acquisition can reveal about the continued accessibility of innate properties. The limited scope of this chapter does not permit us to rehearse the points of convergence and controversy reflected in the literature without oversimplifying and distorting the complex issues (see White 1996 for an insightful overview). However, concisely stated, the candidate positions on the matter include no access to UG, partial access to UG, and full access to UG, with differences and similarities in first and second language attainment marshaled in evidence (Birdsong 1992; Bley-Vroman 1990; Clahsen and Muysken 1986; Coppetiers 1987; Hawkins and Chan 1997; Schachter 1989, 1990, 1996; Smith and Tsimpli 1995; White 1989, 1996).

As expected, much productive research on second language attainment has been focused on the possibility of resetting parameters and the pursuant clustering of language-specific properties (i.e., properties that are not "learned" separately, but are "triggered" as a reflex of a single parameter switch). One of the parameters receiving significant attention in second language research has been the Null Subject Parameter, which clusters a number of superficially unrelated properties in languages such as Spanish. It was thought that learners' experience with (and analysis of) null subject sentences, which are readily available in the input (e.g., Spanish *Hablo inglés* "I speak English"), would be sufficient to trigger knowledge of other Spanish-language phenomena such as postverbal positioning of the subject and long-distance wh-extraction. However, studies of adult learners reveal a lack of clustering of the properties of the parameters at issue. Moreover, learners do not demonstrate the anticipated abrupt change of a parametric shift; instead, the shift is characteristically gradual. Yet, such findings have not been interpreted as precluding a UG access account, but rather, as endorsing the dissociation of null subjects from other properties previously associated with the parameter (de Miguel 1993; Pérez-Leroux and Glass 1997), or as evidence of the influence of the first language on the second language learner's mental representation of the target language (Al-Kasey and Pérez-Leroux 1998). Thus, attention has turned to the interaction of UG and first language knowledge in characterizing the initial mental state of the adult learner, accordingly viewed as fundamentally different from that of a child learner (Schwartz 1998).

Another important thread of initial-state research concerns the existence of nonlexical or functional categories, an issue inspired by developments in generative grammar (where functional projections are postulated to be the locus of cross-linguistic variation—but see Juffs 1996) and by parallel research in first language acquisition (see, e.g., the edited anthologies of Lust, Hermon, and Kornfilt 1994; Lust, Suñer, and Whitman 1994; and Clahsen 1996). Multiple positions have been defended, from full transfer of the first language grammar to adoption of specific aspects of first language representations (Epstein, Flynn, and Martohardjono 1998; Hawkins and Chan 1997; Schwartz and Sprouse 1994, 1996; Smith and Tsimpli 1995; Vainikka and Young-Scholten 1994, 1996, 1998; White 1985). Particularly prevalent are studies on the feature valuations (strong/weak value assignment, feature checking, and matching) that yield effects of word order, for example, those that relate to verb movement (Bruhn de Garavito and Montrul 1996; Mandell 1998; Valenzuela 2002), and those that relate to movement of syntactic phrases (Camacho 1999). Recent research has also converged on the study of direct and indirect object clitics, proposed as the spell-out of agreement projections (Montrul 1999a; Sánchez and Al-Kasey 1999) and what their acquisition indicates about UG access (Duffield and White 1999) and about parameters (Montrul 1999a). Such debates regarding feature specification and feature strength of functional projections have further confirmed that research in second language acquisition has much to reveal about the structure of language.

Analyses of adult second language grammars also entertain hypotheses of what constitutes the learner's final state (at "completion" of learning). It is patently obvious that adult learners differ from children in ultimate attainment, that is, in marked contraposition to child language acquisition, success for adults is exceptional, and most second language learners fossilize on an early interlanguage grammar (see Sorace 1993, 1996, 1999, 2000a for relevant discussion on the distinction between incompleteness and divergence in adult attainment). Furthermore, while learners may master aspects of linguistic knowledge that could not be acquired based solely on evidence from the second language input, their end-state grammars differ from the target and differ from those of other learners who share the same first language, though all may be constrained by UG (Toth 2000). Important questions of ultimate attainment have focused on maturation—for example, is there a decline in access to UG at puberty? (Obler and Hannigan 1996; Johnson and Newport 1991)—others on the question of near-native competence—for example, are near-native speakers' mental representations indistinguishable from those of native speakers of the target language? (Bruhn de Garavito 2002; White and Genesee 1996).[5]

Corresponding to the concerns over the mental representations that underlie parameter-setting and initial- and final-state studies are concerns pertaining to the process by which second language grammars are constructed. As expressed by Klein and Martohardjono (1999), in a generative model, the developmental changes evinced in the course of acquisition reflect grammar restructuring. Thus, in contemporary studies it is deemed important to study the progression by which learners move from one knowledge-state to another. In fact, the Minimalist Program (Chomsky 1993, 1995) and its antecedents (Borer 1984; Chomsky 1991) laid the requisite foundation for the study of knowledge shifts. Within the restricted framework of Minimalism, lexical learning is ascribed a central role in grammar construction.[6] Like first language acquisition (see Wexler and Manzini 1987), second language acquisition (see Archibald 1998; Newson 1990; Herschensohn 2000) is analyzed in terms of lexical learning, and learners are shown to exhibit knowledge of the structural effects of lexical class (see Dekydtspotter, Sprouse, and Anderson 1997).[7] Thus, where differences between languages had been interpreted within the Principles and Parameters paradigm in terms of a small number of specific parameters that typically encoded clusters of properties and descriptive generalizations (e.g., null subject languages allow free inversion), in the Minimalist model, parameters are expressed as features of functional entities within the lexicon. So conceived, parameters are not reset instantaneously, but piecemeal, as the lexicon is progressively mastered. In addition, as lexical learning is gradual, the coverage of a parameter will be less wide-ranging in nature, and second language learners may maintain conflicting settings of a parameter in the course of acquisition (see Bruhn de Garavito and Montrul 1996; Hertel and Pérez-Leroux 1999; Montrul 1999a; and Toth 2000).[8] The prominence of the lexicon in Minimalism is mirrored in the important body of research that has investigated the acquisition of verbs and their associated argument structures in adult second language acquisition (see Montrul 1998, 2002a).

Innovations in the Minimalist Program have also highlighted the importance of economy, eliminating superfluous constructs, including unnecessary levels of representation, and striving for optimal derivations. Appealing to issues of economy in language acquisition, Platzack (1996) submits that since the overt checking that is motivated by strong features is a costly operation, the initial hypothesis of the child learner must be that all syntactic features are weak, and that language acquisition represents the gradual adjustment of feature values toward the target language.[9] More important in the present context, in accordance with this Initial Hypothesis of Syntax, strong values once acquired cannot be lost. In second language acquisition, then, strong values of the first language will be transferred to the second language, a hypothesis that is confirmed in certain interlanguage patterns (see Sánchez and Giménez 1998; Camacho, Paredes, and Sánchez 1997).

Of course, a comprehensive survey of issues in generative second language acquisition research warrants attention to additional themes, notable among these the nature of the input (i.e., triggering data) available to the learner, the conditions under which parameters can be (re)set, the methodologies employed in accessing learner competence, the evaluation of linguistic data, and the psychological constructs invoked in characterizing the acquisition process—none of these crucial themes is adequately covered here. Nevertheless, the preceding paragraphs leave little doubt but that research in second language acquisition and research in UG are inherently related. And the ensuing discussion will make evident that Spanish second language acquisition data provides fertile ground for confronting and advancing theories of Spanish language syntax.

3.0   Selected Issues in Spanish Second Language Acquisition

Having laid the broad context for our work, we now turn to a discussion of some of the central issues in the study of Spanish second language acquisition, culled from the recent and current literature. While some of the extant research aims at testing issues of Spanish first language acquisition, the majority of the studies reviewed here expressly examine interlanguage grammars in their own right. It merits noting at the outset that the survey is not exhaustive by any means, nor does it integrate the results of numerous and varied studies; rather, the discussion is devoted to the presentation of selected issues: null elements, clitics, word order, and predicate argument structures.[10] Still, however delimited in its scope, we hope that this review will serve to encapsulate the progress that has been made in our understanding of Spanish second language syntax.

3.1   Null Elements (Subjects, Objects, and Determiners)

The study of the Null Subject Parameter has been at the center of discussions on parameter resetting and access to UG since the work of Liceras (1989). Subsequent work of the past decade or more traces the evolution from the study of parametric clusters to a more careful analysis of the mechanisms involved in the acquisition of null subjects that includes the role of transfer of properties from the first language, the notion of gradual resetting, and other aspects of grammatical restructuring.

   In their study of the Null Subject Parameter, Al-Kasey and Pérez-Leroux (1998) analyzed the Spanish language forms of English-speaking adult learners and found that the learners initially transfer English-language settings into Spanish; however, over time, there is evident a shift to the null subject grammar of Spanish: null thematic and expletive subjects emerge simultaneously. Evidence of this shift comes from null subjects in learners' oral speech and from an interpretation task in which learners correctly matched sentences such as (1) and (2) with pictures denoting referential and generic meanings. The results of this study demonstrate that these two properties are clustered and may be reset as a single parameter, although the process of resetting is gradual and occurs following an initial period of transference.

1. *A Pedro le gusta su cometa azul. Esta es divertida de volar.*
   "Pedro likes his blue kite. This is fun to fly."

2. *A Pedro le gusta su cometa azul. Es divertido volar.*
   "Pedro likes his blue kite. It is fun to fly."

A somewhat different approach to the Null Subject Parameter is put forth in Pérez-Leroux and Glass (1997). These authors redirect research from traditional parametric values such as the acquisition of verbal morphology, null expletives, and subject-verb inversion to test two novel hypotheses on the distribution of null and overt subjects. The first hypothesis is that the distribution of null and overt subject pronouns in contrastive focus environments should be learned by native speakers of English because it parallels the distribution of unstressed and stressed pronouns in their native language: in Spanish, a contrastive focus interpretation requires an overt pronoun and precludes a null pronoun, as illustrated in (3b); in English a contrastive focus interpretation requires a stressed pronoun and precludes an unstressed pronoun, as shown in (4). The second hypothesis holds that if access to UG is not available in adult language acquisition, the Overt Pronoun Constraint that bans a variable reading of overt pronouns (Montalbetti 1984), as illustrated in (5), should be less readily learned by English-speaking adults, since their native language lacks a similar constraint.

> 3a. *¿Quién cree Juan que ganará el premio?*
> "Who does Juan think will win the prize?"

> 3b. *Juan$_i$ cree que él$_{i/}$*pro$_i$ ganará el premio.*
> Juan$_i$ thinks that he$_{i/}$*pro$_i$ will win the prize.

> 4. John$_i$ pushed Peter$_j$ and then HE$_{j/*i}$ kicked HIM $_{i/*j}$.

> 5a. *Nadie$_i$ dice que pro$_{i/j}$ ganará el premio.*
> "Nobody says that s/he will win the prize."

> 5b. *Nadie$_i$ dice que él$_{*i/j}$ ganará el premio.*
> "Nobody says that s/he will win the prize."

Separate tasks were designed for testing each hypothesis. As a measure of knowledge of the effects of contrastive focus on overt versus null pronoun selection, participants listened to a story and answered a questionnaire based on it. And as a measure of their knowledge of the pronoun restriction, a translation task was administered. The findings confirm both hypotheses: advanced learners of Spanish are sensitive to the focus constraint on the distribution of null versus overt subject pronouns and to the effects of the Overt Pronoun Constraint, the latter finding leading Pérez-Leroux and Glass to conclude that UG is accessible to adult learners.

Other studies have also shifted in focus from the clustering of parametric values and associated phenomena to additional characteristics of null subjects, e.g., the distinction between the pragmatic-semantic devices that provide the identification for null subjects and the morphosyntactic requirements that license them. Liceras and Díaz (1998), Liceras, Díaz, and Maxwell (1998), and Liceras, Díaz, Laguardia, and Fernández (1998), have pioneered this approach to the study of null subjects. Liceras and Díaz (1999) and Liceras, Valenzuela, and Díaz (1999) contrast the conditions that allow for null subjects in child acquisition, in particular the null subjects observed in first language acquisition of non-subject drop languages such as English, with the conditions operating in the second language Spanish grammar of adult speakers of non-null subject languages. Null subjects in child language have been attributed to the nonactivation of the pragmatic principle that equates a root sentence with a full CP (Rizzi 1994). Liceras and Diaz (1999) present evidence that this principle is fully activated in adult nonnative grammars: interlanguage grammars contain null subjects in root and embedded clauses as well as in wh-questions, even at early stages, as the following Spanish interlanguage sample from a French speaker illustrates:

6. *¿Dónde vives?*
   "Where do you live?"

Liceras and Díaz thus propose that the differences between null subjects in the second language acquisition of Spanish and the first language acquisition of non-null subject languages do not stem from the inoperativity of the root CP principle, and must instead be accounted for by reference to the operation of other principles. In an effort to uncover such principles, these researchers analyzed spontaneous Spanish speech data from adult native speakers of non-null subject languages such as English and French and of native speakers of [+topic drop] languages such as colloquial German, Chinese, and Japanese.[11] The results reveal no substantial evidence of early transfer of the first language properties in the Spanish of French and English speakers—null subjects can be found in their early productions (this in contraposition to the findings of Al-Kasey and Pérez-Leroux [1998] presented earlier). However, in the case of native speakers of [+topic drop] languages, Liceras and Díaz found an overuse of overt subject pronouns that identify the null subjects in the interlanguage. The researchers interpret such subject pronoun identification as evidence that local restructuring of the native grammar has taken place, and based on this analysis, propose that adult learners have recourse to mechanisms other than UG to identify null subjects.

In addition to null subjects, null objects, and null determiners have also generated interest in the Spanish second language acquisition literature. Two such studies examine the occurrence of these null elements in the Spanish interlanguage of adult native speakers of Quechua in a situation of language contact. Camacho, Paredes and Sánchez (1997) found strong evidence in favor of initial transfer of the Quechua pronominal value for null objects into Spanish, as illustrated by the response in (7b) from their low proficiency group data. They also found null objects in the oral production data of speakers with intermediate and high levels of proficiency, although as proficiency increases, null objects are less frequent and are constrained to [-human], [-definite] features. Camacho, Paredes and Sánchez argue that this is possible because Quechua, the first language, has a constraint on its object agreement markers that allows them only if the referent is [+human]. Learners assume that agreement markers are only possible with [+human] referents in Spanish and, when clitics emerge (as the heads of AgrOP) in their second language Spanish, they are correlated with [+human] referents; only gradually do learners begin to correlate these with [+definite] referents.

7a. *¿Qué hace, la mata (el lobo) o no la mata a la oveja$_i$?*
   "What does the wolf do, does it kill or not kill the sheep?"

7b. *Sí, mata e$_i$, sí, mata e$_i$.*
   "Yes, it kills it, yes it kills it."

Sánchez and Giménez (1998) analyze null determiners (assumed to be heads of DP, following the proposal of Longobardi [1994] for bare NPs) in the Spanish productions of Quechua-speaking learners. As shown in (8–9), Quechua has null definite determiners; in contrast, Spanish has overt definite determiners and allows for null determiners in generic NPs in object position and in NP complements of prepositions, but disallows them in NPs in subject position.

8. [e *Warmi-Ø*] [e *sapatu-ta*] *rantirqan* [*amigu-(n)-wan*]
    [e woman- Ø] [e shoe-acc] bought [friend-(3p)-comitative]
    "A/the woman bought a/the shoe(s) with a (her) friend(s)."

9. [*La/una/*e mujer*] *compró* [*los/unos/e zapatos*] *con* [*los/unos/e desconocidos*]
    "The/a/*woman bought the/some/e shoes with the/some/e unknown people."

The Spanish interlanguage forms of adult native-speakers of Quechua, exemplified in (10–11), showed that null determiners are favored by syntactic context and occurred in NP objects of verbs and more frequently in NP objects of prepositions (the latter increase attributed to (N-to-D-to-) P incorporation); this was the case for all speakers, irrespective of age and frequency of exposure to Spanish.

10. *El chiquito quiere agarrar venado.*
    The little one wants to catch [e] deer
    "The kid wants to catch (the) deer."

11. *Hay dos sapitos con perrito.*
    There are two frogs with [e] dog
    "There are two frogs with (the) dog(s)."

Such data support the hypothesis that certain syntactic mechanisms from the first language are available to adult learners, especially if the input is compatible with them.

3.2   Clitics

Continuing in the line of research above outlined are studies on the acquisition of clitics[12] and related parametric properties. As noted previously, the issue of the acquisition of a clustering of properties by Spanish second language learners has generated much research. As with the study of null elements, there has been a transition from a perspective that emphasized the resetting of a clustering of surface phenomena to the analysis of the resetting of functional features.

Bruhn de Garavito and Montrul (1996) investigate the acquisition of accusative clitics and related phenomena by French-speaking learners of Spanish.[13] As illustrated in (12), French and Spanish differ in the distribution of direct object clitics with infinitivals: whereas French allows only proclitics with infinitivals, Spanish allows only enclitics with infinitivals or proclitics with inflected verbs.

12a. *Je veux acheter le./*Je le veux acheter./Je veux l'acheter.*

12b. *Quiero comprarlo./Lo quiero comprar./*Quiero lo comprar.*
   "I want to buy it."

Bruhn de Garavito and Montrul assume Kayne's (1991) account of the differential distribution. Following Kayne, the French verb moves to an INFN node above VP and the clitic adjoins to V+INFN, yielding the word order clitic+infinitival. But in Spanish, V+INFN raises to left-adjoin to the CL+T cluster, yielding the enclitic form. Notably, on Kayne's analysis, this latter property of the syntax of Spanish is related to the licensing PRO in *si* structures and to placement of adverbs:

13a. *María no sabe si [PRO ir al cine].*
   "María doesn't know whether to go to the cinema."

13b. *Hablar bien el español es difícil.*
   "It is difficult to speak Spanish well."

These properties of Spanish are treated as a parametric cluster by Bruhn de Garavito and Montrul, who hypothesize that success in resetting these properties would be evidence in favor of access to UG. Their findings reveal some evidence of the acquisition of Spanish infinitival raising and PRO control in *si* sentences, although the results were less clear-cut with respect to placement of clitics, quantifiers, and adverbs. The study yields little support in favor of simultaneous resetting of the cluster of properties hypothesized to be associated with verb movement; instead, the findings suggest a gradual resetting of the parameter, with the possibility of dual grammars in one speaker.[14]

Montrul (1999a) examines the acquisition of a set of properties associated with dative clitics, assumed to head AgrIOP in Spanish. Based on Lightfoot's (1991) diachronic account of the loss of dative case in the development of English, Montrul proposes that languages such as English lack AgrIOP and overt dative case. On Lightfoot's parametric account, the loss of AgrIOP made it possible for English to have constructions such as Exceptional Case Marking, preposition stranding, double objects, and indirect passives. Montrul proposes to extend this analysis to the second language acquisition of Spanish by English speakers (Montrul 1996, 1997). Adopting Schwartz and Sprouse's Full Transfer/Full Access model for the initial state, she hypothesized that in Spanish second language learning, acquisition of dative clitics should trigger the unlearning of the English constructions associated with the lack of AgrIOP. (The French-speaking learners need not postulate new functional structure in accommodating the Spanish language input.) In testing this hypothesis, two tasks were administered to English- and French-speaking learners of Spanish with different levels of proficiency. A written elicited production task tested the acquisition of dative clitics, and a grammaticality judgment task, incorporating items such as in (14), tested the additional properties.

14a. *María cree Juan ser un buen amigo.*
   "María believes Juan to be a good friend."

14b. *¿Qué es el libro sobre?*
"What is the book about?"

14c. *Juan dio María un regalo.*
"Juan gave Mary a present."

14d. *María fue dada un regalo.*
"Mary was given a gift."

The results of this study showed that all learners produced dative clitics, but not all of the proposed effects, calling into question the status of the clitic as the appropriate trigger for parameter resetting.[15] There was also attested some evidence of transference: the French speakers outperformed the English speakers in rejecting ungrammatical sentences; however, French speakers did not transfer their native grammar in its entirety (contrary to the Full Transfer/Full Access hypothesis), as they, like the English speakers, experienced difficulty in accepting sentences that are grammatical in the native language. As in the previous study (Bruhn de Garavito and Montrul 1996), these findings favor a resetting of a subset of the cluster of parametric properties; learners showed evidence of discrete and systematic unlearning of some but not all of the other constructions associated with the AgrIOP parameter.[16] The findings likewise favor a process of gradual resetting, as evidenced in the coexistence of dative and nominative subjects in the data from English speakers.

Alternatives to the study of a cluster of properties associated with clitics have also been put forth in the literature. Duffield and White (1999) have proposed that successful acquisition of accusative clitic placement in Spanish second language acquisition is attainable for native speakers of languages with either a different distribution for clitics, such as French, or with no clitics, such as English. In Spanish, accusative clitics left-adjoin to main and auxiliary tensed verbs, as shown in the examples in (15); they may left-adjoin to the tensed verb or appear to the right of the infinitival in restructuring sentences, as in (16); and they may only appear to the left of the conjugated verb in causative sentences, as in (17). In contrast, English lacks syntactic clitics, and French permits accusative clitics to left-adjoin to tensed verbs, but it allows only for a medial position for the verb in restructuring sentences (see example 12a).

15a. *Juan la encuentra completamente estúpida.*
"Juan finds her completely stupid."

15b. *Mario los ha asesinado dentro de un auto.*
"Mario them has assassinated inside of a car."

16a. *Marta las quiere comprar con cheque.*
"Marta them wants to buy with a check."

16b. *Marta quiere comprarlas con cheque.*
"Marta wants to buy them with a check."

17. *El profesor los hace escribir mucho.*
    "The professor makes them write a lot."

Duffield and White hypothesized that if universal syntactic properties determine clitic placement and these are accessible to adult learners, English and French speakers should be equally successful in acquiring clitic placement. They used an online sentence-matching task and an off-line grammaticality judgment task to test for acquisition of Spanish clitic placement among French- and English-speaking learners. The two tasks converged in uncovering few transfer effects; both groups had acquired clitic placement with main verbs and auxiliaries. However, clitic-climbing in restructuring and causative sentences presented difficulties for both groups. Duffield and White conclude that successful acquisition of clitic placement with main and auxiliary verbs is evidence in favor of access to UG and that the difficulties noted for clitic climbing are consistent with a base-generation analysis of clitics (Sportiche 1996) rather than with a movement analysis (Kayne 1975).

Sánchez and Al-Kasey (1999) assume a different line of inquiry for direct object clitics, drawing on analyses of direct object clitics as agreement markers that head the functional projection AgrOP (Suñer 1988; Franco 1993; Everett 1996). These researchers proposed that English lacks clitics because the functional features of AgrO are never spelled out. In Spanish, on the other hand, these features may be spelled out under specific conditions. For example, clitics are obligatory in constructions in which the direct object complement is a pronoun, as in (18), and in clitic left dislocation structures, as in (19).[17] And in some varieties of Spanish, AgrO may be spelled out when the direct object complement is [+ human, + definite, +specific], as in (20).

18. **(La) vi a ella.*
    CL saw her
    "I saw her."

19. *La casa *(la) pagamos a plazos.*
    "The house *(CL) we pay in installments."

20. *La vi a María.*
    CL saw Maria
    "I saw her."

Sánchez and Al-Kasey hypothesized that in order to acquire the distribution of direct object clitics in Spanish, English speakers must gradually acquire the full specification for the functional features of AgrO, which include person, number, definiteness, and specificity. In order to test this hypothesis, they elicited data from English-speaking learners of Spanish, by administering a picture-based oral production task and a picture-sentence matching questionnaire. If learners demonstrated clitics in their oral productions but were unable to produce clitic-doubling structures or recognize clitics as licensers of clitic left dislocation constructions, this would be evidence of the incomplete specification of AgrO features. In the task that tested for recognition of clitics as licensers in dislocated structures, the picture-sentence matching activity included items such as a picture of a young girl opening a door and a selection of three candidate descriptions:

> 21a. *La niña la abre la puerta.*
>
> The girl CL opens the door

> 21b. *La puerta la niña la abre.*
>
> The door the girl CL opens

> 21c. *La niña la puerta la abre.*
>
> The girl the door CL opens
>
> "The girl opens the door."

Results showed that at initial and intermediate stages of acquisition, adult English-speaking learners of Spanish have a partial specification for AgrO, as indicated by their failure to produce clitic left dislocation and clitic-doubling constructions, as well as their failure to recognize clitics as licensers in the former structures; this was attested by their strong preference for sentences such as (21a). The data also revealed a lack of sensitivity to definiteness and specificity features among beginning and intermediate learners and some instances of clitic-doubling among more advanced learners. There were no strong pronouns in the narratives, ruling out transfer from the first language, but there was evidence of an avoidance strategy of DP repetition, indicating learners' awareness of the incomplete feature specification of AgrO.

3.3   Word Order

Investigations of word order in Spanish second language acquisition have witnessed the now familiar pattern of evolution: the literature is characterized by a shift from early explorations of clusters of parametric values toward studies that focus on specific properties of functional categories and on the constraints that the learner's extant knowledge of lexical classes imposes on the development of second language syntactic knowledge.

A main difference in word order at the clausal level can be ascribed to the head direction and verb-movement parameters. Languages such as English and Spanish are head-initial (i.e., complements follow their heads), whereas others (e.g., Japanese) are head-final. With respect to verb movement, however, English and Spanish differ: English demonstrates a negative value for the verb movement parameter, while Spanish demonstrates a positive value of the parameter (Pollock 1989). González (1997) examines these similarities and differences, as reflected in surface word orders. As shown in (22), English is strictly SVO in declaratives, whereas Spanish allows for alternatives in the ordering of major constituents—SVO, OVS, OSV, and SOV are felicitous, as in (23)—the latter syntactic options achieved by raising of the verb (and object displacement) through the functional projections that articulate INFL (see Déprez 1994).[18]

> 22a. She arranged the flowers.

> 22b. *The flowers arranged she.

22c. *The flowers she arranged.

22d. *She the flowers arranged.

23a. *El entusiasmo vence la dificultad.*
"Enthusiasm defeats difficulties."

23b. *Unos libros compró Juan.*
"John bought some books."

23c. *Dicen que al dictador el pueblo lo repudia.*
"They say that the people rejected the dictator."

23d. *Don Fermín sus espuelas las sacó de la sala.*
"Don Fermín took his spurs from the room."

González predicts that if UG access is available to adults, English-speaking learners of Spanish will prefer SVO order (consistent with the shared head-initial parameter) at early stages and will progressively reset the parameter to the Spanish value for the verb-move-ment parameter, thus allowing for alternate orders; furthermore, she predicts that learn-ers' interlanguage development will be similar to the stages observed in first language ac-quisition.[19] In her study, she presented learners with sentences representative of the four word orders and asked them to identify the subject and object of each. Confirming the predictions, the results of the interpretation task indicated that SVO is the most easily ac-quired order, and the more advanced learners (third and fourth year) are more successful with the non-English structures. Moreover, the first and second-year learners followed the same acquisitional order as do children: SVO, SOV, OSV, and finally, OVS. The findings are interpreted as suggestive of access to parameter settings different from those of the native language.

Mandell (1998) has also investigated the resetting of the verb-movement parameter among native speakers of English acquiring Spanish. Following Suñer (1994), Mandell as-sumes that the [+raise] value of the verb-movement parameter determines (optional) sub-ject-lexical verb inversion in yes/no questions (24a), (obligatory) inversion with thematic-wh questions (24b), and (optional) adverbial placement between lexical verbs and object NPs (24c). None of these properties is found in English: subject-lexical verb inversion is impos-sible in yes/no questions and in questions with wh-fronting, and adverbs cannot appear be-tween lexical verbs and their objects. Mandell's experimental study investigated whether learners' judgments would reveal a pattern in which these properties clustered around verb-movement.

24a. *¿Marta quiere café?/¿Quiere Marta café?*
Marta wants coffee/Wants Marta coffee
"Does Marta want coffee?"

24b. *¿Qué quiere Marta?/*¿Qué Marta quiere?*
What wants Marta/What Marta wants
"What does Marta want?"

24c. *Ponen frecuentemente las cartas en la otra caja.*
They-put frequently the letters in the other box
"They frequently put the letters in the other box."

The results of the grammaticality judgment and dehydrated sentence tasks showed a progression of parameter-related syntactic acquisition across proficiency levels. Resetting occurs in two steps: V-to-COMP is acquired first, as evidenced by beginning and intermediate learners' acceptance of subject-lexical verb inversion in thematic-wh questions and then yes/no questions;[20] and at more advanced stages learners show evidence of short (V-to-AGR) movement, as illustrated by adverb placement.[21] Only on acquiring the latter surface property may learners be said to have acquired the second language parameter setting.

The possible resetting of the verb-raising parameter is also central to Bruhn de Garavito's (2002) study of the dissociation between control in the domain of morphology and knowledge of word order. This dissociation has been attributed to a deficit in the articulation or feature specification of functional categories (Beck 1998; Eubank et al. 1997; Hawkins and Chan 1998) on one hand, and to a problem of access to correct surface forms (Lardiere 1998; Prévost and White 2000) on the other. In contributing to this debate, Bruhn de Garavito examines beginning and intermediate Spanish second language learners' recognition and production of person morphology and their knowledge of permissible and required patterns of word order in the placement of adverbs and in question formation. The study comprised four tasks: a vocabulary task in which participants were asked to give translation equivalents of verbs; an oral production task in which participants retold a story in Spanish, prompted by verbal cues; a recognition task in which participants identified the subject of a clause, as in (25); and a grammatical preference task of sentence pairs representing contrasting word orders for verb placement, as in (26) and adverb placement, as in (27–29).

25. *Ernesto, Pablo y yo nadamos todos los días, pero solamante* _____ *juega al tenis.*
(a) *Pablo* (b) *Pablo y Ernesto* (c) *yo* (d) *Pablo y yo* (e) NA
"Ernesto, Pablo and I swim every day, but only _____ plays tennis."
(a) Pablo (b) Pablo and Ernesto (c) I (d) Pablo and I (e) NA

26a. *¿Qué lee Gustavo por la tarde?*
what reads Gustavo in the afternoon
"What does Gustavo read in the afternoon?"

26b. *¿Qué Gustavo lee por la tarde?*

27a. *Ernesto prepara rápido la sopa.*
Ernesto prepares rapidly the soup
"Ernesto rapidly prepares the soup."

27b. *Ernesto rápido prepara la sopa.*

28a. *Pablo estudia cuidadosamente los verbos.*

Pablo studies carefully the verbs

"Pablo carefully studies the verbs."

28b. **Pablo cuidadosamente estudia los verbos.*

29a. *Ernesto siempre quema completamente la sopa.*

Ernesto always burns completely the soup

"Ernesto always completely burns the soup."

29b. **Ernesto completamente quema siempre la sopa.*

Both beginning and intermediate learners revealed a higher proportion of errors for production (nearly twice as high) than for recognition of verbal forms. Those learners who had acquired person morphology in Spanish behaved as did native controls in the preference tasks, distinguishing grammatical from ungrammatical sentences in each test category—word order in questions, word order in relation to short adverbs, long adverbs, and two adverbs. The latter findings demonstrate that learners have acquired V-to-Agr raising, or, consonant with the Full Access Hypothesis, learners are able to reset the verb-raising parameter.

Camacho (1999) provides a different perspective on parameter resetting in accounting for word order variation, distinguishing between parametric values that can be reset and those that cannot be successfully reset because of target evidence that is compatible with the setting of the first language. In this study, Camacho analyzes the Spanish second language forms of native speakers of Quechua; as shown in (30), the canonical word order in clauses with sentential focus is SVO in Spanish and SOV in Quechua:

30a. *Juana estudia antropología.*

"Juana studies anthropology."

30b. *Luwis tanta-ta miku-yka-n.*

Luis bread-acc is eating

"Luis is eating bread."

Camacho argues that the Spanish interlanguage of Quechua speakers is characterized by transfer of two independent parameters—the possibility of licensing null objects with definite/specific antecedents (see Camacho, Paredes, and Sánchez 1997), and a feature triggering object movement for sentential focus that yields SOV word order. Spanish data from adult learners in early stages of acquisition support this view: the data illustrate responses such as (31b) that include fronted objects that are licensed by a null object pronoun, as in the first language. The data also show fronted topics, as in (32), which are disallowed in the target Spanish grammar:

31a. *¿Y tú vuelves a Ayacucho para ayudar a tus padres en la chacra?*

"Do you return to Ayacucho to help your parents on the farm?"

31b. *Sí claro, maíz (. . .) para sembrar.*
Yes, sure, corn to plant
"Yes, sure, to plant corn."

31c. *Maíz ᵢ [PP para [₁ₚ sembrar pro ᵢ]*

32. *Hay veces con las ropitas me ayudan . . . ropitas usadas pa' mis hijitos me dan.*
Sometimes with clothes CL help clothes used for my children CL give
"Sometimes they help me with clothes, used clothes for my children they give me."

Camacho concludes that only the word order parameter can be reset, as the Quechua setting is inconsistent with the target Spanish language grammar. However, because Spanish shows some evidence of null objects as variables, surface evidence compatible with the interlanguage grammar renders the null object parameter of Quechua very difficult to reset.

In another study of this same Quechua-speaking population, Camacho and Sánchez (1996) consider the word order in Spanish interlanguage possessive constructions. Quechua is characterized by the order possessor-possessed (and by genitive case on the former and person agreement on the latter, as shown in [33a]); in Spanish, the order is reversed although genitive case and agreement are present, as evident in (33b). In the Spanish interlanguage of Quechua speakers in the earlier stages of acquisition, the surface order of these constructions resembles the distribution attested in Quechua (cf. 34). The similarities to Spanish with respect to the grammatical feature of person agreement lead learners to hypothesize that the structures are identical, and hence they transfer the possessor-possessed order into Spanish, and only at subsequent stages is this hypothesis modified (see Escobar 1994; Paredes 1995).

33a. *Nuqa-q ritratu-y/Nuqa-nchis-pa ritratu-nchis*
I-gen. picture-1pl /We-1pl.include.gen. picture-1pl.include.
"(Of me) my picture"/"(Of us) our picture"

33b. *La foto mía/tuya/nuestra/vuestra*
the picture 1stp.sg.fem./2ndp.sg.fem./1stp.pl.fem./2ndp.pl.fem.
"My/your/our picture"

34a. *De mi esposo su hermana*
of my husband his sister
"My husband's sister"

34b. *De mi mi papá es carnicero*
of me my father is butcher
"My father is a butcher."

34c. *Los paisanos me llevaron a su casa de mi tía.*
The countrymen me took to her house of my aunt
"The countrymen took me to my aunt's house."

Such data are interpreted as demonstrating that transfer of word order is crucially dependent on transfer of the feature specifications of functional categories, such as person agreement.

Valenzuela (2002) also considers whether native-like attainment is possible in Spanish second language acquisition or whether adult English-speaking learners are constrained to the features and feature valuations of the native language. The syntactic target—the preverbal topic construction— is characterized by formal features [±operator] and [±recursive], which distinguish English from Spanish. In English, both generic and specific topics are expressed with a null operator, as illustrated in (35). Spanish demonstrates a similar pattern for generic preposed topics, but specific preposed topics must appear in a clitic left dislocation construction, as in (36) (cf., Cinque 1990). A second difference between the native and target grammars concerns recursion of TopP: as shown in (37), topics may be iterated in Spanish, but not in English (cf., Rizzi 1997). Thus, ultimate attainment would be confirmed if the English-speaking learners of Spanish were shown to have acquired the [operator] and [recursive] features and specifications that are implicated in the form and interpretation of topic constructions.

35a. Vitamins, I take everyday.

35b. Your book, I bought.

36a. *Vitaminas tomo todos los días.*
    Vitamins I-take every day.

36b. *Tu libro, *(lo) he comprado.*
    Your book *(CL) I-have bought.

37a. *Un libro, a Enrique, le regalé en Navidades.*
    A book, to Enrique, CL I-gave at Christmas.

37b. *A book, to Enrique, I gave at Christmas.

Sentence completion and oral grammaticality judgment tasks testing these properties of topic constructions were administered to ten native Spanish-speaking controls and nine advanced English-speaking learners who had achieved near-native grammars in Spanish. Group results unveil advanced learners' native-like competence with respect to the [recursive] feature, a feature not instantiated in the native language. However, different patterns emerged for the items assessing acquisition of the [operator] feature. There was no statistical difference between learners and controls with [+specific] preposed topics—learners accurately produced and accepted specific topics with a clitic. However, the learners differed significantly from the control group with [-specific] preposed topics; they overgeneralized the clitic construction. It is important to note, however, that individual results demonstrate that the latter construction was also problematic for one member of the control group. Taken together, Valenzuela interprets the results as suggesting that ultimate attainment is possible: the near-native speaker group behaved statistically similar to the native controls in evincing knowledge of the [recursive] feature, and a subset of the individual learners patterned with a native control in their variable behavior with respect to the specifications of [operator] feature.

Hertel and Pérez-Leroux (1999) explored the role of the verb class in the acquisition of Spanish word order among adult learners. As illustrated in (38–39), unergative and unaccusative verbs demonstrate differential patterns of word order and concomitant semantic values.

Unergatives

38a. SV order: neutral or focused predicate

Susana telefoneó.

"Susana telephoned."

38b. VS order: focused subject

Telefoneó Susana.

"Susana telephoned."

Unaccusatives

39a. SV order: focused predicate

Susana llegó.

"Susana arrived."

39b. VS order: neutral or focused subject

Llegó Susana.

"Susana arrived."

These authors designed two experimental studies to test the learnability of the semantic values and the discourse factors involved in free inversion.[22] The first experimental condition was a grammaticality judgment task administered to beginning and advanced learners as well as to a comparison group of native speakers. All groups preferred inversion with unaccusatives to inversion with unergatives, demonstrative of a sensitivity to verb class. The second study reported was based on an oral narration task in which advanced and intermediate learners were asked to retell a children's story. Again, inversion with unergatives was rare for all groups. Based on these results, Hertel and Pérez-Leroux submit that adult learners possess knowledge of syntax-semantics correspondences that may not be salient in the input, a finding that supports access to UG.

3.4 Argument Structure

Additional studies of lexical knowledge in Spanish second language acquisition have focused on argument structure. Montrul (1998) conducted a longitudinal study on the acquisition of Spanish psychological predicates, e.g., *gustar* "to like," by native speakers of English and French. In Spanish, subjects of such verbs are dative-marked, as observed in (40–41). Moreover, they occupy the surface subject position and are therefore available to control adjunct-clause PRO, as shown in (41). Lastly, experiencer subjects in Spanish are obligatorily doubled by a clitic pronoun, this in contrast to indirect objects, for which clitic-doubling may be optional. In English, experiencer subjects surface only as nominative or accusative NPs; in French they are dative-marked, but cannot be doubled by a clitic. Montrul proposes that at the level of D-structure, experiencers must be projected higher than themes in all three languages (Grimshaw 1994). However, at S-structure experiencers across these languages differ with respect to the case assigned to them, the position in which this case is assigned, and their need of clitic-doubling. Given the cross-linguistic differences outlined, Montrul tested several hypotheses. In particular, she hypothesized that French-speaking learners should be able to assign dative case to experiencers, as in their first language; they might initially treat them as indirect objects and treat clitic-doubling as optional. Furthermore, she postulated that English speakers might initially assign nominative case to experiencers; but if first language influence is characteristic only of initial stages of acquisition, dative case should be accepted at later stages of acquisition.

40a. *A Juan le gusta la música.*
    To Juan-dat CL-3s-dat pleases the music-nom
    "Juan likes music."

40b. *Sin PRO_i saber por qué a Juan_i le gusta María.*
    Without to know why to Juan-dat 3s-dat pleases Maria
    "Without knowing why, Juan likes Maria."

41. *A Juan_i le gusta María sin PROi saber por qué.*
    To Juan CL-3s-dat pleases María without knowing why
    "Juan likes María without knowing why."

In testing for experiencer control of adverbial-clause PRO, Montrul presented learners with questions of the type in (42) and the selection of responses in (43). An additional preference task was used to probe the subjects' preference for dative over other cases with experiencers of unaccusative verbs and for clitic-doubling in sentences with dative experiencers.

42. *¿Quién no sabe por qué?*
    "Who doesn't know why?"

43a. *Juan*

43b. *María*

43c. *Cualquiera de los dos (Juan o María).*
    "Either one of the two (Juan or María)."

The results showed that the learners' native language plays an important role in the acquisition of the surface properties of Spanish. The French learners demonstrate an advantage over English-speaking learners with respect to dative case assignment. At the same time, the data provided evidence of learners' knowledge of the differences between unaccusative verbs and ditransitive verbs, given that both language groups preferred doubling with experiencers more often than with indirect objects. The English-speaking learners presented a much lower acceptance of dative clitics, and at the initial stages preferred nominative over dative experiences. Finally, at later stages of acquisition there were significant improvements in acceptance of dative experiencers in both groups. Montrul interprets these results as indicative of native language influence on second language acquisition, and gradual grammatical restructuring.

In a more recent article, Montrul (1999b) investigated the acquisition of unaccusative verbs in the Spanish interlanguage of Turkish and English speakers. The goal of this study was to determine whether learners differentiate semantically and syntactically between different unaccusative verb classes such as the alternating class (e.g., *romper* "to break"), the paired class (e.g., *morir* "to die" and *matar* "to kill"), and the unpaired class of unaccusatives and unergatives (e.g., *desaparecer* "to disappear" and *llorar* "to cry," respectively). The first class of verbs is optionally transitive, and in detransitivitized form, requires the detransitivizing clitic *se,* as illustrated by the examples in (44). Turkish patterns with Spanish in requiring an overt morphological marker as a detransitivizer; but in English, the class of alternating verbs does not require overt morphology. The second and the third verb classes also exist in Turkish and English; errors with paired and unpaired unaccusative and unergative verbs, attested in first and second language acquisition, consist mainly of causative uses of these verbs. Montrul proposed that adult learners incorrectly map all unaccusative verbs to the bi-eventive template of alternating verbs when they have not yet acquired the relevant aspects of meaning for transitivity.

      44a. *El cocinero derritió la manteca.*
          The cook melt-PAST the butter
          "The cook melted the butter."

      44b. *La manteca se derritió/Se derritió la manteca.*
          The butter REFL melt-PAST/REFL melt-PAST the butter
          "The butter melted."

Two hypotheses are tested in Montrul's study. First, if the adult learning process is constrained by the first language, English-speaking and Turkish-speaking learners should distinguish between unaccusative and unergative verbs and between the three classes of unaccusative verbs. They should also transfer the argument structure of these verbs from the native language. Second, if absolute transfer is not the case, then adult learners should behave as first language acquirers and they should accept causative errors with intransitive verbs. The results of a picture-sentence matching test showed that Turkish-speaking and English-speaking intermediate learners know that unaccusative alternating verbs alternate in transitivity and that paired and unpaired unaccusatives and unergatives do not. Nevertheless, learners accept causative errors with intransitives, incorrectly mapping them to transitive templates, as in first language acquisition. These results may be interpreted as posing a challenge to the Full Transfer/Full Access Hypothesis of Schwartz and Sprouse (1996); however, the author also acknowledges that these intermediate participants may have emerged from the "full transfer" into the "full-access" stage. In addition, the results indicate that transference is not uniform across interlanguage domains: transference effects were attested at the level of morphosyntax, but they were absent at the level of argument structure.

Montrul (2002a) examines further the effects of the native language on the acquisition of argument structure among adult learners. Of particular interest in this study are the representation and development of learners' knowledge of the semantic and syntactic classification of verbs. Montrul examined two classes of verbs that alternate in transitivity. In English and Spanish, verbs that denote change of state participate in a causative and inchoative alternation, as shown in (45). The inchoative variant behaves differently from other unaccusative verbs and unergative verbs which do not alternate in transitivity or allow an extra argument, as shown in (46–47).

> 45a. John broke the mirror./The mirror broke.
>
> 45b. *Juan rompió el espejo./El espejo se rompió.*
>
> 46a. John arrived./*The policeman arrived John.
>
> 46b. *Juan llegó./*El piloto llegó a Juan.*
>
> 47a. John smiled./*Mary smiled John.
>
> 47b. *Juan sonrío./*María sonrió a Juan.*

Agentive verbs of manner of motion in English and Spanish alike are unergative and do not normally appear in the transitive form (48). However, English verbs of motion permit transitive (causative) behavior in the presence of a prepositional phrase (49).

> 48a. The soldiers marched. /*The captain marched the soldiers.
>
> 48b. *Los soldados marcharon./*El capitán marchó a los soldados.*
>
> 49a. The captain marched the soldiers to the tents.
>
> 49b. *El capitán marchó a los soldados hasta el campamento.*

Assuming that the native language constrains second language lexical representations in early interlanguage development (cf., Schwartz and Sprouse 1996), English may be the source of Spanish learners' overgeneralization of the transitivity alternation with manner of motion verbs, and Spanish may be the source of undergeneralization of the alternation in English second language acquisition). In testing Spanish and English learners' knowledge of the behavior of change-of-state and manner-of-motion verbs, four tasks were administered—a cloze test, a translation task, a picture judgment task, and a grammaticality judgment task—in two studies, a Spanish study and an English study. While all learners distinguished between manner-of-motion verbs and change-of-state verbs, the transitive alternation that affords the lexical causative was overgeneralized in second language Spanish and undergeneralized in second language English, confirming full transfer for these intermediate learners. Such findings confirm that the native language limits the hypotheses entertained by the learners at initial stages of development, i.e., full transfer. In discussing subsequent convergence towards the target grammar (full access), Montrul suggests that while undergeneralization errors demonstrated by learners of English may be unlearned with positive evidence, the overgeneralization errors attested in the behavior of learners of Spanish may be more difficult to overcome, and may require additional learning of aspectual properties of verbs and phrases.

Also concerned with the development of Spanish second language morphosyntactic knowledge, Toth (2000) investigates the varied functions of the morpheme *se,* all of which emerge from its role in suppressing a verbal argument. As shown in (50–51), *se* renders the anticausative, passive, reflexive, and reciprocal meanings of the alternator and accusative classes (see Levin and Rappaport Hovav 1995).

Alternator Class: [NP [V NP], [e [V NP]

50a. *María abrió la puerta.*
"Mary opened the door."

50b. *La puerta se abrió.*
"The door opened."

50c. *La música relajó a Marta y María.*
"The music relaxed Martha and Mary."

50d. *Marta y María se relajaron.*
"Martha and María relaxed."/"Marta and María relaxed themselves/each other."

Accusative Class: [NP [V NP]

51a. *Juan pagó la cuenta.*
"Juan paid the bill."

51b. *Se pagó la cuenta.*
"The bill was paid."

51c. *Juan se pagó.*
"Juan paid himself."

Toth reasons that in acquiring targetlike mappings of lexical items onto surface meanings, learners must acquire knowledge of the argument structures of specific verb classes. In examining how this knowledge is acquired, Toth considers the factors that may constrain learners' hypotheses regarding the distribution of *se:* second language input data, explicit instruction, first language transfer, and UG-derived knowledge.

Following a week of explicit form-focused instruction, English-speaking learners were assessed on grammaticality judgment and production tasks. Results support the catalytic benefits of increased input and explicit instruction in the construction of the second language grammar (Ellis 1994). However, the relation between explicit instruction and second language development cannot be direct, inasmuch as learners' performance did not always lead to new knowledge structures (Pienemann 1988). Also evidenced was a preference for *se* forms that could not be ascribed to transfer: *se* was consistently overgeneralized with the class of unaccusatives (which share linking rules with intransitive alternators). These latter results are interpreted as pointing to an implicit UG-derived sensitivity to verbal semantics (cf. similar findings reported in Hirakawa 1995, Sorace 1995). Taken together, these results yield evidence that learners avail themselves of multiple and internal knowledge sources in the construction of target grammars.

3.5   Summary

We have observed that research on the acquisition (or resetting) of parameters associated with null subject pronouns and direct and indirect object clitics has been favored as evidence in sustaining or disclaiming a main role for UG in Spanish second language acquisition. However, the issue of transference has also been shown to have garnered ample consideration, especially in view of hypotheses regarding the transference of functional projections and the (re)specification of syntactic features that motivate and license specific derivations. In broad terms, the lines of analysis that have emerged from the research surveyed herein may be summarized as follows:

1. Gradual resetting of (a subset of the properties associated with) parametric values is evidenced in studies of null subjects (Pérez-Leroux and Glass 1997; Al-Kasey and Pérez-Leroux 1999), clitics (Bruhn de Garavito and Montrul 1996; Duffield and White 1999; Montrul 1998), and verb movement (Bruhn de Garavito 2002; González 1997; Mandell 1998).

2. Transfer of functional features and parametric values at the initial and even at further stages of acquisition is supported by investigations on null categories and word order (Camacho, Paredes and Sánchez 1997; Sánchez and Giménez 1998; Camacho 1999).

3. Evidence for an incomplete specification of functional categories has been found in work on clitics (Sánchez and Al-Kasey 1999).

4. Restructuring of the morphological properties of the first language takes place in the licensing of null subjects and topic constructions in the second language (Liceras and Díaz 1999; Valenzuela 2002).

5. Knowledge of argument structure guides second language acquisition (Hertel and Pérez Leroux 1999; Montrul 1998, 1999b, 2002a; Toth 2000).

As should be evident, linguistic theory serves as a source of explanation in second language acquisition research. That said, a comparative purview of these subdisciplines of linguistic study reveals that research in second language acquisition has not kept in step with syntactic inquiry. For example, recent years have witnessed significant study of the structure of Spanish; among the aspects studied are wh-movement, the formation of yes-no questions, complementation, negation and negative polarity items, quantifier raising, and scopal interactions—all areas of syntactic knowledge that remain open for detailed study in Spanish second language acquisition.

A significant issue not noted in the foregoing review of the research literature concerns research design of studies of interlanguage competence. Researchers of Spanish second language acquisition have commonly focused on adults in academic settings; notable exceptions are Camacho, Paredes, and Sánchez (1997) and Sánchez and Giménez (1999), whose studies are centered on learners in naturalistic settings of language contact. To be sure, contrastive study of learners acquiring languages in academic settings and learners acquiring languages in contact situations could lead to a better understanding of the role that input plays in guiding the acquisition of syntax. Likewise, as expressed by James Lantolf, research seeking to shed light on individual grammars should draw on individual performance data rather than performance data drawn from unnatural groupings, as is common in generative second-language studies. Another important theme not touched on is the variation in the grammars of native speakers (e.g., instructors in language classrooms and speech community peers) who provide input for learners. Dialectal variation is observed in the syntactic phenomena at issue in some of the studies reviewed, though it is seldom treated as a potential confounding variable. For example, clitic-doubling of DPs is widespread in Latin America (Lipski 1994); it is not limited to Río de la Plata Spanish, as some of the literature intimates; and the distribution of null versus overt subjects is subject to much variation among speakers of Caribbean Spanish.

4.0 Avenues for Future Investigation

The ensuing discussion brings to the fore further issues that can potentially contribute to the evolution of the field by providing new insights from cognate areas of inquiry, specifically, language attrition, language variation, and child and adult bilingualism. As with second language acquisition, these studies concern (internally and externally induced) grammar change and concurrent, competing grammars within an individual learner. We must point out that these areas have been deliberately singled out as they coincide with the interests of the present authors; we apologize in advance if we offend by omission of additional areas that promise pertinent findings.

Of potential import to the understanding of Spanish second language acquisition is the study of Spanish native language decline. It is by now well established that some speakers may neutralize morphological endings and avoid complex structures in the decline of native language proficiency (Silva-Corvalán 1986, 1991, 1994; Sorace 1990; Hernández-Chávez 1993; Martínez 1993; Seliger 1996; de Bot 1999). Toribio (2001c) presents a syntactic-theoretical investigation that seeks to determine whether such innovations and tendencies reflect changes in competence, that is, in the abstract formal values that motivate specific derivations and license derived objects of the native language (see Sharwood Smith and Van Buren 1991 for similar perspectives).[23] The study examines the degree of well-formedness of Spanish language forms in the oral and written storytelling texts of Spanish-English bilinguals who demonstrate reduction of Spanish language use. The transcripts reveal that several of the participants studied were able to maintain the integrity of their subordinate Spanish language; any deviations, where they exist, are deviations in performance (e.g., in the temporary unavailability of particular lexical items) while aspects of Spanish language competence appear to remain stable.[24]

There was one noteworthy participant in whose linguistic performance recidivism to English was most pronounced. As shown in (52), this speaker's oral speech demonstrates numerous simplifications of verbal paradigms, and feminine gender morphology is often rendered with a default masculine form. In like manner, more complex forms and structures, e.g., reflexive and subjunctive morphology and clitic-doubling, are eliminated. In addition, there are verbs and constructions modeled on the dominant language (English), e.g., *esperar para Caperucita Roja a llegar,* literally "wait for Little Red Riding Hood to arrive."

52a. *Los enanitos mataron al reina . . .*
"The dwarfs killed the queen." [cf. *a la reina*]

52b. *Ella nunca supió . . .*
"She never knew . . ." [cf. *supo*]

52c. *Dijo a alguien . . .*
"She told someone that she was . . ." [cf. *le dijo a alguien*]

52d. *La ardillita contó al hunter . . .*
"The squirrel told the hunter . . ." [cf. *le contó al cazador*]

52e. *El lobo encontró con ella . . .*
"The wolf ran into her . . ." [cf. *se encontró*]

Toribio notes, however, that while specific syntactic structures and morphological manifestations may be prone to variability, underlying formal features seem resistant to deterioration or respecification. Thus, nonnative verbal affixation need not itself signal a lack of knowledge of the formal morphological features. The data in (53), produced in a writing task, attest to the availability of strong verbal features in the speaker's grammar, as evidenced in adverb placement, the licensing of null and postverbal subjects, and other verb-second structures:

53a. *Y todos estaban muy feliz que . . . vivió, sobrevivió, todo que pasó con ella* [*sic*].
"And everyone was happy that she lived, that she survived, all that happened with her."

53b. *Cuando llegó Caperucita Roja ella vió que no era su abuelita.* [*sic*]
"When Little Red Riding Hood arrived, she saw that it was not her grandmother."

Such data lend further confirming evidence to the proposal of native language acquisition and attrition put forth in Platzack (1996), previously discussed. Speaking specifically to attrition, Platzack's Initial Hypothesis of Syntax tells us that a speaker would not forget where the strong features are to be found in her first language even when she has been out of practice for a long time (1996:383). Corroborating this hypothesis, the participant referenced above made significant errors related to nominal and adjectival agreement and verbal inflections. However, there were attested no errors that indicated that the strong verbal feature setting of the native language had been lost: the participant knows that the Spanish verbal feature is strong, despite the fact that her inflectional morphology is deficient.[25] Such findings suggest that while differences between proficient and attritted (or interlanguage) speech productions might exist, these may lie outside the scope of a computational system (Sorace 2000b; Toribio forthcoming). Thus, even in the foregoing cases in which speakers exhibit decidedly nonnativelike performance, it can be argued that target-deviant forms do not accurately reflect nonnativelike competence (i.e., formal feature values) (Lardiere and Schwartz 1997; Lardiere 1998).

Montrul (2002b) further advances this line of inquiry by considering the deficits that may be evidenced in the semantic features of aspectual morphology of early and late Spanish-English bilinguals. She addresses the subtle preterit/imperfect distinctions in bilinguals' performance in oral and written narratives and on two meaning-interpretation tasks, with the aim of distinguishing between faulty morphology in production (a superficial problem of mapping) from impairments in the interpretation of aspect (incomplete knowledge of semantic features). The four tasks, separated into two studies, were administered to twenty monolingual Spanish-speakers, thirty-one U.S.-born simultaneous and early bilinguals, and eight Latin American-born late child bilinguals. The first study tested participants' recognition of appropriate preterit and imperfect forms in a fill-in-the-blank narrative. A second task tested their use of preterit and imperfect forms in the retelling of the Little Red Riding Hood fairytale in the past tense. The second study tested participants' acquisition of the preterit/imperfect contrast in a sentence conjunction judgment task that required them to assess as logical or illogical sentence predicates of accomplishment, achievement and state:

54a. *La clase era* (IMP) *a las 10 pero empezó a las 10:30.*

54b. *La clase fue* (PRET) *a las 10 pero empezó a las 10:30.*
"The class was at 10 but started at 10:30."

55a. *Los González vendían* (IMP) *la casa pero nadie la compró.*

55b. *Los González vendieron* (PRET) *la casa pero nadie la compró.*
"The Gonzalezes were selling/sold the house but nobody bought it."

56a. *Pedro corría* (IMP) *la maratón de Barcelona pero no participó.*

56b. *Pedro corrió* (PRET) *la maratón de Barcelona pero no participó.*
"Pedro used to run/ran the Barcelona marathon but he did not participate."

A second task examined participants' knowledge of the meanings associated with the preterit/imperfect contrast through judgments on contextualized true/false statements. The sample in (57) exemplifies a condition concerning stative verbs that change meaning in the preterit; other conditions concerned the habitual versus one-time event interpretation, and the generic versus specific subject interpretation.

57a. *Ana va a la boda de sus amigos Carlos y Carolina. Ana no tiene novio. Carolina le presenta a Roberto. Ana y Roberto bailan toda la noche.*
Ana conocía a Roberto: Verdadero/Falso

57b. *Ana va a la boda de sus amigos Carlos y Carolina. Ana no tiene novio. Carolina le presenta a Roberto. Ana y Roberto bailan toda la noche.*

Ana conoció a Roberto: Verdadero/Falso

"Ana goes to the wedding of her friends Carlos and Carolina. Anna doesn't have a boyfriend. Carolina introduces Roberto to Ana. Ana and Roberto dance all night long.

Ana knew Roberto: True/False

Ana met Roberto (for the first time): True/False"

Montrul's study is significant for its theoretical scope and its methodological rigor. Equally significant are the interpretations of the results and broad application of the findings. Results indicate statistical differences between the monolingual and early bilingual groups on production and judgment tasks; there was no statistical difference between the late learners and the monolingual group. Thus age of onset of bilingualism appears to play a role in ultimate attainment of semantic features. This finding confirms Sorace's (2000a) claim that attrition affects [+interpretable], but not [-interpretable] features (cf., Bruhn de Garavito 2001, Toribio 2001c). Furthermore, there was much variation among the bilingual speakers within and across the groups in production and/or interpretation; some bilinguals, Montrul concludes, may never converge on the Spanish system. This variability is typical of second language acquisition, and requires attention to the input received by the early bilinguals. Moreover, the patterns of divergence—more pronounced with stative verbs in the preterite and with achievement verbs in the imperfect— invite closer examination of specific stages of first and second language acquisition and their potential correlates in language erosion.

The "permeability" (read: violability) of first language grammars in situations of language contact is also explored in Sánchez (1997). In that work, Sánchez analyzed the distribution of direct object pronouns in the elicited oral production of two groups of bilingual students aged ten to seventeen. The first group included bilinguals whose first language experiences were in Quechua. The second group comprised bilinguals for whom Spanish was the first language acquired (see also Sánchez 1999b). She found that among bilinguals living a language contact situation a shift in the definiteness and specificity features of the Spanish null object pronouns had taken place. Whereas in Spanish null objects are only allowed with generic antecedents that are nondefinite and nonspecific as shown in (59), in Quechua null objects are allowed with [± indefinite, ± antecedents], as illustrated by the examples in (59).

58a. *¿Compraste pan$_i$?*

Buy-2p.sg. bread

"Did you buy bread?"

58b. *Sí, compré.*

Yes bought-2p.sg. e$_i$

"Yes, I bought some."

59a. *Warmi-ta$_i$ riku-rka-nlei?*

Woman-acc see-past-2p.sg.

"Did you see a/the woman?"

59b. *Manam e$_i$ riku-ra-ni-chu.*

Not e$_i$ see-past-1p.sg.-neg

"I did not see her."

The results of the study showed that both groups of bilingual students had null objects with [+definite] and [+specific] antecedents in their oral production. Example (60) is drawn from the oral production of bilinguals whose first language is Quechua. These bilinguals also demonstrated null pronouns with [-definite, +specific] antecedents as illustrated by example (61), from the oral production of bilinguals whose first language is Spanish.

60. *Nomás sacas [todas las yerbas]$_i$ y después que sacas pro$_i$ echas abono.*

Just take-2p.sg. all the herbs and after that take2-p.sg. pro put 2p.sg. fertilizer

"You just pull out all the herbs and after you pull them out you put fertilizer."

61. *(A) La Cenicienta en la vicharra le echó [un plato de arroz]$_i$ en la ceniza e la Cenicienta recogía pro$_i$ llorando.*

(To) the Cinderella in the kitchen threw-3p.sg. a dish of rice in the cinders and the Cinderella picked-3p.sg. pro up crying.

"(And) in the kitchen she threw Cinderella a plate with rice in the cinders and Cinderella picked it up crying."

This study demonstrates that this contact variety of Spanish resets the parametric value of null objects to a pronominal with a wider range definiteness and specificity for its antecedent. Sánchez interprets these results as evidence in favor of the dominance of less marked or less restricted feature specifications in the grammar of bilinguals (see also Sánchez 1999a). (In line with Platzack's proposal, the findings can be viewed as evidence in favor of the pervasiveness of a strong feature that licenses the null definite pronoun.)

In another study of Andean Spanish, Sánchez (1996) considers word order variation in the distribution of restrictive adjectives and relative clauses. As noted, Spanish is head-initial, and accordingly, modifiers appear in postnominal position; but Quechua is head-final, with modifiers in prenominal position. Early stages of Spanish interlanguage evidence transference of the order of Quechua, i.e., restrictive adjectives appear in prenominal positions, contrasting with (the target forms and) the order attested in later stages.

62a. *El zorro tiene grande diente.*

The fox has big-sg. tooth-sg.

"The fox has big teeth."

62b. *Yo le he preguntado [ahí viene [varios] . . .*

I CL-dat. have asked [there come [several]]

"I have asked several who come from there . . ."

The analysis proffered supports the existence of a functional projection, Pred(icate) Phrase (Bowers 1993), which mediates between D and Agr in modification structures, rendering the structure of an adjectival modification structure as in (63).

63. D [$_{PredP}$ Pred [$_{AgrP}$ [[AP] Agr [NP]]]

Sánchez proposes that in Standard Spanish Agr has strong features (as attested by the agreement morphology on nouns, adjectives, and determiners) and it incorporates to Pred. These strong features trigger NP-movement to SpecPred. Quechua, on the other hand, bears weak Agr features, as attested by the lack of gender and obligatory number morphology. In Quechua, then, there is no trigger for NP-movement to SpecPredP. On this view, parametric variation (and interlanguage grammars) is characterized by XP-movement (triggered by strong features) rather than to head movement/incorporation (see Kayne 1994). In short, early stages of adult acquisition evidence a lack of a strong feature specification for Agr, which must be reset at later stages (again, consonant with Platzack's hypothesis).

Another language contact phenomenon that is pertinent to the study of adult second language acquisition is *code-switching*. Code-switching refers to the ability on the part of bilinguals to alternate between their linguistic codes in the same conversational event (see Toribio and Rubin 1996; Gumperz and Toribio 1999). Contrary to common assumptions, code-switching is common among the most proficient bilinguals and has been revealed to be rule-governed.[26] For example, Spanish-English bilinguals will converge on the judgment that the sentences in (64) represent possible code-switches, whereas those in (65) do not, although they may be unable to account for the differential judgment (see Toribio 2000c, 2001b).

64a. *Al cumplir ella los veinte años, el rey invitó* many neighboring princes to a party.
   "On her twentieth birthday, the king invited/many neighboring princes to a party."

64b. Since she was unmarried, he wanted her to choose *un buen esposo.*
   "Since she was unmarried, he wanted her to choose/a good husband."

64c. Princess Grace was sweet *y cariñosa con todos.*
   "Princess Grace was sweet/and affectionate with everyone."

64d. *Juro por Dios que te casaré con el primer hombre* that enters this room!
   "I swear by God that I will marry you with the first man/that enters this room!"

65a. *Very envious and evil, the *reina mandó a un criado que matara a la princesa.*
   "Very envious and evil, the/queen sent a houseboy to kill the princess."

65b. *Out of compassion the houseboy abandoned *la en el bosque.*
   "Out of compassion the houseboy abandoned/her in the forest."

65c. *La reina le ofreció a Blancanieves una manzana que había* laced with poison.
   "The queen offered Snow White an apple that she had/laced with poison."

65d. *En la cabina vivían siete enanitos que* returned to find Snow White asleep.
   "In the cabin there lived seven dwarfs that/returned to find Snow White asleep."

65e. *Los enanitos intentaron pero no* succeeded in awakening Snow White.
   "The dwarfs tried but did not/succeed in awakening Snow White."

Such judgments about the utterances that result from intrasentential code alternations are proffered by proficient bilinguals, who possess advanced competence in the two component language systems. But results revealed by research in infant and later childhood bilingualism suggest that a child's increased competence in the component languages correlated with increased sensitivity to adultlike code-switching norms. Meisel (1989, 1994) maintains that *language mixing,* broadly defined as the indiscriminate combinations of elements from each of the component languages, is most frequent during a very early phase of language acquisition, owing to limited competence in both languages, but as the child acquires greater competence in the two languages, the language contact attested (if any at all) increasingly takes the form of rule-governed code-switching. That is, code-switching requires elaborate grammatical knowledge of two language systems, and as young children may lack such grammatical competence, their early language alternations cannot be classified as instances of adultlike code-switching (see Köppe and Meisel 1995).[27]

Studies such as those cited immediately above lead Rubin and Toribio (1996) to hypothesize that regardless of his or her age, the bilingual's language mixing/code-switching ability serves as a measure of his or her syntactic competence in the component languages. Of course, studies of code-switching in the adult second language classroom are uncommon, since prescriptive norms are imposed (but see Rakowsky 1989; Toribio et al. 1993; Bhatia and Ritchie 1998; Sunderman and Toribio 2000).

Code-switching is stigmatized in most learning contexts, and teachers and learners themselves generally relate it to a lack of language proficiency.[28] It is not surprising that code-switching, so perceived, is of little interest to second language research programs, which are concerned primarily with second language achievement. In considering adult language learners, Toribio (2001a) predicts that a correlation will obtain between speakers' level of second language proficiency and their sensitivity to the grammatical constraints governing code-switching; the central guiding question addressed in that study is whether, and if so, how second language learners acquire the properties that define structural coherence and allow them to render well-formedness judgments for code-switched forms.[29] This exploration takes on particular significance given that learners receive no evidence that could guide them in rendering such judgments, and therefore results consistent with those observed among competent bilinguals could be imputed to unconscious, abstract linguistic knowledge.

Based on learners' rejection of sentences predicted to be ill-formed, Toribio concludes that advanced participants have access to the grammatical knowledge that includes the information necessary for rendering a judgment on the impossibility of code-switched forms. In marked contrast, the beginners do not appear to render such judgments on the basis of abstract linguistic principles. Unlike the advanced counterparts, who rely on unconscious linguistic knowledge to assess the status of ill-formed code-switched sentences, the beginners appear to employ a strategy of translation in assessing the grammaticality status of code-switched sentences (see Bhatia and Ritchie 1998). The intermediate group manifested response behaviors similar to those of both the advanced and beginners, though statistically indistinguishable from the latter.[30] These results make evident that less advanced learners do not have complete access to the grammatical knowledge that must be invoked in making these judgments; for the advanced participants, this grammatical knowledge includes the abstract features that define code-switching coherence. Note that the developmental cline hypothesized by Toribio and Rubin and confirmed by Toribio is compatible with Herschensohn's Constructionism model of second language acquisition. Herschensohn makes explicit the conformity: reinterpreting her proposal in Toribio and Rubin's terms, she states, "L2ers can be seen to be multicompetent, albeit incomplete bilinguals, who build their knowledge through the acquisition of the morpho-lexicon with all of its features" (2000:222). In other words, the major difference among learners resides, again, in the articulation (and concomitant differentiation) of the lexicon.

Finally, studies of language variation, both synchronic and diachronic, are also germane to investigations in second language acquisition.[31] Current research converges on the observation that from the perspective of grammatical theory, investigations of intrasystem variation (inter- and intradialectal variation) have as much to reveal about the structure of human language as comparative and typological study (Benincà 1989; Uriagereka 1999). Studies of *microvariation* endeavor to discover how speakers combine elements from their two systems when processing "mixed" dialect-standard sentences (Henry 1995, 1997; Wilson and Henry 1998). Addressing microvariation in Spanish, Toribio (2000a, 2000b) brings generative grammar to bear on the analysis of variation in the positional licensing of null and overt referential and expletive pronouns and in the positional licensing of lexical subjects in interrogative, nonfinite clauses, and experiencer constructions in Caribbean Spanish. For example, speakers of Dominican varieties of Spanish are observed to produce utterances such as those in (66), which depart markedly from the norm such as that prescribed in second language classrooms.

66a. *Ellos me dijeron que yo tenía anemia. . . . Si ellos me dicen que yo estoy en peligro cuando ellos me entren la aguja por el ombligo, yo me voy a ver en una situación de estrés.*

"They told me that I had anemia. . . . If they tell me that I am in danger when they put the needle in my belly-button, I am going to find myself in a stressful situation."

66b. *Ellos querían renovar el centro para el turismo y ello hay mucha gente que lo opone.*

"They wanted to renovate the center for tourism and there were many people who opposed it."

66c. *¿Cuánto un médico gana?*

"How much does a doctor earn?" [cf. *¿Cuánto gana un médico?*]

66d. *No hay donde yo sentarme.*

"There is nowhere for me to sit." [cf. *No hay donde sentarme (yo).*]

66e. *Yo no me gusta la gente que hable así.*

"I don't like that people talk that way." [cf. (A mí) no me gusta la gente que hable así.]

66f. *Déjame yo salir temprano.*

"Let me leave early." [cf. *Déjame salir temprano.*]

Importantly, these forms exist alongside standard forms in the speech of the individual (recall the discussion of intrasubject variability reported in Bruhn de Garavito and Montrul 1996, Montrul 1999b, and Toth 2000). Such variation, in which two I-languages correspond to one E-language, clearly have much to reveal of the development of our understanding of language restructuring in general (Muysken 2000).

To conclude, we maintain that by examining language decline and intrasystem variation as rule-governed (i.e., rather than merely as target-deviant forms) and by comparing the language alternations of child and adult learners with those of incipient and proficient bilinguals, a better understanding of linguistic knowledge and the potential for language acquisition throughout the lifespan will be achieved.

ACKNOWLEDGMENTS

We would like to express our gratitude to Rafael Salaberry for the invitation to participate in this book project and to Barbara Lafford for her patience and judicious advice as we prepared the manuscript. We would also like to thank José Camacho and James Lantolf for their insightful and encouraging comments on this work. Finally, we owe a special debt of appreciation to Gabriela Zapata for her careful reading of the document.

NOTES

1. Pathological development excepted, all children achieve a largely uniform language system (the adult-state competence) that is rich and highly complex, including knowledge of very subtle properties of the language.

2. Linguistic *competence* in this context is understood relative to *performance;* competence refers to the speaker's tacit knowledge of the structure of the language, rather than the speaker's actual use of language (performance) in concrete situations (Chomsky 1965).

3. It merits noting that the linguistic principles of UG are thought to constitute a theory of the organization of the initial state of the language learner, a theory of the human faculty for language (Crain and Thornton 2000). In other words, UG postulates principles that are specific to grammar formation, rather than by appeal to general principles of learning or cognitive growth. There are, however, researchers who depart from this position. For example, McLaughlin and Heredia (1996) propose that second language acquisition is guided by principles of learning that are applied in all cases of the development of complex skills.

4. See Gregg (1996) for thorough discussion of the questions pursued in second language acquisition research.

5. A related issue in discussions of first versus second language attainment is the postulation of a *critical period* for language acquisition. See chapter 1 of this volume for further discussion of the critical (or sensitive) period.

6. On this view, the language faculty consists of two components: a computational system and a lexicon; the computational system is composed of invariant principles, with language-specific variation restricted to functional elements and general properties of the lexicon.

7. Note that if this conception proves correct, the debate as to whether knowledge in second language acquisition is derivable from the first language or directly from Universal Gram-

mar is essentially moot, as Dekydtspotter, Sprouse, and Anderson (1997) reason. Yusa (1999) coincides in this view that access to the computational principles that derive the first language is indistinguishable from access to Universal Grammar.

8. Within this framework, then, the task of the child and the adult learner involves the learning of lexical items and their idiosyncratic properties and establishing target-specific settings for parameters, in accordance with UG principles. This view of the process of second language acquisition is formalized in Herschensohn's (2000) model of constructionism, according to which adult acquisition represents a relearning process that consists in three stages, progressing from transfer of the first language settings, through underspecification of morphological features, to more targetlike feature specifications and derivations. Although the proposed stages cannot be neatly defined, what is significant is that, as with primary language acquisition, the lexicon is at the core of second language acquisition, and "grammatical realignment" is a function of mastery of lexical features of the functional categories of the second language.

9. Strong morphological features must be checked and eliminated prior to Spell-Out, but weak morphological features remain after Spell-Out—in fact, by the economy principle duly termed Procrastinate, they must remain—and are checked instead at the level of LF, a less costly operation.

10. Other well-studied phenomena such as tense and aspect are not considered in this paper, but are taken up in detail in chapter 2 of this volume. Chapter 3 also devotes a section to looking at Spanish subjunctive L2 studies carried out within a generative framework.

11. Liceras and Diaz (1999) propose that although INFL features are strong in French and could license null subjects, identification of null subjects is not possible. Note that the French data included child (age 12) data.

12. See chapter 4 of this volume for further discussion of the acquisition of Spanish L2 clitics.

13. The study was, in fact, bidirectional, including Spanish-speaking learners of French. We limit our discussion to the interlanguage data from French learners of Spanish.

14. Interested readers should consult Roeper (1999) for a thought-provoking analysis of bilingualism in language development.

15. Despite confusion among English speakers as regards the optional nature of dative clitics with indirect objects in Spanish, they all appeared to have acquired clitics with dative experiencers, where they are obligatory.

16. Note that this state of affairs does not preclude coherent clustering of properties, for some of these surface phenomena may also involve other parameters and processes (e.g., reanalysis).

17. Sánchez and Al-Kasey (1999) distinguish clitic left dislocation structures from topicalization or focus structures. This sentence is produced with a normal intonational pattern.

18. Note that object movement in Spanish is often accompanied by a clitic-doubling.

19. Comparison child data are drawn from Echeverría (1978).

20. According to Mandell, the preponderance of wh- and yes/no questions in the language classroom prompts grammatical restructuring.

21. Consult White (1992) for similar differences between long and short verb-movement.

22. These studies served as pilots for Hertel (2000).

23. To date, the study of native language attrition has, with notable exceptions, been focused largely on the socio-psychological factors that enter into language loss, e.g., differential patterns of usage, amount and frequency of cross-linguistic contact, and individual and community attitudes towards the language varieties at issue. Parallel to these studies, which are firmly grounded in sociolinguistics, are research endeavors carried out within the discipline psycholinguistics, where scholars have examined the changes in linguistic perception, retrieval, and processing attendant to language attrition and the mechanisms and models that may best accommodate these.

24. The narrative texts illustrate various and complex constructions, e.g., independent and subordinate clauses, sequencing of indicative and subjunctive verbal forms, relativization, pronominalization, clitic-doubling, verb-raising, and adverb placement, all indicative of a stable Spanish-language system.

25. Such findings confirm the dissociation between the dissolution of inflectional affixation and syntactic knowledge of formal features (see Gavruseva and Lardiere 1996; Lardiere 1998). In other words, overt agreement and the use of finite verb forms are the result of a lexical choice, not particular feature values.

26. The status of intrasentential code-switching had been much disputed in the early literature. Some linguists viewed it as indicative of imperfect language acquisition, extreme cross-linguistic interference, or language erosion, and numerous others despaired of finding any constraints on what Lance (1975) called a "willy-nilly" combination of language forms (but see Toribio 2000c, 2000d). However, subsequent studies have revealed that code-switching is rule-governed and systematic (see Lipski 1985; Poplack 1980, 1983), demonstrating grammatical regularities that reflect the operation of underlying syntactic restrictions (see MacSwan 1999 for an overview).

27. Rubin and Toribio (1996) further explore Meisel's contention that grammatical constraints on code-switching can only operate once the child has access to certain properties of grammars, most importantly functional features, which crucially define coherence. They note, however, that this early stage does indeed conform to a pattern specified by universal principles, i.e., the bilingual child does not demonstrate a "wild" grammar, but a transitional competence (read: interlanguage) in which functional structure may be present but remain specified for functional features. McClure (1981) found that children who are not equally proficient in Spanish and English code-switch predominantly at the word level, usually choosing to switch nouns, while those children possessing equal proficiency in the two languages choose to code-switch at higher constituency boundaries within the sentence (see Zentella 1997). McClure concludes that "just as the monolingual improves his control over his verbal resources with age, so too does the bilingual. Further, just as there is a developmental pattern in the monolingual's syntactic control of his language, so too may such a pattern be found in the bilingual's control of the syntax of code-switching, which begins with the mixing of single items from one code into discourse in the other and culminates in the codechanging of even more complex constituents" (1981:92).

28. In fact, most teaching methodologies try to suppress this type of first-language usage, because it is viewed as harmful to the acquisition process. In this context, code-switching is viewed not as a legitimate linguistic behavior, but as a failure on the part of the learner even to attempt a second language form.

29. These investigations assume some version of the functional head constraint of Belazi, Rubin, and Toribio (1994). This constraint, grounded in the system of categories of Chomsky (1986) and the relations proposed in Abney (1987), dictates that the semantic and syntactic features of a functional element must match the corresponding features of its complement; the functional head constraint merely extends the scope of f-selection to include language indexing. Thus, like all other relevant features (e.g., finiteness and mood in subordinate clauses, and number and gender in noun phrases), the (language) feature of a complement f-selected by a functional element, must match the corresponding (language) feature of that functional head. See Toribio (2001a) for discussion of the syntactic-theoretical status of such a feature.

30. In brief, the judgment task seemed to require intermediate-level learners to draw on knowledge that they did not fully yet master. Thus, though they demonstrate some tendency to rely on innate knowledge in rendering their judgments, resulting in the higher percentage of accurate judgments than their beginner counterparts, the intermediates' scores did not approximate those of the advanced participants and were statistically distinct from them.

31. The reader should consult Battye and Roberts (1995) and van Kemenade and Vincent (1997).

WORKS CITED

Abney, S. 1987. The English noun phrase in its sentential aspect. Ph.D. diss., MIT.

Archibald, J. 1998. Lexical parameters and lexical dependency: Acquiring L2 stress. In *The generative study of second language acquisition,* eds. S. Flynn, G. Martohardjono, and W. O'Neill, 279–301. Hillsdale, NJ: Lawrence Erlbaum.

Al-Kasey, T., and A. T. Pérez-Leroux. 1998. Second language acquisition of null objects. In *The generative study of second language acquisition,* eds. S. Flynn, G. Martohardjono, and W. O'Neill, 161–85. Hillsdale, NJ: Lawrence Erlbaum.

Battye, A., and I. Roberts. 1995. *Clause structure and language change.* New York: Oxford University Press.

Beck, Maria-Luise. 1998. L2 acquisition and obligatory head movement: English-speaking learners of German and the local impairment hypothesis. *Second Language Research* 20:311–48.

Belazi, H., E. Rubin, and A. J. Toribio. 1994. Code switching and X-bar theory: The functional head constraint. *Linguistic Inquiry* 25:221–37.

Benincà, P. 1989. *Dialect variation and the theory of grammar.* Dordrecht: Foris.

Bhatia, T., and W. Ritchie. 1998. Language mixing and second language acquisition: Some issues and perspectives. In *The development of second language grammars: A generative approach,* eds. E. Klein and G. Martohardjono, 241–65. Amsterdam: John Benjamins.

Birdsong, D. 1992. Ultimate attainment in second language acquisition. *Language* 68:706–55.

Bley Vroman, R. 1990. The logical problem of foreign language learning. *Linguistic Analysis* 20:3–49.

Borer, H. 1984. *Parametric syntax.* Cambridge, MA: MIT Press.

Bowers, J. 1993. The syntax of predication. *Linguistic Inquiry* 24:591–656.

Bruhn de Garavito, J. 2002.The (Dis)association between morphology and syntax: The case of L2 Spanish. Forthcoming in *Studies in the acquisition of Spanish and Portuguese*, ed., S. Montrul. Somerville, MA: Cascadilla Press.

Bruhn de Garavito, J., and S. Montrul. 1996. Verb movement and clitic placement in French and Spanish as a second language. In *Proceedings of the 20th Annual Boston University Conference on Language Development,* vol. 1, eds. A. Streamfellow, D. Cahana-Amitay, E. Hughes, and A. Zukowski, 123–34. Somerville, MA: Cascadilla Press.

Camacho, J. 1999. From SOV to SVO: The grammar of interlanguage word order. *Second Language Research* 15:115–32.

Camacho, J., and L. Sánchez. 1996. De mi padre, su padre: The syntax of word order transfer and person agreement in Andean L2 Spanish. In *Proceedings of the 20th Annual Boston University Conference on Language Development,* vol. 1, eds. A. Stringfellow, D. Cahana-Amitay, E. Hughes, and A. Zukowski, 155–66. Somerville, MA: Cascadilla Press.

Camacho, J., L. Paredes, and L. Sánchez. 1997. Null objects in bilingual Andean Spanish. In *Proceedings of the 21st Annual Boston University Conference on Language Development,* vol. 1, eds. E. Hughes, M. Hughes, and A. Greenhill, 55–66. Somerville, MA: Cascadilla Press.

Chomsky, N. 1965. *Aspects of the theory of syntax.* Cambridge, MA: MIT Press.

———. 1981. *Lectures on government and binding.* Dordrecht: Foris.

———. 1986. *Barriers.* Cambridge, MA: MIT Press.

———. 1991. Some notes on economy of derivation and representation. In *Principles and parameters in comparative grammar,* ed. R. Friedin, 417–54. Cambridge, MA: MIT Press.

———. 1993. A minimalist program for linguistic theory. In *The view from building 20,* eds. K. Hale and S. J. Keyser, 1–52. Cambridge, MA: MIT Press.

———. 1995. *The minimalist program.* Cambridge, MA: MIT Press.

Cinque, G. 1990. *Types of A'-dependencies.* Cambridge, MA: MIT Press.

Clahsen, H. 1996. *Generative perspectives on language acquisition.* Amsterdam: John Benjamins.

Clahsen, H., and P. Muysken. 1986. The availability of Universal Grammar to adult and child learners: A study of acquisition of German word order. *Second Language Research* 2:93–119.

Coppieters, R. 1987. Competence difference between native and near-native speakers. *Language* 63:544–73.

Crain, S., and R. Thornton. 2000. *Investigations in Universal Grammar.* Cambridge, MA: MIT Press.

de Bot, K. 1999. The psycholinguistics of language loss. In *Bilingualism and migration,* eds. G. Extra and L. Verhoeven, 345–61. Berlin: Mouton de Gruyter.

Dekydtspotter, L., R. Sprouse, and B. Anderson. 1997. The interpretive interface in L2 acquisition: The process-result distinction in English-French interlanguage grammars. *Language Acquisition* 6:297–332.

de Miguel, E. 1993. Construcciones ergativas e inversión en la lengua y la interlengua español. In *La lingüística y el análisis de los sistemas no nativos,* ed. J. Liceras, 178–95. Ottawa: Dovehouse Editions.

Déprez, V. 1994. Parameters of object movement. In *Studies on scrambling: Movement and non-movement approaches to free word order phenomena,* eds. N. Corver and H. van Riemsdijk, 101–52. New York: Mouton de Gruyter.

Duffield, N., and L. White. 1999. Assessing L2 knowledge of Spanish clitic placement: Converging methodologies. *Second Language Research* 15:133–60.

Echeverría, M. S. 1978. *Desarrollo de la comprensión infantil de la sintaxis española.* Concepción: Universidad de Concepción.

Ellis, R. 1994. *The study of second language acquisition.* Oxford: Oxford University Press.

Epstein, S., S. Flynn, and G. Martohardjono. 1998. The strong continuity hypothesis: Some evidence concerning functional categories in adult L2 acquisition. In *The generative study of second language acquisition,* eds. S. Flynn, G. Martohardjono, and W. O'Neil, 61–77. Mahwah, NJ: Lawrence Erlbaum.

Escobar, A. M. 1994. Andean Spanish and bilingual Spanish: Linguistic characteristics. In *Language in the Andes,* eds., P. Cole, G. Hermon, and M. D. Martín, 51–73. Newark, DE: Latin American Studies.

Eubank, L., J. Bischof, A. Huffstutler, P. Leek, and C. West. 1997. Tom eats slowly cooked eggs: Thematic verb raising in L2 knowledge. *Language Acquisition* 6:177–99.

Everett, D. 1996. *Why there are no clitics.* Dallas: Summer Institute of Linguistics.

Flynn, S. 1996. A parameter-setting approach to second language acquisition. In *The handbook of second language acquisition,* eds. W. Ritchie and T. Bhatia, 121–58. New York: Academic Press.

Flynn, S., G. Martohardjono, and W. O'Neil. 1998. *The generative study of second language acquisition.* Mahwah, NJ: Lawrence Erlbaum.

Franco, J. 1993. On object agreement in Spanish. Ph.D. diss., University of Southern California.

Gavruseva, L., and D. Lardiere. 1996. The emergence of extended phrase structure in child L2 acquisition. In *Proceedings of the 20th Annual Boston University Conference on Language Development,* vol. 1, eds. A. Stringfellow, D. Cahana-Amitay, E. Hughes and A. Zukowski, 225–36. Somerville, MA: Cascadilla Press.

González, N. 1997. A parametric study of Spanish L2 acquisition: Interpretation of Spanish word order. In *Contemporary Perspectives on the Acquisition of Spanish,* vol. 1, *Developing grammars,* eds. A. T. Pérez-Leroux and W. Glass, 133–48. Somerville, MA: Cascadilla Press.

Gregg, K. 1996. The logical and developmental problems of second language acquisition. In *Handbook of second language acquisition,* eds. W. Ritchie and T. Bhatia, 49–81. New York: Academic Press.

Grimshaw, Jane. 1994. Lexical reconciliation. *Ligua* 92, nos. 1–4 (April):411–30.

Gumperz, J., and A. J. Toribio. 1999. Code-switching. In *The MIT encyclopedia of the cognitive sciences,* eds. F. Keil and R. Wilson, 118–19. Cambridge, MA: MIT Press.

Hawkins, R., and C. Chan. 1997. The partial availability of Universal Grammar in second language acquisition: The "failed functional features hypothesis." *Second Language Research* 13:187–226.

———. 1998. The partial availability of Universal Grammar in second language acquisition: The "failed functional features hypothesis." *Second Language Research* 13:287–326.

Henry, A. 1995. *Belfast English and Standard English.* Oxford: Oxford University Press.

————. 1997. Viewing change in progress: The loss of V2 in Hiberno-English imperatives. In *Parameters of morphosyntactic change,* eds. A. van Kemenade and N. Vincent, 273–96. Cambridge: Cambridge University Press.

Hernández-Chávez, E. 1993. Native language loss and its implications for revitalization of Spanish in Chicano communities. In *Language and culture in learning: Teaching Spanish to native speakers of Spanish,* eds. B. Merino, H. Trueba, and F. Samaniego, 58–74. Washington, DC: Falmer Press.

Herschensohn, J. 2000. *The second time around: Minimalism and L2 acquisition.* Amsterdam: John Benjamins.

Hertel, T. 2000. The second language acquisition of Spanish word order: Lexical and discourse factors. Ph.D. diss., Pennsylvania State University.

Hertel, T., and A. T. Pérez-Leroux. 1999. The second language acquisition of Spanish word order for unaccusative verbs. In *Proceedings of the 23rd Annual Boston University Conference on Language Development,* vol. 1, eds. A. Greenhill, H. Littlefield, and C. Tano, 228–39. Somerville, MA: Cascadilla Press.

Hirakawa, M. 1995. L2 acquisition of English accusative constructions. In *Proceedings of the 19th Annual Boston University Conference on Language Development,* vol. 1, eds. D. MacLaughlin and S. McEwen, 407–18. Somerville MA: Cascadilla Press.

Johnson, J., and E. Newport, E. 1991. Critical period effects on universal properties of language: The status of subjacency in the acquisition of a second language. *Cognition* 39:215–58.

Juffs, A. 1996. Parameters in the lexicon, language variation, and language development. In *Proceedings of the 20th Annual Boston University Conference on Language Development,* vol. 1, eds. A. Stringfellow, D. Cahana-Amitay, E. Hughes and A. Zukowski, 407–18. Somerville, MA: Cascadilla Press.

Kayne, R. 1975. *French syntax: The transformational cycle.* Cambridge, MA: MIT Press.

————. 1991. Romance clitics, verb movement and PRO. *Linguistic Inquiry* 22:647–86.

————. 1994. *The antisymmetry of syntax.* Cambridge, MA: MIT Press.

Klein, E., and G. Martohardjono. 1999. *The development of second language grammars: A generative approach.* Amsterdam: John Benjamins.

Köppe, R., and J. Meisel. 1995. Code-switching in bilingual first language acquisition. In *One speaker, two languages,* eds. L. Milroy and P. Muysken, 276–301. Cambridge: Cambridge University Press.

Lance, D. 1975. Spanish/English code-switching. In *El lenguaje de los Chicanos,* eds. E. Hernández-Chávez, A. Cohen, and A. Beltramo, 138–53. Arlington, VA: Center for Applied Linguistics.

Lardiere, D. 1998. Dissociating syntax from morphology in a divergent L2 end-state grammar. *Second Language Research* 14:359–75.

Lardiere, D., and B. Schwartz. 1997. Feature-marking in the L2 development of deverbal compounds. *Journal of Linguistics* 33:327–53.

Levin, B., and M. Rappaport Hovav. 1995. *Unaccusativity: At the syntax-lexical semantics interface.* Cambridge, MA: MIT Press.

Liceras, J. 1989. On some properties of the "pro-drop" parameter: Looking for missing subjects in non-native Spanish. In *Linguistic Perspectives on Second Language Acquisition,* eds. S. Gass and J. Schachter, 109–33. New York: Cambridge University Press.

Liceras, J., and L. Díaz. 1998. On the nature of the relationship between morphology and syntax: Inflectional typology, f-features and null/overt pronouns in Spanish interlanguage. In *Morphology and its interfaces in second language knowledge,* ed. M. L. Beck, 307–38. Amsterdam: John Benjamins.

————. 1999. Topic-drop versus pro-drop: Null subjects and pronominal subjects in the Spanish L2 of Chinese, French, German and Japanese speakers. *Second Language Research* 15:1–40.

Liceras, J., L. Díaz, B. Laguardia, and R. Fernández. 1998. Licensing and identification of null categories in Spanish nonnative grammars. In *Theoretical analyses on Romance languages,* eds. J. Lema and E. Treviño, 263–82. Amsterdam: John Benjamins.

Liceras, J., L. Díaz, and D. Maxwell. 1998. Null subjects in non-native grammars. In *The development of second language grammars: A generative approach,* eds. E. Klein and G. Martohardjono, 113–49. Amsterdam: John Benjamins.

Liceras, J., E. Valenzuela, and L. Díaz. 1999. L1/L2 Spanish grammars and the pragmatic deficit hypothesis. *Second Language Research* 15:161–90.

Lightfoot, D. 1991. *How to set parameters.* Cambridge, MA: MIT Press.

Lipski, J. 1985. *Linguistic aspects of Spanish-English language switching.* Tempe: Arizona State University Center for Latin American Studies.

————. 1994. *Latin American Spanish.* New York: Longman.

Longobardi, G. 1994. Reference and proper names: A theory of N-movement in syntax and in logical form. *Linguistic Inquiry* 25.4:609–65.

Lust, B., G. Hermon, and J. Kornfilt. 1994. *Binding, dependencies, and learnability.* Hillsdale, NJ: Lawrence Erlbaum.

Lust, B., M. Suñer, and J. Whitman. 1994. *Heads, projections and learnability.* Hillsdale, NJ: Lawrence Erlbaum.

MacSwan, J. 1999. *A minimalist approach to intra-sentential code switching.* Cambridge: Cambridge University Press.

Mandell, P. 1998. The V-movement parameter: Syntactic properties and adult L2 learners of Spanish. *Spanish Applied Linguistics* 2:169–97.

Martínez, E. 1993. *Morpho-syntactic erosion between two generational groups of Spanish speakers in the United States.* New York: Peter Lang.

McClure, E. 1981. Formal and functional aspects of the code-switched discourse of bilingual children. In *Latino language and communicative behavior,* ed. R. Duran, 69–94. Norwood, NJ: Ablex.

McLaughlin, B., and R. Heredia. 1996. Information-processing approaches to research on second language acquisition use. In *The Handbook of Second Language Acquisition,* eds., W. Ritchie and T. Bhatia, 213–28. San Diego: Academic Press.

Meisel, J. 1989. Early differentiation of languages in bilingual children. In *Bilingualism across the lifespan: Aspects of acquisition, maturity, and loss,* eds. K. Hyltenstam and L. Obler, 13–40. Cambridge: Cambridge University Press.

————. 1994. Code-switching in young bilingual children: The acquisition of grammatical constraints. *Studies in Second Language Acquisition* 16:413–39.

Montalbetti, M. 1984. After binding. Ph.D. diss., MIT.

Montrul, S. 1996. The second language acquisition of dative case: From absolute L1 influence to optionality. In *Proceedings of the 20th Annual Boston University Conference on Language Development,* vol. 1, eds. A. Stringfellow, D. Cahana-Amitay, E. Hughes, and A. Zukowski, 506–17. Somerville, MA: Cascadilla Press.

————. 1997. On the parallels between diachronic change and interlanguage grammars: The L2 acquisition of the Spanish dative case system. *Spanish Applied Linguistics* 1:87–113.

————. 1998. The L2 acquisition of dative experiencer subjects. *Second Language Research* 8:27–61.

————. 1999a. Activating AgrIOP in second language acquisition. In *The development of second language grammars: A generative approach,* eds. E. Klein and G. Martohardjono, 81–107. Amsterdam: John Benjamins.

————. 1999b. Causative errors with unaccusative verbs in L2 Spanish. *Second Language Research* 15:191–219.

————. 2002a. Agentive verbs of manner of motion in Spanish and English as second languages. *Studies in Second Language Acquisition* 23:171–206.

————. 2002b. Incomplete acquisition and attrition of Spanish tense/aspect distinctions in adult bilinguals. *Bilingualism: Language and Cognition* 5:39–68.

Muysken, P. 2000. *Bilingual speech.* Cambridge: Cambridge University Press.

Newmeyer, F., and S. Weinberger. 1998. The ontogenesis of the field of second language learning research. In *Linguistic theory in second language acquisition,* eds. S. Flynn and W. O'Neil, 34–46. Dordrecht: Kluwer.

Newson, M. 1990. Dependencies in the lexical setting of parameters: A solution to the undergeneralisation problem. In *Logical issues in language acquisition,* ed. I. Roca, 177–98. Dordrecht: Foris.

Obler, L., and S. Hannigan. 1996. Neurolinguistics of second language acquisition and use. In *Handbook of second language acquisition,* eds. W. Ritchie and T. Bhatia, 509–23. New York: Academic Press.

Paredes, L. 1995. Clitics in Andean Spanish. Ph.D. diss., University of Southern California.

Pérez-Leroux, A. T., and W. Glass. 1997. OPC effects on the L2 acquisition of Spanish. In *Contemporary perspectives on the acquisition of Spanish,* vol. 1, *Developing grammars,* eds. A. T. Pérez-Leroux and W. Glass, 149–65. Somerville, MA: Cascadilla Press.

Pienemann, M. 1988. Psychological constraints on the teachability of languages. In *Grammar and second language teaching: A book of readings,* eds. W. Rutherford and M. Sharwood Smith, 85–106. Rowley, MA: Newbury House.

Platzack, C. 1996. The initial hypothesis of syntax: A minimalist perspective on language acquisition and attrition. In *Generative perspectives on language acquisition,* ed. H. Clahsen, 369–414. Amsterdam: John Benjamins.

Pollock, J.-Y. 1989. Verb-movement, UG and the structure of IP. *Linguistic Inquiry* 20:365–424.

Poplack, S. 1980. Sometimes I'll start a sentence in English y termino en español: Toward a typology of code-switching. In *Spanish in the United States: Sociolinguistic aspects,* eds. J. Amastae and L. Elías-Olivares, 230–63. Cambridge: Cambridge University Press.

―――. 1983. Bilingual competence: Linguistic interference or grammatical integrity? In *Spanish in the U.S. setting: Beyond the Southwest,* ed. L. Elías-Olivares, 107–29. Roslyn, VA: National Clearinghouse for Bilingual Education.

Prévost, P., and L. White. 2000. Missing surface inflection or impairment in second language acquisition? Evidence from tense and agreement. *Second Language Research* 16:103–33.

Rakowsky, A. 1989. A study of intra-sentential code-switching in Spanish-English bilinguals and second language learners. Ph.D. diss., Brown University.

Rizzi, L. 1994. Early null subjects and root null subjects. In *Language acquisition studies in generative grammar,* eds. T. Hoekstra and B. Schwartz, 151–76. Amsterdam: John Benjamins.

―――. 1997. The fine structure of the left periphery. In *Elements of Grammar,* ed. L. Haegman, 281–337. Dordrecht: Kluwer.

Roeper, T. 1999. Universal bilingualism. *Bilingualism: Language and Cognition* 2:169–86.

Rubin, E., and A. J. Toribio. 1995. Feature checking and the syntax of language contact. In *Contemporary research in Romance linguistics,* eds. J. Amastae, G. Goodall, M. Montalbetti, and M. Phinney, 177–85. Amsterdam: John Benjamins.

―――. 1996. The role of functional categories in bilingual children's language mixing and differentiation. *World Englishes* 15:385–93.

Sánchez, L. 1996. Word order, predication and agreement in DPs in Spanish, Southern Quechua and Southern Andean bilingual Spanish. In *Grammatical theory and romance languages: Selected papers from the 25th Linguistic Symposium on Romance Languages,* ed. K. Zagona, 209–18. Amsterdam: John Benjamins.

―――. 1997. Why do bilingual Spanish and Spanish in contact varieties drop definite objects? In *Proceedings of the GALA 97 Conference on Knowledge and Representation,* eds. A. Sorace and C. Sheylock, 148–53. Edinburgh: University of Edinburgh Press.

―――. 1999a. Null objects and D° features in contact Spanish. In *Formal perspectives on Romance linguistics: Selected papers from the 28th Linguistic Symposium on Romance Languages,* eds. J. M. Authier, B. Bullock, and L. Reed, 227–42. Amsterdam: John Benjamins.

―――. 1999b. Morphosyntactic representations in L1 and L2/bilingual speakers in language contact situations. Paper presented at the 1999 Conference on L1 and L2 Acquisition of Spanish and Portuguese and Third Hispanic Linguistics Symposium, Georgetown University.

Sánchez, L., and T. Al-Kasey. 1999. The role of clitic-doubling in the acquisition of L2 Spanish. *Proceedings of the generative approaches to second language acquisition '97 conference.* McGill University.

Sánchez, L., and M. Giménez. 1998. The L2 acquisition of definite determiners: From null to overt. In *Proceedings of the 22d Annual Boston University Conference on Language Development,* vol. 2, eds. A. Greenhill, M. Hughes, H. Littlefield, and H. Walsh, 640–50. Somerville, MA: Cascadilla Press.

Schachter, J. 1989. Testing a proposed universal. In *Linguistic perspectives on second language acquisition,* eds. S. Gass and J. Schachter, 73–88. Cambridge: Cambridge University Press.

————. 1990. On the issue of completeness in second language acquisition. *Second Language Research* 6:93–124.

————. 1996. Maturation and the issue of Universal Grammar in second language acquisition. In *Handbook of second language acquisition,* eds. W. Ritchie and T. Bhatia, 159–93. New York: Academic Press.

Schütze, C. 1996. *The empirical base of linguistics: Grammaticality judgments and linguistic methodology.* Chicago: University of Chicago Press.

————. 1998. On two hypotheses of "transfer" in L2A: Minimal trees and absolute L1 influence. In *The generative study of second language acquisition,* eds. S. Flynn, G. Martohardjono, and W. O'Neil, 35–59. Mahwah, NJ: Lawrence Erlbaum.

Schwartz, B. 1998. On two hypotheses of "transfer" in L2A: Minimal trees and absolute L1 influence. In *The generative study of second languge acquisition,* eds. S. Flynn, G. Martohardjono, and W. O'Neill, 35–39. Mahwah, NJ: Lawrence Erlbaum.

Schwartz, B., and R. Sprouse. 1994. Word order and nominative case in non-native language acquisition: A longitudinal study of L1 Turkish German interlanguage. In *Language acquisition studies in generative grammar,* eds., T. Hoekstra and B. Schwartz, 317–68. Amsterdam: John Benjamins.

————. 1996. L2 cognitive states and the full transfer/full access model. *Second Language Research* 12:40–72.

Seliger, H. 1996. Primary language attrition in the context of bilingualism. In *Handbook of second language acquisition,* eds. W. Ritchie and T. Bhatia, 605–25. New York: Academic Press.

Sharwood Smith, M., and P. Van Buren. 1991. First language attrition and the parameter setting model. In *First language attrition,* eds. H. Seliger and R. Vago, 17–30. Cambridge: Cambridge University Press.

Silva-Corvalán, C. 1986. Bilingualism and language contact. *Language* 62:587–608.

————. 1991. Spanish language attrition in a contact situation with English. In *First language attrition,* eds. H. Seliger and R. Vago, 151–71. Cambridge: Cambridge University Press.

————. 1994. *Language contact and change.* Oxford: Clarendon Press.

Smith, N., and I. M. Tsimpli. 1995. *The mind of a savant: Language learning and modularity.* Oxford: Blackwell.

Sorace, A. 1990. Indeterminacy in first and second languages: Theoretical and methodological issues. In *Individualizing the assessment of language abilities,* eds. J. de Jong and D. Stevenson, 127–53. Philadelphia: Multilingual Matters.

————. 1993. Incomplete versus divergent representations of unaccusativity in non-native grammars of Italian. *Second Language Research* 9:22–47.

————. 1995. Acquiring linking rules and argument structures in a second language: The unaccusative/unergative distinction. In *The current state of interlanguage: Studies in honor of William E. Rutherford,* eds. Lynn Eubank, Larry Selinker, and Michael Sharwood Smith, 153–75. Amsterdam: John Benjamins.

————. 1996. The use of acceptability judgments in second language acquisition. In *The handbook of second language acquisition,* eds. W. Ritchie and T. Bhatia, 375–409. New York: Academic Press.

————. 1999. Initial states, end-states, and residual optionality in L2 acquisition. In *Proceedings of the 23rd Annual Boston University Conference on Language Development,* vol. 2, eds. A. Greenhill, H. Littlefield, and C. Tano, 666–74. Somerville, MA: Cascadilla Press.

————. 2000a. Syntactic optionality in non-native grammars. *Second Language Research* 16:93–102.

————. 2000b. Differential effects of attrition in the L1 syntax of near-native L2 speakers. In *Proceedings of the 24th Annual Boston University Conference on Language Development,* vol. 2, eds. A. Do, L. Domínguez and A. Johansen, 719–25. Somerville, MA: Cascadilla Press.

Sportiche, D. 1996. Clitic constructions. In *Phrase structure and the lexicon,* eds. J. Rooryck and L. Zaring, 213–76. Dordrecht: Kluwer.

Sunderman, G., and A. J. Toribio. 2000. Converging evidence for a syntactic-theoretical constraint in bilingual speech. Paper presented at Generative Approaches to Second Language Acquisition, MIT.

Suñer, M. 1988. The role of AGR(eement) in clitic-doubled constructions. *Natural Language and Linguistic Theory* 19:511–19.

————. 1994. V-movement and the licensing of argumental wh-phrases in Spanish. *Natural Language and Linguistic Theory* 12:335–72.

Toribio, A. J. 2000a. Setting parametric limits on dialectal variation. *Lingua* 110:315–41.

————. 2000b. Minimalist ideas on parametric variation. In *NELS 30: Proceedings of the North East Linguistics Society,* eds. M. Hirotani, A. Coetzle, N. Hall, and J.-Y. Kim, 627–38. Amherst: University of Massachusetts.

————. 2000c. Spanglish?! Bite your tongue! Spanish-English code-switching among US Latinos. In *Reflexiones 1999,* ed. R. Flores, 115–47. Austin, TX: Center for Mexican American Studies.

————. 2000d. Code-switching and minority language attrition. In *Spanish applied linguistics at the turn of the millennium,* eds. R. Leow and C. Sanz, 174–93. Somerville, MA: Cascadilla Press.

————. 2001a. On the emergence of code-switching competence among second language learners. *Bilingualism: Language and Cognition* 4:203–31.

————. 2001b. Accessing Spanish-English code-switching competence. *International Journal of Bilingualism* 5:403–36.

————. 2001c. On Spanish-language decline. In *Proceedings of the 25th Annual Boston University Conference on Language Development,* vol. 2, eds. A. Do, L. Domínguez, and A. Johansen, 768–79. Somerville, MA: Cascadilla Press.

————. forthcoming. Unilingual code and bilingual mode: The Spanish of Spanish-English bilinguals. *International Journal of Bilingualism.*

Toribio, A. J., and E. Rubin. 1996. Code-switching in generative grammar. In *Spanish in contact,* eds. J. Jensen and A. Roca, 203–26. Somerville, MA: Cascadilla Press.

Toribio, A. J., R. Roebuck, J. Lantolf, and A. Perrone. 1993. Syntactic constraints on code-switching: Evidence of abstract knowledge in second language acquisition. Unpublished manuscript, Cornell University.

Toth, P. 2000. The interaction of instruction and learner-internal factors in the acquisition of L2 morphosyntax. *Studies in Second Language Acquisition* 22:169–208.

Uriagereka, J. 1999. Irreversible language loss. Paper presented at the Annual Meeting of the Eastern States Conference in Linguistics, University of Connecticut at Storrs.

Vainikka, A., and M. Young-Scholten. 1994. Direct access to X-theory: Evidence from Korean and Turkish adults learning German. In *Language acquisition studies in generative grammar,* eds., T. Hoekstra and B. Schwartz, 265–316. Amsterdam: John Benjamins.

———. 1996. Gradual development of L2 phrase structure. *Second Language Research* 12:7–39.

———. 1998. The initial state in the L2 acquisition of phrase structure. In *The generative study of second language acquisition,* eds. S. Flynn, G. Martohardjono, and W. O'Neil, 17–34. Mahwah, NJ: Lawrence Erlbaum.

Valenzuela, E. 2002. The acquisition of topic constructions in L2 Spanish. In *Proceedings of the 26th Annual Boston University Conference on Language Development,* eds., A. Do, S. Fish, and B. Skarabela, 723–33. Somerville, MA: Cascadilla Press.

van Kemenade, A., and N. Vincent. 1997. *Parameters of morphosyntactic change.* Cambridge: Cambridge University Press.

Wexler, K., and M. Manzini. 1987. Parameters and learnability in binding theory. In *Parameter setting,* eds. T. Roeper and E. Willams, 41–76. Dordrecht: Reidel.

White, L. 1985. The "pro-drop" parameter in adult second language acquisition. *Language Learning* 35:47–62.

———. 1989. *Universal Grammar and second language acquisition.* Amsterdam: John Benjamins.

———. 1992. Long and short verb movement in second language acquisition. *Canadian Journal of Linguistics* 37:273–86.

———. 1996. Universal Grammar and second language acquisition: Current trends and new directions. In *Handbook of second language acquisition,* eds. W. Ritchie and T. Bhatia, 85–120. New York: Academic Press.

White, L., and F. Genesee. 1996. How native is near-native? The issue of ultimate attainment in adult second language acquisition. *Second Language Research* 12:233–65.

Wilson, J., and A. Henry. 1998. Parameter setting within a socially realistic linguistics. *Language in Society* 27:1–21.

Yusa, N. 1999. Multiple-specifiers and wh-island effects in L2 acquisition: A preliminary study. In *The development of second language grammar: A generative approach,* eds. E. Klein and G. Martohardjono, 289–315. Amsterdam: John Benjamins.

Zentella, A. C. 1997. *Growing up bilingual.* Malden, MA: Blackwell.

8

Cognitive Perspectives

Cognitive Perspectives on the Acquisition of Spanish as a Second Language

PAOLA E. DUSSIAS   Pennsylvania State University

1.0   Introduction

The purpose of this chapter is to provide an overview of current research on various cognitive approaches to second language learning in Spanish. The first section discusses several cognitive models, paying attention to a number of dichotomies that have informed the field: product-oriented versus process-oriented approaches, explicit versus implicit knowledge, focus on input versus focus on output, Processing Instruction versus traditional and meaning-based output, and attention to form versus attention to meaning. Where relevant, I analyze how models have dealt with these dichotomies and how empirical studies have provided (or not provided) support for the proposed theoretical tenets. In the second part of this chapter, I discuss research on sentence processing in Spanish-English learners at various levels of proficiency (i.e., advanced second language learners and Spanish-English bilinguals), for this topic reveals basic general cognitive processes that may inform general theoretical approaches with an emphasis on cognition.[1]

2.0   Cognitive Accounts of Second Language Acquisition

Cognitive accounts of second language acquisition all agree that language learning engages the same cognitive systems (perception, memorization, information processing, etc.) that are involved in other kinds of learning. This is often explained by invoking the metaphor that learning a language is seen as essentially no different from learning how to play an instrument or how to ride a bicycle. Where the accounts differ is on whether they focus on the relationship between explicit and implicit knowledge, the relationship between input and implicit knowledge, or the relationship between L2 knowledge and output (Ellis 1994).

In this section, I review cognitive models whose claims have been empirically tested using data from Spanish second language learners. I begin with a discussion of the differ-

ences between product-oriented versus process-oriented approaches to second language acquisition research. Under this rubric, I review several interlanguage studies and Krashen's
distinction between *acquisition* and *learning.* Although admittedly Krashen's ideas are in-
natist in nature, in explaining the contrast between *acquisition* and *learning,* Krashen draws
on the constructs of *implicit* and *explicit,* which are cognitive in nature (Ellis 1994). Subsequently, I briefly touch on Andersen's Nativization Model and Pienemann's Processability
Theory, ending with a discussion of the contrast between comprehensible input and comprehensible output by presenting the theoretical tenets and pedagogical implications of
"input processing" versus "output practice" models of language acquisition.

2.1 Product-Oriented Versus Process-Oriented Approaches

According to Lafford (2000), the early literature on the acquisition of Spanish by second language learners is characterized by a comparison of the differences between native and target languages, inasmuch as it was believed that these differences were responsible for learners' errors. Early research tended to be descriptive, introspective, and pedagogical in nature,
with little attention paid to the actual performance of students. With the growing recognition that the grammars learners constructed on their way to acquiring the target language
were systematic and ruled-governed, the product-oriented approach to the study of Spanish second language acquisition was replaced by a process-oriented approach, where the object of study became not what learners should be doing (a comparison of L2 products with
target language use) but rather how learners constructed their L2 systems. Early morpheme
acquisition studies were abandoned and replaced by studies dealing with explanations of
the systematic variation in learners' interlanguage. In what follows, I will briefly review a
number of research studies that have investigated the acquisition of specific grammatical
aspects and lexical meanings by second language learners of Spanish within an interlanguage framework. As will be seen, these studies have sought to explain the evolution of
learners' interlanguage by proposing the existence of a number of internal strategies (e.g.,
Selinker 1972) utilized during the L2 acquisition process.

2.1.1 Interlanguage as a Set of Internal Strategies

Selinker (1972) coined the term *interlanguage* to refer to both the internal mechanism that
learners have constructed at a single point in time as well as to the interconnected systems
that characterize the learners' progress over time. Early interlanguage theory was concerned, among other things, with the cognitive processes that were responsible for the hypotheses constructed by second language learners about the structural properties of the target language. Partly on the basis of errors found in the speech of language learners,
Selinker (1972) identified the following five processes:

1. Language transfer: some rules of the interlanguage may result from the transfer of semantic or grammatical features from the first language.
2. Overgeneralization: some linguistic forms of the interlanguage may be the result of
   overgeneralization of the rules of the target language.

3. Transfer of training: some linguistic forms of the interlanguage may result from the training process employed to teach the second language.

4. Strategies of second language learning: some linguistic forms of the interlanguage may result from a specific approach to the material to be learned.

5. Strategies of second language communication: some linguistic forms of the interlanguage may result from specific ways in which learners learn to communicate with speakers of the target language.

Examples of studies that have sought to examine different aspects of Spanish interlanguage development are VanPatten (1987), Ryan and Lafford (1992), Guntermann (1992), Andersen (1986), Lafford and Collentine (1989), Lantolf (1988), DeKeyser (1991), and Frantzen (1991). In this section, I will focus on the first three of these studies, for together they provide a comprehensive examination of stages of transitional competence that second-language learners of Spanish exhibit in the development of two formal features of the language: the copulas *ser* and *estar*.[2]

The first in-depth study of the development of the Spanish copulas *ser* and *estar* by second language learners was conducted by VanPatten (1987). Through the analysis of longitudinal data collected from six classroom learners of Spanish, as well as grammaticality judgments and classroom observations, VanPatten found five different stages in the development of Spanish copulas:

1. Absence of copula in learner speech
   María baja. "Mary short."

2. Selection of *ser* to perform most copula functions
   Juan es estudiando. "John is studying."
   El libro es aquí. "The book is here."
   María es enferma. "Mary is ill."

3. Appearance of *estar* with present progressive
   Juan está estudiando. "John is studying."

4. Appearance of *estar* with locatives
   El libro está aquí. "The book is here."

5. Appearance of *estar* with adjectives of condition
   María está enferma. "Mary is sick."

VanPatten argues that these transitional stages cannot be explained either by classroom teaching approaches or by sequence of instruction. The *sequence-of-instruction* account, for example, predicts that forms that are taught first are acquired first. Given that the use of the copula *estar* with adjectives of condition was taught from the first days of instruction and was used through the course of instruction, one would expect learners to exhibit a certain degree of mastery of this form at early stages of language development. Likewise, if teaching approaches were responsible for the different stages of development, we would expect the concurrent emergence of both copulas in the interlanguage of these learners, inasmuch as *ser* and *estar* as well as their usage were presented early in the instructional curriculum. A more likely explanation, offered by VanPatten, is to account for these stages of transitional competence via the interaction of four factors known to be involved in second language acquisition:

1. Simplification—copula omission or overuse of *ser* for both copulas.
2. Communicative value—copulas tend to be omitted because they generally do not add any real information to the message contained in a sentence.
3. Frequency in input—*ser* appears to be overwhelmingly more frequent than *estar* in the readings aimed at first-year students.
4. L1 transfer—*ser* appears in the interlanguage of English-speaking learners for a prolonged period because of the existence of only one copula in English.

In a related study, Ryan and Lafford (1992) sought to examine the extent to which VanPatten's (1987) findings could be generalized to other language learning settings. Analysis of transcriptions from elicited oral interviews revealed that sixteen beginning-level students in a study abroad context acquired the Spanish copulas and their uses in ordered stages, much in the same way as described in VanPatten (1987). The only real difference between the two studies lay in the order of the acquisition of the locative and conditional uses. Whereas Van-Patten found that the locative uses of *estar* are learned first, Ryan and Lafford found mastery of *estar* in conditional contexts to precede mastery of *estar* in locative contexts.

Guntermann (1992), also looking at development of *ser* and *estar* over time, found only partial support for the stages of acquisition postulated by VanPatten (1987). Data collected from oral interviews to evaluate the proficiency of nine Peace Corps volunteers in Spanish revealed that the copula omission characteristic of stage I was not brief (as stated in Van-Patten 1987), but rather was still present in the language samples of advanced speakers of Spanish. Guntermann attributes this result to learners employing simplification as a means to use the least complex forms and rules to express the most meanings and to expand their ability to use language.

The studies investigating the development of the Spanish copula by second language learners show striking similarities in their results despite their methodological differences and the interlearner and intralearner variability that characterizes second language acquisition research. The convergence of results strongly suggests that the acquisition of *ser* and *estar* involves identifiable stages of development. Although studies such as these undoubtedly contribute some of the best descriptive work in SLA research, there are a number of shortcomings surrounding this type of work.

First, although these studies acknowledge that the first language plays a role during the learning of a second language, they typically do not articulate what this role is. That is, no account is given to explain in what ways the L1 and the L2 contribute to the specific structure of the interlanguage, and nothing is said about the qualitative ways in which the system learners build at a given point in time differs from that of the native speaker.

Second, the typology used to explain the different stages of development observed in the learners' interlanguage is itself more a descriptive statement than an explanation of the processes involved in the development of a second language. To say, for example, that a particular type of linguistic behavior is due to simplification does not really explain why simplification occurs. It may be the case that learners simplify because they have not yet acquired a particular form. Or it may be that learners are unable to access the particular form in the production of specific linguistic utterances. The fact that simplification can reflect the processes of either acquisition or production raises the need to distinguish between what learners "know" at a particular stage in their language development and what they do. One way to address this issue would be to use instruments of data collection whose hypothesized properties allow researchers to tap into these two types of linguistic behavior (e.g., grammaticality judgments versus naturalistic data).

Third, one of the explanations given for the early selection of *ser* over *estar* to perform most copula functions was to suggest that frequency of occurrence in the input could have played a role. That is, learners may have overextended the uses of *ser* simply because it appeared more frequently in the readings of first-year classroom students, making it easier for learners to perceive (see VanPatten 1987). Although it is reasonable to suggest that frequency is linked to the attention and internalization of linguistic forms, the frequency of occurrence of *ser* and *estar* in the readings in question remained unattested.

Fourth, when data is collected by means of a single instrument—as was the case in Ryan and Lafford (1992) and Guntermann (1992)—the variability in learner language produced in different contexts is ignored. To take an example, Schmidt (1980) used free oral production, imitation, written sentence-combining and grammaticality judgments to study second-verb ellipsis (e.g., Peter is eating an apple and Paul an orange). The findings revealed that learners always included the second verb in free oral production but omitted it in other samples of their language in proportion to the degree of monitoring that the tasks allowed.[3] Given this finding, it seems appropriate that studies investigating developmental sequences use two or more instruments to collect data.

Despite these limitations, the discovery that there are testifiable developmental patterns in second language acquisition of a syntactic, lexical, and semantic nature is important, for any theory of second language acquisition will need to account for such developmental patterns.

2.1.2 The Implicit Versus Explicit Contrast in Interlanguage Studies

According to Krashen (1981, 1982), adult second language learners may either "acquire" or "learn" a second language. *Acquisition* is an unconscious process that occurs when learners engage in meaningful interactions in natural communication settings in the second language, with no attention to form. *Learning,* on the other hand, is the conscious process of studying and attending to form and rules; both error detection and error correction are central here in that learning results in "knowing about language." Although Krashen failed to supply a clear definition of conscious and unconscious, he identified *conscious learning* with the ability to provide grammaticality judgments based on rules. In contrast, *unconscious learning* was identified with the ability to provide grammaticality judgments based on "feel." In this respect, then, conscious learning is associated with explicit knowledge whereas unconscious learning is associated with implicit knowledge.

Studies that have sought to examine the explicit/implicit distinction have typically equated learners' explanations of grammatical rules with explicit knowledge and learners' use of the same grammatical features in production with implicit knowledge.[4] A recent study investigating the explicit/implicit dichotomy is VanPatten and Mandell (1999). Although the study investigated the influence of structure type on how learners judge L2 sentences, it nevertheless examined the question of learners' explicit and implicit knowledge and how this knowledge is represented in the mind of the learner. In this study, a group of sixty-four second language learners of Spanish was shown sentences that contained different types of morphosyntactic errors. Relevant to our discussion are Type I sentences, sentences containing errors for which learners regularly receive explicit instructions and corrective feedback in the L2 classroom, and Type III sentences, sentences containing errors for which learners are neither taught nor for which they receive corrective feedback (i.e., errors that, according to some prevailing theories of linguistic analysis, result because of violations of principles of Universal Grammar).

The learners were asked to provide a judgment (i.e., correct or incorrect), to correct the sentences, and in each case to state whether their judgment was based on largely "feel," "known rule," or "guess." Results showed that subjects' correctly rejected the ungrammatical sentences the majority of the time. In addition, most subjects reported that grammaticality judgments of Type I sentences were based on knowledge of a rule about which they had received instruction, and those of Type III sentences were based on feel. These results showed that learners relied on different sources of information when providing grammaticality judgments. Explicit knowledge of rules was used when subjects were judging sentences containing errors for which they had received explicit classroom instruction, whereas implicit knowledge was used when judging sentences with errors for which no attention to form was available. These findings suggest that explicit rules constitute part of the available knowledge to L2 learners, and tentatively provide some legitimacy of the cognitive distinction between explicit and implicit learning postulated by Krashen.

There are, however, a number of limitations associated with VanPatten and Mandell's (1999) study. Recall that the researchers set out to test whether learners' L2 judgments strategies could be grouped according to the type of structure that the L2 learners were judging. For morphosyntactic structures about which learners regularly receive explicit instruction in the L2 classroom (i.e., Type I sentences), the prediction was that learners would report significantly more use of "known rules." Conversely, for structures that are neither taught nor for which learners receive corrective feedback (i.e., Type III sentences), the hypothesis was that learners would report significantly more use of "feel" than "known rule." However, subjects were not asked to formulate a rule for cases in which they indicated that judgment was based on "known rule." Therefore, one cannot rule out the possibility that learners may have judged a sentence as ungrammatical based on "feel," but remembered having received some type of explicit instruction about the structure, and consequently reported having made the judgment based on "known rule" instead.

Another possibility is that learners may have engaged in the use of other strategies, such as translation, analogy, or semantics, to arrive at a judgment, and somehow equated this to the concept of "known rule." An added problem is that no control group (i.e., native speakers of Spanish) was available to compare the results obtained for the second language learners. This baseline comparison seems necessary in light of the fact that a central assumption in the study is that second language learners rely on "feel," much as native speakers do, when faced with structures that learners come to learn not because they have received explicit instruction, but because of interactions between Universal Grammar and input data. Although the results obtained in the study point in the right direction, without the native speaker data it is not possible to determine the degree of similarity in the behavior of native speakers and second language learners.

Finally, a glance at the materials reveals that some of the sentences assumed to be impossible in Spanish (e.g., *Yo honestamente no entiendo tu problema* "I honestly don't understand your problem"; *Una flor fea creció en el jardín* "An ugly flower grew in the garden"; *Café no hay para el desayuno* "There is no coffee for breakfast") have varying degrees of acceptability. Some sentences are encountered in everyday conversations, whereas others are marginally acceptable or used only in some highly marked contexts. Given that not all the experimental sentences had the same level of acceptability, the validity of the judgments provided by the second language learners is questionable.

Although the results of VanPatten and Mandell's (1999) study have been compromised by the limitations outlined here, investigations of this nature play a significant role because the relationship between explicit and implicit knowledge continues to be an important issue in the discussion of the role of consciousness and attention in second language acquisition.

2.1.3   Andersen's Nativization Model

Whereas interlanguage theory sought to answer the question of the processes that were responsible for interlanguage construction and the nature of the interlanguage continuum, Andersen's Nativization Model (1979, 1983, 1990) investigated how learners created and restructured their interlanguage system. He distinguished between two processes, *nativization* and *denativization*. Nativization involves assimilation as learners make the input conform to their own internalized view of what constitutes the L2 system. This process results in the type of pidginization characteristic of early language acquisition. On the other hand, denativization consists of accommodation to the external system and results in the kind of depidginization evident in later stages of second language acquisition (McLaughlin 1987; Ellis 1994).

More recently, based on research on the L2 acquisition of English and Spanish, Andersen (1990) has proposed seven operating principles that specify the processes, cognitive principles and communicative strategies that operate during second language acquisition. These are: the One-to-One Principle, the Multifunctionality Principle, the Formal Determinism Principle, the Distributional Bias Principle, the Relevance Principle, the Transfer to Somewhere Principle, and the Relexification Principle. To illustrate how the principles work, an in-depth look at one of the principles, Formal Determinism, is in order. This principle states that "when the form-meaning relationship is clearly and uniformly encoded in the input, the learner will discover it earlier than other form-meaning relationships and will incorporate it more consistently within his interlanguage system" (55). Support for this principle comes from plural subject-verb agreement in Spanish. Andersen observes that the verbal markers *–mos* and *–n* for first and third person respectively are acquired before the first person singular marker *–o*. He explains this by noting that the plural markers in question are invariably used across the entire verbal inflection paradigm, whereas the singular inflection *–o* is restricted to present indicative. According to formal determinism, the consistency and transparency of these plural markers in Spanish promote their early discovery (see also Andersen 1983, 1984, 1986, and 1990 for further evidence for the principles using Spanish second language acquisition data).

Outside of Andersen's own research, one aspect of the interlanguage of second language learners of Spanish that has found support for the proposed operating principles is the development of the prepositions *por* and *para*.[5] Lafford and Ryan (1995), for example, found that the functions of "purpose" and "beneficiary" (both of which carry the meaning of "goal") associated with *para* surface early in the language of the learners. According to Lafford and Ryan, this can be explained by invoking Andersen's (1989) One-to-One Principle. The principle states that "interlanguage systems should be constructed in such a way that an intended underlying meaning is expressed with one clear invariant surface form (79)." This is illustrated here, since the meanings encoded in the function of "goal" are expressed invariantly by the form *para*. Lafford and Ryan also reported a number of nonnative uses of *por* and *para*. The most common use was "substitution," and was explained as a manifestation of the Naïve Lexical Hypothesis and Andersen's Relexification Principle. The first principle is seen at work in the speech of learners who equated *por* with English "for," as in *El piso tiene tres habitaciones por dormir* "The apartment has three rooms <u>for</u> sleeping." Andersen's Relexifixation Principle states that second language learners use the native language structure with items from the second language. This principle may explain learners' use of *por* + finite verb in place of the English "to" + infinitive verb as exemplified in *por habla español con chicas* "to speak Spanish with girls," even though the particular forms of the verb in Spanish and English do not correspond.

Andersen's operating principles were formulated to explain why certain linguistic forms typically appear in learners' second language production before others. There are, however, several well-known criticisms associated with these principles. First, the principles are not mutually exclusive, and so it becomes difficult to test each one of them separately (see Dulay and Burt 1974 and Larsen-Freeman 1975 on a similar criticism made to Slobin's 1973 list of operating principles). In addition, we do not know the weight to be attached to each principle when they are in conflict (Ellis 1994). Because of this, it is difficult to predict or to explain the emergence of certain linguistic forms in the learners' interlanguage. Given this state of affairs, it seems reasonable to seek out other theories that would enable us to explain, for example, the underlying patterns of behavior evidenced in the development of *por* and *para,* as well as the development of other morpheme types, in second language learners of Spanish.[6]

2.1.4 Pienemann's Processability Theory

In general, Processability Theory claims that fluent language-processing speed can be achieved because different components of the language production device operate automatically and without conscious attention (Johnston 1995). In the case of subject-verb agreement, for example, the appearance of the verb ending crucially rests on information created before the verb is uttered—for example, person and number marking on the subject noun. Subject-verb agreement can only occur if this information is stored and subsequently becomes available when the verb is produced. For adult native speakers of a language, it is assumed that these processes are highly automated and that there is a special memory buffer—a grammatical buffer—dedicated to the storage of such information, which, because of its task-specific nature, is accessible only to automated plans. The situation for second language learners is quite different. Because L2 learners do not possess automated procedures for the production of the target language, they do not have access to the task-specific grammatical buffer. What the second language learner processor needs to do, then, is to keep the transfer of syntactic information from its storage source to the memory buffer to a minimal level. The more information to be transferred, the less space there will be for other memory-dependent processes, including word access. What this means, then, is that linguistic information such as tense is expected to surface prior to, say, subject-verb agreement.

Following this line of reasoning, Pienemann (1998) proposes five hierarchical procedures, which form the backbone of Processability Theory. *Word/lemma access* is the first procedure and simply involves the access and production of words. This is a prerequisite for *lexical categorization,* in which specific grammatical characteristics such as person, number, and gender are associated with the lexical entry, along with certain semantic information. *Phrasal procedure* is the third procedure and refers to a process that is dependent on an adequate lexical entry for the phrasal head. In essence, this procedure yields agreement within a single phrase, such as a noun, verb, or adjective phrase. Upon completion of the procedures carried out within a single phrase, the role of that phrase within an utterance can be assigned and the phrase can be properly inserted within a sentence frame or structure. The assigning of phrasal function and the storing of sentential information occurs in the *S-procedure,* the fourth procedure. Finally, the *subordinate clause procedure* involves an exchange of grammatical and semantic information between a subordinate clause and the main clause.

According to the model, the development of grammatical structure will occur as learners systematically overcome the constraints identified in processing strategies. These strategies are also involved in L1 production and can only be accessed in the L2 incrementally. Based on the work on L2 German and English, Pienemann and his colleagues have suggested that not all linguistic items are developmental in the sense that acquisition occurs at a particular stage of the learner's development. Some are *variational,* in that the learners may or may not acquire them and can be acquired at any stage of development.

The predictive paradigm established by Pienemann's theory finds support in data from the interlanguage of second language learners of German, Japanese, and Spanish. For Spanish, Johnston (1995) presents preliminary data from language samples gathered from a variety of learners of Spanish in Australia that indicate the existence of the stages for the acquisition of word order outlined in table 8.1 (examples of stage I are not provided in Johnston (1995) given that they are too simplified to be of interest). At stage II, we evidence the use of strictly serial word order for the mapping of semantic roles onto surface forms. Interphrasal procedures such as subject-verb agreement are blocked at this stage. This is precisely what we would expect at the stage of category procedures. At stage III, we note the emergence of phrasal morphemes. Because S-procedures rely on the input from phrasal procedures, the former can only develop after the latter have emerged. Therefore, we do not expect the development of interphrasal operations (such as subject-verb agreement), unless intraphrasal operations have emerged. This is precisely what the data show. Stages IV and

Table 8.1

Examples of the Interlanguage of Spanish L2 Learners

Stage	Language Sample
Stage II	*De universidad llaman Macarthur Institute* "From university they call Macarthur Institute." [canonical word order]
Stage III	*Son simpáticos.* "They are nice." [intraphrasal agreement]
Stage IV	*En Australia se necesitan buenas buenos puntos.* "In Australia good points are needed." [interphrasal agreement]
Stage V	*Les dije que no hablaba español.* "I told them that X did not speak Spanish." [obj-clitic]

Source: Johnston 1995.

V show the development of interphrasal procedures such as subject-verb agreement and clitic placement.

We saw earlier that the identification of stages of development is of little value for theory construction unless a principled explanation for them is given. In this respect, Processability Theory makes an important contribution to second language acquisition research. By proposing hierarchical procedures and processing strategies, it explains why learners pass through the stages of development that they do. In addition, it offers researchers a mechanism to form hypotheses about which structures will be acquired at which stage of development. The result is a model that has both explanatory and descriptive adequacy.

There are, however, a number of criticisms associated with the model. First, the model rests on the assumption that learners overcome the processing constraints specific to a particular stage to move onto the next stage. However, no explanation is given of why or how learners overcome the processing constraints (Larsen-Freeman and Long 1991). An additional problem, noted in Ellis (1994), relates to the notion of acquisition. Pienemann and his colleagues define *acquisition* in terms of "first appearance" of a grammatical feature in production. Although this notion has been accepted for some time now in theories that underscore the importance of processing operations, Pienemann fails to provide quantitative and qualitative criteria to be met by the learner's production, in order to ascertain the operation of a predicted processing strategy. Finally, the model says nothing about how learners come to comprehend grammatical structures, nor does it tell how the comprehension and production mechanisms interact (Ellis 1994).

Before leaving this section, it is important to note some points about the role of instruction in the development of learner language under Pienemann's model. Pienemann and his associates have for some time now maintained that whereas some linguistic features can be taught successfully at various points in the learner's development (e.g., vocabulary), others cannot be affected by instruction because they are internally driven—determined by general constraints on how human beings process information and develop increasingly more complex levels of automation in speech production. In the latter case, Pienemann maintains that learners cannot be made to "leapfrog over stages" unless they are developmentally ready to do so, and he proposes to align teaching objectives with stages of acquisition. This proposal, known as the Teachability Hypothesis (Pienemann 1985), finds support in a number of studies. Pienemann (1998), for example, presents evidence that teaching interventions *can* accelerate the rate at which language is learned and can increase the number of structures a learner can produce only if the learner is "ready" to learn. Although this is an attractive proposal from a pedagogical stance, its main difficulty arises with the fact that, as Lightbown (1985) has pointed out, our current knowledge of natural acquisition sequences is still quite limited to make specific recommendations about whether particular forms can be taught and when.

2.2   The Role of Input and Output

Most researchers would not dispute that input—or exposure to the target language systems via oral and written data—is necessary for language acquisition to take place. Krashen (1982) views this as the single most important factor in second language acquisition, in that it answers the critical question of how languages are acquired. More recently, VanPatten (1991, 1996) has proposed a model of second language acquisition, dubbed "Input Processing," (IP) that focuses on the relationship between input and input processing strategies and their impact on the developing knowledge of the second language learner.[7]

2.2.1   Processing Instruction versus Traditional and Meaning-Based Output

The IP model is an account of intake derivation that occurs in working memory during on-line comprehension. It rests on four hypotheses about L2 input processing strategies that underpin the competition existing between attention to form and attention to meaning in a system characterized by learners' limited attentional capacity. These hypotheses are provided in table 8.2 (from Lee and VanPatten 1995).

A fundamental claim made in the model is that because processing is more effortful for early-stage learners, obtaining meaning from the input more efficiently involves processing lexical items and ignoring grammatical items (number markers, verb and noun inflections), particularly when the latter are very low in communicative value (i.e., learners can ignore them and still understand the utterance). Accordingly, in the early stages of language acquisition, learners' processing of grammatically encoded information will be limited unless that information has relatively high communicative value.

In some respects, the Input Processing Model, as currently formulated, is somewhat limited. VanPatten refers to the notion that beginning learners simply ignore inflectional items when these are low in communicative value and pay attention to the roots of content words because they are high in communicative value (see, for example, Lee and VanPatten 1995). What remains unclear is exactly how early-stage learners determine what is high and what is low in communicative value in the target language. In other words, when beginning learners encounter the sentence *Nosotros comemos en la playa* "We eat at the beach," what mechanism does the learner draw on to determine that it is the initial *com-* in *comemos,* as opposed to, say, *come-* or even *comem-,* that carries substantive meaning? Also, VanPatten refers to morphological items as having different levels of meaningfulness and claims that limited attentional capacity drives the learner to ignore less meaningful morphology.

Table 8.2

Hypotheses about L2 Input-Processing Strategies

H1. Learners process input for meaning before they process it for form.

  H1a. Learners process content words in the input before anything else.

  H1b. Learners prefer processing lexical items to grammatical items (e.g., morphology) for semantic information.

  H1c. Learners prefer processing more meaningful morphology before less or non-meaningful morphology.

H2. In order for learners to process form that is not meaningful, they must be able to process informational value or communicative content at no or little cost to attention.

H3. Learners tend to process input strings as agent-action-object or subject-verb-object, assigning agent or subject status to the first noun phrase they encounter.

H4. Learners may process phrases and recurring patterns as whole unanalyzed chunks, especially if phonological properties help to delimit these phrases.

Source: Lee and VanPatten 1995:97.

However, the model does not account for how learners determine different degrees of morphological meaningfulness or how the processing mechanism determines what to ignore. If the meaning conveyed in the grammatical form is also encoded lexically, the form is said to be low in communicative value. No account is given, though, of how the processing mechanism identifies this information, which is crucial to later processing of the linguistic input in accordance with the limited resources the processor has available.

VanPatten's Input Processing Model and the principles contained therein have motivated a particular type of focus on form instruction called Processing Instruction. Central to his instructional model is the idea that the key to restructuring the learner's interlanguage system lies in focusing learner attention on structural aspects of the input data, as they become intake. VanPatten maintains that this is not possible with traditional approaches to instruction, which are typically characterized by the presentation of grammatical information plus some form of output practice. Rather than manipulating the learner's output to affect change in the developing system, VanPatten suggests that instruction ought to focus on altering how learners process the input.

Processing Instruction receives support from a number of empirical studies that have found a learning advantage when instruction is aimed at affecting how learners perceive and process input rather than when it is focused on having learners practice the language via output (see, for example, Van Patten and Cadierno 1993; Cadierno 1995; Cheng 1995, 2002; VanPatten 1996, 2000, 2002a). In a recent study, Farley (2001) investigated the relative effects of input-based Processing Instruction versus meaning-based output instruction by looking at the acquisition of the Spanish subjunctive of doubt. The twenty-nine participants in this study were assigned to either a processing-instruction or meaning-based output instruction treatment. Processing Instruction consisted of activities structured in a deliberate attempt to force learners to attend to the targeted forms for meaning. Meaning-based output instruction consisted of meaning-based output activities similar to those found in traditional approaches to grammar instruction, with the difference that they were not mechanical in nature. Scores on sentence-level tasks involving the interpretation and production of the Spanish subjunctive of doubt revealed that both types of instructions brought about improved performance on the assessment tasks; however, the performance of the meaning-based output group declined over time on the interpretation task, while the Processing Instruction group showed no such decline. Farley interprets this finding as evidence for the superiority of Processing Instruction over other types of instruction. The pedagogical implications of VanPatten's Input Processing Model, however, have been challenged in a number of studies.[8]

2.2.2   Attention to Form versus Attention to Meaning

The development of an input-based acquisition model of the type described coupled with the claim that language acquisition takes place when learners engage in meaningful conversational interactions (Long 1983; Hatch 1992; Pica, Young, and Doughty 1987) raises the question of whether learners can focus on form while attending to the propositional meaning of an utterance. Whereas some researchers have maintained that acquisition is a subconscious process, resulting from sufficient exposure to meaningful and comprehensible input in the target language (see, for example, Krashen 1982), others take the position that formal features of language must be consciously registered by the learner for successful acquisition to occur. Schmidt (1990, 1994), for example, has argued that adult second language requires attention to form in the input. Schmidt does not discard the possibility of incidental or subconscious learning but states that this is possible only when task demands focus the learner's attention on the relevant features of the input (Schmidt 1988).[9] DeKeyser, agreeing with a weaker version of this *focus on form* position, notes that "some kind of focus on form is useful to some extent, for some students, at some point in the learning process" (1998:42).

Given that focus on form requires conscious processing and that conscious processing is in turn effortful, if learners are asked to attend to form while also processing the input for meaning, a negative effect should surface in the comprehension process. To explore this hypothesis, VanPatten (1990) asked Spanish language learners (N = 202) to listen to one of four paragraphs and to perform one of four tasks: Listen to a passage for content only; listen to the passage for content while at the same time noting all instances of the word *inflación*; listen to the passage for content and to note all instances of the definite article *la*; listen to the passage for content and simultaneously noting the verb morpheme *–n*. Comprehension of the passage was assessed by asking the participants to recall the passage in English. It was predicted that if a disruption in attention to content, caused by attention to form, affected comprehension, participants would produce less complete recall protocols, as measured by the raw number of idea units produced. Overall, the results revealed that there was no significant drop in recall scores when participants were asked to listen for content and note a lexical item simultaneously. However, subjects' recall scores decreased significantly when they listened for content while simultaneously noting a grammatical morpheme, indicating that they had difficulty attending to form that did not contribute substantially to the meaning of the input.

Although interesting, the findings could have resulted not from a legitimate difficulty associated with the simultaneous attention to content and form, but from the saliency, or lack thereof, inherent in the different linguistic items that the subjects were asked to attend to. That is, subjects may have experienced a drop in recall scores when listening for content and noting a grammatical morpheme, not because they experienced trouble attending to form per se, but simply because the grammatical morphemes that they were asked to tally were less salient—were significantly shorter, lacked stress, and the like— than the lexical items. Also, detection of the content word may have been facilitated by the fact that the word that the participants were asked to listen for (*inflación*) is an English cognate. In order to argue for a genuine "competition" between meaning and form, the materials need to be closely controlled, so that the sole difference is the aspect being investigated.

An additional limitation deals with the instrument used for data collection. Although the study makes a number of assertions about what second language learners do during real time language processing, the instrument used for data collection is an off-line task. To overcome this limitation, it is necessary to use data collection instruments that have been documented to tap more directly into online language processing. For example, eye tracking would be a more suitable candidate, as much has been written about eye-movement records as well as how eye-movement data can inform research on attention and language processing.

2.2.3   Recasts in L2 Acquisition

The debate on focus on form versus focus on meaning raises the question of whether there is linguistic input that can be utilized in language acquisition, which draws learners' attention to particular forms while at the same time avoids the interruption of the flow of communication (i.e., keeps focus on meaning). One obvious candidate is the use of recasts, defined as the reformulation of a learner's ungrammatical utterance while maintaining a focus on meaning (for a complete review of the role of recasts in language acquisition, see Nicholas, Lightbown, and Spada, 2001).

Ortega and Long (1997) compared the effects of positive evidence (models) and implicit negative evidence (recasts) on the learning of two structures by thirty L2 Spanish speakers. The structures under investigation involved Spanish object topicalization (label used by authors) (*La guitarra la tiene Pepe*/The guitar, Pepe has it) and Spanish adverb placement (*Elena toma a veces café*/Elena drinks sometime coffee). The treatment (models and recasts) and the structures (object topicalization and adverb placement) were crossed and counterbalanced across four groups, so that each group was exposed to both treatment types as well as to both structures. In the recast condition, participants were given the names of six items and a set of six pictures of people. The task was to hear the name of an object, to assign it to one of the six people, and to inform a partner about who had received the object. In the modeling condition, participants heard sentences containing information about who was assigned to each object, and to repeat the information aloud so that a partner could match the objects with the correct people. Comparisons between scores in a pretest and a posttest, each containing a grammaticality judgment task and a picture-description oral production task, revealed that models and recasts had no learning effect on object topicalization, but that recasts produced a greater effect on the learning of adverb-placement in Spanish than did models. These results provide partial support for the claim that adult second language learners are able to learn from implicit negative feedback. Some caution needs to be taken when interpreting these findings, given that, as the authors rightly point out, the posttest was administered shortly after the treatment session. Therefore, it is not possible to assess the long-term effect of recasts on learning. In addition, it is not clear that the modeling treatment actually engaged learners in the processing of the structures they were producing. That is, it is conceivable that the learners were repeating the structures without paying attention to form or meaning. In this respect, it is possible that the recast condition and the model condition were not truly comparable.

In a recent empirical study, Leeman (2003) examined the role of recasts, negative evidence, and enhanced saliency in the development of the Spanish noun-adjective agreement system. The treatment was provided by the researcher to each of the participants in a one-time experimental sitting, while the two worked together to complete an object placement task and a catalogue shopping task. During the first part of each task, the learner was required to provide directions to the researcher, while the researcher provided the learner with feedback that varied according to the treatment group in which the learner belonged (i.e., recast group, negative evidence group, and enhanced salience group). Examples of each feedback type are provided below:

Recast

NNS: *En la mesa hay una taza rojo.
"On the table there is a red [incorrect gender ending] cup."

R: Um hmm, una taza roja. ¿Qué más?
"Uh, huh, a red cup [correct gender ending]. What else?"

Negative Evidence

NNS: *En la mesa hay una taza rojo.
"On the table there is a red [incorrect gender ending] cup."

R: Um hmm, pero tú dijiste una taza rojo. ¿Qué más?
"Uh, huh. But you said a red [incorrect gender ending] cup. What else?"

Enhanced Saliency and Control Group

NNS: *En la mesa hay una taza rojo.
"On the table there is a red [incorrect gender ending] cup."
R: Um hmm, ¿Qué más?
"Uh huh. What else?"

In the second part of the treatment task, learners were asked to respond based on the researcher's directions. This exposed all learners to positive evidence as well, but for the enhanced group stress and intonation were used to enhance the salience of the target form (e.g., *La manzana roja está en la mesa* "the RED [correct gender ending emphasized] apple is on the table"). All other groups received unenhanced input. Gains on the development of the Spanish noun-adjective agreement system were assessed via a comparison between pretest scores and two posttest scores—an immediate posttest and a one-week delayed posttest. The findings revealed that negative evidence alone had little or no effect on the development of agreement abilities in L2 Spanish learners, and that recasts and enhanced saliency produced significant gains, when compared to a control group. However, in the delayed posttest, only the enhanced saliency group significantly outperformed the control group on gender agreement scores.

The results of this study make an important contribution with respect to the types of linguistic feedback that best draw learner's attention to particular forms in the input, and at the same time suggests directions for further research. It is important to find out, for example, whether learners actually view statements such as *Tú dijiste X* ("You said X") as a type of negative evidence that informs about the acceptability of an utterance, or whether they simply view it a restatement of what the interlocutor said. In this same vein, the length of the treatment may have been insufficient for negative evidence to influence language development. The fact that the delayed posttest occurred only a week after treatment also needs to be further modified to include longer lapses of time, given that as it stands, the beneficial outcome of enhanced saliency over the other types of feedback can only be framed in the context of largely short-term gains. Finally, given the emerging interest in the role of enhancement in second language acquisition, the exact role that saliency played in the recast treatment group in this study needs to be carefully examined.

2.3 Summary of Findings on Cognitive Issues Discussed

In section 2 we have briefly reviewed cognitive models of language development whose tenets have been tested using Spanish second language acquisition data. Some models, originally proposed to account for L1 acquisition, have subsequently been used in SLA research—as is the case with Andersen's Operating Principles. Others, such as Pienemann's Processability Theory, have developed from work undertaken in SLA research. We saw that some theories generate precise hypotheses that can be systematically tested, whereas others offer researchers a more general picture of how second language acquisition occurs. In part because the study of second language acquisition is a recent field of inquiry, it is not yet possible to construct a comprehensive cognitive theory of SLA. The theories examined above vary greatly not only in scope but also in the type of data for which they try to account. Current work aims at evaluating these different theories by testing the hypotheses that they advance. This type of work eventually leads to the collapse of some cognitive models and the revision of others.

To varying degrees, the theories presented above seek to explain the extent to which individual learners conform to target-language forms (i.e., ultimate level of proficiency that learners reach). For example, Pienemann's model places second language learners in a continuum that reflects the learners' orientation toward the learning task. At one end, learners have a segregative attitude toward target language speakers and the target culture. At the other, learners have an integrative orientation, which arises when the learner desires to assimilate into the L2 culture or when the learner has an instrumental need to learn the L2. Where learners place on this continuum constrains learning outcomes.

In the next section, we will examine the Competition Model of sentence parsing and an intriguing proposal, put forth by Fernández (1995, 1999), to account for ultimate attainment in L2 learning. Fernández takes the position that language learning is driven by an innate mechanism (i.e., Universal Grammar) that is dedicated to language and operates independently of more general cognitive processes. Fernández proposes that incomplete second language attainment may come about when learners use L1 parsing strategies that are not optimal to develop the underlying grammar of the target language. She reasons that if parsing strategies are inadequate to process incoming language in the L2, learners may be missing input that is crucial to building the linguistic system in the second language. To explore this proposal, it is first necessary to understand exactly how second language learners parse input in their L2. We now turn to a discussion of the Competition Model of sentence parsing by second language learners, as this topic unveils yet another dimension of cognition and second language acquisition.

3.0   Sentence Parsing by Spanish-English Speakers

3.1   The Competition Model

Much of the initial work on sentence processing in Spanish-English speakers is grounded in the Competition Model[10] (Bates and MacWhinney 1982, 1987). The model is primarily concerned with grammatical performance (as opposed to competence) and aims at explaining how speakers determine relationships among elements in a sentence. To capture particular relationships between surface forms and associated functions, which are crucially characterized as one-to-many mappings, (e.g., the function of "agent of an action" can be signaled through different form devices such as word order, case, and agreement), the notion of cue is brought into play. Sentence processing is seen as a competition among various cues, each contributing to a different resolution in sentence interpretation.

Within this framework, languages vary as a function of the presence or absence of the relative strengths of form-function mappings and of specific form types (e.g., rich agreement, overt case assignment). For example, Spanish and English are languages in which the canonical word order is assumed to be subject-verb-object (SVO). Presumably, because word order in English is rigidly of the form SVO, native speakers of English rely primarily on word order to encode the meaning of "agency" in sentences with canonical word order. In English, then, word order is said to be high in cue validity, since it is a reliable cue to sentence meaning. In noncanonical word orders, English speakers are said to display a reliable tendency to choose the second noun in a sentence as the agent, resulting in a marked bias for OSV and VOS interpretations. Spanish, on the other hand, allows for wider word-order permutations than English. Given this, word order in Spanish is said to be low in cue validity; speakers have to rely on other sources of information such as morphological agreement—the strongest cue—and on semantics—the second most influential cue in Spanish—for adequately determining, say, the subject noun phrase in a sentence. In cases where different sources of information come into conflict, the Competition Model predicts that Spanish speakers will rely primarily on morphological cues at the expense of word order information, whereas English speakers are expected to behave in the opposite fashion.

With this background, we now turn to issues of second language processing from the perspective of the Competition Model. Because processing strategies differ for monolingual English and Spanish speakers, researchers of this persuasion ask how Spanish-English bilinguals perform syntactic processing in each of their languages. As Hernández, Bates, and Ávila (1994) have indicated, there are four possible patterns of behavior that one can logically expect to observe from these speakers when processing language in the monolingual mode. The first one, *differentiation,* is used to describe cases where speakers adopt separate strategies for processing each language, corresponding to the strategies used by monolingual speakers of those languages. *Forward transfer* refers to the use of first language (L1) strategies in processing the second language (L2), and is likely to be evidenced in speakers who are more dominant in their first language than in their second language. The term *backward transfer* denotes cases in which speakers use L2 strategies to process the L1. Finally, *amalgamation* describes situations in which speakers apply to both languages a set of strategies derived from the two languages.

In a study of sentence interpretation strategies, Hernández, Bates, and Ávila (1994) investigated the real-time costs of sentence interpretation in Spanish-English early bilinguals using a reaction-time measure. The study aimed at investigating the saliency of syntactic, semantic and morphological cues on the processing strategies used by early Spanish-English bilinguals (i.e., speakers who reported speaking their second language by age eleven). The participants (N = 100) read sentences on a computer screen, similar to "The pencil is eating the donkey," and were asked to choose which of the two nouns carried out the action of the sentence by pressing a button corresponding to the side of the screen on which the picture of a noun had previously appeared.

Analysis of the *choice data* and the *reaction time data* revealed that, overall, English monolinguals relied on word-order cues to assign the role of agent—followed by agreement and animacy. Spanish monolinguals, on the other hand, used agreement—followed by animacy and word order. For bilinguals tested in English and Spanish, however, agreement was by far the strongest cue to subjecthood in both languages, followed by word order and animacy. For the bilingual participants, this pattern of preference reflects a combined effect of Spanish and English monolingual processing strategies, with Spanish providing stronger cues than English. In general, the results in Hernández, Bates, and Ávila (1994) suggest that Spanish/English bilinguals fall "in between" the monolinguals of both languages, apparently having developed a compromised or amalgamated set of strategies for processing Spanish and English (see also Wulfeck et al. 1986 for similar results).

Why bilinguals use the same strategies for processing two different linguistic systems is a matter of speculation at this point. We know that, based on numerous social and linguistic factors, the bilingual moves along a continuum of language activation that ranges from a monolingual language mode, where the bilingual deactivates one language, although never totally, to a bilingual language mode, where both languages are activated, although perhaps to differing degrees (Grosjean 2001). It may be possible, then, that the managing of two linguistic systems becomes too costly for the language processing mechanism of these bilinguals and that the bilingual processor seeks ways of optimizing the resources it has available. One feasible way of doing this is by partially merging or amalgamating the processing strategies of the two languages. This *processing trade-off,* although not ideal as a solution from a monolingual perspective, may be the most beneficial in terms of cost-effectiveness from a bilingual perspective (Hernández, Bates, and Ávila 1994).

Clearly, the processing trade-off hypothesis needs further testing. This is particularly so given that the findings reported in Hernández, Bates, and Ávila (1994) could reflect some type of postsyntactic processing of sentences. As stated earlier, in order to study the processes involved during sentence interpretation more directly, Hernández, Bates, and Ávila used a reaction-time measure. However, the time measurement reflected the collective time it took subjects to read a sentence, to make a decision regarding the agent of the sentence and to press a button indicating the decision. Because subjects were not given a time constraint to complete the task, it is possible that they may have made an initial decision regarding the agent role in a sentence but reversed it before pressing the button. Hence, the results could still very well reflect off-line decisions.

To access the workings of the sentence processor properly, it is crucial to tap the processing of sentence structure as it unfolds. What is needed, then, is the use of speedier tasks or more precise or sophisticated measures of online sentence processing that would permit us to investigate more accurately the effects of cue validity and cue conflict on sentence interpretation. We also need to investigate other aspects of sentence processing where the two languages under investigation have been shown to differ in some other respects. If indeed amalgamation is a strategy that the bilingual processor uses to reduce the costs associated with managing two linguistic systems, it should apply also when memory and time constraints require the processor to quickly structure material to preserve it in a limited-capacity memory. Below, we turn to a discussion of sentence processing as it occurs under these constraints, by looking at the strategies that Spanish-English second language learners employ when processing structures that are temporarily ambiguous. As will be shown, amalgamation is a strategy that extends beyond sentence interpretation, into the domain of syntactic analysis or parsing.

3.2 Processing Temporarily Ambiguous Sentence

The first study to investigate explicitly the processing strategies used by Spanish-English learners during the parsing of modifiers (i.e., sentence with the structure NP1-of-NP2-RC) is Fernández (1995) (see also Fernández 1998, 1999, 2000). The study is concerned with the fundamental question of explaining why adult learners seem to be only partially successful at acquiring a second language. Fernández suggests that incomplete second language attainment may come about when learners use L1 parsing strategies that are not optimal to develop the underlying grammar of the target language.

In order to test this proposal, Fernández (1995) examined the responses to ambiguous English sentences by monolingual English speakers, early Spanish-English bilinguals (i.e., native Spanish speakers who had learned English before age ten), and late Spanish-English bilinguals (i.e., native Spanish speakers who had learned English after the age of ten). A questionnaire was used to present subjects (total N = 45) with sentences such as this, where the prepositional phrase in the complex NP was an argument of the first noun[11]:

Roxanne read the review of the play that was written by Dianne's friend.

In sentences of this type, the ambiguity arises because the relative clause ("that was written") can be attached high to "the review" (early closure) or attach low to "the play" (late closure). The sentences in the questionnaire were immediately followed by a question ("What was written by Diane's friend?") that was designed to probe the subject's preferred attachment, and by two possible answers ("the play" and "the review"). Subjects were asked to circle the phrase best suited to answer the question. Fernández (1995, 1999) found that the strongest preference for low attachment was displayed by the English monolinguals (for similar results in English monolingual speakers see Cuetos and Mitchell 1988; Mitchell and Cuetos 1991; Mitchell and Brysbaert 1998), followed by the early bilingual group and then by the late bilingual group. Fernández also reported that language proficiency seemed to be the best predictor of attachment preferences. That is, subjects who rated their Spanish proficiency higher than their English proficiency favored high attachment. Subjects who rated English as their dominant language tended to show a preference for low attachment. Somewhat unexpected was the correlation obtained for subjects who rated both languages equally high (approximately half of the early bilinguals). Seemingly, some preferred high attachment and others preferred low attachment.

On the basis of the findings obtained for the late bilingual group, Fernández (1999) suggested that L2 processing strategies might be hard to learn after puberty. This in turn may be one of the reasons leading to the irregular or incomplete attainment of a second language by adult learners. Fernández reasoned that adult learners might transfer some of their L1 processing strategies when processing L2 input. In cases where the L1 strategies may not be suitable for assigning the appropriate structure to the L2 input, learners may end up with an incomplete (or erroneous) representation of the L2 grammar. Moving briefly to the patterns of behavior that one can expect to observe from second language learners when processing language in the monolingual mode, the data from the late bilinguals suggest that these learners have used their L1 parsing routines when processing L2 input, showing evidence of forward transfer (Fernández 1995, 1999).

Because Fernández (1995, 1999) did not test learners in their two languages, it was not possible to determine whether they would use the same strategies when reading Spanish as they did for English, or whether they would employ a different set of strategies. In order to answer this question, Dussias (1998) investigated the attachment preferences by late Spanish and English learners reading English and Spanish sentences with the structure NP1-of-NP2-RC. Subjects (N = 32) were presented with two questionnaires, one in Spanish and one in English, containing sentences similar to the ones used in Fernández (1995). Each sentence was followed by a question and two possible answers, and subjects were asked to circle either one of two responses as the correct answer for the question.

The results for the English monolinguals showed a clear preference for low attachment, complying with late closure. This group was found not to differ significantly from the late learners, indicating that these participants too had a general preference for low attachment. Results for the Spanish questionnaire showed that, as expected, the Spanish monolinguals gave answers indicating that they had attached the relative clause to the higher noun considerably more times than to the lower noun. However, most of the late Spanish and English learners preferred, once again, low attachment over high attachment.

Because the questionnaire data could not guarantee that the choices readers make represent actual "first pass" commitments, Dussias (1998) conducted an additional experiment to test the learners' attachment preferences online while reading Spanish sentences. Data were collected using a self-paced reading task. The materials were designed so that some experimental sentences would have a plausible meaning only if readers attached the relative clause low into the structure (e.g., *El perro mordió al cuñado de la maestra que vivió en Chile con su esposo* "The dog bit the brother-in-law of the teacher [fem.] who lived in Chile with her husband") and others would be plausible only if they chose high attachment (e.g., *El perro mordió a la cuñada del maestro que vivió en Chile con su esposo* "The dog bit the sister-in-law of the teacher [masc.] who lived in Chile with her husband").

The results for the control group (i.e., Spanish monolinguals) showed the conventional bias for high attachment (for similar results with Spanish monolingual speakers, see also Cuetos and Mitchell 1988; Carreiras and Clifton 1999). Interestingly, for the late learners of English whose first language was Spanish, the sentences favoring high attachment took significantly longer to read than the one favoring low attachment. This result replicated the questionnaire findings reported above and suggested that, contrary to what would ordinarily be expected, these learners had a genuine preference for low attachment when reading in Spanish, their native language. Results for the late learners of Spanish whose native language was English indicated a trend toward favoring low attachment; however, this preference was not statistically significant.

Taken together, the findings reported in Dussias (1998) support the hypothesis that the cognitive demands placed on the language processor may be responsible for the low attachment preference reported earlier for the late learners, while reading stimuli in Spanish and English. That is, because (1) managing two linguistic systems produces costs for the language system in the form of delays in processing time (for supporting evidence, see, e.g., Grosjean 1985, 1994, 1997; Obler and Albert 1978; Soares and Grosjean 1984; Mägiste 1979), and (2) the parser's tendency is always to adopt the *least-effortful* option (see Fodor 1998), the bilingual parser will naturally choose operations such as *late closure* (i.e., low attachment) that give rise to the most simple and most quickly derived analysis, thereby minimizing processing load. This would explain why a majority of speakers in Dussias (1998) applied late closure when reading English and Spanish.

Put together, the results reported in this section suggest that some second language speakers show evidence of amalgamation and forward transfer during sentence processing, whereas other learners prefer to use only one type of strategy (i.e., late closure) to parse in their two languages. This may indicate that in addition to amalgamation, the use of a single parsing strategy to process two languages is another resource that the bilingual processor uses to decrease the costs associated with managing two linguistic systems. The findings also offer some preliminary support to the proposal that second language learners do not always process target structures using the same strategies that monolingual speakers do.

4.0 Conclusion

In this chapter I have reviewed current cognitive models of second language acquisition, and in doing so I have presented some of the issues being dealt with by proponents of these models. Constructs such as language transfer, which were characteristics of early interlanguage studies, although redefined over the years, continue to find support in recent research studies. Similarly, cognitive distinctions, such as Krashen's explicit and implicit knowledge, find some legitimacy in Spanish second language acquisition data. The study of these constructs, however, has taken a step back by the interest sparked in recent years in the study of other variables that affect second language acquisition. We saw, for example, that one aspect of second language acquisition currently under intense dispute is the role of output in the acquisition process. Whereas some researchers maintain that production will aid acquisition only when the learner is pushed (Swain 1985, 1993, 1995), VanPatten and his colleagues maintain that production practice may either aid in the development of fluency and accuracy or may act as a focusing device that draws learners' attention to the input as mismatches are observed (VanPatten and Cadierno 1993; VanPatten 2002a). This debate currently occupies a focal position in second language acquisition circles partly because of the implications it carries for classroom instruction. Input-oriented theories advocate an emphasis on classroom activities that first attempt to impact the learner's interlanguage system via a focus on input, and only later give the learner the opportunities to develop productive abilities. Output-oriented models, on the other hand, encourage instruction where the teacher takes a more active role in pushing students from the beginning to produce more extensive and more accurate language samples.

This chapter has also reviewed research studies that address sentence processing by Spanish and English second language learners. This research, which finds its origins in the Competition Model, was primarily concerned with investigating whether second language speakers used the same syntactic and semantic cues as monolingual speakers did during sentence processing. Currently, much of the impetus is being directed at the study of parsing strategies by second language learners, with the goal of explaining (1) whether incomplete second language attainment may come about when learners use L1 parsing strategies that are not suitable for the development of the underlying grammar of the target language, and (2) the effects of second language learning on sentence parsing.

Clearly, there is much ground to be covered yet. We are only at the beginning stages of understanding, for example, the impact that text enhancement has on learners' development of grammatical and lexical knowledge, and its implications for a theory of attention allocation and noticing. Similarly, given that recall tasks are often used in second language research studies to assess the effects of different types of classroom language instructional approaches on acquisition, further research is needed in which modality (e.g., written versus aural) is treated as a variable that might be responsible for the conflicting results reported in the literature on Spanish SLA (the pioneering work of Leow 1995 and Mecartty 2001 are two cases in point). Finally, few studies have dealt with topics addressing other areas of Spanish second language-related cognitive behavior such as speech perception, lexical access in word recognition, relations between phonological and orthographic/visual representations, sentence processing, discourse comprehension, language production, attention, and capacity theory. The relative lack of research in these directions may owe in part to the fact that the psycholinguistic study of Spanish in native speakers is itself relatively new; only recently have scholars begun to look at contrasting properties of Spanish to help test the generality of the language processing mechanisms that have been proposed and to refine their descriptions. However, as our understanding of Spanish native language processing becomes clearer, so should our future endeavors into the investigation of these aspects of language processing in Spanish-English second language speakers. This new direction of research will contribute not only by deepening our understanding of the processes that govern language processing in speakers of two languages, but it also will allow us to examine under different perspectives and using different sets of data, the validity and generality of current monolingual language processing theories, with the purpose of formulating models capable of accounting for monolingual as well as bilingual behavior.

NOTES

I am indebted to Jacqueline Toribio for invaluable comments during the preparation of this document.

1. It is important to note that although Cognitive Theory views interaction as playing a role in SLA, given that this topic is covered in chapters 6, 9, and 10 of this volume, our focus here will be primarily the structuring of the individual's cognitive system.

2. See chapter 5 of this volume for further discussion of the acquisition of the Spanish copulas *ser* and *estar*.

3. See also Larsen-Freeman (1975) and LoCoco (1976) for additional discussions on the effect of task on learner language.

4. See DeKeyser (1995) for additional discussion.

5. See chapter 5 of this volume for further discussion of the acquisition of the Spanish prepositions *por* and *para*.

6. One such theory is Myers-Scotton's Matrix Language Model (1993), and, more recently, Myers-Scotton and Jake's 4-M Model (Myers-Scotton and Jake 2000, 2001).

7. See chapter 10 of this volume for further discussion of the impact of various instructional approaches on the acquisition of Spanish as a second language.

8. For additional discussion see Salaberry (1997); Collentine (1998, 2002); Farley (2002); and chapter 3 of this volume; Grove (1999) and chapter 10 of this volume; DeKeyser et al. (2002); see VanPatten (2002b), for a response to DeKeyser et al. (2002).

9. In light of Schmidt's Noticing Hypothesis, Leow (2001) found no significant benefit of written input enhancement over unenhanced input. Overstreet (2002), on the other hand, found

that textual enhancement *and* communicative value of the target item affect comprehension as measured by a free recall task and a form recognition task. For additional discussion on the role of awareness and attention in SLA, see Leow (1997, 1999a, 1999b, 1998, 2000,) and chapter 10 of this volume.

10. See chapter 3 of this volume for further discussion of the Competition Model.

11. Fernández (1995, 1999) also tested sentences where the prepositional phrase (PP) in the complex NP was an adjunct to the first noun (e.g., "The crowd cheered for the singer with the guitarist that was awarded a medal"). However, given that the results for these types of sentences were generally similar to those for sentences where the PP was an argument of the first noun, they will not be discussed here.

WORKS CITED

Andersen, R. W. 1979. Expanding Schumann's pidginization hypothesis. *Language Learning* 29:105–19.

———. 1983. *Pidginization and creolization as language acquisition.* Rowley, MA: Newbury House.

———. 1984. The one-to-one principle of interlanguage construction. *Language Learning* 34:77–95.

———. 1986. El desarrollo de la morfología verbal en el español como segundo idioma. In *Adquisición de lenguaje/Aquisição da linguagem,* ed. J. Meisel, 115–38. Frankfurt: Vervuert.

———. 1989. The theoretical status of variation on interlanguage development. In *Variation in second language acquisition,* vol. 2, *Psycholinguistic issues,* eds. S. Gass, C. Madden, D. Preston, and L. Selinker, 46–64. Philadelphia: Multilingual Matters.

———. 1990. Models, processes, principles and strategies: Second language acquisition inside and outside the classroom. In *Second language acquisition—Foreign language learning,* eds. B. VanPatten and J. F. Lee, 45–68. Clevedon: Multilingual Matters.

Bates, W., and B. MacWhinney. 1982. Functionalist approaches to grammar. In *Language acquisition: The state of the art,* eds. E. Wanner and L. R. Gleitman, 173–218. New York: Cambridge University Press.

———. 1987. Competition, variation and language learning. In *Mechanisms of language acquisition,* ed. B. MacWhinney, 157–93. Hillsdale, NJ: Lawrence Erlbaum.

Cadierno, T. 1995. Formal instruction from a processing perspective: An investigation into the Spanish past tense. *Modern Language Journal* 79:179–93.

Carreiras, M., and C. Clifton. 1999. Another word on parsing relative clauses: Eyetracking evidence from Spanish and English. *Memory and Cognition* 27.5:826–33.

Cheng, A. C. 1995. Grammar instruction and input processing: The acquisition of *ser* and *estar.* Ph.D. diss., University of Illinois, Urbana-Champaign.

———. 2002. The effects of processing instruction on the acquisition of *ser* and *estar. Hispania* 85.2:308–23.

Collentine, J. 1998. Processing instruction and the subjunctive. *Hispania* 81:576–87.

———. 2002. On the acquisition of the subjunctive and authentic processing instruction: A response to Farley. *Hispania* 85.4:879–88.

Cuetos, F., and D. C. Mitchell. 1988. Cross-linguistic differences in parsing: Restrictions on the use of the late closure strategy in Spanish. *Cognition* 30:73–105.

DeKeyser, R. M. 1991. Foreign language development during a semester abroad. In *Foreign language acquisition research and the classroom,* ed. B. L. Freed, 104–19. Lexington MA: D. C. Heath.

———. 1995. Learning second language grammar rules: An experiment with a miniature linguistic system. *Studies in Second Language Acquisition* 17:379–410.

———. 1998. Beyond focus on form: Cognitive perspectives on learning and practicing second language acquisition. In *Focus on form in classroom second language acquisition,* eds. C. Doughty and J. Williams, 42–63. Cambridge: Cambridge University Press.

DeKeyser, R. M., M. R. Salaberry, P. Robinson, and M. Harrington. 2002. What gets processed in processing instruction? A commentary on Bill VanPatten's "Processing instruction: An update." *Language Learning* 52.4.

Dulay, H., and M. Burt. 1974. A new perspective on the creative construction processes in child second language acquisition. *Language Learning* 24:253–78.

Dussias, P. E. 1998. The use of the late closure strategy in fluent Spanish-English bilinguals. Paper presented at Linguistic Colloquium on Bilingualism, University of Arizona, Tucson.

Ellis, R. 1994. *The study of second language acquisition.* Oxford: Oxford University Press.

Farley, A. 2001. Authentic processing instruction and the Spanish subjunctive. *Hispania* 84:289–99.

———. 2002. Processing instruction, communication value, and ecological validity: A response to Collentine's defense. *Hispania.* 85.4:889–95.

Fernández, E. M. 1995. Processing strategies in second language acquisition: Some preliminary results. Paper presented at 3d Generative Approaches to Second Language Acquisition Conference, City University of New York.

———. 1998. Language dependency in parsing: Evidence from monolingual and bilingual processing. *Psychologica Belgicae* 38:197–230.

———. 1999. Processing strategies in second language acquisition: Some preliminary results. In *The development of second language grammars: A generative approach,* eds. E. C. Klein and G. Martohardjono, 217–39. Amsterdam: John Benjamins.

———. 2002. Bilingual sentence processing: Relative clause attachment in English and Spanish. Ph.D. diss., CUNY Graduate Center.

Fodor, J. D. 1998. Learning to parse? *Journal of Psycholinguistic Research* 27:285–319.

Frantzen, D. 1991. The emergence of subjunctive/indicative accuracy in written Spanish. Paper presented at the Central States Conference, Indianapolis.

Grosjean, F. 1985. The bilingual as a competent but specific speaker-hearer. *Journal of Multilingual and Multicultural Development* 6:299–310.

———. 1994. Individual bilingualism. *Encyclopedia of language and linguistics,* 1656–60. Oxford: Pergamon.

———. 1997. Processing mixed languages: Issues, findings, and models. In *Tutorials in bilingualism,* eds. A. M. B. de Groot and J. F. Kroll, 225–54. Mahwah, NJ: Lawrence Erlbaum.

———. 2001. The bilingual's language modes. In *One mind, two languages: Bilingual language processing,* ed. J. Nicol, 1–22. Oxford: Blackwell.

Grove, C. 1999. Focusing on form in the communicative classroom: An output-centered model of instruction for oral skills development. *Hispania* 82:817–29.

Guntermann, G. 1992. An analysis of interlanguage development over time: Part II, *ser* and *estar. Hispania* 75:1294–303.

Hatch, E. 1992. *Discourse and language education.* Cambridge: Cambridge University Press.

Hernández, A. E., E. A. Bates, and L. X. Ávila. 1994. On-line sentence interpretation in Spanish-English bilinguals: What does it mean to be "in between"? *Applied Psycholinguistics* 15:417–46.

Johnston, M. 1995. Stages of the acquisition of Spanish as a second language. *Australian Studies in Language Acquisition* 4:2–28.

Krashen, S. 1981. *Second language acquisition and second language learning.* Oxford: Pergamon.

————. 1982. *Principles and practices in second language acquisition.* Oxford: Pergamon.

Lafford, B. 2000. Spanish applied linguistics in the twentieth century: A retrospective and bibliography (1900–99). *Hispania* 83:711–32.

Lafford, B., and J. Collentine. 1989. An analysis of access errors in the speech of intermediate students of Spanish. *Lenguas Modernas* 16:143–62.

Lafford, B., and J. M. Ryan. 1995. The acquisition of lexical meaning in a study abroad context: The Spanish prepositions *por* and *para. Hispania* 78:522–47.

Lantolf, J. P. 1988. The syntactic complexity of written texts in Spanish as foreign language: A markedness perspective. *Hispania* 71:933–40.

Larsen-Freeman, D. 1975. The acquisition of grammatical morphemes by adult ESL students. *TESOL Quarterly* 9:409–30.

Larsen-Freeman, D., and M. Long. 1991. *An introduction to second language acquisition research.* London: Longman.

Lee, J. F., and B. VanPatten. 1995. *Making communicative language teaching happen.* New York: McGraw-Hill.

Leeman, J. 2003. Recasts and second language development: Beyond negative evidence. *Studies in Second Language Acquisition* 25.1.

Leow, R. P. 1995. Modality and intake in second language acquisition. *Studies in Second Language Acquisition.* 17:79–90.

————. 1997. Attention, awareness, and foreign language behavior. *Language Learning* 47:467–506.

————. 1998. Toward operationalizing the process of attention in second language acquisition: Evidence for Tomlin and Villa's (1994) fine-grained analysis of attention. *Applied Psycholinguistics* 19:133–59.

————. 1999a. Attention, awareness, and focus on form research: A critical overview. In *Meaning and form: Multiple perspectives,* eds. J. F. Lee and A. Valdman, 69–98. Boston: Heinle and Heinle.

————. 1999b. The role of attention in second/foreign language classroom research: Methodological issues. *Advances in Hispanic Linguistics: Papers from the 2nd Hispanic Linguistics Symposium,* eds. F. Martínez-Gil and J. Gutiérrez-Rexach, 60–71. Somerville, MA: Cascadilla Press.

————. 2000. A study of the role of awareness in foreign language behavior: Aware vs. unaware learners. *Studies in Second Language Acquisition* 22:557–84.

————. 2001. Do learners notice enhanced forms while interacting with the L2? An online and offline study of the role of written input enhancement in L2 reading. *Hispania* 84:496–509.

Lightbown, P. 1985. Can language acquisition be altered by instruction? In *Modeling and assessing second language acquisition,* eds. K. Hyltenstam and M. Pienemann, 101–12. Clevedon: Multilingual Matters.

LoCoco, V. 1976. A comparison of three methods for the collection of L2 data: Free composition, translation and picture description. *Working Papers on Bilingualism* 8:59–86.

Long, M. 1983. Native speaker/non-native speaker conversation and the negotiation of comprehensible input. *Applied Linguistics* 4:126–41.

McLaughlin, B. 1987. *Theories of second-language learning.* London: Edward Arnold.

Mägiste, E. 1979. The competing language systems of the multilingual: A developmental study of decoding and encoding processes. *Journal of Verbal Learning and Verbal Behavior* 18:79–89. New York: Newbury House.

Mecartty, F. 2001. The effects of modality, information type and language experience on recall by foreign language learners of Spanish. *Hispania* 84.2:265–78.

Mitchell, D. C., and M. Brysbaert. 1998. Challenges to recent theories of cross-linguistic variation in parsing: Evidence from Dutch. In *Sentence processing: A cross-linguistic perspective,* ed. D. Hillert, 313–55. New York: Academic Press.

Mitchell, D. C., and F. Cuetos. 1991. Restrictions on late closure: The computational underpinnings of parsing strategies in Spanish and English. Unpublished manuscript, University of Exeter.

Myers-Scotton, C. 1993. *Dueling languages: Grammatical structures in codeswitching.* Oxford: Oxford University Press.

Myers-Scotton, C., and J. L. Jake. 2000. Testing the 4-M model: An introduction. *International Journal of Bilingualism* 4:1–8.

————. 2001. Explaining aspects of codeswitching and their implications. In *One mind, two languages: Bilingual language processing,* ed. J. Nicol, 84–116. Oxford: Blackwell.

Nicholas, H., P. Lightbown, and N. Spada. 2001. Recasts as feedback to language learners. *Language Learning* 61.4:719–58.

Obler, L., and M. Albert. 1978. A monitor system for bilingual language processing. In *Aspects of bilingualism,* ed. M. Paradis, 156–64. Columbia, SC: Hornbeam Press.

Ortega, L., and M. Long. 1997. The effects of models and recasts on the object topicalization and adverb placement in L2 Spanish. *Spanish Applied Linguistics* 1.1:65–86.

Overstreet, M. H. 2002. The effect of textual enhancement on second language learner comprehension and form recognition. Ph.D. diss., University of Illinois, Urbana-Champaign.

Pica, T., R. Young, and C. Doughty. 1987. The impact of interaction on comprehension. *TESOL Quarterly* 21:737–59.

Pienemann, M. 1985. Learnability and syllabus construction. In *Modeling and assessing second language acquisition,* eds. K. Hyltenstam and M. Pienemann, 23–76. Clevedon: Multilingual Matters.

————. 1998. *Language processing and second language development—processability theory*. Amsterdam: John Benjamins.

Ryan, J. M., and B. Lafford. 1992. Acquisition of lexical meaning in a study abroad environment: *Ser* and *estar* and the Granada experience. *Hispania* 75:714–22.

Salaberry, M. R. 1997. The role of input and output practice in second language acquisition. *Canadian Modern Language Review* 53:422–51.

Schmidt, M. 1980. Coordinate structures and language universals in interlanguage. *Language Learning* 30:397–416.

Schmidt, R. 1988. The role of consciousness in second language learning. Plenary address delivered at the Eight Second Language Research Forum, University of Hawaii at Manoa.

————. 1990. The role of consciousness in second language learning. *Applied Linguistics* 11:129–58.

————. 1994. Deconstructing consciousness is search of useful definitions for applied linguistics. *AILA Review* 11:11–26.

Selinker, L. 1972. Interlanguage. *International Review of Applied Linguistics* 10:209–31.

Slobin, D. I. 1973. Cognitive prerequisites for the development of grammar. In *Studies of child language development,* eds. C. A. Ferguson and D. I. Slobin, 175–208. New York: Holt, Rinehart and Winston.

Soares, C., and F. Grosjean. 1984. Bilinguals in a monolingual and a bilingual speech mode: The effect on lexical access. *Memory and Cognition* 12:380–86.

Swain, M. 1985. Communicative competence: Some roles of comprehensible input and comprehensible output. In *Input and second language acquisition,* eds. S. Gass and C. Madden, 235–53. Cambridge, MA: Newbury House.

————. 1993. The output hypothesis: Just speaking and writing aren't enough. *Canadian Modern Language Review* 50:158–64.

————. 1995. Three functions of output in second language learning. In *Principles and practice in applied linguistics: Studies in honor of H. G. Widdowson,* eds. G. Cook and B. Seidlhofer, 125–44. Oxford: Oxford University Press.

VanPatten, B. 1987. Classroom learners' acquisition of *ser* and *estar.* In *Foreign language learning: A research perspective,* eds. B. VanPatten, T. Dvorak, and J. F. Lee, 19–32. Cambridge, MA: Newbury House.

————. 1990. Attending to form and content in the input: An experiment in consciousness. *Studies in Second Language Acquisition* 12:287–301.

————. 1991. Grammar instruction and input processing. Paper presented at the special colloquium on the role of grammar instruction in communicative language teaching, Concordia University and McGill University, Montreal.

————. 1996. *Input processing and grammar instruction*. Norwood, NJ: Ablex.

————. 2000. Processing instruction as form-meaning connections: Issues in theory and research. In *Form and meaning: Multiple perspectives,* eds. J. F. Lee and A. Valdman, 43–68. Boston: Heinle and Heinle.

————. 2002a. Processing instruction: An update. *Language Learning* 52.4:755–803.

————. 2002b. Processing the content of IP and PI research. A response to DeKeyser, Salaberry, Robinson and Harrington. *Language Learning* 52.4:825–31.

VanPatten, B., and T. Cadierno. 1993. Explicit instruction and input processing. *Studies in Second Language Acquisition* 15:225–43.

VanPatten, B., and P. Mandell. 1999. How type of structure influences the ways in which L2 learners render grammaticality judgments. Unpublished manuscript, University of Illinois.

Wulfeck, B., L. Juárez, E. Bates, and K. Kilborn. 1986. Sentence interpretation strategies in healthy and aphasic bilingual adults. In *Language processing in bilinguals: Psycholinguistic and neuropsychological perspectives,* ed. J. Vaid, 199–219. Hillsdale, NJ: Lawrence Erlbaum.

9

Sociocultural Perspectives

Sociocultural Theory and the Acquisition of Spanish as a Second Language

MARTA ANTÓN   Indiana University-Purdue University, Indianapolis

FREDERICK J. DICAMILLA   Indiana University-Purdue University, Indianapolis

JAMES P. LANTOLF   The Pennsylvania State University

1.0   Introduction

The purpose of this chapter is to examine the contribution of sociocultural theory to the understanding of how people learn Spanish as a second language. Sociocultural theory is concerned with the relationship between language and mind and is based principally on the work of the Russian psychologist L. S. Vygotsky. One of the principal claims of the theory is that language activity, including both speech and writing, functions as the chief mediating mechanism for human cognitive activity. In other words, the higher mental functions are organized and subordinated to language activity, which imbues humans with the capacity to organize such intentional processes as voluntary memory and attention, planning, rational thought, and learning. These higher functions originate externally in social interaction but beginning in early childhood they gradually take on an intramental, or psychological, perspective during ontogenetic development of the person. The ability to speak internally to oneself as a means of regulating one's mental operations qualitatively changes human thought. Thus, the study of how language activity shapes human behavior on both the social (between individuals) and psychological planes (within individuals) is critical to the sociocultural perspective.

Our discussion here focuses on the application of the principles of sociocultural theory to the acquisition of Spanish as a second language. To carry out the project, we will first present an overview of the major statements of the theory. We will then briefly review the research informed by sociocultural theory that focuses primarily on the acquisition of Spanish.[1] Finally, we will discuss some of the criticisms of sociocultural theory, the challenges such studies pose, and future avenues of research in this domain.

2.0 The Theoretical Framework

The most fundamental concept of sociocultural theory is that the human mind is *mediated.* Vygotsky (1978, 1987) argued that just as humans do not act directly on the physical world but rely instead on tools and labor activity, which allows us to change the world, and with it the circumstances under which we live, we also use symbolic tools, or signs, to mediate and regulate our relationships with others and with ourselves and thus change the nature of these relationships. The task of psychology, in Vygotsky's view, is to understand how human social and mental activity is organized and regulated by culturally constructed artifacts. A particularly powerful example in this regard is found in the impact of new metaphors on the way people think and behave. For instance, for nearly four decades researchers have conceived of and studied human minds as if they were computational devices, a perspective that would have been impossible until the development of computers during the middle years of the twentieth century.

2.1 Genetic Domains

Sociocultural theory recognizes four genetic domains: *phylogenesis,* concerned with differences between humans and other life forms; *sociocultural evolution,* whose focus is on the history of the development and impact of artifacts by human cultures (e.g., literacy, numeracy, computing devices, etc.); *ontogenesis,* interested in how children internalize mediational means to regulate their own physical and mental activity as they mature into adulthood; and *microgenesis,* concerned with development over relatively short time spans, as when participants are trained to criteria prior to the start of a psychology experiment, or when students internalize some aspect of a second language. The lion's share of research attention has focused on ontogenesis and to a somewhat lesser extent on microgenesis. Much of the research to be reported on here is concerned with these two domains. Most of the research has been carried out in the ontogenetic domain where the focus has been on exploring the ways in which abilities such as voluntary memory are formed in children through the integration of mediational means into the thinking process.

2.2 Unit of Analysis

Sociocultural theory clearly rejects the notion that thinking and speaking are one and the same thing. It also rejects what some now call the communicative view of language (see Carruthers and Boucher 1998), which holds that thinking and speaking are completely independent phenomena, with speaking serving only as a means of transmitting already formed thoughts. Sociocultural theory argues that thinking and speaking, though separate, are tightly interrelated in a dialectic unity in which publicly derived speech completes privately initiated thought. Thus, thought cannot be explained without taking into account how it is organized and controlled through symbolic means. To break the dialectic unity between thinking and symbolic activity is to forego any possibility of understanding human mental capacities, much in the same way, as Vygotsky observed, that independent analysis of oxygen and hydrogen fails to generate an explanation of water's capacity to extinguish fire.

What is needed, then, is a unit of analysis that preserves the dialectic unity of the elements (thinking and speaking)—a domain of sociocultural research that has been controversial; unfortunately, space does not permit us to explore this interesting area of debate (see Wertsch 1985). Suffice it to say that most contemporary scholars agree with some version of the position expressed by Wertsch (1998), who argues that the appropriate unit of analysis is *tool-mediated, goal-directed action.*

2.3   Zone of Proximal Development

Culturally specified forms of mediation develop in what Vygotsky referred to as the *zone of proximal development* (ZPD). According to Vygotsky (1978, 1987), all higher mental abilities appear twice in the life of the individual: first on the intermental plane in which the process is distributed between the individual, some other person(s) and/or cultural artifacts, and later on the intramental plane in which the capacity is carried out by the individual acting via psychological mediation. It must be emphasized again that the ZPD is not a physical place situated in time and space; rather, it is a metaphor for observing and understanding how mediational means are made available, recognized and ultimately internalized by the individual.

Determining the ZPD of an individual, however, is not necessarily an easy task. The accepted view is that the ZPD is based on what a person can achieve when acting without external mediation, which may be in the form of the assistance or support from someone else or with the aid of cultural artifacts, including such devices as computers, paper and pencil, or even speech that has been externalized. From a sociocultural perspective, a person acting with the external support of physical or symbolic artifacts is considered to be engaged in collaborative activity just as much as is the person interacting socially with other individuals. The difference is that in the former case, the other individuals are distanced in space and/or time, whereas in the latter they are not.

Culture, then, can be considered as the presence of distal others through the artifacts they make available to the members of a community living at a given time and in a given space. With regard to expertise, it is frequently the case that people working together are able to co-construct contexts in which expertise emerges as a feature of the group rather than of any given individual within the group. This is important, for without such a possibility it is difficult to imagine how expertise of any kind could arise. The ZPD then can be thought of as the collaborative construction of opportunities for individuals to change. Borrowing from the work of Gibson, van Lier (1996) characterizes these opportunities as *affordances,* while Swain and Lapkin (1998) call them "occasions for learning."

2.4   Regulation, Inner Speech, and Private Speech

According to Vygotsky, "Any higher mental function necessarily goes through an external stage in its development because it is initially a social function. . . . Any higher mental function was external because it was social at some point before becoming an internal, truly mental function" (1981:162). In the earliest stages of ontogenesis of individuals, the mental and physical behavior of children is heavily influenced by the physical objects in their environment. Thus, children are easily distracted and moved away from an in-progress activity by such things as the sudden ringing of a bell or the appearance of a bright object that catches their eye. Adults and older children are generally able to resist if not ignore completely such potential intrusions into ongoing activity. Vygotsky characterized the succumbing of children to environmental factors as *object regulation*. In other words, the behavior of children in the early stages of development is often easily subordinated to the presence of physical entities in the immediate surroundings. As Luria's (1981) research showed, at this point, it is usually difficult if not impossible for children to be controlled, or regulated, by the speech activity of others. It's interesting to note that Luria's experiments with young children (aged 2–3 years) showed that they react only to the acoustic (e.g., volume) of other's speech and not to the semantic content of that speech.

As children mature, however, their behavior gradually becomes subordinated to the semantic properties of the speech of adults and older peers. This stage of development is known as *other regulation*. Eventually, children are able to use their own external speech to regulate their own mental and physical activity. This ability signals the beginnings of the process through which forms of regulation deployed by others are appropriated by the individual, as she subordinates her behavior to her own speech activity. Eventually, speech directed at the individual by the individual (i.e., self-talk or *private speech*) is internalized as *inner speech* and the individual is able to regulate her behavior from the inside (see Diaz and Berk 1992; Zivin 1979; John-Steiner 1992; Soskin and John-Steiner 1963). Thus, the person is said to be a *self-regulated* individual.

As we will see in the discussion of various studies described in this chapter, the analysis of speech plays an important part in sociocultural theory research because it often indicates the extent to which one is object-regulated, other-regulated, or self-regulated as a language learner. Thus, for example, private speech, recognized often by its highly abbreviated syntax, elliptical reference, and odd uses of tense and aspect, provides insight into the mental operations of learners as they attempt to be self-regulated in the performance of cognitively difficult tasks, which is when it most commonly occurs. Similarly, the speech between individuals involved in a learning interaction reveals how language serves not only a communicative function but a cognitive function as well.

Another, and perhaps the most important, function of private speech is its role in the internalization of external means of mediation from the social, or interpersonal to the mental, or intrapersonal domain. According to Kozulin (1990:116), "the essential element in the formation of higher mental functions is the process of internalization," and as Luria argues, it is through this process that the social nature of people comes to be their psychological nature as well" (Luria 1979:45).

Internalization is a key concept in Vygotsky's theory, because it is through this process that the Cartesian mind/world dualism is overcome. According to Gal'perin (1967:28–29), through internalization what is originally an external and nonmental form of activity becomes mental; thus, the process "opens up the possibility of bridging this gap" [between the nonmental and the mental]. It is important to emphasize that internalization does not mean that something literally is "'within the individual' or 'in the brain,'" but instead "refers to the subject's ability to perform a certain action [concrete or ideal] without the immediately present problem situation 'in the mind'" (Stetsenko 1999:245) and with an understanding that is derived from, but independent of, "someone else's thoughts or understandings" (Ball

2000:250–51). Thus, on this view, mental activity is carried out "on the basis of mental representations, that is, independently of the physical presence of things" (Stetsenko 1999:245).

With regard to L2 learning, internalization is the process through which learners construct a mental representation of what was at one point physically (acoustic or visual) present in external form. This representation, in turn, enables them to free themselves from the sensory properties of a specific concrete situation. Again, to cite Stetsenko, the formation of intrapersonal processes "is explained as the transition from a material *object-dependent* activity (such as the actual counting of physical objects by pointing at them with a finger in the initial stages of acquiring the counting operation) to a material *object-independent* activity (when a child comes to be able to count the objects without necessarily touching them or even seeing them)" (1999:245–55).

The theoretical implications of internalization are clear. For one thing, recent work on social-constructionist models of learning and interactional competence theory of language proficiency, which either establish links to sociocultural theory, or argue for compatibility with the theory, overlooks the central role of internalization in Vygotsky's thinking (see, for example, Hall 1993; He and Young 1998; Johnson 2001; Rogoff 1995). These theories, as interesting and as important as they are with their focus on local and situated learning and proficiency, foreground social and discursive factors and while not denying the relevance of the intrapersonal mental plane, nevertheless exclude it from their theorizing. Consequently, as Valsiner and Van der Veer (2000:6) put it, such theories are "upwardly" reductive and, as a result, fail to deal appropriately with the Cartesian dualism that in Vygotsky's view was at the heart of the crisis in psychology.

2.5   Scaffolding and Intersubjectivity

An important concept related to collaboration is scaffolding. The concept has its roots in Vygotsky's notion of the ZPD but was actually first proposed by Wood, Bruner, and Ross (1976). Originally it served as a metaphor for the interaction between an expert and a novice engaged in a problem-solving task. According to Wood, Bruner, and Ross (1976:90), scaffolding involves the expert taking control of those portions of a task that are beyond the novice's current level of competence, thus allowing the learner to focus on the elements within his or her range of ability. Scaffolding is manifested primarily through the semiotically mediated interactions that occur between the novice and the expert. Stone (1993) discusses various ways of analyzing scaffolding as semiotic interactions, including among other things, the role of utterances that "presuppose some as yet unprovided information" (Stone 1993:171). Rommetveit (1974, 1979) refers to this process as *prolepsis,* in which utterances serve to challenge a listener/learner to partake of the speaker's/expert's view of a problem-solving situation; that is, to construct with the expert, a shared perspective, or *intersubjectivity* (Rommetveit 1985). According to Wertsch (1985:159), intersubjectivity is achieved when "interlocutors share some aspect of their situation definitions," that is, when individuals working in collaboration define the objects (both concrete and abstract), events and goals of a task in the same way. Moreover, the "overlap" in definitions of situation that constitute intersubjectivity may occur at many different levels, thus creating various levels of intersubjectivity (Wertsch 1985:159).

3.0   Sociocultural Theory and Spanish as a Second Language

Many of the key elements of sociocultural theory discussed here have formed the basis of numerous studies of second language learning in general, and as a result much has been learned about how language addressed both to oneself and to others functions as a psychological tool for language learners. So, for example, the work of Frawley and Lantolf (1985) and McCafferty (1992, 1994) and the ongoing research of De Guerrero (1987, 1994, 1999) have revealed that learners use private speech (L1 and L2) when faced with cognitively difficult tasks in the language learning process and that it is often abbreviated, elliptical, and may vary according to cultural background.

In the study of how language mediates learning between individuals, the work of scholars such as Donato (1994), Aljaafreh and Lantolf (1994), Swain and Lapkin (1998), De Guerrero and Villamil (1994), and Villamil and De Guerrero (1996) has contributed to our understanding of how dialogue functions as a cognitive tool not only between teachers and their students but also between students working in collaboration to learn a language. A good many of the early studies of Second Language Learning (SLL) from the perspective of sociocultural theory focused on English. Recent years, however, have seen a number of studies that deal with Spanish growing out of this larger body of work. In what follows we will briefly summarize this work and more recent research on Spanish L2.[2]

3.1   Private Speech

One of the first studies on the acquisition of Spanish as a foreign language informed by sociocultural theory was, in fact, among the earliest studies on the acquisition of any nonnative language carried out from this theoretical perspective. This was Lantolf and Frawley's (1984) replication of Frawley and Lantolf's (1985) research on the function of private speech by ESL speakers.[3]

Frawley and Lantolf (1985) show how twenty-one early ESL learners and nine native-speaking children of English deploy private speech (in English) as a way of maintaining and regaining self-regulation in a storytelling task. The properties of the private speech revealed attempts by the speakers to gain control over the structure of the task by externalizing the macrostructure of the story (27), to use past tense to distance the events in the story as a way of gaining some perspective on how to relate the story depicted in a series of drawings (31), and to externalize affective markers such as laughter and sighs as a way of manifesting frustration at their inability to relate the story in a language they did not control (39). In addition, the speakers, unlike more proficient users of the language, frequently introduced characters into the story through use of pronouns instead of lexical nouns. Consequently, it was difficult for the listener to keep track of who was doing what. Finally, Frawley and Lantolf noted that the early ESL speakers and the native-speaking children consistently used the present progressive to describe the actions of the characters, which gave the impression that they were describing a series of photographs rather than relating a story. Advanced ESL (N = 6) and native speakers (N = 10) of the language used the historical present as they related a coherent narrative.

In the replication study, with intermediate classroom learners of Spanish as a foreign language, Lantolf and Frawley (1984) found that not only was this group unable to carry out the task of relating a coherent narrative based on the pictures, but it also used virtually no private speech. Instead the speakers produced what looked very much like responses to the traditional grammatical exercises that characterize many FL classrooms. This suggests, among other things, that the circumstances under which learning happens greatly influence the nature of the learning process. In other words, as Lantolf and Frawley (1984) argue, the Spanish students had no opportunity to engage in natural everyday discourse practices of the target speech community. For them, the language was little more than a school subject to be studied on a par with other subjects, such as math, history, physics, and the like.

The ESL learners, on the other hand, had the opportunity to engage in social speech with proficient users of the language in the everyday world in which people rely on language as a tool for mediating each other and themselves through the activity of living. As Vygotsky proposed, the origins of private speech are found in social speech. Because the Spanish students did not have much opportunity to participate in the kind of linguistically mediated social interactions available to the ESL students either inside or outside of the classroom setting, it is understandable that they would not develop private speech in this language and as a consequence would have difficulties regulating themselves through this language (Lantolf and Frawley 1984).

3.2   Reading Comprehension and Recall

As part of a larger study, Roebuck (1998) analyzes the written recall protocols of thirty-two elementary and intermediate-level English-speaking learners of Spanish at an American university after reading a difficult newspaper article in Spanish. Roebuck explores L2 reading comprehension and recall processes as mediated by language. Consistent with sociocultural principles, the study assumes that language "represents the externalized activity of the mind in the face of cognitive difficulty" (34). The linguistic analysis of the written protocols reveals that learners engage in both social and private activity. That is, even though the learners were supposedly writing with a communicative purpose (to demonstrate to others their comprehension of the text), the language in the protocols provides evidence of private writing, writing that reflects how learners attempt to complete a difficult task (see DiCamilla and Lantolf 1994).

Roebuck finds examples of the following features in the learners' written protocols: macrostructure (i.e., externalized knowledge about the organization, structure, topic, etc. of a particular type of discourse), odd uses of tense and aspect, epistemic stance (this refers to the use of devices such as metacomments, modals, and vague language, devices used to create some distance from information that the speaker is uncertain about), reference (including ambiguous pronominal reference, abbreviation and focus or continued reference to an item which appears to be redundant), externalization of information about the text, and online editing. The examples of private writing in the protocols are indicative of the difficulty of the task for most learners. What is interesting, though, is that private writing functions in some cases as a strategy that allows learners to gain control and eventually complete the task. Importantly, the analysis shows that private writing uncovers the learner's orientation toward the task. Roebuck notes that it is evident in the data that orientation may change during the performance of the task as learners react to the cognitive challenges of the task. Thus, the same task may result in different activity by different individual learners.

3.3   Lexical Organization

The topics of lexical organization and the acquisition of Spanish from a sociocultural perspective are dealt with by Grabois (1997, 1999). Two central ideas of sociocultural theory inform this research. One is Vygotsky's distinction between sense *(smysl)* and meaning *(znachenie)*. Although the former term refers to all the psychological associations to one word in our consciousness, the latter is the most stable and precise part of sense. Thus, the sense of a word varies as the individual engages in different activities, whereas its meaning, or conceptual content, tends to remain stable. The second relevant notion is Vygotsky's foundational claim that words not only have their own meaning but are also simultaneously embedded in a network of other related words that form the conceptual structure that members of a culture internalize in accordance with their everyday and educational experiences. Different cultures have different conceptual organizations. These facts are important because as private speech goes underground as inner speech it loses its formal properties, and what we are left with is meaning only. The question then is whether a change in the material circumstances under which people use language, as in the case of immigrants becoming permanent residents of another country, will have an effect on the lexical organization of a second and even a first language and by implication, result in a reorganization of inner speech.

Using a complex word association methodology, Grabois (1999) explores the conceptual networks of very proficient (L1 English) speakers of Spanish as a second language with regard to such abstract concepts as *happiness, love, fear, power,* and *death.* Data from five different groups (N = 32 per group) of participants (native Spanish speakers, expert speakers of Spanish as L2 [the immigrant group], L2 Spanish study-abroad learners, learners of Spanish as a foreign language in a classroom environment, and native English speakers) reveal quantitative and qualitative differences in their lexical/conceptual structure. The quantitative analysis shows that the expert L2 Spanish speakers consistently showed high correlations with native Spanish speakers, which suggests that it is in fact possible for L2 learners to approximate the lexical/conceptual organization of native speakers of the L2, under appropriate circumstances, such as extended or permanent residency in the community. Importantly, the study-abroad students and the classroom-only learners failed to show similar correlations with the native Spanish-speaking participants.

Perhaps most intriguing of all was that Grabois (1997) uncovered suggestive, although certainly not overwhelming, evidence that the L1 English-speaking immigrants in Spain show some signs of restructuring of their native lexicon. As Grabois points out (1997:165), although many of these individuals spoke Spanish most of the time in their daily lives, they also continued to use English to some extent.[4] Extended, permanent residency in another culture has an effect on the way an individual's native lexicon is organized. The implication of these results is that lexical organization can be acquired in an L2 through linguistic mediation and participation in the L2 community. Grabois's (1997) exploration of the effect of gender in the acquisition of L2 lexical organizations shows that gender is not as significant as language group.

3.4 Language Play

Lantolf (1997) studies the functions of language play in the acquisition of Spanish as a second language. He proposes that language play is one of the functions of private speech. The phenomenon of language play has been widely explored in child L1 studies, but it is an area about which we know little in adult L2 learning. Vygotsky thought that play has a role in language development because it creates a zone of proximal development in which the child behaves above his age and his daily conduct. In this article, Lantolf argues that language play has an important role in L2 learning. One of the things learners do is play with what they "notice" in the input, which serves as a means to appropriate linguistic elements that have been noticed. The data reported in the study come from a cross-sectional survey administered to students of Spanish as a foreign language and to ESL learners. Whereas all the ESL subjects were at an advanced level of language proficiency, the students of Spanish ranged from the beginning to the advanced level. The questionnaire asked students to report on their own language play activity. Some examples of what was meant by language play, such as talking out loud to oneself in the language, repeating phrases silently, making up sentences or words in the language, imitating sounds, having snatches of the language pop into one's head, and the like, were given in the questionnaire.

The results of the study indicated that language play occurred at a higher frequency in advanced level students of Spanish. Lantolf hypothesizes that language play may decrease or stop entirely as linguistic competence increases. This would explain why advanced students of Spanish play with language more than ESL advanced students, whose competence in the language, by virtue of having more exposure and more opportunities to use the target language, is more developed than that of foreign language students. Low-proficiency Spanish language learners reported low frequency of language play. Lantolf speculates that this may be attributed to lack of motivation to learn the language since most of these learners explicitly indicated that their only reason to study Spanish was to fulfill a university language requirement.

Another important result of the survey is that conversation seems to stimulate language play more than pattern drills and grammar study. Learners also self-report that language play has a positive effect on their confidence in the use of the language. The study also informs us on the types of language play that learners use. Based on the information provided by the survey, Lantolf develops a theory of language play adopting MacWhinney's (1985) dialectic model of acquisition. In the context of language learning, the concepts of thesis, antithesis, and synthesis are redefined. Thesis is the hypothesis that a learner has about language; antithesis refers to some information that does not match the learner's hypothesis. Synthesis is the learner's attempt to resolve the noticed mismatch between thesis and antithesis, and language play is viewed as the activity of trying to regain balance. As learners increase their proficiency in the language, the potential mismatch between their system and the target language decreases; thus the chances of creating a state of disequilibrium are reduced. Consequently, engagement in language play decreases or disappears in advanced language learners.

Broner and Tarone (2001) present evidence of two types of language play: language play as fun (ludic) as described in Cook (1997, 2000) and language play as rehearsal (Lantolf 1997), in the classroom interaction of three fifth-grade students of Spanish in an immersion program. They identify channel cues (e.g., presence of laughter, shift in voice, etc.) that distinguish both types and postulate different roles for both types of language play in second language acquisition. Although both types share some features (both lack communicative intent, they involve exercise of linguistic imagination, etc.), they differ in purpose, specifically internalization in the case of rehearsal vs. amusement in the case of ludic language play. Language play as rehearsal, as described by Lantolf (1997), allows learners to compare their interlanguage system to the forms they "notice" in the environment. On the other hand, ludic language play seems not to be necessary for second language acquisition but may contribute to it in several ways. Because it entails affective response, it may make L2 utterances more noticeable. Also, it may provide the opportunity to role-play. More important, it may foster the acquisition of forms situated in the students' developmental path (Tarone 2000). As proficiency increases, ludic language play tends also to increase, while language play as rehearsal decreases and eventually disappears.

Lantolf has recently begun to collect actual samples of private speech in which adult learners of foreign languages, including Spanish, exhibit intrapersonal speech in which they appear to be playing and experimenting with their new language in an attempt to internalize it (see Lantolf, in press). Below we consider two examples of such speech produced by a classroom learner of Spanish in a North American university setting. The relevant utterances are identified as private speech based on the criteria established by Saville-Troike (1988) in her study of children learning English as a second language and utilized by Ohta (2001) in her research on adult learners of Japanese as a foreign language. The criteria include speech produced at a reduced volume, often whispered, and with no response from a potential interlocutor. Often the speech was produced while the course instructor was addressing the class as a whole or a particular student other than the participant. The Spanish recordings were made over a two-week period in which the participant, enrolled in a fourth-semester intermediate-level course, agreed to wear a microphone attached to a Sharp mini-disc recorder.

In the first example, the learner, L, along with her class, is engaged in an exercise aimed at distinguishing between the true passive and constructions using *estar* followed by an adjective, which students often confuse with the passive. L simultaneously and privately repeats the correct preposition required in the adjectival construction following an incorrect response produced by another student, C.

> C [addressing the teacher]: And we wanna say *las montañas están cubiertas . . . *por nieve?*
>
> "the mountains are covered . . . *by snow"
>
> L: *De, de* [simultaneously providing along with the instructor, but in a low voice, the correct preposition]

C confuses the construction in which the past participle *cubiertas* functions as an adjective with the true passive construction. He does not recognize that the verb in this case is *estar,* which occurs with descriptive adjectives, and not *ser* "to be" required in the passive. L clearly seems to understand the construction. However, she then over-generalizes the preposition from this construction to constructions with the true passive, as in the next excerpt, in which the instructor unsuccessfully prompts L to respond with the appropriate preposition.

> T: *Mi pintura favorita . . .* "my favorite painting"
>
> L: *¿Fue pintada *de Monet?* "was painted *from Monet"
>
> T: *¿Fue pintada . . .?* "was painted . . ."?
>
> L: **¿De Monet?* "*from Monet"?
>
> T: *Por . . .* "by"
>
> L: *Por, no de* [privately, while overlapping T's correction] "'by,' not 'from'"
>
> T: *Mi pintura favorita fue pintada por Monet* "My favorite painting was painted by Monet."
>
> L: [while T moves on to work with other students] From, from, from.

L immediately repeats the correct preposition *por* silently to herself and then tells herself in Spanish that *de* in the passive construction is incorrect, *no de.* In L's whispered repetition of the English preposition at the conclusion of the exchange she is telling herself that Spanish *de* means "from" in English, which of course it does in some cases, but not in any of the constructions at issue. Thus, L has formulated a nice way of distinguishing for herself the two prepositions. The problem with this strategy is that in Spanish *de* also has the English equivalent "of," as well as "with" or even "by," no doubt the source of the difficulty in the first place. Instructing herself that *de* can be rendered as "by" in English, at least on some occasions, would, no doubt, have complicated matters for L, since she would then be faced with two forms in the L2 with the same meaning. It makes things less complicated to assign different meanings to different forms (avoidance of synonymy), as Andersen's (1984) "one-to-one principle" proposes. Another English equivalent of *de,* frequently occurring at the early stages of instruction, is "from," as in *¿De dónde es Ud.?* Thus, it is not too surprising that L selects this option as a way of keeping things straight, as it were. The problem, un-fortunately, is that L's strategy is likely to cause her difficulties in the future, if she wants to produce something like "The road is covered with snow," which she would likely render as **El camino está cubierto con/por nieve.*

Although research on private speech and internalization is important because of its potential to provide access to the learning process in "flight," to paraphrase Vygotsky (1987), it is imperative that future research establish a relationship, as was in fact done in Saville-Troike's (1988) study, between the forms learners experiment with in their private speech and the forms they deploy in their public performances in the L2.

3.5 Collaborative Interaction

Several studies have focused on the nature of collaborative interaction among learners of Spanish while performing various communicative tasks in a classroom environment. Platt and Brooks (1994) use the sociocultural framework to question the validity of the term *acquisition-rich environment* for several reasons: it assumes that it is possible to establish a priori when an environment provides opportunities for language learning; it does not accurately represent the important role of learners as primary interactants in communicative task-based situations in the language classroom; it does not portray the wide range of functions performed by all the utterances occurring in learner–learner talk; and, finally, it does not specify what learners actually acquire.

The study examines collaborative interaction in ESL and FL classrooms including learners of Spanish. The analysis of the talk that takes place between two intermediate university-level learners of Spanish performing a paired jigsaw task shows that besides *negotiated interaction* the task elicits important strategic activity. The authors highlight how language is used by the learners to define the situation, that is, the learners externalize for themselves and create a shared view of the goals of the activity. The interaction also reveals the use of metatalk or talk about their own talk. In the particular case the authors are studying, learners talk about their frustration at their perceived lack of proficiency in Spanish that prevents them from completing the task in an expedient way. The authors speculate that this type of talk serves the purpose of allowing learners to achieve "intersubjective states." In the interaction among learners there are also instances of private speech in the form of whispering to oneself. The authors note that much of the interaction among the learners in their study occurs in L1, which learners, especially at the lower proficiency levels, use as the only mediational tool fully available to them. The authors conclude that "environments" are created and constituted dialogically by learners. The joint speech activity that develops during problem-solving tasks does not merely serve the purpose of transferring messages, but it gives learners opportunities to "enhance the psychological processes that underlie regulation or psychological autonomy" (508).

Brooks and Donato (1994) also examine learners' talk during a problem-solving task from a sociocultural perspective. They claim that the dominant encoding-decoding view of student exchanges obscures the investigation of learners' talk by constraining it to comprehension of input and the construction of mental linguistic representations. Studies of this sort do not properly describe how speaking activity serves as a strategic psychological tool for "cognizing and constructing tasks, meanings and shared situational definitions" (263). In this article the authors study the interaction of eight pairs of third-year high school English-speaking learners of Spanish who were asked to complete a two-way information gap task. The authors focus their analysis on the role of speech as an agent in the creation of a "shared social reality." In particular, they illustrate how learners' talk serves three functions of speaking: speaking as object regulation, speaking as shared orientation, and speaking as goal formation. Speaking as object regulation refers to the way speech makes it possible for learners to control the task. Learners' discourse reveals instances of metatalk, or talk about the task itself and the language that constitutes the task. Utterances such as "I like that word," "I know what you are talking about," and "I don't know what that means" are examples of metatalk. The authors argue that, although this kind of talk is often discouraged in second language classrooms because it is seen as irrelevant and most often it takes place in L1, its occurrence is important in that it allows learners to establish intersubjectivity.

With respect to the use of L1, the authors comment that "it is a normal psycholinguistic process that facilitates L2 production and allows the learners both to initiate and sustain verbal interaction with one another" (268). Speaking as shared orientation refers to how speaking creates a "shared social reality," a mutually agreed-on perspective of the task. It is closely related to the previous function in that it contributes to the establishment of intersubjectivity. It serves the purpose of focusing attention on the problem to be solved and on how to proceed about it. Speaking as goal formation relates to the formation of individual or common objectives and plans of action during the interaction. Sometimes learners need to discuss the goals of their activity. The authors conclude that in learner–learner interaction, learners attempt to gain control (self-regulate in Vygotskian terms) of the task by constructing it through dialogue and developing a mutual understanding of the language and task demands. The analysis of discourse within the sociocultural framework shows the "impossibility of discussing L2 performance apart from cognition (e.g. planning, monitoring, etc.) as is often done in second language acquisition research" (271). Because cognition is dialogically constructed, it is possible to observe it directly in interaction.

In a follow-up study, Brooks, Donato, and McGlone (1997) analyze the development of certain features of learners' language across tasks. As in their previous studies, the authors challenge the primacy given to message exchange and use of communicative strategies for the negotiation of meaning in research studies using information-gap activities. They argue that the focus on communication as simply message exchange has prevented researchers from uncovering important psycholinguistic and semiotic processes and has failed to give an accurate representation of what goes on in learner–learner interaction. Looking at interaction between learners from a sociocultural perspective, speaking emerges as a cognitive tool that humans use to control themselves, others and objects in tasks that present difficulties. In the language classroom, speaking assists learners in gaining control of the foreign language and the task itself. The authors maintain that it is possible to develop self-regulation in a second language when learners are given the opportunity to engage in collaborative problem-solving activity repeatedly across time in situations where students are allowed to use language as a psychological tool.

In their study, the authors highlight the following features of learner language: metatalk or talk about their own talk, metacognition or talk about how to do the task, students' use of English, and students whispering to themselves. The following examples of metatalk found in this study were much like those found in Brooks and Donato (1994): "That's a good word," "Let me think of another way to say this," and "I don't know how to say this in Spanish." Metacognition or talk about task procedures is revealed in statements such as "You can say *número tres,* and that way we know what we are talking about," "I don't know if I'm right," and the like. Examples of whispering to self in the data included subvocalized L2 words, counting out numbers, affective reactions to the task, and openings and closing of episodes with utterances such as "Let's see . . ." "Okay . . ." "Now what?"

Brooks, Donato, and McGlone were interested in investigating the development of these aspects of learners' language when students have multiple opportunities to engage in similar tasks over time. Their subjects in this case were six third-semester learners of Spanish in a classroom environment who participated in five jigsaw tasks. The authors analyzed learners' interactions during the first, third, and fifth tasks. What they found was a general decrease of these features as learners gained familiarity with the task. With respect to metatalk, the authors note that it allows learners to reflect on the task and their linguistic resources and thereby gain control over their own communication. Looking at the development of metatalk across tasks, the authors find not only that its occurrence decreases in frequency but also that there is a shift from using English to using Spanish. Also, statements revealing metacognition or talk about task decrease across tasks. In fact, they almost disappeared by the fifth task. It is not surprising that this happens when students have reached a common orientation toward the task and have become familiar with task goals and procedures. In previous studies, the authors had already established the important supportive role played by the L1 as a mediator of metacognitive strategies. The authors note that of the four language features studied, the use of English presents the most dynamic developmental profile. They observe how the use of English progressively disappears from the interaction. Across groups there is a 77 to 91 percent reduction in English utterances.

The authors also observed the occurrence of private speech in the form of whispering to oneself in both L1 and L2. Because, according to sociocultural theory, private speech can serve the function of planning, guiding, and directing individual actions in a task, the authors view whispering to oneself during collaborative interaction as "a form of semiotic mediation that enables second language learners to gain control of themselves, the new language, and the task" (532). Interestingly, this aspect of the learners' language also decreases as task familiarity increases. What these findings imply is that learners achieve self-regulation in tasks when they have opportunities to engage in similar tasks across a period of time. Looking at these language features across time reveals clear developmental patterns in language learners' discourse.

Along these same lines, the work of DiCamilla and Antón (1997) and Antón and DiCamilla (1998) has focused on the collaborative interaction of five dyads of beginning-level adult learners of Spanish in a classroom context working in collaborative writing tasks. Students regularly wrote individual compositions in class. On three occasions, students were asked to write collaboratively. The writing sessions were conducted in a language laboratory where students' interactions were recorded. The authors examined specific features (e.g., repetition, sentence types, modal verbs) of student interactions in order to determine the social and cognitive functions of the subjects' utterances in the performance of the three collaborative writing assignments. The research addresses the general question of how language, whether native language or target language, functions as the principal mediating device in the process of learning a second language in a classroom setting. In particular, the authors focus on the semiotics of scaffolding and intersubjectivity, which the authors view as two critical components in effective collaboration within the ZPD.

As stated in the introduction to this chapter, scaffolding involves one individual taking control of those portions of a task that are beyond a less proficient partner's current level of competence, thus allowing the less proficient individual to focus on the elements within his or her range of ability (Wood, Bruner, and Ross 1976). As recent studies show, however, learners involved in collaborative learning tasks take on and exchange the roles of more or less proficient partners as the tasks unfold. *Intersubjectivity* is achieved when "interlocutors share some aspect of their situation definitions," that is, when individuals working in collaboration define the objects (both concrete and abstract), events and goals of a task in the same way (Wertsch 1985:159). The research of Antón and DiCamilla has sought to answer the following questions: How do the learners use language to construct and hold in place scaffolded help? How do the learners use language to achieve and maintain intersubjectivity? Answers to these questions are expected to provide greater insight into the psychological functions of specific features of language and language use.

DiCamilla and Antón (1997) find that, much as it happens in L1 conversation discourse (Tannen 1989), repetition plays a functional role in the creation of discourse in an L2 collaborative setting. In this study, repetition refers to any restatement of the content or form of the task previously mentioned in the discourse (in either L1 or L2) by a member of the dyad. Although many previous studies on the role of interaction in second language learning recognize the important role of repetition in making input comprehensible and negotiating meaning, there had not been much research trying to understand the sociocognitive role of repetition in interaction in the L2 classroom. The authors argue that the role of repetition in L2 acquisition may be better understood if undertaken from a sociocultural perspective. The qualitative analysis of learners' collaborative interaction demonstrates that repetition plays a critical cognitive role in scaffolding and in creating and maintaining intersubjectivity, thus allowing learners to perform the task, attain their goals, and realize their levels of potential development.

The data collected for this study reveal that in some cases repetition is used as a cognitive strategy by which learners externalize knowledge, and by repeating it, they hold in place the scaffolded help that learners offer each other. Like a space in a scaffold from which one may work, repetition creates a cognitive space in which learners hold on to what they have constructed up to that point, what they know and are sure of while they keep their focus of attention on, think and hypothesize about, and evaluate new forms. In the interaction, repetition emerges as one of the devices used by learners to mediate the collective construction of the scaffold. This study makes the metaphor of scaffolding more robust by providing an answer (or, at least, a partial answer) to the question of what semiotic mechanisms play a role in learning in scaffolded instruction (Stone 1993:176).

Another function of repetition found to be important is that of establishing and maintaining intersubjectivity. Repetition enables learners to speak with virtually one voice, creating discourse that appears more like a monologue than a dialogue, as "two voices coming into contact and interanimating one another" (Wertsch 1991:73). Repetition sparks this interanimation. As students repeat each other's phrases, words, and even syllables, they accept what the other offers without any comment or discussion. Repetition links their discourse and thus their minds in a shared perspective of the task, giving learners joint ownership as they complete it.

Based on the same set of data, Antón and DiCamilla (1998) explore the social and cognitive functions performed by the native language in the collaborative interaction of beginning-level learners of Spanish. This study expands the view of the role of the native language in second language learning beyond that of merely a source of language transfer. The qualitative analysis of learners' interactions demonstrates that the native language is used as a powerful tool of semiotic mediation both on the interpsychological (between individuals) plane and the intrapsychological (within individuals) plane. On the interpsychological plane, use of the native language enables learners to collaborate effectively by providing each other with scaffolded help (Wood, Bruner, and Ross 1976) and by facilitating intersubjectivity (Rommetveit 1985), or a shared perspective of the task at hand. Within individuals, the native language emerges as a cognitive tool in problem resolution while learners are engaged in collaborative work.

On the interpsychological plane, learners use their native language to provide each other with scaffolded help. The authors observed, for example, that learners use the L1 to enlist and keep each other's interest in the task, to develop strategies for managing the task, to focus on the goals of the task, to highlight important elements of the task, to discuss solutions to specific problems, and to explain and build on their partial solutions to the problems they face. Further, the learners' L1 was found to be a critical tool for accessing linguistic forms in the second language. For example, expressions such as "I don't know the word for —" or "I don't remember the word for —" indicate the search for lexical items in the L2. Often, these utterances triggered a semantic analysis of the word they are seeking, a cognitive and communicative strategy that results in the learners jointly accessing lexical items in the L2. Learners also resorted to their native language when they tried to make sense of the meaning or form of the text and when they evaluated the text in the L2 either in the form of translation or externalizing their explicit knowledge about the L2.

In addition to the cognitive functions mentioned above, the authors argue that the L1 of their subjects served important social functions as well. At least with learners of low L2 proficiency, the use of the native language appears to be necessary to create a social space that aids learners in achieving intersubjectivity and thus effective collaboration. In the interaction, English modal verbs and questions emerged as two important linguistic devices in the establishment of intersubjectivity. Modal verbs perform dual social and cognitive functions in the collaborative speech of second language learners by encoding both politeness and hypotheticality. Thus, expressions such as "You could say—" "Would you say—?" serve simultaneously to foster a polite social atmosphere and to create a cognitive stance that facilitates learners' attempts to help each other as they work through the task. Questions and other utterances marked for hypotheticality enable learners to work on the cognitive plane with ideas and on the social plane with polite forms that invite the listener to engage in the task and participate in problem solving. The L1 also contributes to the establishment of intersubjectivity by giving learners a way to control the setting of goals and subgoals and limiting the task in progress.

Finally, at the individual level, L1 is used sometimes as the vehicle of private speech when faced with a cognitively difficult task. Private speech in collaborative interaction takes different forms. Sometimes it is communicative in appearance, that is, it is an utterance that might well have been addressed to someone else but is identified as self-addressed because it is not interpretable in the course of the interaction. In other instances, its form is more elliptical; because language is directed to oneself, there is no need to overtly state the thought. Antón and DiCamilla observed learners using L1 to pose and answer self-addressed questions (e.g., *es* or *está? Es*), to use reference in ways that indicate one's own private perspective (e.g., "our walk" versus "the walk"), and to switch from the use of modal verbs to more assertive statements (e.g., "we can say" versus "let's just say") (1998:334–37). Based on such evidence, the authors conclude that learners often rely on their L1 to externalize their thoughts as they attempt to be self-regulated in the language-learning task at hand.

In the following section we conclude our overview of sociocultural research into Spanish language learning by focusing on current research by two of this chapter's authors, Antón and DiCamilla. Following that we will consider certain problems that this approach to second language learning presents and the challenges it faces in offering a theoretical framework for explaining how individuals learn a second language, in particular for our purposes Spanish as a second language.

4.0   Collaborative Interaction among Advanced Learners of Spanish

More recent research by Antón and DiCamilla (1999, 2000) focuses on similar issues, namely the investigation of the discursive mechanisms deployed in the creation of scaffolding and establishment of intersubjectivity in the collaborative interaction of adult native speakers of English enrolled in an upper-level Spanish course. Antón and DiCamilla (1999, 2000) replicate the methodology of their two previous studies with learners who are at advanced levels of proficiency in the L2, Spanish.

In the collaborative interaction of the ten advanced-level learners of Spanish examined in Antón and DiCamilla (1999, 2000), the L2 is used for a variety of social and cognitive functions serving the purpose of jointly constructing a scaffold that allows them to successfully complete the activity. The talk that is part of the activity also serves to establish and maintain intersubjectivity, which is necessary to be able to carry out the activity. Some of the communicative mechanisms that contribute to achieving effective collaboration include repetition, use of modals, and questioning. Although these mechanisms are similar to those we have observed in the interaction of beginning-level learners engaged in the same tasks, the crucial difference is that advanced-level learners are able to deploy the L2 for such functions. The L2 emerges in the interaction as the principal mediating device to negotiate meaning, language forms, and task goals and procedures, thus offering opportunities to use the L2 in ways that may not be available in a noncollaborative setting. Beginning-level learners generally rely on their L1 for most, if not all of these functions.

Given that, from our theoretical perspective, language functions not merely as a means for expressing prefabricated thoughts but as a cognitive tool that organizes and guides our mental life, pedagogies that proscribe the use of the L1 in the classroom risk interfering with the learning process. We want to be clear that we are not supporting a laissez-faire approach to language teaching in which students are allowed to use their L1 at will and as an easy substitute for the L2. We are arguing, however, that there is a role for the L1 in L2 learning and this is as a psychological mediating tool. In other words, from our vantage point, if learners can learn to use the L2 as a primary means of social communication, the fact that they need to rely on their L1 for mental regulation should not be a cause for concern. Even though some of the advanced learners examined in the data considered here were apparently able to mediate each other through the L2 in the specific activities at issue, this does not mean that these learners will be able or will even want to regulate themselves through the L2. The research of Pavlenko and Lantolf (2000) shows how mentally and emotionally debilitating it can be to develop private speech in a second language, even for someone who immigrates into a second culture. The work of Swain and Lapkin (1998) similarly shows that French immersion students prefer to regulate themselves through their L1 even when they clearly have the proficiency in their L2 to use this language instead.

5.0   Conclusion and Future Directions

There has been growing interest in the implications of sociocultural theory for second language learning and use, but a great deal more work remains to be done. As attractive as this theory may be, it is of course, like any theory worth considering, not without its problems. For one thing, scholars working within SCT are not in full agreement on what the unit of analysis for the study of mind should be. Many were following the proposal of Wertsch (1998) that this unit should not be the word, as Vygotsky originally proposed, but mediated action. However, in the latest volume of Vygotsky's *Collected Works* (2000), there appears a previously unpublished paper that makes a fairly convincing argument that sign, not as understood by Saussure, as a stable entity, but as interpreted by Vološinov and Bakhtin as a unit that is malleable according to the needs of the circumstances should be reintroduced as the appropriate theoretical unit for the study of mind.

Specifically with regard to L2 research, Mitchell and Myles (1998:161) argue that SCT does not present a clear picture of the "nature of language as a formal system." In general this is an accurate assessment of the situation. However, not all SCT researchers would see this as a shortcoming of the theory, since the theory is a psychological and not a linguistic theory. To be sure, this does not preclude the need to show the kinds of linguistic theories it is compatible with. These theories, however, need not be those that take language to be a formal system. Lantolf (2000a) suggests, for instance, that sociocultural theory might very well be compatible with Hopper's (1998) notion of "emergent grammar" rather than with more recognized formal theories such as Chomsky's.

Collaborative learning, though a fruitful area of inquiry, presents particular challenges for sociocultural research. One of the most important of these is the question of how to determine unambiguously the distinction between social and private speech in learners' interactions, or indeed whether such a distinction can be made. Wells (1998:349) argues that when we are examining dialogic activity, no clear distinction can be made between social and private speech and that utterances spoken aloud in a dialogue have "both an inner and outer orientation, one or the other of which has greater salience on any particular occasion." Such a more finely tuned distinction has important implications for sociocultural research into collaborative language learning because scholars undoubtedly will still want to ascertain, for example, when a learner's speech in collaborative activity has a greater inner orientation and, as a result, what this reveals about the mental operations of the learner and the extent to which the learner is self-regulated in the language learning process.

Despite such issues, research on collaborative learning in the language classroom certainly has been informative and, therefore, should continue. It is equally important, however, for sociocultural scholars interested in second language learning to expand the scope of their work in order to pay attention to the process of internalization. It is not enough to understand how learners interact and negotiate intersubjectivity and collaboratively construct scaffolding, but we need to know the consequences of these activities on learning at the level of the individual. We want to make it clear that in adopting this stance, we are not supporting the binary distinction between the "autonomous" individual and the social world in which the individual lives, which is pervasive in SLA research[5] (see, for example, Ellis 1997:244). There is no place for "autonomous" beings in sociocultural theory. The problem has been, however, that even though the theory insists on a seamless and necessary dialectic link between the social and the individual, the lion's share of SLA research has focused on the social and not on the dialectic link between social and individual. One likely reason for this, of course, is that it is often easier to conduct research on social interaction than it is on the process through which individuals internalize social interactions. A potentially fruitful area of research in this regard, however, has been suggested by Lantolf (2000a) on the importance of private speech in the internalization process.

In closing, let us observe that although in recent years there has been some research into the acquisition of Spanish as a second language from a sociocultural perspective, especially regarding collaborative interaction, this area of inquiry has not been as productive as it has been in the acquisition of other languages. We hope that the research reported in this chapter will encourage more Spanish L2 studies, in both second and foreign language contexts. Lantolf (2000b) singles out some areas of both theoretical and pedagogical interest in which more research is needed in general with respect to second language learning and sociocultural theory. Among them, he mentions the role of metatalk in L2 learning (particularly with respect to the transition between L1 and L2), the role of private speech in language learning, with special attention to the methodology for collecting this type of data, and the effect of artifact mediation (particularly technology) on learning another language. To this agenda we must add the need for intensive research on internalization. The countless number of people trying to learn Spanish, in every variety of settings, provides very fertile ground for the exploration of all of these issues. The outcomes of such studies would undoubtedly contribute to our understanding of a growing phenomenon, namely the learning of Spanish as a second language.

NOTES

1. See chapters 6 and 10 of this volume for further discussion of Spanish L2 studies carried out within a sociocultural framework.

2. For a critical survey of the general L2 research carried out within sociocultural theory, see Lantolf (2000b).

3. Even though the publication dates of the two articles in question appear to show that the replication study predates the original work, it is only because as it turned out, it took longer for the original study to appear in print. In fact, this study was originally presented as a paper at the 1983 TESOL convention held in Toronto.

4. A recent study by Pavlenko and Lantolf (2000) documents that under circumstances in which an individual immigrates to a new speech community and culture and in so doing is compelled to abandon her native language as a means of social interaction, it is indeed possible for one's inner speech to shift completely from L1 to L2.

5. Ellis (1997:244), for example, while recognizing the contribution of sociocultural research to our understanding of second language learning, nevertheless argues that the learner

as "autonomous processor" metaphor is still needed to account for how learning happens inside the head. Lantolf (2000a), in responding to Ellis, claims that the metaphor is not needed because of the dialectic unity of social and individual and to sustain the metaphor is to sustain an unproductive dualism—a dualism that some, such as Firth and Wagner (1997), have also criticized.

WORKS CITED

Aljaafreh, A., and J. P. Lantolf. 1994. Negative feedback as regulation and second language learning in the zone of proximal development. *Modern Language Journal* 78:465–83.

Andersen, R. 1984. The one-to-one principle of interlanguage construction. *Language Learning* 34:77–95.

Antón, M., and F. DiCamilla. 1998. Socio-cognitive functions of L1 collaborative interaction in the L2 classroom. *Canadian Modern Language Review* 54:314–42.

———. 1999. The discursive features of the collaborative interaction of language learners: A sociocultural perspective. Paper given at the American Association for Applied Linguistics Annual Conference, Stamford.

———. 2000. L1 function in student collaborative discourse across three levels of Spanish proficiency: A sociocultural perspective. Paper given at the American Association for Applied Linguistics Annual Conference, Vancouver.

Ball, A. F. 2000. Teachers' developing philosophies on literacy and their use in urban schools: A Vygotskian perspective on internal activity and teacher change. In *Vygotskian perspectives on literacy research: Constructing meaning through collaborative inquiry,* eds. C. D. Lee and P. Smagorinsky, 226–55. Cambridge: Cambridge University Press.

Broner, M. A., and E. E. Tarone. 2001. Is it fun? Language play in a fifth-grade Spanish immersion classroom. *Modern Language Journal* 85:363–80.

Brooks, F. B., and R. Donato. 1994. Vygotskyan approaches to understanding foreign language learner discourse during communicative tasks. *Hispania* 77:262–74.

Brooks, F. B., R. Donato, and J. V. McGlone. 1997. When are they going to say 'it' right? Understanding learner talk during pair-work activity. *Foreign Language Annals* 30:523–41.

Carruthers, P., and J. Boucher. 1998. Introduction: Opening up options. In *Language and thought: Interdisciplinary themes,* eds. P. Carruthers and J. Boucher, 1–18. Cambridge: Cambridge University Press.

Cook, G. 1997. Language play, language learning. *ELT Journal* 51:224–31.

———. 2000. *Language play, language learning.* Oxford: Oxford University Press.

De Guerrero, M. C. M. 1987. The din phenomenon: Mental rehearsal in the second language. *Foreign Language Annals* 20:537–48.

———. 1994. Form and function of inner speech in adult second language learning. In *Vygotskian approaches to second language research,* eds. J. P. Lantolf and G. Appel, 83–116. Norwood, NJ: Ablex.

———. 1999. Inner speech as mental rehearsal: The case of advanced L2 learners. *Issues in Applied Linguistics* 10:27–55.

De Guerrero, M. C. M., and O. S. Villamil. 1994. Social-cognitive dimensions of interaction in L2 peer revision. *Modern Language Journal* 78.4:484–96.

Diaz, R. M., and L. E. Berk, eds. 1992. *Private speech: From social interaction to self-regulation.* Hillsdale, NJ: Lawrence Erlbaum.

DiCamilla, F. J., and M. Antón. 1997. The function of repetition in the collaborative discourse of L2 learners. *Canadian Modern Language Review* 53:609–33.

DiCamilla, F. J., and J. P. Lantolf. 1994. The linguistic analysis of private writing. *Language Sciences* 16:347–69.

Donato, R. 1994. Collective scaffolding in second language learning. In *Vygotskian approaches to second language research,* eds. J. P. Lantolf and G. Appel, 33–56. Norwood, NJ: Ablex.

Ellis, R. 1997. *SLA research and language teaching.* Oxford: Oxford University Press.

Firth, A., and J. Wagner. 1997. On discourse, communication, and (some) fundamental concepts in SLA research. *Modern Language Journal* 81.3:285–300.

Frawley, W., and J. P. Lantolf. 1985. Second language discourse: A Vygotskyan perspective. *Applied Linguistics* 6:19–44.

Gal'perin, P. Ya. 1967. On the notion of internalization. *Soviet Psychology* 5:28–33.

Grabois, H. 1997. Love and power: Word associations, lexical organization and L2 acquisition. Ph.D. diss., Cornell University.

———. 1999. The convergence of sociocultural theory and cognitive linguistics: Lexical semantics and the L2 acquisition of love, fear, and happiness. In *Languages of sentiment: Pragmatic and cognitive approaches to understanding cultural constructions of emotional substrates,* ed. G. B. Palmer and D. Occhi, 201–33. Amsterdam: John Benjamins.

Hall, J. K. 1993. The role of oral practices in the accomplishment of our everyday lives: The sociocultural dimension of interaction with implications for the learning of another language. *Applied Linguistics* 14:143–66.

He, A., and R. Young. 1998. Language proficiency interviews: A discourse approach. In *Talking and testing: Discourse approaches to the assessment of oral proficiency,* eds. R. Young and A. He, 1–24. Amsterdam: John Benjamins.

Hopper, P. 1998. Emergent grammar. In *The new psychology of language: Cognition and functional approaches to language structure,* ed. M. Tomasello, 155–75. Mahwah, NJ: Lawrence Erlbaum.

Johnson, M. 2001. *The art of non-conversation: A reexamination of the validity of the oral proficiency interview.* New Haven: Yale University Press.

John-Steiner, V. 1992. Private speech among adults. In *Private speech: From social interaction to self-regulation,* eds. R. M. Diaz and L. E. Berk, 285–96. Hillsdale, NJ: Lawrence Erlbaum.

Kozulin, A. 1990. *Vygotsky's psychology: A biography of ideas.* Cambridge, MA: Harvard University Press.

Lantolf, J. 1997. The function of language play in the acquisition of L2 Spanish. In *Contemporary perspectives on the acquisition of Spanish,* eds. W. R. Glass and A. T. Pérez-Leroux, 3–24. Somerville, MA: Cascadilla Press.

———. 2000a. Going out of my head: The role of private speech in second language learning. Plenary lecture presented at the International Conference on Language and Mind, National University of Singapore.

———. 2000b. Second language learning as a mediated process. *Language Teaching* 33:79–96.

————. In press. Intrapersonal communication and internalization in the second language classroom. In *Vygotsky's theory of education in cultural context,* eds. A. Kozulin, V. S. Ageev, S. Miller, and B. Brindis. New York: Cambridge University Press.

Lantolf, J. P., and W. Frawley. 1984. Second language performance and Vygotskyan psycholinguistics: Implications for L2 instruction. In *The Tenth LACUS Forum 1983,* eds. A. Manning, P. Martin, and K. McCall, 425–40. Columbia, SC: Hornbeam Press.

Luria, A. R. 1979. *The making of mind: A personal account of Soviet psychology.* Cambridge, MA: Harvard University Press.

————. 1981. *Language and cognition.* New York: Wiley.

MacWhinney, B. 1985. Hungarian language acquisition. In *The cross-linguistic study of language acquisition,* ed. D. Slobin, 1069–155. Hillsdale, NJ: Lawrence Erlbaum.

McCafferty, S. 1992. The use of private speech by adult second language learners: A cross-cultural study. *Modern Language Journal* 76.2:179–88.

————. 1994. The use of private speech by adult ESL learners at different levels of proficiency. In *Vygotskian approaches to second language research,* eds. J. P. Lantolf and G. Appel, 117–34. Norwood, NJ: Ablex.

Mitchell, R., and F. Myles. 1998. *Second language learning theories.* London: Arnold.

Ohta, A. S. 2001. *Second language acquisition processes in the classroom: Learning Japanese.* Mahwah, NJ: Lawrence Erlbaum.

Pavlenko, A., and J. P. Lantolf. 2000. Second language learning as participation and the (re)construction of selves. In *Sociocultural theory and second language learning,* ed. J. P. Lantolf, 155–78. Oxford: Oxford University Press.

Platt, E., and F. B. Brooks. 1994. The "acquisition-rich environment" revisited. *Modern Language Journal* 78.4:497–511.

Roebuck, R. 1998. *Reading and recall in L1 and L2: A sociocultural approach.* Stamford, CT: Ablex.

Rogoff, B. 1995. Observing sociocultural activity on three planes: Participatory appropriation, guided participation, and apprenticeship. In *Sociocultural studies of mind,* eds. J. V. Wertsch, P. de Río, and A. Alvarez, 139–64. New York: Cambridge University Press.

Rommetveit, R. 1974. *On message structure: A framework for the study of language and communication.* New York: Wiley.

————. 1979. On codes and dynamic residuals in human communication. In *Studies of language, thought and verbal communication,* eds. R. Rommetveit and R. M. Blakar, 163–75. Orlando, FL: Academic Press.

————. 1985. Language acquisition as increasing linguistic structuring of experience and symbolic behavior control. In *Culture, communication, and cognition,* ed. J. V. Wertsch, 183–204. Cambridge: Cambridge University Press.

Saville-Troike, M. 1988. Private speech: Evidence for second language learning strategies during the "silent" period. *Child Language* 15:567–90.

Soskin, W. F., and V. John-Steiner 1963. The study of spontaneous talk. In *The stream of behavior: Explorations of its structure and content,* ed. R. G. Barker, 228–81. New York: Appleton-Century-Crofts.

Stetsenko, A. P. 1999. Social interaction, cultural tools and the zone of proximal development: In search of a synthesis. In *Activity theory and social practice: Cultural historical approaches,* eds. S. Chaiklin, M. Hedegaard, and U. J. Jensen, 235–52. Aarhus: Aarhus University Press.

Stone, C. A. 1993. What is missing in the metaphor of scaffolding? In *Contexts for learning: Sociocultural dynamics in children's development,* eds. E. Forman, N. Minick, and C. A. Stone, 169–83. Oxford: Oxford University Press.

Swain, M., and S. Lapkin.1998. Interaction and second language learning: Two adolescent French immersion students working together. *Modern Language Journal* 83.3:320–38.

Tannen, D. 1989. *Talking voices: Repetition, dialogue, and imagery in conversational discourse.* Cambridge: Cambridge University Press.

Tarone, E. 2000. Getting serious about language play: Language play, interlanguage variation, and SLA. In *Interaction of social and cognitive factors in SLA: Proceedings of the 1999 Second Language Research Forum,* eds. B. Swierzbin, F. Morris, M. Anderson, C. Klee, and E. Tarone, 31–54. Somerville, MA: Cascadilla Press.

Valsiner, J., and R. Van der Veer. 2000. *The social mind: Construction of the idea.* Cambridge: Cambridge University Press.

van Lier, L. 1996. *Interaction in the language curriculum: Awareness, autonomy, and authenticity.* London: Longman.

Villamil, O. S., and M. C. M. de Guerrero. 1996. Peer revision in the L2 classroom: Social-cognitive activities, mediating strategies, and aspects of social behavior. *Journal of Second Language Writing* 5:51–75.

Vygotsky, L. S. 1978. *Mind in society: The development of higher psychological processes.* Cambridge, MA: Harvard University Press.

———. 1981. The genesis of higher mental functions. In *The concept of activity in Soviet psychology,* ed. and trans. J. V. Wertsch, 144–88. Armonk, NY: M. E. Sharpe.

———. 1987. *The collected works of L. S. Vygotsky,* vol. 1. New York: Plenum Press.

———. 2000. *The collected works of L. S. Vygotsky,* vol. 6. New York: Plenum Press.

Wells, G. 1998. Using L1 to master L2: A response to Antón and DiCamilla's "Socio- cognitive functions of L1 collaborative interaction in the L2 classroom." *Canadian Modern Language Review* 54.3:343–53.

Wertsch, J. V. 1985. *Vygotsky and the social formation of mind.* Cambridge, MA: Harvard University Press.

———. 1991. *Voices of the mind: A sociocultural approach to mediated action.* Cambridge, MA: Harvard University Press.

———. 1998. *Mind as action.* Oxford: Oxford University Press.

Wood, D., J. S. Bruner, and G. Ross. 1976. The role of tutoring in problem solving. *Journal of Child Psychology and Psychiatry* 17:89–100.

Zivin, G., ed. 1979. *The development of self-regulation through private speech.* New York: Wiley.

Part III

Methodological Perspectives

10

Instruction

The Role of Instruction in Spanish Second Language Acquisition

CHARLES GROVE   West Chester University of Pennsylvania

1.0   Introduction

This chapter will focus on state-of-the-science approaches to instruction that aim to facilitate the acquisition of Spanish as a second language.[1] Although national standards[2] for instruction and the proficiency movement have helped Spanish language practitioners to define both content emphases for their classrooms and general objectives of instruction, there remains little consensus about which specific types of classroom activities most effectively promote development of this proficiency across skills or language acquisition in general.[3] An historical overview of the role of instructional methodologies of the second half of the twentieth century reveals that trends in foreign language instruction have shifted a number of times toward varying—often contradicting—definitions of what it means to teach and practice a language with the goal of developing real-world, functional skills in using it as a system of communication. Grittner (1990:10) employs a bandwagon metaphor to describe these movements in foreign language instruction that evoke "a·fervent commitment to a single, unified theory of teaching [whose] demonstrated results . . . are far superior to those of any other previous approach."

The disagreement along these lines is especially evident to practitioners who teach Spanish at the novice and intermediate levels, where consumer demand driven by burgeoning enrollments has given rise to a wide range of instructional materials. The activities included in the texts most commonly used in today's communicative classroom vary greatly, both in the relative emphasis that is placed on the provision and formal properties of instructional input, and the manner in which interaction and student production, or output, is defined relative to comprehension-based tasks. Important differences include the shape and sequencing of pedagogical grammar information, organizational frameworks of small and whole group interactive tasks, instructor specifications and opportunities for the provision of requisite input in the target language, the criteria for quantity and quality of student-generated output, and the techniques that materials systematically employ for eliciting student responses and class participation in general.[4] These basic differences in instructional materials tend to reflect assertions rooted in the theories of second language acquisition on which they are purportedly based.

Although "method" continues to be a term commonly used in teacher education programs to refer to an a priori set of classroom behaviors implemented regularly toward an articulated objective, Long (1991) argues that "it is no exaggeration to say that language teaching methods do not exist—at least, not where they would matter, in the classroom" (39). He cites four reasons for "avoiding the methods trap." Among these are an overlapping of prescribed classroom practices across articulated methods, a demonstrated lack of consistency in the implementation of methodologically prescribed practices by instructors, a lack of evidence that any one method is significantly more effective than any other, and a fatal disjunction between the analytic construct of a method and the observable classroom practices of the teacher trainees who have been trained to implement it (39–40). In effect, these basic inadequacies associated with the teaching method construct have posed—and continue to pose—challenges for both researchers, who attempt to compare learning outcomes associated with the implementation of specific methods or technique clusters, and teachers, who wish to use the research to inform the instructional choices they make in their classrooms.

In light of Long's insights regarding the pitfalls of discussing instructional approaches in terms of cogent methods, this chapter will focus on design features that are operationalized in the research, including Long's notion of *a focus on form,* and will review the SLA components of major classroom approaches that have greatly influenced the instruction of Spanish as a foreign language in the United States, up to the present. A comprehensive model of SLA proposed by Gass and Selinker (2001) will be presented and utilized as a framework for purposes of comparison and analysis. An understanding of the primary variables of SLA research—input, intake, the integration of new knowledge, and output—as well as current theories regarding how these elements are thought to relate, gives the practitioner a platform from which newly proposed theories, associated materials, technologies, and instructional techniques may be evaluated. With this knowledge, they may also gain some associated protection against what Larsen-Freeman and Long (1991:220–21) refer to as "seductive but inadequate theory-based prescriptions for the classroom."

2.0   Focus on Form: In Search of a Grammar for Communication

A consideration of the weaknesses associated with the construct of "teaching methodology," as well as the challenges these weaknesses pose to conducting fruitful classroom research on their effectiveness, has initiated a serious rethinking of traditional modes of organizing the instructional content of language teacher education programs away from the notion of method and toward an emphasis on the nature and efficacy of specific classroom practices outside of methodological confines. With regard to the role of grammar in foreign language (FL) instruction, for example, the debate has currently shifted to a discussion of the utility of *a focus on form* in instructed second language acquisition. Long (1991) first makes the distinction between a *focus on forms* in instruction, the systematic attention to grammatical aspects of the target language (TL) in a traditional sense, and a *focus on form,* instruction that endeavors to contextualize attention to the formal properties of the language within communicative interactions. Evidence suggests that though a focus on form in instruction does not influence the route of acquisition (acquisition order), both rate (or the speed of acquisition) and ultimate level of linguistic attainment may benefit.

However, even as researchers like DeKeyser (1998) note that there is considerable agreement that "some kind of focus on form (FonF) is useful to some extent, for some forms, for some students, at some point in the learning process," there are clearly few, if any, definitive classroom-ready answers available to practitioners who have an interest in facilitating their students' TL skills development via a focus on form (42). In their edited volume on the topic, Doughty and Williams (1998) additionally point out that "there is considerable variation in how the term *focus on form* is understood and used" (5). The editors conclude that some attention to form-function relationships in instruction is desirable, but the precise nature of the form-focused instructional process is left undetermined.

Long's (1991:44) initial discussion, however, clearly describes what a focus on form is *not:* "The practice of isolating linguistic items, teaching and testing them one at a time" via techniques like display questions and repetition drills, which comprise a traditional focus on forms. Beyond this criterion, Long is careful to point out certain caveats regarding this design feature: (1) a focus on form serves as one of a range of relevant features that differentiate instructional program types, syllabus models, tasks or tests; (2) instructional environments that emphasize an overt focus on form may do so in a variety of ways, and to differing degrees; (3) learners will frequently fail to notice form in situations where instructors or materials encourage noticing, and vice versa; and (4) "Some degree of awareness of form and a focus on meaning may not be mutually exclusive on some tasks" (43–44).

As the roles assigned to input, intake, the integration of new knowledge, and output are examined in the context of instructed Spanish SLA, the motivating question of what constitutes an effective focus on form for purposes of facilitating real-world proficiency is also necessarily integrated. For as Garrett (1986:135) first noted, "Given the goal of communicative competence, neither the learning of meaningless form, nor the learning of arbitrarily imposed rules of correctness, nor the learning of the workings of a system will help the students. When grammar is so defined, the point has to be conceded: learning grammar does not promote communicative competence."[5]

The focus-on-form discussion in the literature can be viewed, in part, as a continuing search for a newly defined notion of grammar that is optimally aligned with the communicative, proficiency-based outcomes adopted by the field in the 1980s. Though major studies have often been conducted in the ESL context,[6] researchers in Spanish, in particular, have also contributed enormously to this discussion, most notably in the work of Terrell, who together with Krashen broke new ground in communicative teaching with the creation of the Natural Approach (Krashen and Terrell 1983). More recently, the work of VanPatten (1993, 1996, and 2002), VanPatten and Cadierno (1993), and others has led to greater insight into possible modes of form-focused instruction through the development and testing out of the Input Processing Model of SLA and Processing Instruction. Finally, investigations of the role of learner interaction in both Spanish and ESL (Pica 1992; Gass and Varonis 1994; Lantolf 1997; Donato 1994; Brooks and Donato 1994) have brought attention to the crucial role

Figure 10.1

A Model of Second Language Acquisition

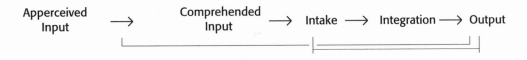

Source: Adapted from Gass and Selinker 2001:401.

played by communicative exchanges between students in the promotion of language acquisition in instructed settings. Following the overview of an integrated model of SLA and pertinent definitions, each of these contributions will be discussed in subsequent sections.

3.0 Second Language Acquisition: Integrated View and Key Definitions

Gass and Selinker (2001) propose an integrated model of second language acquisition,[7] which effectively incorporates the primary variables that are investigated and discussed in the current literature, while proposing several additional processes through which these components connect as acquisition takes place (see fig. 10.1). Figure 10.1 places *input,* or a body of second language data to which learners are exposed, at the starting point of the acquisition process. In this model, *apperceived input,* where apperception is defined as "the process of understanding by which newly observed qualities of an object are related to past experiences" (2001:400), is established as a kind of priming device for the subsequent analysis of data as *comprehended input.* By virtue of frequency in the input, prior knowledge, or experience, the learner may notice a form as apperceived input due to its particular features (400–402). As differentiated from apperceived input, *comprehended input* goes a step beyond noticing, to analyzing the form. The phonemic quality of stress as a marker of past time in Spanish (*hablo* "I speak" versus *habló* "he spoke"), for example, may be noticed (apperceived input) as being important by virtue of its frequency in the input and distinguishing acoustic features. At the level of comprehended input, however, the learner may analyze the input, hear the post-stem stress, and associate it with particular meaning, that is, past time.

Corder (1967) differentiates input from *intake,* which is defined as a subset of input to which the learner attends, and may therefore use for acquisition. In contrast, Gass and Selinker (2001:406) refer to intake as "the process of assimilating linguistic material" and "the mental activity that mediates between input and [learner] grammars." To the extent that input alone does not directly contribute to grammar formation, then, "input and intake refer to two fundamentally different phenomena" (406). The authors suggest that several key modes of learner-internal processing of second language rules, including hypothesis formation, hypothesis testing, hypothesis rejection, hypothesis modification, and hypothesis confirmation, occur at the level of intake.

Integration in the Gass and Selinker model may result from intake in situations where development of the second language grammar takes place. According to their view, hypothesis confirmation or rejection during intake results in integration, whereas input that is not completely understood, analyzed, or processed is not integrated and may be placed in *storage* for later use.[8] In situations where information contained in the input has already been incorporated into learner grammar, it may serve the important purpose of *rule strengthening* or *hypothesis reconfirmation.* Here, the authors suggest that "part of becoming a fluent speaker of a second language involves the automatic retrieval of information from one's knowledge base. The knowledge base is developed through practice or repeated exposures to exemplars" (407–8).

Like Swain (1985, 1993, 1995), Gass and Selinker assign a causal role to *output,* or learner production of the second language, in SLA as they argue that "the output component represents more than the product of language knowledge; it is an active part of the entire learning process" (410). This recursive model demonstrates how output actually feeds into the development of other components in the model, such as intake and comprehended input. For example, the model demonstrates how output provides the learner with essential opportunities to test out hypotheses in their developing grammar systems, which, coupled with feedback, may link output with intake in SLA processes (see fig. 10.1). In addition, output production is thought to force the learner to engage in an analysis of the formal properties of the second language system that extends beyond semantics (i.e., getting the gist) to the level of morphosyntax (i.e., noticing and internalizing the grammar). Figure 10.1 demonstrates how this function of output in SLA may link opportunities for learner production with comprehended input.

This integrated model will serve as an organizational framework in the sections that follow. The discussion will flow chronologically and will emphasize the strategies that have been most widely popularized via broad-based instructional materials publication in Spanish, with attention to techniques that have been frequently utilized in classroom-based empirical studies of Spanish, ESL and other languages. In this overview, major models of SLA will be presented and referenced to the integrated Gass and Selinker model. In addition, reactions to these models—along with several clarifications regarding the assertions and counterassertions that have arisen in the literature—will be addressed.

4.0   Input and Output in the Spanish Foreign Language Classroom

If SLA researchers categorically agree on anything, it is the fact that input is a necessary ingredient in successful acquisition (cf. Larsen-Freeman and Long 1991; Gass and Selinker 2001). It can be argued that one of Krashen's principal contributions to the classroom with his Monitor Model is the attention he has brought to the importance of input in the acquisition process, and to the form and function of varieties of comprehensible input that seek to enhance learner comprehension via simplification (Hatch 1983; Wong Filmore 1985; Wing 1987; Frey 1988). Moreover, a review of important publications from the 1980s to the present reveals the considerable extent to which Krashen's ideas have influenced the field of instructed second language acquisition. Many researchers and theorists working in Spanish and ESL have debated or attempted to fine-tune or build on Krashen's original model. In addition, much-debated issues raised in his earlier works (e.g., Krashen 1982) are frequently used as an important point of reference in more current research (VanPatten 1993; Loschky

1994; Leow 1993; DeKeyser and Sokalski 1996; Swain and Lapkin 1995; Lee and Rodríguez 1997; Lee 1998).

Krashen's Monitor Model has also won great popularity, especially among Spanish practitioners, through its continued and widespread implementation via the Natural Approach.[9] To some extent, this popularity may result from the satisfying, if specious, answers it offers to many of the complex questions associated with the endeavor of language teaching, including the role of grammar instruction, the importance of input and use of the target language as the primary mode of instruction, error correction, and output production. For these reasons, the Monitor Model and Natural Approach are briefly reviewed below, along with several major reactions and critiques. In particular, the discussion that follows will focus on how the constructs of input and output have developed over time, from Krashen's notions up to the present discourse on noticing and a focus on form in instructed SLA.

4.1 The Natural Approach and Monitor Model: An Overview

Facing a classroom process void created by the move away from audiolingual drilling, and a growing dissatisfaction with the grammar-based cognitive code method,[10] Tracy Terrell resorted to a modified form of the Direct Method to teach a first-year Dutch course at the university level. The resulting paper (Terrell 1977) initiated a movement in foreign language teaching, particularly in Spanish, that continues to influence the field in profound ways more than twenty years later. Underlying Terrell's Natural Approach is an attempt to reexamine the principal objective of instructed second language acquisition. Communicative competence in a second language, according to Terrell, "mean(s) that a student can understand the essential points of what a native speaker says to him in a real communicative situation and can respond in such a way that the native speaker interprets the response with little or no effort and without errors that are so distracting that they interfere drastically with communication" (1977:326). Reacting against the renewed "cognitive" interest in rule instruction and systematic mastery of the TL grammar, Terrell redefines the goal of elementary language instruction according to his definition of communicative competence, and argues that the field must lower standards for structural accuracy in production as expectations for the acquisition of communicative competence are raised.

The Natural Approach is closely associated with the Monitor Model of second language acquisition and its five hypotheses[11] as developed by Krashen. This marriage of theory and practice is elaborated in Krashen and Terrell (1983), and serves as the basis for the elementary Spanish text and instructional materials published as *Dos mundos: A communicative approach* (1986, 1990, 1994, 1998, 2001). As implied by its name, this approach holds that second languages are acquired "naturally," given sufficient exposure to language input over time. Key to this theory of SLA is that input be both comprehensible and of an appropriately challenging level, aligned with the level of an individual (i), but slightly more advanced ($+1$). Input must also be made available to the learner in a low-anxiety environment, or under conditions of a low affective filter. An important point of criticism of the Monitor Model has been the untestability of many of the constructs associated with its hypotheses (e.g., the acquisition/learning distinction, $i + 1$). The general lack of empirical research regarding both the model and the approach is due in large part to the untestable nature of these hypotheses. An overview of several major critiques of the Monitor Model will follow in sections 5.0, 6.0, and 7.0.

4.2   Input and Output in the Natural Approach

Perhaps the most distinguishing feature of the Natural Approach is its emphasis on the provision of copious comprehensible input in a positive affect environment. In the *Instructor's manual to accompany Dos Mundos,* Terrell et al. (1994) justify an emphasis on the development of comprehension skills via input and a corresponding de-emphasis of output at beginning levels of instruction, claiming both that "[the students'] anxiety levels will be lower, and their comprehension of spoken Spanish will develop faster" (84). Terrell (1991:52) additionally notes that "the major implication of [Krashen's] 'input model' is that learners' output is supposedly based directly on the input they process and store," a notion that runs contrary to assertions regarding output made by Swain (1985, 1995, 1998), Gass and Selinker (2001), and others. With regard to oral output and learner production in general, Krashen and Terrell (1983) initially identify two pertinent Natural Approach principles:

1. Comprehension precedes production. The approach provides for a *silent period,* lasting "from a few hours to several months" in which learners may elect to completely refrain from producing the TL.

2. Production emerges in stages. Natural Approach materials are designed and sequenced with these stages in mind such that initial activities, those of the *silent/pre-speech period* (Stage 1), generally require no verbal response, or a simple yes/no answer. *Early production* (Stage 2) activities call for single word responses, or a forced choice option. *Speech emergence* (Stage 3) activities increasingly require combination responses of two or more words, through phrases, sentences, toward the ultimate goal of "more complex discourse" (1983:20–21).

As a result, classroom formats associated with the Natural Approach emphasize the provision of comprehensible input that is both nonthreatening and potentially interesting to the learner. Narration series and other drawings, comprehension signaling tasks, Total Physical Response (TPR) activities, personal interviews, and pedagogically modified readings and listening passages comprise the majority of instructional materials, all geared toward facilitating the provision (by the instructor) of personally relevant, comprehensible input that will promote acquisition.

4.3   Focus on Form in the Natural Approach: An Expanded Role for Explicit Grammar Instruction

Terrell's (1977) original position on the role of traditional grammar instruction, including deductive rule explanation, form-focused practice and error correction, was that it was useful solely for facilitating learning, and that it should be well planned and highly structured for out-of-class study. As a result, Natural Approach pedagogical grammar explanations and associated exercises are appended at the end of each chapter, clearly set apart from the oral (acquisition-oriented) activities to which they are referenced.

However, this position is later modified by Terrell (1991:53), where "explicit grammar instruction" (EGI) is loosely defined as "the use of instructional strategies to draw the students' attention to or focus on form and/or structure." Here, Terrell diverges from the Monitor Model as he defines three additional roles for EGI, including its utility (1) as an "advance organizer" that facilitates comprehension and segmenting of the input; (2) as a "meaning-form focuser" that helps the learner connect morphologically complex forms with their semantic meaning; and (3) as a provider of forms for monitoring, which may serve as added input for the learner to the extent that these are produced in output (58). This modified stance combines well with the Gass and Selinker model, where EGI may be viewed as a means of facilitating both the "prior experience" that the authors suggest enables apperception, and the required level of analysis that constitutes comprehended input via the association of meaning and form. In revising his position, Terrell also suggests that output may serve a causal function in SLA, to the extent that the role of production in SLA is expanded to incorporate its utility as a viable source of additional, auto-input.

5.0   An Expanded Role for Practice

McLaughlin (1978, 1987, 1990) objected to Krashen's distinction between acquisition and learning, pointing out that "arguments on either side [of acquired vs. learned knowledge] depend on subjective, introspective and anecdotal evidence" (1978:318). As an alternative, McLaughlin posited a model built on the distinction between *controlled* and *automatic* processes, with roots in principles of cognitive psychology. An automatic process can be defined as any mental operation that occurs without the need for conscious initiation. Perhaps the most cited illustration of automatization is that of learning to drive. Initially, the learner is hesitant, carrying out procedures as if he or she were acting with regard to a mental checklist. Such hesitation is characteristic of controlled processes, which in the initial stages of learning "will be adopted and used to perform accurately though slowly" (1978:319). As the procedures are performed repeatedly (practiced), however, the operation becomes more fluent or *automatic* in nature.

McLaughlin's Information Processing Model suggests that in L2 acquisition, "controlled processes lay down the stepping stones for automatic processing as the learner moves to more and more difficult levels" (319). These initial controlled processes result in output characterized by slow speech, delayed reaction times to linguistic stimuli, and false starts. However, "as the situation becomes more familiar, always requiring the same sequence of processing operations, automatic processes will develop, attention demands will be eased, and other controlled operations can be carried out in parallel with automatic processes as performance improves" (1978:319).

Cognitive processing models make no distinction between language acquisition and the acquisition of any other skill. Within this paradigm, language learning is considered much like learning to type or play piano inasmuch as these models do not recognize the function of any specialized language acquisition device in the brain. Similar to learning any complex skill, acquiring a second language requires the mastery of both *high-order tasks* and *low-order subtasks,* the former being defined by McLaughlin as creative expression and topic choice, and the latter as appropriate use of lexicon and morphosyntactic inventory (1987:135).

Information Processing models view the teaching of language as providing the student with the opportunity to automatize language skills through practice. Gatbonton and Segalowitz (1988) define creative automatization as "placing students in settings where they repetitively desire to use target utterances as appropriate responses in genuine communicative situations" (476). Practice toward automatized language use involves placing students in linguistic situations, and consequently providing the opportunity for a sequence of processing operations to be performed until they become familiar to the learner. While practice according to processing models does involve repetition and stimulus-response sequences, it differs from the audiolingual notion of practice in its emphasis on meaningful, creative language use.

6.0 An Expanded Role for Output as a Focus on Form

In the late 1980s, scholars began to turn their attention toward output in SLA research. Chaudron (1988) suggested that the limited findings regarding the influence of production on learning outcomes might be a result of the failure of researchers to account for the *quality* of student output (as opposed to the impact of quantity), in addition to faulty research design. Similarly, Crookes (1991) noted that studies of second language comprehension greatly outnumbered those of production, reporting that "neglect of second language production is likely to continue unless there is a steady pressure to assert its importance and to make the somewhat scattered findings generally accessible" (114).

A primary researcher and proponent of output, Swain (1985, 1993, 1995, 1998; Swain and Lapkin 1995) develops a formalized version of the Output Hypothesis as an addition (rather than an alternative) to Krashen's Input Hypothesis. In proposing her Output Hypothesis, Swain agrees that input is an essential element in successful SLA, but she goes on to make a compelling case for the role of comprehensible output as another important causal variable. She finds that input fails to account for certain features of French immersion students' second language proficiencies, and that although comprehensible input is necessary for acquisition to occur, it is not sufficient to ensure that the outcome will be native-like performance. Her observations lead her to suggest that in addition to exposure to comprehensible input, learners need to engage in the production of comprehensible output in order to attain native levels of accuracy. Considering learner production in isolation from input, Swain (1985:248–49) points to three basic roles of comprehensible output in SLA:

1. Output provides the opportunity for meaningful (contextualized) use of one's linguistic resources in the process of negotiating meaning. Especially valuable is the "pushed language use" resulting from negative input arising in situations of communication breakdown. (Pushed language use requires the learner to find alternative means of expressing the desired message.)

2. Output is useful in that it provides the learner with opportunities to test out linguistic hypotheses to see if they work.

3. Production "may force the learner to move from semantic processing to syntactic processing." Learners can comprehend L2 messages without syntactic analysis of the

input that they contain. Production acts as a trigger that forces attention to the linguistic means of expression.

Swain (1993:160–61) discusses the pedagogical implications of her Output Hypothesis and cites first the obvious "necessity of providing learners with considerable in-class opportunities for speaking and writing." She adds, however, that "just speaking and writing are not enough. Learners must be pushed to make use of their resources; they need to have their linguistic abilities stretched to their fullest; they need to reflect on their output and consider ways of modifying it to enhance comprehensibility, appropriateness and accuracy."

Grove (1999) explores in detail the ways in which Swain's notion of *pushed output* translates into an output-centered focus on form in the context of a first-year Spanish course. Contrary to the specifications of the Natural Approach, an output-centered approach to teaching emphasizes the necessity for building appropriate, meaningful opportunities for production into instruction from the start. Coupled with feedback, this emphasis on production represents a contextualized focus on form supported by raised expectations for progress in proficiency development. Through placing increased output demands on learners in the context of communicative interactions, learners are required to notice the formal properties of the language they produce, to test linguistic hypotheses, and to reformulate their output in the direction of the target norm in situations where errors may occur.

In the Gass and Selinker (2001) model, a process is proposed whereby the learner goes from noticing a form in the input (apperceived input), to analysis of the form (comprehended input), to integration of the form into the developing grammar (intake). In this analysis, output has been identified as a way to bring about desirable noticing among learners. The result is a nonlinear, recursive SLA model in which output is viewed as an integral part of the process, rather than as solely product of successful acquisition. Similarly, Swain (1995, 1998) suggests that production has a consciousness-raising effect, which focuses learners on "gaps" or problems in the ways they conceptualize the L2 system. She posits several levels of noticing, where "learners may simply notice a form in the target language due to frequency or salience of the features themselves. Or as proposed by Schmidt and Frota (1986) in their "notice the gap principle," learners may notice "not only the target language form itself but also that it is different from their own interlanguage" (66). Swain and Lapkin (1995) address this question, and demonstrate how output production can effectively get learners to notice these gaps and advance from a mode of semantic to syntactic processing, that is, to the point of making a consideration of the grammatical form of their output.

Finally, Swain and Lapkin (1995) point to a metalinguistic function of output, defined as certain interactive production tasks—i.e., think-aloud protocols or private speech—which induce learners to reflect about the language they use such that the L2 becomes not only the tool, but also the object of linguistic construction. Lantolf (1997) also refers to *language play* in the context of L2 Spanish acquisition, which constitutes linguistic experimentation on the part of learners as they are engaged in acquisition processes. This function of learner output and interaction is consonant with current constructivist theories of learning, as reviewed later in the chapter (section 9.0) with studies relating to interaction and SLA.

7.0   An Expanded Notion of Input: The Input Flood as a Focus on Form

The notion of comprehensible input and the facilitation of intake have been among the most frequently debated issues arising in response to the Monitor Model (e.g., Gregg 1984; Higgs 1985; White 1987; White et al. 1991; Trahey and White 1993; Leow 1993). Gass and Selinker (2001:404) are careful to differentiate their notion of *comprehended input* from that of Krashen's *comprehensible input* to the extent that "comprehensible input is controlled by the person providing input . . . whereas comprehended input is learner controlled; that is, it is the learner who is or who is not doing 'work' to understand . . . and [who] ultimately controls intake." In addition, they argue that the dichotomous aspect of Krashen's construct is misleading, since comprehension may take place at various levels, most typically at the semantic level.

White (1987) argues for a "tightening up" of Krashen's notion of input.[12] She cites evidence to demonstrate a need for *negative input* (or information regarding how the second language does *not* function) in situations where learners operate with erroneous hypotheses about the target system, which positive evidence alone (in the form of comprehensible input) cannot disprove. For example, native speakers of English who acquire Spanish as a second language would require negative evidence to notice that insertion of the nominative (subject) pronoun, while permissible, is not compulsory in the L2, as is the case in the L1.[13]

With regard to positive and negative evidence as input, Trahey and White (1993) investigate the acquisition of adverb placement by fifty-four French-speaking ESL students. Subjects were exposed to a two-week *input flood* designed to make a selected form (adverbs) salient through enhanced frequency in the input. Comprising stories, games, and exercises as positive evidence, the input flood was introduced to learners over a two-week period without negative evidence. The study finds that although positive L2 input did affect subjects' interlanguage, "this input was not sufficient to drive out forms that are permitted in the L1 but not in the L2" (201). These findings support the need for negative evidence, or information about what is *not* grammatical, in cases where learner interlanguage contains a rule that is more general than the rule of the target language.

White and Evans (1998) also integrate a focus on form into an ESL course via an input flood technique as they investigate two levels of explicitness in focus in the teaching and acquisition of English participial adjectives (he is interest*ed*/interest*ing*) and passive constructions with thirty-three learners. Experimental group 1 (flood) was exposed to an input flood "in the form of artificially increased incidence of the form in focus," with no explicit rules or corrective feedback (141). The input flood materials utilized in the study included a text that was modified to contain three times the original number of participial adjectives, and a survey that was similarly loaded with questions and tasks in the passive voice. Experimental group 2 (instructed) was exposed to the same input flood, with an additional integration of both explicit instruction and corrective feedback. A control group was also established for purposes of comparison.

The pretest/posttest design found differing results across several tasks, which included grammaticality judgments (GJ), sentence completions (SC), and picture-driven narratives. In the case of participial adjectives, the instructed group significantly outperformed both the flood and control groups on the GJ and SC tasks. The flood-group score outcomes were slightly higher than those of the control group, but these differences were not significant. Passive voice results demonstrated a more frequent, though not necessarily accurate, use of the form by both instructed and flood subjects. In addition, both the instructed and flood groups significantly outperformed their control counterparts on this sentence completion task. White and Evans (1998) interpret these results as an indication that "a focus on form is indeed useful and should be integrated into communicative curricula" (155). They caution, however, that learner readiness, including an awareness of form emergence stages, as well as the nature of the form itself must be considered by a teacher in determining appropriate instructional practice.

8.0   Apperceived Input/Noticing: Input Enhancement as a Focus on Form

Sharwood Smith (1991) first refers to a learner external (instructional) process as *consciousness raising* (CR),[14] or "a deliberate focus on the formal properties of language with a view to facilitating the development of L2 knowledge" (118). He suggests that such a focus on form may be implemented to varying degrees along two dimensions: *elaboration* and *explicitness*. CR activities that are *less elaborate* are brief, lasting only a few seconds (i.e., a short signal to indicate a learner error, a single spontaneous explanation of an error). Alternately, CR activities that are *more elaborate* are programmed into a learning sequence, such as a short signal used repeatedly to indicate the same error or a recurring explanation format used throughout a semester sequence. The second dimension, that of *explicitness,* involves "the sophistication and detail of the consciousness raising process" (119). Facial expressions or simple visual cues characterize the low end of this dimension, whereas complex grammar rules are considered more highly explicit. These dimensions are useful for purposes of characterizing options for implementing a focus on form in language instruction by way of alternate modes of feedback. The term *input enhancement* is later introduced by Sharwood Smith (1993) as preferable to consciousness-raising, in that CR focuses on the observable manipulation of input by teachers without accounting for functions of learner-internal processes of attention. Input enhancement reveals how instructors "enhance" certain features in their input. According to Sharwood Smith, "What is desired is not so much noticing the signal as acting on it, that is, learning something from it" (1991:121).

White (1998) investigated input enhancement in the context of ESL instruction and acquisition of third person singular possessive determiners (PDs) *his* and *her* by eighty-six francophone learners. In this study, input enhancement is operationalized via *typographical enhancement,* including the enlargement, boldfacing, and/or italicizing of pertinent forms as they occur naturally in a written text:

> Once upon a time there was a king. *He* had a beautiful young daughter. For *her* birthday, the king gave *her* a golden ball that *she* played with every day (White 1998:107).

The author notes that "typographical enhancement, proposed by Sharwood Smith (1981, 1991) and investigated by Doughty (1988, 1991), is considered to be the 'visual equivalent of stress and emphasis' in spoken input" (Doughty 1988:87–88; cited in White 1998:91). Three groups of learners participated in the study under the conditions of *Enhanced plus* (E+), where a typographically enhanced input flood was coupled with extensive reading and listening activities, *Enhanced* (E), in which learners were exposed to a typographically enhanced input flood alone, and *Unenhanced* (U), where an input flood without typographical enhancement was utilized. Data were collected through a pre/post-picture description task, which was administered three times: both immediately before and after a two-week treatment period, and again six weeks later as a delayed posttest.

The findings demonstrate that learners across groups profited from instruction in terms of their ability to more frequently and accurately produce *his* and *her* in the description task. White notes, however, that "although accuracy ratios overall followed the predicted order, that is, Group E+ >> Group E >> Group U, the within-group variance [among learners in the same group] canceled out most of the predicted between-group effects at the two posttests" (101). She goes on to note that while typographical enhancement of selected input features may positively influence the rate of acquisition, "implicit FonF may not be adequate in cases involving L1–L2 contrasts," as in the case of PDs in French and English (106). It is suggested that in these situations of contrast, a more explicit mode of instruction, combined with input enhancement techniques, may be required to effectively promote linguistic development that results from noticing and knowledge integration.

On the other hand, Leow (2001) notes that not all studies of input enhancement have found positive results for this type of external textual manipulation For instance, Leow (1997) studied the effects of input enhancement on adult Spanish L2 learners' reading comprehension and intake. Fourteen college-level second-semester students of Spanish were exposed to texts of different lengths with and without enhancement and then participated in comprehension and a multiple-choice recognition task. A significant effect on reading comprehension (but not on intake) was found for text length. However, external manipulation of the text (enhancement) showed no significant effects on comprehension or intake.

In order to address the methodological shortcomings of prior research on the effects of enhanced written input (lack of "concurrent data on learners' attentional processes while interacting with the L2 input" [2001:497]) Leow used both *online* (concurrent, during exposure) and *offline* (after exposure) data collection procedures to study this phenomenon. Think-aloud (online) protocols were gathered from thirty-eight college-level learners of Spanish reading enhanced and unenhanced texts. The results of their performance on immediate and delayed recognition and production tasks showed no significant benefits of enhanced over unenhanced written input for readers' intake or comprehension, or for the amount of noticing of Spanish formal command forms that participants reported.

In the Gass and Selinker model, knowledge integration refers to the process of moving from apperceived and comprehended input to intake. Input enhancement may therefore be viewed as a means of integrating a focus on form in instruction by deliberately highlighting crucial input features toward increasing their saliency for eventual intake by the learner. Processing Instruction, proposed by VanPatten (1993 and elsewhere), represents a widely researched possibility in this regard and will be reviewed in the following section as intake and the integration of new knowledge in SLA are addressed.

9.0   Intake and Knowledge Integration: Psycholinguistic Representations

The psycholinguistic view of adult learners as "limited capacity processors" of information serves as the context in which Leow (1993, 1995, 1997, 1998) investigates the relationship among attention, awareness, intake and exposure to simplified input in instructed Spanish SLA.[15] According to this perspective, the relative complexity of input interacts in crucial ways with learner attention resources, and affects their ability to notice competing stimuli in the input without a cognitive overload. Proponents of simplification argue that exposure to simplified input enables greater comprehension and noticing. To the extent that learners are not overloaded with complicated input, they are free to attend to more forms and structures, a condition that is thought to affect intake positively. A counterassertion suggests that although simplified input may facilitate greater comprehension of the communicative content of input, it does not necessarily function to draw learner attention to formal properties of the language, that is, does not facilitate intake via enhanced noticing.

Leow (1993) addressed the effects of simplification in relation to two variables: type of linguistic form (present perfect or present subjunctive) and learner experience (one or four semesters of study) in the context of a university-level Spanish program. Subjects (N = 137) in two groups were exposed to either simplified or unsimplified input texts, which comprised modified authentic readings selected for their use of the forms in question and reduced in length by the researcher. Other modifications included the conversion of verb forms to increase their frequency in the texts, a conjoining of sentences to ensure that unsimplified texts required more complex processing among learners in that group. The findings suggest that "simplification does not appear to have a facilitating effect on learners' intake of linguistic items contained in the input" (345). In addition, more advanced learners (fourth semester) demonstrated a superior ability to manipulate their attentional resources "in order to take in significantly more linguistic items in written input than learners with less language experience" (345). Leow proposes that these findings provide empirical support for the use of unedited authentic readings in the Spanish (FL) classroom.

9.1   Input Processing and Processing Instruction: An Overview

VanPatten (1993, 1996, 2002) has developed a psycholinguistic model of SLA that addresses the incorporation of new knowledge into the developing system. In its initial presentation, VanPatten's (1993) Input Processing (IP) model of second language acquisition suggests that the essential key to accessing and modifying learner grammar—to facilitating developmental change—lies in focusing learner attention on certain salient structural features of input data as it becomes intake. The transition from stage I to stage II in figure 10.2 represents input processing, or the conversion of input to intake, where intake is defined as "that subset of the input that is comprehended and attended to in some way." A second set of processes

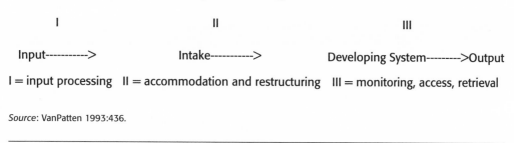

Figure 10.2
Input Processing Model

I   II   III

Input---------->   Intake---------->   Developing System--------->Output

I = input processing   II = accommodation and restructuring   III = monitoring, access, retrieval

Source: VanPatten 1993:436.

(II), called accommodation and restructuring, "are those that mediate the incorporation of intake into the developing system." A final set of processes (III) "involves making use of the developing system to create output" (436). Whereas "traditional instruction" has focused on stage III in this process, with instruction involving explanation plus some form of output practice, VanPatten proposes Processing Instruction (PI) as a mode of introducing IP principles to instructional practice, where the aim is to "direct learners' attention to relevant features of grammar in the input and to encourage form-meaning mappings that in turn result in better intake" (1993:438). The *structured input activity* draws learner attention to formal properties of input data as it becomes intake (I in fig. 10.2) and requires the noticing and discrimination of forms as a means of bringing a focus on form to the classroom.

VanPatten and Cadierno (1993) conducted the first empirically based study of the effects of PI versus traditional instruction (TI) on the acquisition of Spanish clitic direct object pronouns. Their design comprises a pretest/posttest classroom-based investigation in which they compare sentence-level comprehension and production outcomes of 129 university Spanish learners instructed via input processing and "traditional instruction," defined here as deductive rule explanation plus oral production practice involving an isolated morphosyntactic feature. The experimental instructors were given two instructional packets, PI and TI, for use during the two-day treatment implementation process.

Subjects in the PI group first received a deductive explanation regarding the grammatical concepts of subject and object and their accurate interpretation, "followed by explanations of important points to keep in mind about the positions of object pronouns in Spanish" (231). Explanation was followed by two types of PI, in which learners: (1) demonstrated if they had correctly assigned argument structure in a sample sentence, and (2) responded to the communicative content of a sample sentence in a personalized way to demonstrate whether they had accurately noticed and analyzed the form in question. In the traditional group, subjects also received explicit grammar instruction regarding the form and position of direct object pronouns in a sentence. This instruction emphasized linguistic form and content rather than strategies for their accurate interpretation. Grammar explanation was followed by oral and written practice activities that emphasized sentence-level use and manipulation of pertinent forms.

The primary research questions motivating this study relate to the relationship between the way subjects process input and the possible influence of this processing on their developing systems of competence. Posttest results on sentence level interpretation and production tasks reveal significant improvements for the PI group on both tasks, while traditional group subjects made significant gains on the production task alone. The authors interpret these results as support for the more limited utility of traditional instruction, including output practice, in the development of *learned,* rather than acquired, knowledge, and more fluent access to the developing system at the moment of performance. With regard to processing instruction, it is argued that "explicit grammar instruction should first seek to make changes in the developing system via focus on input and only afterward should instruction provide opportunities for developing productive abilities" (239). This position suggests that input processing leads to L2 acquisition, or the development of competence, while traditional instruction—including the production of output—results in learned knowledge and enhanced performance.

9.2 Input Processing: Recent Clarifications

VanPatten and Cadierno (1993) and input processing in general have initiated considerable debate in the literature. VanPatten (2002) cites several studies (Cadierno 1995; Cheng 1995[16]; Farley 2000[17]; Benati 2000) that have tested the extent to which the findings of VanPatten and Cadierno (1993) may be generalized to other structures (and languages), with positive results. Major counterarguments have focused on issues including the incompatibility of IP with predictions of skill acquisition theory (DeKeyser and Sokalski 1996), potential research design flaws (DeKeyser and Sokalski 1996; Salaberry 1997), theoretical inadequacies (Salaberry 1997), IP specifications for the role of output in SLA (Salaberry 1997; Grove 1999), and a failure to replicate the findings of VanPatten and Cadierno (DeKeyser and Sokalski 1996; Salaberry 1997; Collentine 1998).

    In response, VanPatten (1996, 2002) has issued clarifications of the IP model while both examining other researchers' efforts to replicate VanPatten and Cadierno (1993) and reexamining and providing support for the IP model and the initial study itself. Answering Salaberry (1997), Sanz and VanPatten (1998) clarify the intended scope of PI and the role that output plays in the input processing model. They emphasize that PI—as it has been developed by VanPatten and Cadierno (1993), Lee and VanPatten (1995), and VanPatten (1996)—is much less prescriptive than has been suggested, pointing out that the need for output-based practice has been addressed throughout the literature on input-processing and PI. According to Sanz and VanPatten, PI is most accurately viewed as "*an adjunct to* communicative language teaching and/or to comprehension-based approaches . . . [and] a type of focus on form that serves to enhance comprehension-based approaches (e.g., immersion, the Natural Approach)" (264).

    These points are reemphasized by VanPatten (1996, 2000, 2002), where he presents additional principles that pertain to IP. These include the crucial role of the working memory (and its limitations) in psycholinguistic models of SLA and the import of the communicative value of a form,[18] word order, and sentence position in determining which forms in the input are noticed by the learner during real-time comprehension, and which are likely to be overlooked or misinterpreted as a result of the application of one or more of the specified principles. PI is further defined as "a type of grammar instruction or focus on form derived from the insights of IP . . . [which] uses a certain type of input to push learners away from the non-optimal processing strategies [defined by the aforementioned principles]" (8).

With regard to debate over the utility of output in SLA, VanPatten (2002) notes that "a focus on IP in acquisition does not suggest there is no role for output . . . [which] may play a role as a focusing device that draws learners attention to something in the input as mismatches are noted and it may play a role in the development of both fluency and accuracy" (762). Specifying a function for output in SLA, he argues, "does not mean that input has any less of a role to play in acquisition" (762). Salaberry (1997) also addresses as questionable the debate of input vs. output by positing a more crucial role for interaction in SLA, and by minimizing the importance of the distinction between input and output processing as a platform for the construction of theory or pedagogical practice. He argues that "the need to engage in meaningful interaction—*more likely* to occur in natural settings and *less likely* so in academic settings—will lead the learner to engage in more active processing of L2 meaning and grammatical from. Hence *the distinction* between input and output processing is not consequential for language development, because *both processes* are involved in the development of form-meaning connections" (440).[19] The following section addresses this point through the integration of input and output into an overview of the two approaches to understanding the role of interaction in SLA. Associated studies of the ways in which interaction may affect language development are also reviewed.

10.0   Two Approaches to Understanding Interaction in Instructed SLA

Cooperative learning tasks, including interviews, information-gap tasks,[20] and situation role-plays as primary formats, have been widely implemented by language teaching practitioners since the mid-1980s as a means of placing their students at the center of the communicative teaching/learning endeavor. Long and Porter (1986) list several advantages that may be associated with the integration of cooperative formats into the language classroom. These include increased practice opportunities, improved quality of output, a more positive affective climate, and enhanced motivation among learners.

Long (1996) further emphasizes a crucial role for conversational interaction in his *interaction hypothesis,*[21] where he argues that "*negotiation for meaning,* and especially negotiation work that triggers *interactional adjustments* by the NS [native speaker] or more competent interlocutor, facilitates acquisition because it connects input, internal learner capacities, particularly selective attention, and output in productive ways" (451–52). According to this hypothesis, meaning negotiation in the context of interaction may serve the function of directing learner attention to gaps that exist between the developing linguistic system and the target-language reality. Gass and Selinker (2001:295) state that "learning may take place 'during' the interaction, or negotiation may be an initial step in learning; interaction may serve as a priming device, thereby representing the setting of the stage for learning rather than being a forum for actual learning."

Recent studies conducted on the effects of interaction on the acquisition of Spanish[22] include Ortega and Long (1997),[23] which explores the utility of implicit negative feedback in the acquisition of object topicalization and adverb placement among thirty undergraduate

Spanish students, an investigation of the development of turn-taking organization and discourse structure by Spanish immersion students (Lynch 1998),[24] and, most recently, a study of the relationship between interaction in the Spanish classroom and interlanguage development (Garcia and Asención 2001), reviewed below. Additional studies in ESL have focused on the effects of interaction on linguistic development, possible relationships between input enhancement strategies and enhanced comprehension during interaction, and the utility of interaction and associated modifications within native speaker and nonnative speaker dyads.

While interaction is globally viewed as an important variable in successful SLA, we can nevertheless distinguish between two developing lines of research in this area: (1) a linguistic approach, which emphasizes the analysis of formal modifications made by learners as they interact to overcome communicative difficulties; and (2) a sociocultural approach, which utilizes a Vygotskyan framework to understand cognitive development as a by-product of interaction as it occurs within a social context. Sections 10.1 and 10.2 review major studies conducted within these two frameworks, respectively.

10.1   Interaction as a Negotiation of Linguistic Form

The first of these approaches is deductively presented by Lightbown and Spada (1993; summarized by Lee 2000:5):

1. Interactional modification makes input comprehensible;
2. Comprehensible input promotes acquisition. Therefore,
3. Interactional modification promotes acquisition.

To the extent that the development of real-world proficiency has replaced linguistic analysis as the primary goal of instruction, group and pair work activities that promote the negotiation of personally relevant meaning among learners have become synonymous with effective pedagogy, based in large part on this reasoning. Pica et al. (1996:60) summarize this view of interaction as a negotiation of linguistic form by noting that "a growing body of evidence shows that participation in interaction can play an even broader and more theoretically important role in the learning process by assisting language learners in their need to obtain input and feedback that can serve as linguistic data for grammar building and to modify and adjust their output in ways that expand their current interlanguage capacity."

While attitudes in the field regarding negotiated interaction and cooperative work in the classroom tend to be positive, Doughty (1998:137) is careful to point out that "though these conditions seem favorable for language acquisition, it must be admitted that there is, as yet, no direct evidence that group work contributes to sustained interlanguage development." Nevertheless, the findings of several major studies conducted with ESL learners have contributed in significant ways to our understanding of the role-negotiated interaction in SLA, with some associated implications for classroom practice that may be useful in the Spanish (FL) context.

In their ESL study of native speaker (NS) and nonnative speaker (NNS) interactions, Gass and Varonis (1994) examined the potential lasting effects of input and interaction on learners' linguistic development. The authors contextualized this study with data from Gass and Varonis (1989), which demonstrated adjustments that are made as a result of NNS–NNS interactions. Nonnative learners were sent together as pairs into the field to tape record themselves completing a communicative task. The authors found that a predominance of modifications made as a result of NNS–NNS interactions (89 percent) were made in the direction of the target language norm. These findings support the notion that interactions between nonnative speakers may have a positive impact on accuracy in linguistic development.

With regard to the effects of NS–NNS interactions, Gass and Varonis (1994) examined conversations containing either modified or unmodified input[25] from sixteen dyads as they completed a direction-giving task involving the placement of objects on a picture board. The authors introduced the additional independent variable of interactive/noninteractive exchanges into the study by controlling subjects' use of requests for repetition, clarification, and comprehension checks in specified subgroups. Their findings indicate that in situations where native speakers and nonnative speakers interact, the conditions of modified input and interaction enhance nonnative comprehension on task performance. "Furthermore, the opportunity to *interact* when receiving directions in turn enables the [nonnative speaker] to provide better directions on a subsequent trial" (294). Whereas modified input increased nonnative speakers' comprehension of directions, however, the condition of unmodified input better enabled nonnative speakers to provide clearer directions in subsequent tasks. These results lend additional support to the efficacy of interaction in promoting both comprehension and oral production in instructed SLA.

Pica et al. (1996) also investigated ESL learner interactions with other learners as compared with interactions with native speakers. This study explored the extent to which the need for modified input, form-focused feedback and output modification were addressed in the conversational exchanges of five nonnative learner dyads across a series of communicative exchanges, including jigsaw and storytelling tasks. The findings suggest that while NNS dyads resulted in less modified input than learner interactions with native speakers, learner interactions with each other were fruitful in terms of the amount and type of form-focused feedback that was offered by signals of negotiation throughout the exchanges. In addition, subjects were found to produce modified output in qualitatively similar ways and amounts when interacting with either native speakers or fellow learners. In their discussion, the authors propose that "the results of the study suggest both caution and optimism toward learners' interaction in the L2 classroom" (80). With regard to classroom implications, the findings indicate that learners are less valuable to each other as sources of modified input. However, teachers are encouraged to consider learner interaction as potentially useful in terms of the feedback that learners may provide one another in the context of cooperative work.

10.2   Interaction as Collaboration within a Social Context

While negotiation of meaning has been defined in alternate ways in the literature, there is a consistent reference in the approaches outlined in section 10.1 to the prominence of linguistic adjustments. Interaction according to this view is studied via analysis of these modifications (phonological, morphosyntactic, discourse, and/or lexical) as they are made by two or more interlocutors in order to resolve a breakdown in communication, or to facilitate communication in some way.[26]

Other researchers (e.g., Aljaafreh and Lantolf 1994; Lantolf and Appel 1994; Donato 1994; Brooks, Donato, and McGlone 1997; DiCamilla and Antón 1997; Buckwalter 2001) have approached the role of interaction in SLA within a Vygotskyan framework, which emphasizes the influence of social context and collaboration on linguistic and cognitive development. Proponents of this position conduct research that is tied to Vygotsky's (1978, 1986) notion that learning and cognitive development are inherently linked, and that the development of cognition is an outcome of social interaction. According to this model, learners approach the completion of a task with two levels of development: the *actual developmental level,* which comprises the skills and information that learners already control, and the *potential developmental level,* which symbolizes a yet unrealized outcome. By virtue of iterative problem solving via collaboration with a more knowledgeable or capable guide, the learner is thought to develop as the present potential developmental level becomes the next level of actual development. The cognitive distance between these two levels is where development occurs, and is referred to as the *zone of proximal development* (ZPD). *Scaffolding* constitutes the linguistic and social support employed by the more knowledgeable or capable guide—i.e., a peer or teacher—that is structured to facilitate the learner's development through the ZPD to the point where he or she may self-regulate during task performance.

DiCamilla and Antón (1997) utilized a Vygotskyan framework as they investigated the function of repetition among ten adult learners of Spanish as they were collaboratively engaged in a writing assignment. Through an analysis of repetition in learner discourse, the authors sought to demonstrate that "repetition is an important means by which students construct and hold in place scaffolded help while achieving and maintaining intersubjectivity"[27] (614). The data from this study, reported in figure 10.3, comprise the second in a series of six episodes used by the authors to illustrate the role of repetition in the collective construction of a scaffold by language learners. In their analysis of these data, the authors point to the repetition of various accurate and inaccurate forms of the verb *almorzar,* which ultimately leads to the production of desired *almorzamos* ("we eat lunch") form in line 13. Whereas the learners might have been satisfied with the less complex, but accurate *comemos* ("we eat") form produced in line 3, R uses repetition of the erroneous form from line 2 to continue the collaboration. According to the analysis, a repetition of the accurate (but undesired) *almuerzo* ("I eat lunch") form in line 11 "seems to provide the necessary scaffolding to solve the problem of how to say 'we eat lunch' (in line 13)" (621). The authors conclude from this evidence that repetition may be viewed as a feature of semiotic mediation that plays a key, distributive role in scaffolded instruction; by spreading the scaffolding support throughout the interactive event, repetition may "hold the scaffold in place, as it were, creating a cognitive space in which to work (e.g., think, hypothesize, evaluate), and from which to build (i.e., generate more language)" (627–28).

Brooks and Donato (1994) also utilize this framework as they investigate the discourse of eight dyads of secondary-level Spanish learners during an information-gap task. Five "examples" of learner interactions are presented and analyzed to demonstrate the complex ways in which speaking facilitates learning as learners make sense of the task (object regulation), co-construct a shared social reality (shared orientation), and establish individual or cooperative goals for task completion (goal formation). The authors are careful to point

Figure 10.3
Repitition and the Collective Construction of a Scaffold

1. R: Um . . . How do you say "lunch"?

2. T: almuer . . . almuer . . . zamos . . . we eat lunch.

   ([False start] *we have lunch* [incorrect form] . . . *we eat lunch.*)

3. R: oh . . . comemos . . . oh.

   (Oh . . . we eat . . . oh)

4. T: What do you want to say?

5. R: Almuerzos?

   (Lunch? [plural])

6. T: We eat lunch . . . almuer . . . zamos.

   (We eat lunch . . . we eat lunch [incorrect form])

7. R: It's not . . . it's a-l-m-u-r?

8. T: Yeah.

9. R: Now you don't change the "zamos" to "ue" though?

10. T: Right, it's almuer . . . almuerzar.

    (Right . . . it's [false start] *to have lunch)*

11. R: How do you say "almuerzo"? A-l-m-u-e-r-z-o?

    (How do you say "I have lunch"? [spelling])

12. T: Yeah . . . that's "I eat lunch."

13. R: How do you say we . . . almor . . . it's "almorzamos."

    (How do you say . . . [modifying spelling] . . . *it's "We have lunch.")*

14. T: Oh.

15. R: It's "o" to "ue" remember? So we keep it to the "o." Make sense?

16. T: OK. You're so smart.

Source: DiCamilla and Antón 1997:620.

out that the purpose of their analysis diverges in important ways from prior analyses, which tended to focus on "the codification and quantification of discourse patterns that, in the end, remove us from the very material of interest" (265). Rather, Brooks and Donato examine how learner interaction during the task completion "collaboratively influences and builds a shared social reality between the participants" (265). The authors conclude from their analyses that learner interaction involves much more than the encoding and decoding of a message, as research on interaction conducted outside of a sociocultural framework suggests. The observable *metatalk,* often produced in the L1 by novice-level learners, is crucial to the learning process, and "is in fact mediating the participants' control over the language and procedures of the task, each other, and ultimately the self" (271).

Brooks, Donato, and McGlone (1997) extended this research on socioculturally defined aspects of learners' language use through recording and analyzing the interactions of three dyads of third-semester university Spanish learners as they completed five similar jigsaw tasks over a period of approximately 1.5 weeks. More specifically, the authors looked for increases, decreases, or maintenance trends across five administrations of the tasks, with regard to learners' use of the L1, use of *metatalk* (talk about their own talk), use of *metacognitive speech* (talk about task completion), and use of whispering (subvocalized, task-related speech). Discourse analyses of the recorded exchanges revealed how the subjects' use of both Spanish and English during a collaborative task completion constitutes an effort by the learner to develop increased awareness and control of language. According to the authors, "metatalk should not be understood as outside the requirements of the specific speaking task or as off-task behavior as some teachers might characterize it" (529). This constitutes a major point of the study, according to the authors, to the extent that a trend in the data indicates that metatalk—in both target language and the L1—is produced with less frequency by learners over time as they acquire language and become more skilled at completing a task. The authors suggest that a more in-depth understanding by teachers of the language that learners produce during problem-solving tasks is required, so that opportunities for saying "it" right are not inadvertently prevented from entering in the discourse.

10.3   Interaction: An Integrated View

An investigation by Garcia and Asención (2001) attempts to build on prior research in both of these camps by not only quantifying the extent to which interaction has a positive effect on interlanguage development, but also through qualifying via data analysis the precise features of interaction that may account for its effectiveness in SLA. This study of thirty-nine university-level students enrolled in a first-year Spanish course employed a pretest-posttest design to test the effects of small group interaction on both listening comprehension of a narrative text in the present tense, and on the subjects' ability to reconstruct this text using notes. The findings indicate a significant effect for interaction on the listening-comprehension outcomes, with the experimental (interaction) subjects outperforming their control counterparts on a multiple-choice comprehension task.

With regard to the nature of the language utilized by the interaction group, Garcia and Asención confirm the findings of Swain and Lapkin as they note that learners used language "to co-construct the language they need to express the meaning they want and to co-construct knowledge about language" (394). Confirmation and code switching were also observed as interactive strategies, with switches from English to Spanish occurring primarily within verb phrases. The authors hypothesize that these switches may comprise "a strategy for automatizing new verb forms" (394).

To summarize, studies that emphasize interaction as a negotiation of linguistic form find that though learners may be somewhat limited in terms of the quality of input they provide one another, the feedback they offer in the context of interaction is of value to the acquisition process. In addition, NNS–NNS interactions seem to promote linguistic development toward greater accuracy. While modified input leads to greater comprehension, unmodified input and the opportunity to negotiate meaning during interactions lead to enhanced production capabilities.

Research informed by a view of interaction as social collaboration demonstrates how learners provide linguistic support to each other as they interact to meet shared goals. Repetition is revealed as an important tool for constructing and maintaining supportive scaffolding as learning occurs. The crucial role of metatalk in both the first and second languages is additionally emphasized as being relevant and essential to effective performance during small group task completions in instructed environments.

To the extent that primarily qualitative research regarding interaction has been conducted with smaller subject samples, the generalizability of results may be viewed as somewhat problematical. Nevertheless, the findings to date (e.g., Mayo and Pica 2000) generally support a positive role for interaction. Although it is viewed as being beneficial to learners, however, interaction alone is not thought to be a sufficient condition for SLA to occur. Future studies regarding the effects of classroom interaction on SLA processes may benefit from the implementation of a hybrid research design. The strengths of both qualitative and quantitative investigative frameworks may be combined in effective ways in order to answer classroom-specific questions related to interaction.

11.0 Conclusion

This chapter has attempted to illustrate how developing theoretical models and associated perspectives on the roles of input, intake, knowledge integration, output, and interaction in the field of Spanish language acquisition[28] have led to a significant potential growth in the implementation of empirically informed instructional practices. These movements continue to have a major impact on the primary variables of instruction as they occur in the classroom, including the optimal shape and content of a focus on form that supports acquisition and the development of real-world proficiency. In addition, much has been learned about the processes that facilitate linguistic and cognitive development in learners as they interact in increasingly learner-centered classrooms.

Current research leads us to reemphasize that quality input is essential for successful language acquisition to occur. Additional factors, including output production, positive evidence (input flood), input enhancement, negative evidence (corrective feedback), and negotiated interaction have been shown to facilitate a crucial *noticing* among learners. This noticing is thought to assist learners in the endeavor of successfully analyzing input data and recognizing erroneous hypotheses and potential gaps that may exist between the target language and their developing interlanguage systems. Output production and negotiated interaction, in particular, are increasingly viewed as essential variables in successful SLA, not only for their utility as "practice" toward more fluent access of forms for production, but also for their value in promoting noticing and in creating opportunities for the social collaboration that comprises learning.

With few exceptions, however, major Spanish textbooks and published instructional programs frequently make no significant effort to inform prescribed classroom practices with current SLA theory and research findings. In cases where principles of SLA do play a role in materials development, one theoretical model is often emphasized to the exclusion of others. Furthermore, many popular textbook activity formats continue to result in the systematic integration of curricula and classroom practices that are counter-prescribed by the research, i.e., the implementation of a systematic focus on forms via a traditional structural syllabus, strategies that marginalize or deemphasize the provision of TL input, and the continued prevalence of depersonalized, teacher-centered grammar explanation and drilling. As we enter the twenty-first century, we may safely conclude that the enormous disconnect between theoretically informed research and generalized classroom practice continues to pose a serious challenge for the field.

We currently have a clearer vision of functional proficiency as a desired outcome of instruction. Nevertheless, the field is still engaged in the process of gathering more information regarding the specifics of how to organize classroom procedures so that outcomes are maximized. State-of-the-science instructional approaches take into account the research that has informed major model builders. We must continue this line of research, especially the testing out of design features in Spanish classroom-based research, in order to increase our understanding of how to most effectively facilitate SLA in our classrooms. More crucially, the findings of this research must be effectively utilized on a broader scale as a resource for materials development, teacher training, instructional planning and testing.

ACKNOWLEDGMENTS

I would like to thank the editors and anonymous reviewers for their comments on earlier versions of this chapter. While the collective wisdom of outside readers was of considerable utility in negotiating a happy medium regarding a very broad topic, I must take responsibility for any gaps in the final product.

NOTES

1. Attention was paid to major studies using ESL or data from other languages in order to illustrate important issues chosen for discussion in this chapter.

2. See Lafayette (1996) and the National Standards in Foreign Language Education Project (1996). For a discussion of the Five Cs (Communication, Cultures, Connections, Comparisons, Communities) as they relate to classroom instruction, see Shrum and Glisan (2000). For information on the foreign language standards as applied to Spanish see National Standards in Foreign Language Education Project (1999) and Guntermann (2000).

3. While the *ACTFL Proficiency Guidelines* (1986, 1999) and the associated *ACTFL Oral Proficiency Interview* (OPI) are widely known and utilized in the field of world languages in-

struction and assessment, both have been the subject of considerable debate, especially with regard to the validity of the OPI. See Dandonoli and Henning (1990) and Johnson (2000, 2001) for a complete discussion.

4. Compare, for example, formats of grammar-based and oral activities in Terrell et al., *Dos mundos: A communicative approach,* with those of VanPatten et al., *¿Sabías que . . .? Beginning Spanish,* and Knorre et al., *Puntos de partida: An invitation to Spanish.*

5. The framework of communicative competence represents an expansion of Chomsky's original notion of linguistic competence, to include grammatical, sociolinguistic, discourse, and strategic competencies (Canale and Swain 1980; Canale 1983). Bachman (1990) integrates additional components that emphasize the organizational (grammatical and textual) and pragmatic (illocutionary and sociolinguistic) components of communicative competence. Bachman's model has recently been challenged by scholars working in an Interactional Competence Framework (see Johnson 2001 for a discussion of these issues.)

6. The issue of crucial environmental differences across instructed Spanish FL/SL, ESL, and EFL contexts must be considered as research findings are reviewed with an eye toward informing classroom process. Such issues will be addressed as they become relevant in this discussion.

7. For an additional review of classroom research related to SLA, see Lightbown (2001).

8. Malapropisms and misused formulaic utterances (such as *"¡Buena suerte!"* "Good luck!" for *"¡Buenos días!"* "Good morning!" as a greeting) comprise an essential phase in the novice-level learner's developing proficiency.

9. Instructional materials associated with the Natural Approach continue to lead the market in Spanish.

10. Growing out of detailed structuralist descriptions of languages carried out by American linguists including Fries (1948) and Bloomfield (1929), Audiolingualism (ALM) was originally brought to the classroom by methodologists (i.e., Lado 1957), who anchored their notions of classroom process on the principles of structural linguistics and Behaviorist stimulus-response psychology, especially as set forth by Skinner (1957). ALM promoted a view of language as an oral phenomenon, with the ability to orally communicate being the primary objective of the language-learning endeavor. Thus, oral production by learners was a major feature of the ALM classroom. According to the principles of conditioning and reinforcement associated with Behaviorist psychology, however, language learning was viewed as a complex series of habits to be repeatedly drilled until *overlearned* and internalized by the learner. With its emphasis on linguistic habit formation through pattern practice, ALM techniques left little room for student error—or *creative* production.

Dissatisfied with results of the largely mechanical classroom procedure of ALM, practitioners of the mid- to late 1960s experienced a return to traditional modes of grammar-based FL instruction. Described by Carroll (cited in Ellis 1990:38) as a modified, up-to-date grammar translation theory, the *cognitive code method* supported a return to deductive rule learning, and viewed language acquisition as a progression from *competence* to *performance,* from knowledge about the target system to the ability to actively apply this knowledge. The associated structural syllabus was organized to lead students from the known to the unknown in order that new information be associated and integrated with what had been learned previously.

11. These five hypotheses (Acquisition-learning Hypothesis, Natural Order Hypothesis, Monitor Hypothesis, Input Hypothesis and Affective Filter Hypothesis) are discussed in detail in Krashen and Terrell (1983).

12. Higgs (1985) also addresses certain inadequacies that he perceives regarding the input level construct of $i +1$ and its function (according to Krashen) as the essential and sufficient key to the promotion of acquisition when it is offered in a stress-free, affect-appropriate environment. He argues that even while input (i) is offered comprehensibly, the ($+1$) beyond actual learner level is highly problematic to gauge effectively. Here, the author suggests that input level is more likely to be too low in classroom situations (where numerous students operate at multiple levels at any given moment), or too high, and made comprehensible to the learner only by virtue of extralinguistic cues. In the latter case, the formal linguistic properties of the data may be rendered superfluous as students watch for cues (rather than listen to data) in order to comprehend input (200).

13. Leeman (2003) examined the role of negative evidence in the development of Spanish L2 noun-adjective agreement. See chapter 8 of this volume for details of this study. Lin and Hedgecock (1996) looked at the influence of negative (metalinguistic) feedback on the interlanguage systems of Chinese L2 learners of Spanish in Spain. Those with extensive formal training were more successful at incorporating this type of negative feedback than naturalistic learners.

14. See Schmidt (1995) for a complete review of literature on consciousness and foreign language learning.

15. See Leow (2000) for a complete review of attention and awareness research.

16. See also Cheng (2002) for a study of the effects of processing instruction on the acquisition of *ser* and *estar.*

17. Farley (2001) summarizes this dissertation, which finds that contrary to Collentine's (1998) assertion, "PI has an overall greater effect than meaning-based output instruction (MOI) on how learners interpret and produce the Spanish subjunctive of doubt" (289). A rebuttal from Collentine (2002) and a subsequent response from Farley (2002) appeared in the December 2002 issue of *Hispania.*

18. Communicative value is defined as "the relative value a form contributes to overall sentence meaning" (Lee and VanPatten 1995). When a grammatical marker (i.e., [ó]) is made redundant in the context of sentence by virtue of the presence of other forms (i.e., a nominative pronoun and temporal adverb [*él* habló *anoche* "He spoke last night"]), the form is said to possess low communicative value, to the extent that meaning may be derived in the absence of noticing.

19. See VanPatten (2002, in press) and DeKeyser et al. (2002) for further discussion on the effects of processing instruction.

20. An information gap activity involves students in a necessary exchange of information. One student has information that another student needs. Of course, the students must produce language in order to negotiate and eventually resolve the information gap (Brumfit and Johnson 1979).

21. See also Hatch (1978a, 1978b).

22. For a comprehensive overview of these works through 1999, see Lafford (2000).

23. See chapter 8 for a discussion of Ortega and Long (1997).

24. See chapter 6 for a discussion of Lynch (1998).

25. Native speaker participants in each dyad were provided with one of two possible scripts that were made prior to the start of data collection. The unmodified input script was a transcript of two native speakers completing the designated task; the modified input script was a transcript of a native speaker completing the task with a nonnative speaker.

26. See chapters 6, 8, and 9 for more discussion of Spanish L2 interaction studies.

27. According to Wertsch (1985:159), intersubjectivity is achieved when "interlocutors share some aspect of their situation definitions," namely, when individuals working in collaboration define the objects (both concrete and abstract), events, and goals of the task in some way.

28. See endnote 1.

WORKS CITED

Aljaafreh, A., and J. Lantolf. 1994. Negative feedback as regulation and second language learning in the zone of proximal development. *Modern Language Journal* 78:465–83.

Bachman, L. 1990. *Fundamental considerations in language testing.* Oxford: Oxford University Press.

Benati, A. 2000. Processing instruction: Un tipo di grammatica comunicativa per la classe di lingua straniera—il caso del futuro italiano. *Italica* 77:471–94.

Bloomfield, L. 1929. *Language.* New York: Holt, Rinehart and Winston.

Brooks, F., and R. Donato. 1994. Vygotskyan approaches to understanding foreign language learner discourse during communicative tasks. *Hispania* 77:262–74.

Brooks, F., R. Donato, and J. McGlone. 1997. When are they going to say "it" right? Understanding learner talk during pair-work activity. *Foreign Language Annals* 30:524–36.

Brumfit, C., and K. Johnson. 1979. *The communicative approach to language teaching.* Oxford: Oxford University Press.

Buckwalter, P. 2001. Repair sequences in Spanish L2 dyadic discourse: A descriptive study. *Modern Language Journal* 85.3:380–97.

Cadierno, T. 1995. Formal instruction from a processing perspective: An investigation into the Spanish past tense. *Modern Language Journal* 79:179–93.

Canale, M. 1983. From communicative competence to communicative language pedagogy. In *Language and communication,* eds. J. Richards and R. Schmidt, 2–27. London: Longman.

Canale, M., and M. Swain. 1980. Theoretical bases of communicative approaches to second language teaching and testing. *Applied Linguistics* 1:1–47.

Chaudron, C. 1988. *Second language classrooms: Research on teaching and learning.* New York: Cambridge University Press.

Cheng, A. 1995. Grammar instruction and input processing: The acquisition of Spanish *ser* and *estar.* Ph.D. diss., University of Illinois, Urbana-Champaign.

———. 2002. The effects of processing instruction on the acquisition of *ser* and *estar.* *Hispania* 85.2:308–23.

Collentine, J. 1998. Processing instruction and the subjunctive. *Hispania* 81:576–87.

———. 2002. On the acquisition of the subjunctive and authentic processing instruction: A response to Farley. *Hispania* 85.4:879–88.

Corder, S. 1967. The significance of learners' errors. *International Review of Applied Linguistics* 5:161–70.

Crookes, G. 1991. Second language speech production research: A methodologically oriented review. *Studies in Second Language Acquisition* 13:113–32.

Dandonoli, P., and G. Henning. 1990. An investigation of the construct validity of the ACTFL Proficiency Guidelines and oral interview procedure. *Foreign Language Annals* 23:11–22.

DeKeyser, R. 1998. Beyond focus on form: Cognitive perspectives on learning and practicing second language grammar. In *Focus on form in classroom second language acquisition,* eds. C. Doughty and J. Williams, 42–63. New York: Cambridge University Press.

DeKeyser, R., and K. Sokalski. 1996. The differential role of comprehension and production practice. *Language Learning* 46:613–42.

DeKeyser, R. M., M. R. Salaberry, P. Robinson, and M. Harrington. 2002. What gets processed in processing instruction? A commentary on Bill VanPatten's "Processing instruction: An update." *Language Learning* 52.4:805–23.

DiCamilla, F., and M. Antón. 1997. Repetition in the collaborative discourse of L2 learners: A Vygotskyan perspective. *Canadian Modern Language Review* 53:609–33.

Donato, R. 1994. Collective scaffolding. In *Vygotskyan approaches to second language acquisition research,* eds. J. Lantolf and G. Appel, 33–56. Norwood, NJ: Ablex.

Doughty, C. 1988. The effect of instruction on the acquisition of relativization in English as a second language. Ph.D. diss., University of Pennsylvania.

———. 1998. Acquiring competence in a second language: Form and function. In *Learning foreign and second languages: Perspectives in research and scholarship,* ed. H. Byrnes, 128–56. New York: Modern Language Association.

Doughty, C., and J. Williams, eds. 1998. *Focus on form in classroom second language acquisition.* New York: Cambridge University Press.

Ellis, R. 1990. *Instructed second language acquisition: Learning in the classroom.* Cambridge, MA: Blackwell.

Farley, A. 2000. A comparison of processing instruction and meaning-based output instruction in the learning and teaching of the Spanish subjunctive. Ph.D. diss., University of Illinois, Urbana-Champaign.

———. 2001. Authentic processing instruction and the Spanish subjunctive. *Hispania* 84:289–99.

———. 2002. Processing instruction, communicative value, and ecological validity: A response to Collentine's defense. *Hispania.* 85.4:889–95.

Frey, H. 1988. The applied linguistics of teacher talk. *Hispania* 71:681–86.

Fries, C. 1948. As we see it. *Language Learning* 1:12–16.

Garcia, P., and Y. Asención. 2001. Interlanguage development of Spanish learners: Comprehension, production, and interaction. *Canadian Modern Language Review* 57:377–401.

Garrett, N. 1986. The problem with grammar: What kind can the language learner use? *Modern Language Journal* 70:133–48.

Gass, S., and L. Selinker. 2001. *Second language acquisition.* 2d ed. Mahwah, NJ: Lawrence Erlbaum.

INSTRUCTION **315**

Gass, S., and E. Varonis. 1989. Incorporated repairs in nonnative discourse. In *The dynamic interlanguage: Empirical studies in second language variation,* ed. M. Eisenstein, 71–86. New York: Plenum.

———. 1994. Input, interaction and second language production. *Studies in Second Language Acquisition* 16:283–302.

Gatbonton, E., and N. Segalowitz. 1988. Creative automatization: Principles for promoting fluency within a communicative framework. *TESOL Quarterly* 22:473–92.

Gregg, K. 1984. Krashen's monitor model and Occam's razor. *Applied Linguistics* 5:79–100.

Grittner, F. 1990. Bandwagons revisited: A perspective on movements in foreign language education. In *New perspectives and new directions in foreign language education,* ed. D. Birckbichler, 9–43. Lincolnwood, IL: National Textbook Company.

Grove, C. 1999. Focusing on form in the communicative classroom: An output-centered model of instruction for oral skills development. *Hispania* 82:538–50.

Guntermann, G. 2000. *Teaching Spanish with the 5 Cs: A blueprint for success.* Fort Worth, TX: Harcourt College Publishers.

Hatch, E. 1978a. Acquisition of syntax in a second language. In *Understanding second and foreign language learning: Issues and approaches,* ed. J. Richards, 34–69. Rowley, MA: Newbury House.

———. 1978b. Discourse analysis and second language acquisition. In *Second language acquisition: A book of readings,* ed. E. Hatch, 401–35. Rowley, MA: Newbury House.

———. 1983. Simplified input and second language acquisition. In *Pidginization and creolization as language acquisition,* ed. R. Andersen, 64–86. Cambridge, MA: Newbury House.

Higgs, T. 1985. The input hypothesis: An inside look. *Foreign Language Annals* 18: 197–205.

Johnson, M. 2000. Interaction in the oral proficiency interview: Problems of validity. *Pragmatics* 10.2:215–31.

———. 2001. *The art of non-conversation: A reexamination of the validity of the oral proficiency interview.* New Haven: Yale University Press.

Knorre, M., T. Dorwick, A. M. Pérez-Gironés, W. R. Glass, and H. Villareal. 2001. *Puntos de partida: An invitation to Spanish.* 6th ed. New York: McGraw-Hill.

Krashen, S. 1982. *Principles and practice in second language acquisition.* New York: Pergamon.

Krashen, S., and T. Terrell. 1983. *The Natural Approach.* Hayward, CA: Alemany Press.

Lado, R. 1957. *Languages across cultures: Applied linguistics for language teachers.* Ann Arbor: University of Michigan Press.

Lafayette, R., ed. 1996. *National standards: A catalyst for reform.* Lincolnwood, IL: National Textbook Company.

Lafford, B. 2000. Spanish applied linguistics in the twentieth century: A retrospective and bibliography (1900–99). *Hispania* 83:711–32.

Lantolf, J. 1997. The function of language play in the acquisition of L2 Spanish. In *Contemporary perspectives on the acquisition of Spanish,* eds. W. Glass and A. Pérez-Leroux, 3–24. Somerville, MA: Cascadilla Press.

Lantolf, J., and G. Appel, eds. 1994. *Vygotskyan approaches to second language research.* Norwood, NJ: Ablex.

Larsen-Freeman, D., and M. Long. 1991. *An introduction to second language acquisition research.* New York: Longman.

Lee, J. F. 1998. The relationship of verb morphology to second language reading comprehension and input processing. *Modern Language Journal* 82:33–48.

―――. 2000. *Tasks and communicating in language classrooms.* New York: McGraw Hill.

Lee, J. F., and R. Rodríguez. 1997. The effects of lexemic and morphosyntactic modifications on L2 reading comprehension and input processing. *Contemporary perspectives on the acquisition of Spanish,* vol. 2, eds. W. Glass and A. Pérez-Leroux, 135–57. Somerville, MA: Cascadilla Press.

Lee, J. F., and B. VanPatten. 1995. *Making communicative language teaching happen.* New York: McGraw Hill.

Leeman, J. 2003. Recasts and second language development: Beyond negative evidence. *Studies in Second Language Acquisition* 25.1.

Leow, R. 1993. To simplify or not to simplify: A look at intake. *Studies in Second Language Acquisition* 15:333–55.

―――. 1995. Modality and intake in second language acquisition. *Studies in Second Language Acquisition* 17.1:79–89.

―――. 1997. Simplification and second language acquisition. *World Englishes* 16:291–96.

―――. 1998. The effects of amount and type of exposure on adult learners' L2 development in SLA. *Modern Language Journal* 82:49–68.

―――. 2000. Attention, awareness, and focus on form research: A critical review. In *Form and meaning: Multiple perspectives,* eds. J. F. Lee and A. Valdman, 69–96. Boston: Heinle and Heinle.

―――. 2001. Do learners notice enhanced forms while interacting with the L2? An online and offline study of the role of written input enhancement in L2 reading. *Hispania* 84:496–509.

Lightbown, P. 2001. Anniversary article: Classroom SLA research and second language teaching. *Applied Linguistics* 21:431–62.

Lightbown, P., and N. Spada. 1993. *How languages are learned.* Oxford: Oxford University Press.

Lin, Y. H., and J. Hedgecock. 1996. Negative feedback incorporation among high-proficiency and low-proficiency Chinese-speaking learners of Spanish. *Language Learning* 46:567–611.

Long, M. 1991. Focus on form: A design feature in language teaching methodology. In *Foreign language research in cross-cultural perspective,* eds. K. De Bot, R. Ginsberg, and C. Kramsch, 39–52. Amsterdam: John Benjamins.

―――. 1996. The role of linguistic environment in second language acquisition. In *Handbook of second language acquisition,* eds. W. Ritchie and T. Bhatia, 413–68. San Diego: Academic Press.

Long, M., and P. Porter. 1986. Groupwork, interlanguage talk, and second language acquisition. *TESOL Quarterly* 19:207–28.

Loschky, L. 1994. Comprehensible input and second language acquisition: What is the relationship? *Studies in Second Language Acquisition* 16:303–23.

Lynch, A. 1998. Exploring turn at talk in Spanish: Native and nonnative speaker interactions. *Spanish Applied Linguistics* 2.2:199–228.

Mayo, M., and T. Pica. 2000. L2 learner interaction in a foreign language setting: Are learning needs addressed? *IRAL* 38:35–58.

McLaughlin, B. 1978. The monitor model: Some methodological considerations. *Language Learning* 28:309–32.

———. 1987. *Theories of second language learning.* London: Edward Arnold.

———. 1990. Restructuring. *Applied Linguistics* 11:113–27.

National Standards in Foreign Language Education Project. 1996. *National standards for foreign language learning: Preparing for the 21st century.* Lawrence, KS: Allen Press.

———. 1999. Standards for Learning Spanish: A project of the AATSP. In *Standards for FL learning in the 21st century,* 431–474. Lawrence, KS: Allen Press.

Ortega, L., and M. Long. 1997. The effects of models and recasts on the object topicalization and adverb placement in L2 Spanish. *Spanish Applied Linguistics* 1.1:65–86.

Pica, T. 1992. The textual outcomes of native speaker-non-native speaker negotiation: What do they reveal about second language learning? In *Text and context: Cross-disciplinary perspectives on language study,* eds. C. Kramsch and S. McConnell-Ginet, 198–237. Lexington, MA: D. C. Heath.

Pica, T., F. Lincoln-Porter, D. Paninos, and J. Linnell. 1996. Language learners' interaction: How does it address the input, output and feedback needs of L2 learners? *TESOL Quarterly* 30:59–84.

Salaberry, R. 1997. The role of input and output practice in second language acquisition. *Canadian Modern Language Review* 53:422–51.

Sanz, C., and B. VanPatten. 1998. On input processing, processing instruction and the nature of replication tasks: A response to Salaberry. *Canadian Modern Language Review* 54:263–73.

Schmidt, R. 1995. Consciousness and foreign language learning: A tutorial on the role of attention and awareness in learning. In *Attention and awareness in foreign language learning,* ed. R. Schmidt, 1–63. Honolulu: University of Hawaii Second Language Teaching and Curriculum Center.

Schmidt, R., and S. Frota. 1986. Developing basic conversational ability in a second language. In *Talking to learn,* ed. R. Day, 237–326. Rowley, MA: Newbury House.

Sharwood Smith, M. 1981. Consciousness-raising and the second language learner. *Applied Linguistics* 2.2:159–68.

———. 1991. Speaking to many minds: On the relevance of different types of language information for the L2 learner. *Second Language Research* 7:118–32.

———. 1993. Input enhancement in instructed SLA. *Studies in Second Language Acquisition* 15:165–79.

Shrum, J., and E. Glisan. 2000. *Teacher's handbook: Contextualized language instruction.* Boston: Heinle and Heinle.

Skinner, B. F. 1957. *Verbal behavior.* New York: Appleton-Century-Crofts.

Swain, M. 1985. Communicative competence: Some roles of comprehensible input and comprehensible output in its development. In *Input in second language acquisition,* eds. S. Gass and C. Madden, 235–53. Rowley, MA: Newbury House.

———. 1993. The output hypothesis: Just speaking and writing aren't enough. *Canadian Modern Language Review* 50:158–64.

————. 1995. Three functions of output in second language learning. In *Principle and practice in applied linguistics,* eds. G. Cook and B. Seidlhofer, 125–44. Oxford: Oxford University Press.

————. 1998. Focus on form through conscious reflection. In *Focus on form in classroom second language acquisition,* eds. C. Doughty and J. Williams, 64–81. New York: Cambridge University Press.

Swain, M., and S. Lapkin. 1995. Problems in output and the cognitive processes they generate: A step towards second language learning. *Applied Linguistics* 16:371–91.

Terrell, T. 1977. A natural approach to second language learning. *Modern Language Journal* 61:325–37.

————. 1991. The role of grammar instruction in a communicative approach. *Modern Language Journal* 75:52–63.

Terrell, T., et al. 1994. *Instructor's manual to accompany Dos Mundos,* 3d ed. New York: McGraw-Hill.

————. 2001. *Dos mundos.* 5th ed. New York: McGraw-Hill.

Trahey, M., and L. White. 1993. Positive evidence and preemption in the second language classroom. *Studies in Second Language Acquisition* 15:181–204.

VanPatten, B. 1993. Grammar teaching for the acquisition-rich classroom. *Foreign Language Annals* 26:435–50.

————. 1996. *Input processing and grammar instruction in second language acquisition.* Norwood, NJ: Ablex.

————. 2000. Processing instruction as form-meaning connections: Issues in theory and research. In *Form and meaning: Multiple perspectives,* ed. J. F. Lee and A. Valdman, 43–68. Boston: Heinle and Heinle.

————. 2002. Processing instruction: An update. *Language Learning* 52.4:755–803.

————. In press. Processing the content of IP and PI research: A response to DeKeyser, Salaberry, Robinson and Harrington. *Language Learning* 52.4:825–31.

VanPatten, B., and T. Cadierno. 1993. Explicit instruction and input processing. *Studies in Second Language Acquisition* 15:225–44.

VanPatten, B., J. F. Lee, and T. Ballman. 1996. *¿Sabías que . . .? Beginning Spanish.* New York: McGraw-Hill.

Vygotsky, L. 1978. *Mind in society.* Cambridge, MA: Harvard University Press.

————. 1986. *Thought and language.* Cambridge, MA: MIT Press.

Wertsch J. V. 1985. *Vygotsky and the social formation of mind.* Cambridge, MA: Harvard University Press.

White, J. 1998. Getting learners' attention: A typographical input enhancement study. In *Focus on form in classroom second language acquisition,* eds. C. Doughty and J. Williams, 85–113. New York: Cambridge University Press.

White, J., and J. Evans. 1998. What kind of focus on and which forms? In *Focus on form in classroom second language acquisition,* eds. C. Doughty and J. Williams, 139–55. New York: Cambridge University Press.

White, L. 1987. Against comprehensible input: The input hypothesis and the development of L2 competence. *Applied Linguistics* 8:95–110.

White, L., N. Spada, P. Lightbown, and L. Ranta. 1991. Input enhancement and L2 question formation. *Applied Linguistics* 12:416–32.

Wing, B. 1987. The linguistic and communicative functions of foreign language teacher talk. In *Foreign language learning: A research perspective.* eds. B. VanPatten et al., 158–73. Cambridge, MA: Newbury House.

Wong Filmore, L. 1985. When does teacher talk work as input? In *Input in second language acquisition,* eds. S. Gass and C. Madden, 17–50. Rowley, MA: Newbury House.

Afterword

BARBARA A. LAFFORD   Arizona State University

RAFAEL SALABERRY   Rice University

The preceding chapters of this state-of-the-science volume on Spanish second language acquisition take a critical look at touchstone works of the research done in this field since its
inception just over two decades ago. These chapters reveal that although great advances in
the field have taken place during this period, more rigorous research needs to be carried out
in various Spanish SLA subfields.

To borrow a phrase characteristic of the political realm, it may be said that the *state-
of-the-science* of the field of Spanish second language acquisition is *strong.* Researchers in
this field bring more scientific rigor to their studies, both empirical and theoretical. Most authors consistently note not only the shortcomings of the studies that preceded them, but
also recognize the limitations of their own studies (e.g., issues of methodology and generalizability). Premiere journals in the field call upon the best scholars to review articles for
publication, and at professional meetings such as the American Association of Applied Linguistics and the American Association of Teachers of Spanish and Portuguese, represen-
tatives of those journals hold panel discussions to advise scholars on best practices to increase the likelihood of their articles being published.

Within the last two decades, new graduate programs in second language acquisition
and teaching have been created at American universities, largely to meet the demand for
training tenure-track professors, with research specializations in second language acquisition, to direct and supervise language programs at large universities. These new graduate
programs are aware of the fact that the bar is constantly being raised regarding the quality of research that is deemed acceptable for publication in the premiere journals in the field,
and, as a result, have incorporated coursework in research methods and statistics into their
core curriculum. Several of the authors in this volume are, themselves, "products" of those
new programs.

In spite of the fact that the state of our science is strong, there is room for improvement in the way some Spanish second language acquisition studies are carried out. In order
to recognize methodological and content areas in need of attention, each author in this *state-
of-the-science* volume was asked to critically review major works done in their particular

field of expertise. An overview of all their critical comments made us realize that many of the problems with the studies the authors cite are common to several of the works they discussed, regardless of the product, process, or instructional approach they reviewed.

Upon realizing the commonalities found in the critical reviews of several studies in different chapters, we believed that it would be useful to restate these criticisms in the form of a list of guidelines that future Spanish second language researchers can follow in order to avoid some of the methodological shortcomings detailed by the authors of this volume. In this way, the scholarly community can benefit from these insights and take measures to improve the quality of the research yet to be published in the field of Spanish second language acquisition.

To this end, we present (1) a list of guidelines for future Spanish SLA research and (2) a short description of the content areas of Spanish SLA research most in need of scientific investigation in the twenty-first century, which complement suggestions made by authors in the individual chapters. Through this discussion we hope to inform second language professionals of the most pressing needs for carrying out future explorations in our field.

Guidelines for Future Spanish SLA Research

Contextualization of the Research

- Contextualize research studies more extensively within the body of second language acquisition literature on the topic at hand (including key works using data from languages other than Spanish).

- Relate the results of empirical studies more clearly to theoretical models of second language acquisition.

- Explain the inner workings of the theoretical models discussed in order to shed more light on how second language input is processed to form interlanguage systems.

- Strive for explanatory as well as descriptive adequacy when utilizing new or existing SLA models.

- Establish more dialogue among proponents of different SLA models (generative, cognitive and sociocultural) in order to gain more insight into the Spanish SLA data being analyzed.

- Use Spanish second language data to create new models of acquisition and relate those (and current SLA models) to models of language and cognition (especially those with a psycholinguistic base) found in other disciplines (e.g., education and psychology).

Methodological Issues

Sample Selection

- Size: Increase the size of samples of second language learners used in quantitative studies.

- L1 diversity: Use learners of Spanish from various linguistic backgrounds (e.g., Indo-European and well as non-Indo-European languages) in order to gauge the generalizability of the results of the studies.

- Level of the learner: Conduct more studies of learners at various L2 levels to complete the picture of the stages involved in the acquisition of various target language phenomena.

- Native speaker control group: Use control groups of native speakers performing the same task as the Spanish second language learners; recognize that native speaker norms to which Spanish L2 data are compared are inherently variable and that acceptability judgments may vary among native speakers; use native speakers to render acceptability judgments on data produced by learners who have acquired the second language in different learning contexts (e.g., study abroad vs. classroom) so that these data can be understood and interpreted appropriately.

Research Design

- Cross-sectional vs. longitudinal studies: Collect more longitudinal data from one group or a small number of individuals over lengthy periods of time to understand how individuals vary in their journey towards acquisition of the target language.

- Type of methodological approach: Carry out both qualitative and quantitative analyses on Spanish second language data to deepen the understanding of the *processes* at work that help to create the *products* under investigation.

- Individual variation: Investigate more fully the effects of various individual factors on the SLA process, e.g., sex, personality, cognitive orientation, learning style, and discourse style.

- Type of experimental design: Carry out more Spanish L2 studies with true experimental designs (with a randomly chosen control group) to complement the studies already carried out using ex post facto, pre-experimental and quasi-experimental designs.

- Replication studies: Be cautious in characterizing research as a "replication study" unless all of the major research design factors are comparable; researchers need to recognize the extent to which their data can truly be compared to that of another study.

Treatment

- Duration of treatment: Increase the time (duration) of the treatment period to more than a day or two (the typical duration of studies to date).

- Autonomy of treatments: Do not allow the treatment conditions to overlap with each other within a given experiment; for example, when investigating the effects of instruction, the level of analysis should be a "design feature" of instruction and not an entire methodological approach; treatment materials should be constructed so that the only difference between treatments is the variable being studied.

- Timing and number of posttests: Conduct multiple posttests several weeks/months apart to gauge the long-term effects of a given treatment.

Tasks

- Effect of mode: Carry out more contrastive Spanish L2 studies of oral vs. written data taken from the same subjects.

- Number and type of tasks: Include a variety of tasks (e.g., spontaneous data as well as controlled data collection procedures, production data as well as grammaticality judgments) to corroborate results through "triangulation" procedures.

- Effect of task: Spanish second language research needs to recognize the variable effect of different tasks on learner performance (e.g., answering direct questions vs. spontaneous speech); in addition, more study of "carry-over" effects (e.g., influence on one type of task [writing] on the performance of another [oral production task]) is called for.

- Instruments: Recognize the limitations of certain types of data collection instruments (e.g., the ACTFL Oral Proficiency Interview).

- Online protocols: Conduct more Spanish L2 studies in which "online" data is collected during the process of performing a task (e.g., think aloud protocols) instead of relying mostly on "off-line" (measured after the treatment) data gathering procedures.

Threats to Validity

- Validity: Control factors that might threaten internal or external validity (e.g., failure to operationalize concepts [for instance, thresholds of acquisition] or research questions clearly or appropriately; failure to control for other variables that may affect the results and explain them just as well as the variables studied).

- Prior knowledge: Control for subjects' background knowledge (e.g., exposure to other second languages) or prior knowledge of the phenomenon to be studied.

Data Analysis

Statistical Tests

- Multivariate analyses: Conduct more multivariate analyses in order to understand the complexity of the various factors that interact to affect the acquisition process.

Effect of the Context of Learning

- Effect of learning environment: Carry out more studies that contrast the acquisition of Spanish second language phenomena in different learning contexts (e.g., formal classroom vs. immersion [study abroad] contexts).

- Effect of social context: Recognize the effects of the sociolinguistic/pragmatic context present when measuring the use of the target form being acquired in the L2 (e.g., effects of the power and solidarity relationships that exist between the researcher and the learner in the data collection context).

Generalization of Research Findings

- Take measures to insure the use of an appropriate research design and a large enough sample to make possible the generalization of the research results.

As noted earlier, the methodological shortcomings in Spanish second language studies noted by the authors of this volume are being systematically overcome, in great part, due to the existence of newly established or reinvigorated already-established graduate programs that produce Spanish second language scholars who have been trained in proper ways to design and execute quality research.

Areas for Future Spanish L2 Research

Each chapter discusses the type of research application that needs to be addressed in the future for the topics chosen for this volume. We will not belabor those points here. Suffice it to say that in order to understand the complexities involved in the acquisition process, more theoretical and empirically based second language acquisition research needs to be carried out using quantitative and qualitative paradigms from interdisciplinary perspectives on Spanish L2 data collected from various learning environments (e.g., classroom, study abroad, and second language settings).

Although research in the twenty-first century should be carried out on all the themes covered in this book, a careful reading of this volume will point out a special need to pay attention to the effects of different types of interaction and the development of Spanish L2 competence in areas other than grammar—for example, the lexicon and components of Bachman's (1997) model of communicative language ability, as follows.[1] In addition to studying *grammatical competence* (the part of organizational language competence containing knowledge of phonology, morphology, syntax and vocabulary), more L2 research emphasis needs to be placed on the study of *strategic competence* (the cognitive skills involved in language use, such as assessing, planning and execution—e.g., the ability to use communication strategies and negotiate meaning), and the following components of *language competence: textual competence* (the part of organizational competence involving rules of cohesion and rhetorical organization), and both components of *pragmatic competence (illocutionary competence,* involving the interpretation and expression of a wide range of language functions, and *sociolinguistic competence,* the ability to interpret and control the conventions of language use determined by social context, cultural references, dialectal and register differences and figurative language).

It is only through the systematic study of all these components of communicative language ability in various social contexts that SLA researchers will be able to begin to understand the complex phenomena involved in the acquisition of Spanish as a second/foreign language and, in the process, shed more light on how the human mind constructs knowledge (linguistic) structures through a combination of learners' abilities and the processing of environmental input.

NOTE

1. The reader should also consult Johnson (2001) for a critical look at Bachman's model and an overview of the model of Interactional Competence proposed by Hall (1993, 1995), He and Young (1998), and Young (1999).

WORKS CITED

Hall, J. K. 1993. The role of oral practices in interaction with implications for learning another language. *Applied Linguistics* 14:145–66.

———. 1995. (Re)creating our worlds with words: A sociocultural perspective on face-to-face interaction. *Applied Linguistics* 16:206–32.

He, A., and R. Young. 1998. Language proficiency interviews: A discourse approach. In *Talking and testing: Discourse approaches to the assessment of oral proficiency,* eds. R. Young and A. He, 1–24. Amsterdam: John Benjamins.

Johnson, M. 2001. *The art of non-conversation: A reexamination of the validity of the oral proficiency interview.* New Haven: Yale University Press.

Young, R. 1999. Sociolinguistic approaches to SLA. *Annual Review of Applied Linguistics* 9:105–31.

Contributors

Marta Antón (Ph.D. University of Massachusetts–Amherst) is a professor of Spanish linguistics at Indiana University–Purdue University at Indianapolis. She has published articles on second language learning and teaching and is the recipient of the 2001 Indiana Foreign Language Teachers Association and Indiana chapter of the American Association of Teachers of Spanish and Portuguese Teaching Award.

Joseph G. Collentine (Ph.D. University of Texas at Austin), professor of Spanish and chair of the Department of Modern Languages at Northern Arizona University, has devoted his research efforts to understanding factors that influence the acquisition of the mood and complex syntax by second language learners and to identifying instructional strategies and conditions that enhance subjunctive instruction. He is also an active researcher on the efficacy of CALL in the acquisition of Spanish grammar.

Frederick J. DiCamilla (Ph.D. University of Delaware) is a professor of linguistics in the Department of English at Indiana University–Purdue University, Indianapolis (IUPUI). He teaches undergraduate and graduate courses in linguistics and second language acquisition. He has published research on L1 writing and on the acquisition of Spanish as a second language using a sociocultural theoretic perspective.

Paola E. Dussias (Ph.D. University of Arizona) is a professor of Spanish and applied linguistics at The Pennsylvania State University. Her research area focuses on parsing and sentence comprehension processes in bilinguals. She has also conducted research on the use of experimental techniques to study psycholinguistic processes involving code-switched utterances.

A. Raymond Elliott (Ph.D. Indiana University) is a professor of Spanish and chair of the Department of Modern Languages at the University of Texas at Arlington. His areas of specialization include Spanish applied linguistics, second language acquisition, and the acquisition of second language phonological skills. He has published articles and reviews on these topics in premier language journals.

Charles Grove (Ph.D. University of Pittsburgh) coordinates the teacher certification program in world languages at West Chester University, where he is a professor of Spanish and linguistics. He is the author of numerous articles and resources on language teaching, second language acquisition and professional development of language teachers. His most recent work has examined the applications of a social justice framework in the mentoring of student teachers in the public schools.

Adam S. Karp (Ph.D. University of California, Davis) is professor of Spanish at American River College and serves as language laboratory coordinator there. His publications focus on the role of technology in the acquisition of Spanish by second language learners. He is currently exploring the use of wireless technology for interaction within the language classroom environment.

Dale A. Koike (Ph.D. University of New Mexico) is a professor of Spanish and Portuguese linguistics at the University of Texas at Austin, specializing in Spanish discourse analysis and pragmatics and second language acquisition. She has published books and numerous articles on Spanish discourse analysis and pragmatics and Spanish second language acquisition and is the recipient of the 2002 University of Texas Silver Spurs Award for Excellence in Teaching.

Barbara A. Lafford (Ph.D. Cornell University) is a professor of Spanish and linguistics at Arizona State University. She has numerous publications in professional journals related to second language acquisition, applied linguistics, sociolinguistics, and the use of technology in foreign language teaching. She also served as the associate editor for applied linguistics for the journal *Hispania* (1996–2002).

James P. Lantolf (Ph.D. Pennsylvania State University) is professor of applied linguistics and Spanish and director of the Center for Language Acquisition at The Pennsylvania State University. His publications include *Sociocultural Theory and Second Language Learning* (Oxford University Press, 2000). He has served as coeditor of *Applied Linguistics* and will become president of the American Association of Applied Linguistics in 2005.

James F. Lee (Ph.D. University of Texas) is professor of Spanish at Indiana University and serves as the director of Hispanic linguistics and as director of language instruction. He has published many articles on second language reading comprehension and the interrelationship of reading comprehension and input processing. He and Bill VanPatten serve as general editors of the McGraw-Hill Second Language Professional Series.

Silvina Montrul (Ph.D. McGill University) is a professor of Spanish, linguistics, and SLATE at the University of Illinois at Urbana-Champaign. Her research focuses on the second language acquisition of syntax, lexical semantics, and morphology within a generative paradigm. She is the author of numerous articles on the acquisition of verb classes, tense and aspect, and clitics by second language learners of Spanish and Spanish-English bilinguals.

Lynn Pearson (Ph.D. University of Texas at Austin) is a professor of Spanish at Bowling Green State University. Her research interests include second language acquisition of Spanish pragmatics, Spanish dialectology, teacher education, and discourse analysis. Currently, she is working on a study of Spanish language use in northwestern Ohio and a survey of university resources for preparing foreign language teacher candidates.

Rafael Salaberry (Ph.D. Cornell University) is a professor of Spanish applied linguistics at Rice University. He is the author of *The Development of Spanish Past Tense*

Morphology in a Classroom Environment (John Benjamins, 2000) and of several articles on Spanish second language acquisition and research on computer-assisted language learning. His research interests also include language testing, language teaching methodology, and syntactic-semantic-pragmatic interfaces in language acquisition.

Liliana Sánchez (Ph.D. University of Southern California) is a professor of Spanish linguistics at Rutgers University. She is the author of several articles on second language and bilingual acquisition among Quechua-Spanish speakers and of articles on Spanish syntax. She has also worked as a consultant on bilingual education for Peru's Ministry of Education and is coauthor of *Demanda y necesidad de educación bilingüe: Lenguas indígenas y castellano en el sur andino* (Peru Ministry of Education, 2000).

Almeida Jacqueline Toribio (Ph.D. Cornell University) is a professor of linguistics and Spanish linguistics at The Pennsylvania State University. Her major field of inquiry is syntactic theory, and her recent research endeavors include studies in microvariation, language contact, and bilingualism. She is the recipient of a National Endowment for the Humanities fellowship, and is coauthor of numerous articles published in notable compendia and journals.

Caryn Witten (Ph.D. University of Texas at Austin) is a professor of Spanish and humanities at Southeastern Oklahoma State University and is the former recipient of a Fulbright-Hags scholarship to Colombia. She has published articles on pragmatics and other areas of Spanish second language acquisition. Her recent research examines the enhancement of video to improve pragmatic competence in the L2 classroom.

Index